2009
COACH OF THE YEAR CLINICS
FOOTBALL MANUAL

Edited by Earl Browning

COACHES CHOICE™

www.coacheschoice.com

ISBN: 978-1-60679-062-5

ISSN: 1534-925X

Telecoach, Inc. Transcription: Kent Browning, Tom Cheaney, and Dan Haley

Diagrams: Steve Haag

Book layout and cover design: Bean Creek Studio

Front cover photo: Sports Information Department, University of Georgia

Back cover photos: Sports Information Department, University of Georgia (top), Sports Information Department, Florida Atlantic University (bottom)

Special thanks to the Nike clinic managers for having the lectures taped.

Coaches Choice
P.O. Box 1828
Monterey, CA 93942
www.coacheschoice.com

Contents

Contents

THE COUNTER RUN AND PASS SCHEMES

Penn State

It is an honor to be here today representing Joe Paterno and Penn State University. I always enjoy coming back to this area. I played football at East Rutherford High School.

I have a short story to tell before I get started. Recruiting today has gotten out of hand. With the internet and all the rating services, it is a big deal. There are five-star players and four-star players throughout the country according to these services. People can look at the internet and see how many of each player you sign. That is real overkill when it comes to recruiting.

We have had three players start at wide receiver for us as freshmen and play four years. They were three good football players and they went on to play in the NFL. One of those receivers came to Penn State as a five-star player. The other two were walk-ons and did not have a scholarship when they came. One of them was 5'10" and 185 pounds. No one offered him a scholarship coming out of high school. We offered him one after he came on campus.

No one knows how good these players are going to be when you sign them or when they come to you as a walk-on. You do not know how they will develop with their attitudes and work ethics about playing the game.

I am going to talk about the counter play. I will tell you how we teach it, show you some tape of how we execute it, and show you the play-action pass that goes with it.

The counter is probably the play we run most often in our offense. It is a very productive play and has been for a number of years. We only run this play in one direction. We run the counter play to the right. We run most of our plays to the right and left,

but there are two plays we run in one direction. We do that because of execution. We feel we cannot become good at running every play to both sides. That goes back to the reps you get in practice. To become good at this play we only run it to the right.

We feel like we are not predictable with the play because of the different formations we run. We also feel we run enough of our offense both ways to keep the defense honest.

The counter is the same concept and scheme as our half-slide pass protection. That becomes an advantage for your offensive line. They run the counter, but it is the same as another play in execution and technique. On the counter, we pull the tackle but we do not pull him on the half-slide protection.

The right side is the onside and the left side is the offside. When we teach our rules, we begin running against air (Diagram #1). We do not use a defense to start a teaching process. The right tackle has a simple rule, which is like his pass protection scheme. His rule is man-on-outside. When we run this play, he is in a protection scheme and pass sets. The counter play is a draw/counter play. It is designed to look like a pass from the onside tackle. The playside guard's rule is man-on-inside. If he is not covered, he blocks inside. The center is responsible for the backside A gap.

The backside guard is responsible for the backside B gap. The backside tackle pulls and blocks the first linebacker to the playside. There is one exception, but I will point that out as we go along. The tight end to the backside is the cutoff player. He cuts off anything from the C gap to the outside. However, his rules are based on the number of backs in the backfield.

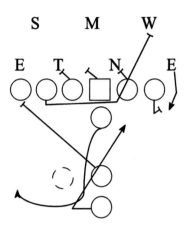

Diagram #1. Counter

If there is a 5-technique defender, he has to cut that player off. If he has a 7-technique, 6-technique, or 9-technique defender, that is his block. If there are two backs in the backfield, he blocks the Sam linebacker if he is uncovered. If we run a one-back counter, the tight end has a one-to-two rule. He jab-steps, momentarily holds off the D-gap defender, then goes up on the Sam linebacker.

The running back slides two steps to the left side, plants, and comes back to the right side. The quarterback opens to the left side and hands the ball to the running back. As he opens to the left, he comes back at an angle off the midline to hand the ball to the running back. After he hands the ball to the running back, he continues to the outside on a naked fake.

In the two-back counter, the fullback cuts off the C gap to the backside. If the tight end is uncovered, he goes through to the Sam linebacker. If he is covered, he works his gap making sure not to cross the face of the fullback coming backside.

We can also run the same play with the quarterback carrying the ball (Diagram #2). From the shotgun set with a back in the right halfback position, he fakes to the running back and follows the tackle into the hole. The running back becomes the cutoff back for the play. We can run the play from a no-back set. We generally try to overload the left side with receivers and counter run with the quarterback coming to the right. We hope to get linebackers or nickel backs moving to the unbalanced set side.

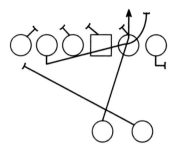

Diagram #2. Q-Counter

When we put the defense into the play, our rules should hold up (Diagram #3). A popular defense we see is 5 technique on the playside tackle and 2 technique by the defensive tackle on the playside guard. In our slide protection, the guard and tackle are responsible for those two defenders. If the down linemen run a twist stunt, they must handle that stunt. We run this play in short yardage as well.

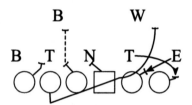

Diagram #3. Twist Scheme

The center has the backside A gap. In this defense, the nose is playing a tight-end-side shade on the center. That is the center's block. The backside guard's rule is to block back on the B gap. He keys the 5-technique defender and watches his inside knee. If the defensive end slants toward the guard, he blocks the 5 technique. If the 5 technique does not come inside, the guard climbs immediately to the linebacker and blocks him from the inside out. The backside tackle pulls for the Will linebacker on the playside.

The pulling tackle cannot be too slow, but he cannot be too fast. Ideally, we want the tackle's first step to be back with his inside foot. His second step is with the outside foot, which he uses to plant. He pushes off that foot and runs downhill aiming for the playside A gap. If he cannot get up into the A gap, he takes the B gap. On some occasions, he may have to go all the way to the outside.

Last year, our tackle on the left side was in a left-handed stance. His footwork was a step up with his left foot, a step back with his right foot, plant the left foot, and run to the playside. That is not ideal, but it timed up well with the play.

The next defense is a 4-3 stack defense (Diagram #4). The playside tackle blocks the man-on rule. The playside guard is uncovered and blocks the playside A gap. The center's rule is to block the backside A gap. If he has a slight shade or 0 technique aligned on him, he steps with his right foot to the playside with his shoulders slightly turned toward the tight end side. The right guard slides inside to the hip of the center and snaps the nose. What we refer to as a "snap" is a shove with both hands on the nose. The guard pushes the nose so he ends up in the backside A gap. The center takes over the block on the nose and the right guard comes up to the stack linebacker.

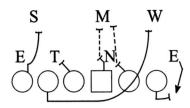

Diagram #4. 4-3 Stack Defense

That is what we would like to have happen. If the nose is too strong and stays in the playside A gap, the guard blocks him and the center goes up on the linebacker.

The backside guard blocks the B gap, which is the 3-technique defensive tackle. He has to be sure he has an inside-out angle on the 3-technique defender. He wants to hit the defender's inside number with his nose. He has an option to step with his inside or outside foot. If he has a tight 3-technique defender, he steps with his inside foot first. He takes a short jab-step with the inside foot and gets his second foot on the ground. He gets his nose on the inside number and drives the defender backside.

If the 3-technique defender is in a wide alignment in the gap, the guard steps with his outside foot. He steps at the near number, brings his inside foot with him, and drives the defender. The whole objective of the footwork is to take care of the inside stunt. If the defender stunts inside, the guard has to get a good piece of the defender so he can turn him over to the center. He does not want the 3-technique defender to get a clear shot on the center. That gives the center a chance to take over the 3 technique, and it allows the guard to move to the next defender that comes to him.

The tackle pulls and the tight end has to apply his rules. This play is a single-back counter. The tight end jab-steps and hits the defensive end. If the defensive end crashes inside, he drives him. If the defensive end stays outside, he jab-steps, punches the end, and releases on the Sam linebacker. If it was a two-back set, the tight end would block the Sam linebacker and the fullback would block the defensive end.

If the center is uncovered and has no piece of the nose, he slides into the backside A gap (Diagram #5). He slides and does not turn his shoulders. If nothing comes into the backside A gap, this allows him to go vertical for the backside linebacker. Nothing else changes on the scheme.

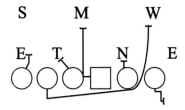

Diagram #5. Uncovered Center

If we go to a triple formation with the tight end on the backside, we often get the linebackers overshifted to the trips set (Diagram #6). The Sam linebacker moves into a 30 alignment over the backside guard. The backside defensive tackle and end play a 5 technique and a 9 technique. The playside tackle pass sets and invites the rusher outside. The playside guard wants to knock the nose into the center's backside A gap. The backside guard steps into his B gap and climbs to the Sam linebacker.

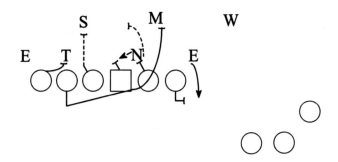

Diagram #6. Overshifted Linebackers

If the playside guard is successful in knocking the nose into the backside A gap, we have a 2-on-1 block on the Sam linebacker or we get an extra blocker. If we get the free blocker, he moves up to the next level. The playside guard and backside guard can get on the Sam linebacker. The tight end blocks the 5 technique and the tackle pulls for the Mike linebacker.

The last look I want to show you is the *Okie* or 3-4 defense (Diagram #7). Anytime the defense has two linebackers to the playside, we make a call. If we block our rules, we are one blocker short on the playside. We put the playside guard and tackle on the defensive end and Will linebacker in a zone blocking scheme. The tackle opens and takes whatever comes to him. If the defensive end charges up the field, the tackle blocks him and the guard takes the Will linebacker. If the defensive end charges inside, the tackle turns him over to the guard and blocks the Will linebacker.

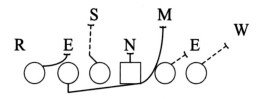

Diagram #7. 3-4 Defense

That leaves the center in a single block on the nose. He takes the nose wherever he can. The backside guard steps to his B gap and climbs to the linebacker if the 5 technique does not slant to the inside. The tight end cuts off the backside. The backside tackle pulls and blocks the playside linebacker. The tackle has to be aware of the center's block on the nose. If the nose works to the

playside, the center drives him in that direction. The pulling tackle may have to go under the center's block to get to the linebacker.

There is no perfect offensive line. We thought we had a good offensive line, but it was a rare occasion when we blocked the play perfectly. If you do not have backs that can make people miss and break tackles, you are in for a long evening. We had a couple of great backs this year that could make people miss and break tackles.

When we align off the line of scrimmage, we want the guards and tackles with their helmets at the bottom of the center's jersey number. To do that, the guards must have their toes aligned on the center's heels. I do not want our line splits to be so wide that we create rush lanes for the defense. However, I do not want to be so tight, that we cannot operate. I want a natural spacing that allows us to create holes. We take the in-between approach to line splits. We want our spacing to be equal between the offensive linemen.

The same thing is true with the distance we are aligned off the ball. If you get too far off the ball, you have the ability to read. However, the impact area is too far. We want to get on defensive linemen quickly. We align off the ball, but we do not take the full distance allowed under the rules of football. Offensive tackles want to be off the ball when they are pass protecting against a wide defensive end.

I want to get into our play-action passing game. Our play-action scheme is built around our naked play. When we run the naked play-action, we block the running play and do not pass protect the quarterback. The object is to fool the defense and get the quarterback on the edge with the ball.

To run this type of play, you do not need a great running quarterback or a great passing quarterback. However, you cannot have a quarterback who cannot get out of his own way. He has to be effective as a runner to get the most from this game. The play-action passing game is essential to making the running game more effective.

I want to show you the principles of the game first. The first thing we tell our receivers is that they must be active when they go down the field. The running backs must make good fakes and become good blockers after the fakes. The quarterback has to make a good fake. However, it is essential for him to get his head around quickly. He cannot have his head down or he misses the blitz coming off the edge unblocked. If he gets his head around and gets enough depth off the fake, he has a chance to make something happen.

If the quarterback is pressured off the edge, the first thing he has to do is get rid of the ball. We do not want to take the sack. If he has any doubt at all, he throws the ball away. We do not want to take a chance and have the ball intercepted. If there is no pressure, the first thing the quarterback does is look deep to his playside receiver (Diagram #8). The playside receiver generally runs a deep comeback or post. We can adjust his pattern according to the game plan. We can also run a double move in this situation.

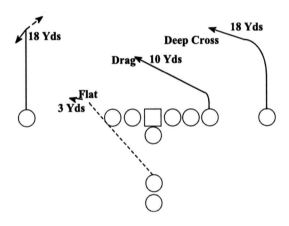

Diagram #8. Play-Action Concept

The second pattern the quarterback wants to throw is the flat. If the pattern is run away from the tight end, the second pattern has to come from the backfield. The inside receiver to the callside runs the flat pattern. The receivers away from the naked side run drag and crossing patterns. To the backside of the pattern, the inside receiver runs the drag pattern and the outside receiver runs the deep cross. In theory, we can run this pattern from any formation. When the receivers know the principles involved, you should not have any problems.

If the play-action is away from the tight end, he runs the flat route. He blocks the C-gap defender

before he releases to the flat (Diagram #9). The outside receiver runs the same pattern as before. If there is an inside receiver to the backside, he runs the drag and the outside receiver runs the deep cross.

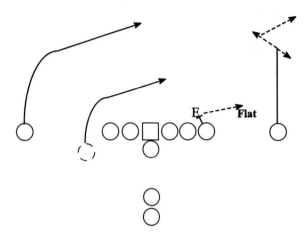

Diagram #9. Play-Action Concept Tight End

The first naked action is off the counter (Diagram #10). We align in a triple-receiver set to the tight end side. We run the one-back counter action to the split end side. The tight end stays in and blocks his assignment on the counter run. The line blocks counter run except the pulling tackle does not turn upfield. All the offensive linemen block their run assignments but do not go downfield. The quarterback fakes the counter and brings the ball to the left. The action of the counter should bring the defender aligned on the inside receiver to the inside. The inside receiver runs an out cut toward the sideline. The outside receiver runs a deep comeback or pattern determined by the scouting report. The split receiver runs the deep cross.

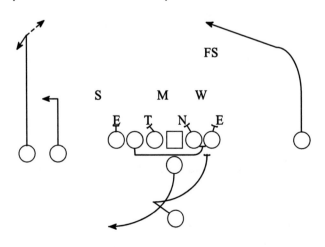

Diagram #10. Counter Naked

9

The most effective play-action pass we throw is the naked off the inside zone play (Diagram #11). This formation is a triple set to the right side. When we run the zone play, we like to bring the H-back in motion across the set to cut off the backside defenders. We can snap the ball and let him track behind the line into the flat. We run the naked pass from the zone play and release the H-back into the flat as the second receiver. The outside receiver runs his route. The tight end runs the drag route and the wide receiver runs the deep cross.

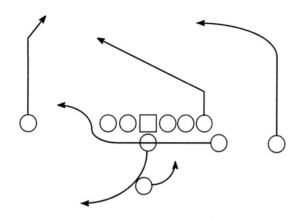

Diagram #11. Inside Zone Naked

The drag pattern by the tight end on this play is deeper because there is a receiver in the flat. Against zone coverage, he wants to climb when he reaches the position of the opposite tight end. The deep cross pattern is 18-yards deep. The quarterback gets 9 to 10 yards of depth after his fake. If the quarterback gets pressure, he throws the flat or throws the ball away. If there is no pressure, he looks at the deep pattern first.

With a three-wide-receiver set, we like the play-action off the outside zone play (Diagram #12). We run the naked play into the twin receiver side. The patterns are the same as before. When we protect these plays, we are using gap protection toward the play-action fake.

When we run the inside zone play, we zone step to the side of the play and cut off the backside edge with the fullback. We can move the fullback into the strong or weak halfback position and run the play away from him. If he is in the I formation, he cuts off

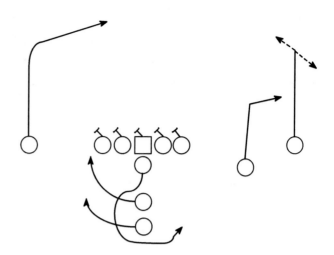

Diagram #12. Outside Naked

opposite the playside. We can also use an H-back in a wing or slot position in motion to cut off the backside.

I want to show you the inside zone play. We spend a lot of time running this play (Diagram #13). It is a very simple play, but it can be very effective. The blocking assignment for everyone on the offensive line is playside gap. If the defender in the playside gap is a down linemen or a walked-up linebacker, the blocker attacks the outside number of the defender aggressively. The fullback goes opposite the play and secures the backside.

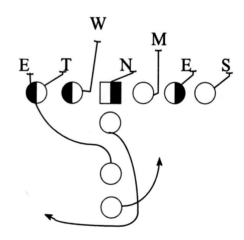

Diagram #13. Inside Zone Fullback

If there is no defender in the playside gap, we call this technique a "stall" player. He does not attack the linebacker off the ball. He works on the line in a stalled position. In the diagram, the playside tackle, tight end, center, and backside tackle have aggressive blocks. The playside guard and backside guard play stall techniques.

The stall technique protects the playside gap. However, they cannot run through the gap or get to the second level too quickly (Diagram #14). When the blocker reaches the second level, we want his shoulders square. When we run the inside zone, we do not marry it to the outside zone. We run those plays differently with different people.

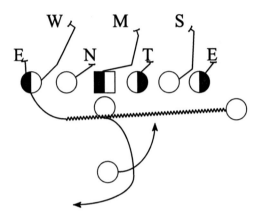

Diagram #14. Inside Zone Tight End

In the second diagram, we run the same play. We use the H-back in motion to cut off the backside. The defense changes and the aggressive techniques and stall techniques also change. In the second zone diagram, the backside guard, playside guard, and tight end have aggressive blocks. The backside tackle, center, and playside tackle have stall techniques. It is important for anyone going vertical to the second level to keep their shoulders square. That prevents the linebacker from going backdoor on the block.

When we run the outside zone, we fly to the edge. The fullback comes to the playside and is the lead blocker. We run the outside zone to the split end side as well as to the tight end side.

The first outside zone I want to show you is to the split end side (Diagram #15). The defense is an under 4-3 defense. The playside guard and tackle have aggressive outside blocks on the 5-technique and 3-technique defenders. The center has no one in his playside gap and flies off the ball through the A gap trying to get to the Will linebacker. The

backside guard uses a "pull cutoff" on the nose. He loops around the center position to get to the playside shoulder of the nose.

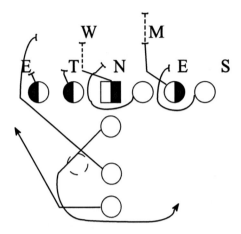

Diagram #15. Outside Zone Split Under

The tackle to the backside flies off the ball working for the playside number of the backside linebacker. The tight end uses a pull-cutoff technique to get to the backside defensive end. The offensive line is aggressive on their blocks. The playside tackle has no help on an inside move by the defender. However, the playside guard has the center coming through the A gap to pick up a slant move by the defender. If the defender slants inside, the playside guard works up to the Will linebacker and the center blocks the slant.

The fullback flows outside the playside tackle looking to clean up on the Will linebacker. We align the fullback in an I formation or queen set to the split end.

If the defense was an over 4-3 defense, the scheme would be somewhat different with the angles of the offensive line (Diagram #16). The playside tackle's block is the same. The guard does not fly outside. He wants to cut off the Mike linebacker. The center blocks the playside A gap. The backside guard and tackle block the defensive tackle and Sam linebacker. The tight end tries to get inside on the Sam linebacker. If he cannot, he climbs to the next level. The fullback goes inside or outside the playside tackle and blocks the Will linebacker.

To the tight end side, the tailback aims at the outside hip of the tight end (Diagram #17). The

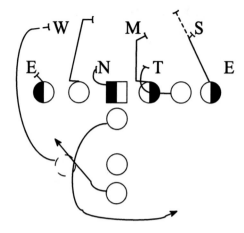

Diagram #16. Outside Zone Split Over

tailback reads the block of the tight end and runs inside or outside his block. Against the under front, the playside guard and tackle run a combination block on the defensive end in the 5 technique. One of them will get off on the inside linebacker.

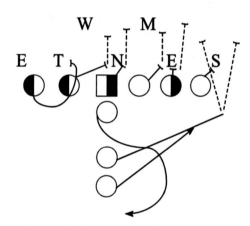

Diagram #17. Outside Zone Tight End Under

The center and backside guard block a combination on the nose with one of them coming off for the backside linebacker. The backside tackle runs a pull-cutoff technique for the backside defensive tackle. The fullback goes inside or outside the tight end's block and seals inside.

Against the over 4-3 defense, the angles change for the linemen (Diagram #18). The playside tackle and tight end run a combination block for the 6-technique defender up to the outside linebacker. The center and playside guard block the combination on the 3-technique tackle and the Mike linebacker. The backside guard uses a pull cutoff for the nose defender. The backside tackle tries to cut off the Will linebacker. The fullback leads the play outside the tight end.

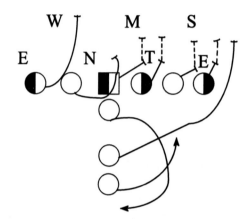

Diagram #18. Outside Zone Tight End Over

When we use the pull-cutoff block, the offensive linemen actually pull behind the line and get their inside shoulder to the outside number of the defender.

I am not going anywhere. If you have questions about what you have seen, come up and talk. Thank you for being here.

COACHING POINTS IN THE PUNTING GAME

Buffalo Bills

Thank you, Earl. It is true I have been coming to this clinic for several years. Earl Ceh has been here for as long as I can remember. I always like to come to this clinic because it is important to me for several reasons. My goal is to be able to give back to the game that has been so good to me over the years.

If I were coaching in a high school situation, this is what I would do to try to help the players. First, on the punt return, catching the ball is the number-one priority. You must teach the kids to catch the football on the punt. It is important for the return men to be able to catch the ball, not just standing there, but on the move as well. With solid catching skills, the return men can do a lot of different things on the punt return.

The punt return is a very dangerous play, in that the ball is in the air and the return men must go to catch the ball. So, those return men need to practice as much as possible to catch the ball from the punter. They need to get the ball into their hands, making sure they secure the ball. The thing we like to work on is running to make the catch. Very few times do we see the ball kicked directly to the return man.

When return men catch the ball from the JUGS® machine, it is as if they are in an activity class. We have a few special drills that we run with our punt returns, and I will show them to you on the films later.

I listed a few things that will increase the probability of catching the ball on the punt. We want to catch the ball with the fingers up. We want to "give" as we catch the ball. This is to cushion the ball with your body, particularly with the soft area under the pads.

We want to keep the hands and eyes set at eye level between the eyes and the ball. We want a natural extension for the ball. We want the hands between the eyes and the ball. The hands and eyes are a natural extension of each other.

We do not go overboard with a lot of points on this area of the punt return because you can make it too rigid. I find the punt returners get too rigid in their segment of catching the ball. It is all a rhythm in one flow. The big point is to catch the ball with their hands.

If the ball hits the plastic on the mask, helmet, or shoulder pads, the probability of them catching that punt is not very good. We want the punt to come down in the middle of the player's face. We want the hands between the eyes and the ball. We want the eyes and hands to be an extension of each other. If the eyes are reaching for the ball, or drifting with their feet, it decreases the probability of them catching the ball. In many cases, we see some players that really have the ability to catch that ball on the punt. But in the scheme of things, if you can get them to set their hands and feet, they have a good chance to make the catch.

I am not talking about the return men to go stiff and tighten up when they are setting to make the catch. They must see the football, set their eyes and feet, and bring the ball into their body. They catch the ball with their hands first. We emphasize the hands first, but it is almost as if they are catching the ball with their hands and body at the same time. If we do not emphasize the hands first, the ball will end up hitting on the plastic, and as I said, it is difficult to make the catch when it hits that plastic.

There is a little give with the knees as they catch the punt. As a result, we do not have the return men perfectly square when they catch the ball. Some coaches want them square, and that is fine. We want them in a modified stance, and we want a little give when they go get the punt.

I tell the receivers on the punt to look at the ball all the way to "security." They will never do that in a game, but we try to enforce this in practice. We want to overexaggerate looking the ball into the secure area.

For the most part, the most skilled players on the field are the defensive corners and receivers. Consequently, they are the best punt returners. They do not practice a lot of ball security. When we work on kicking field goals, or blocking field goals, we do not have any skilled players involved in that phase of the game. We do have a holder, but he is our punter. We do have a couple of corners who come off the edge, but they are not our returners.

When we work on field goals, on any day, we have ball security that day as well. When the rest of the team is working on the field goals, we take our punters and punt-return men, and we work on ball-security drills. Our running back coach runs those drills. The security drills last six or seven minutes. We do the drill twice a week.

Let's look at some of the things that reduce the possibility of catching the punt. If your hands are too low, the ball will hit the return man between the wrist and the elbow. You can make copies of games on TV and see what I am talking about. Our guys do not drop balls in practice, so I do not have any film on them. Nevertheless, you can look at enough games from TV to see what happens when the man catching the ball has his hands too low.

When the ball hits on the forearm, it is going to bounce up. You will see a lot of double catching the ball when this happens. The man catching the ball has his hands too low, so it bounces up, and he has to reach up and pull it back into his hands.

You are better off if the hands are facing the kicker, and the fingers are pointing up. You do not want the back of your wrist facing the ground. You will have a more natural catch with the hands and wrist up, facing the punter.

If the hands are too rigid when you are attempting to catch the ball, it will be difficult to hold onto the punt. All of this is a flow deal, so you have to be careful how you present the techniques to the players. If the knees are rigid and there is no give, given the way the ball comes down, it makes it a tough catch.

Reaching for the ball and drifting with the feet is an absolute no-no! Taking your eyes off the ball is another bad habit. If you get a lot of wind, as we do near the lakes, it can be difficult catching the punts. If we have a windy day, we may say we will not attempt to field certain punts. We have an advantage in that we have the wind almost every day. Therefore, we can practice catching the punts with the wind and against the wind. That can be a totally different phase of the game for each team.

Those are some ideas on catching the punts. I would film my returners catching the punts in practice. You can stand up close on them with a video camera, or you can shoot the video from the side to show them what they are doing with their eyes, where their hands are, and where they are catching the ball.

If you had to make a decision between blocking the punts or returning the punts, which would you do? It is tough for the snappers and the punters to have perfect get-off timing on rhythm. I would put them on blocking the kicks, if I had to choose one or the other. We know certain punts can be difficult to return. We do not always get good punts to return. In addition, as I said, the snaps are not always good. If we know the snapper is not consistent, we will go for more blocks instead of punt returns.

We do not block as many punts now as we used to. We have only blocked two punts in five years since I have been at Buffalo. There are not that many punt blocks in the NFL. It is going down each year. The reason it is going down is because the snappers are so good, the timing and rhythm is so good, and it is difficult to block a punt. It is tough to get back to the kicker because the protection is so good.

Here is a point that will be debatable. You will have to make up your own mind how you want to handle the situation. The question is: should you want to leave your feet in blocking a punt? In watching punts blocked, almost every time, a player leaves his feet when he blocks a punt. There are very few punts blocked where the player blocks the kick on the go without leaving his feet. However, there is some type of extension in blocking punts.

Most coaches tell the punt rusher to only leave his feet after the punter has dropped the ball. They will tell him to go for the area where the ball hits on the punter's shoe when he drops the ball. If he extends a little, he can get to the ball. If he really extends, he can get a large part of the ball. So, there is a phenomenon of extending to get to the ball.

We tell our players to use the Pete Rose slide, just as he would use if he were going into second base. It is a leap slide, where we are extending out as hard and fast as we can. That time will come in most cases. It is best to watch the situation on film to really understand the extension into the ball. If you can get a copy of the block punts, you will see that the blocks happen just as the punter drops the ball. It is tough to work on this technique because of the nature of the extension.

There is a fine line in teaching the extension on the punt block. If you are worried about roughing the punter, you probably should never rush him. It can happen even if you stay on your feet. You see players run into the punter, and you see players blocked into the punter. This is another story, and I do not have time to cover the blocks in this session.

For us, on the attempts to rush the punter, everything comes from the inside out. We want to get up the field and then run a cut, or a speed cut. It is a six- to eight-foot cut toward the punter, who is lined up at 15 yards. You could run a post and then a square inside to get to the punter. As soon as I make a move on the edge of the offensive man, I want them looking back inside for the football. As soon as the ball comes off the punter's hand on the drop, we would like to catch the ball before it hits the punter's foot.

It is like the soccer player who dives to block a shot. We are trying to lay out the same way as he does. Generally, the plant foot and the ball coming off the hand of the punter happen at about the same time.

I am not sure if you can picture this or not, but all the punt rusher is trying to do is to go through a box that is in front of the punter. It is about one yard in front of the punter, and one yard outside on both sides of the punter's foot. You want your body sliding through that box in going for the football.

If you are going to try to block punts, and if you are going to lay out to block the punts, you have to train where to aim for when you lay out. Know the aiming point when you extend. You must practice this to become good at blocking the punts without getting a penalty.

There is a lot of directional punting in our league. As a result, we have to consider the angle the punt blocker is coming from. It is different from a straight-on punt. We say that "second base," where the ball and foot make contact, is in a different spot. You must have the blockers aware of this, and they must see that spot from where the ball is kicked.

If a team does not have a really good snapper, I think the block punt call is a good call. Since it is so very tough to get the snapper, and the punter, and the protection all proper, the punt block can be worth spending time on. If the punter is not good at getting the ball off, then we are going to rush him on the punts.

One thing I want to cover before I get into the film: if I am going to do a punt return, I want to get into the gunners in a position where it is similar to a position we would be if we were dancing. We are not so much concerned with holding him up as much as we are with getting our hands up and getting inside-out position on the outside man.

I coached with the Steelers for a couple of years, and I heard Dick LeBeau talk about a similar position. He said, "The goal and objective in football is always to be on the ballside of your opponent." I still claim that as my position on the punt.

If we are blocking a gunner on a punt return, I want to finish my block on him as I started out on the snap. As we go down the field, I want to keep on the ballside of the defender. I want to end and finish the block exactly the same as when I entered the block. You will see a lot of this in the film that I am going to show.

Many times, you cannot get the fixed position on the defender coming down to cover the punt. Watch our games on Sunday, and you will see the most common penalty called in the NFL is the block in the back on a punt return. You will see two or three of these penalties in a game.

We have almost gone to an off-hand check similar to what a cornerback does against a receiver coming off the line of scrimmage. If I can force the man outside as he comes off the line, I have a chance to nudge him to keep him outside. It is so difficult to get the defender to turn toward the blocker. If we can hand check him to the point where we can keep him out of the middle of the return, we feel we have done a good job.

In teaching the open-field block, and reducing the probability of a penalty is huge. The off-hand check and the nudge block become more important to us than anything else would in this situation.

The thing we do is to train the players on the punt-return team the exact same way as we do with defensive backs. We teach them the same techniques that we teach defensive backs to play on press coverage. For us, everything is press coverage, and it is the off-hand check. It is making a turn where we face the defender, or we do a speed turn where we would turn our back on the man. All of this is involved in a punt return.

Once the defender is going down the field, and we are the defender, he is no different from a receiver going for that pass reception. He is going to the reception point in a pass route. Our blockers are no different from the defensive back trying to stay between the receiver and the ball, just as a corner would do on a pass route. We are playing the man as if we are a defensive back. We are using all the skills a defensive back would use. Keep this in mind as we watch this film.

I hope we will be able to make the next part of the session easy. This is going to be an input session. Let's start the film.

You can use a football on a broomstick or a PVC pipe, and tape it so the football stays on the pipe. You can make the stick or pipe five or six feet long. This is to simulate the snap. Gilman has the gadget for sale, but you can make one as well. We use it for the punt as well as the defense.

If you go to camp or the start of practice, you will find that teams do the same drills repeatedly each day. You all know the basic drills you use to start the season out with. I am not saying this is bad, but you can see them do these same drills all of the time.

What we started doing during this period of the practice schedule is to take one of the individual groups and work on special techniques instead of the same drills they have been doing over and over. If we are in two-a-days, we have a different group in the next session. We continue that process until we have worked with the entire team.

We may do a practice where I work on tackling with one of the groups. We want to steal as much time as possible to get some of the different techniques completed. If you do not do it this way, you have to do it on the fly during the team period.

We want to break up our special-teams units for coaching the same way you do for your offense and defense. We have found this helps us in our practice schedule.

I am going through the film clips fast. I want to make sure you get to see all of the examples I have covered.

It has been a real honor for me to be here. I appreciate you being here. I hope this information will help your players. Thank you.

PROVEN KEYS TO WINNING

Florida State University

Thank you. It is good to be here. I used to come to New Jersey when I was coaching at West Virginia University. Football has always been good in this area.

I left West Virginia in 1976 to go to Florida State University. They had lost 11 straight games. They were about ready to drop football. The record before the 11 games they lost was 1-10, and 3-5. When they lost the 11 games, they fired the coach. They called me to see if I was interested in coming down for a visit to see if I would take the head coaching position. I was only a little interested in going to Florida State. I ended up taking the job and have been there ever since.

You can imagine what it was like getting started that first year. We had to play a lot of games on the road that first year. I think we were the homecoming game for five different teams that year. Everyone wanted a piece of us, and they wanted us as their homecoming game.

To get teams to play us, we had to play teams at their place. We played LSU five games in a row with no games at our place. We played Nebraska four times with none of the games at our place. We played two games at Ohio State with no return games at home. Also, we played Arizona State away three straight years without a game at home.

One of the reasons I took the job at Florida State was that it was closer to my home, which was Alabama. I figured I could coach a couple of years at Florida State and then get a job in the state of Alabama.

The longer I stayed at Florida State the better things got, so I have stayed there all of these years. But we had it hard getting the program going. We had a stadium that seated 41,000 people. We

averaged 17,000 in attendance each year. I knew we had to win, but we also had to put fans in the stands. Football is expected to pay a lot of bills for the athletic department. We had to get good teams to play us at home.

We were getting ready to play our first game at home that first year. We had played two games away, and we had lost them both. We were playing our first home game after those two losses.

In those days, the head coach received 10 complimentary game tickets, and the assistant coaches received four game comp tickets. I had taken my 10 tickets and distributed them to my family and close friends, and I ended up with two extra tickets. I tried to sell those two extra tickets, and I could not find anyone who wanted them. I had tried to give them to the janitor, but he did not want them.

That Friday, I had to go down to the Tallahassee Mall to get a haircut. I decided I would get rid of those tickets. I parked close to the barbershop and got out of my car. I took those two tickets and placed them on the outside of my car. I put them under the wiper blades on the front windshield. I knew someone would take those tickets. I went in to get my haircut.

I came out of the mall in one hour. I could not wait to see if they tickets had been taken. To my surprise, I found six game tickets on my windshield. At that time, I knew we were facing an uphill battle. However, we did make progress and improved the program over the years.

Later, we were fortunate to play Georgia in the Sugar Bowl. Between the end of the season and the Sugar Bowl, our players had their final exams. Our quarterback overslept and missed one of his final exams. At that time, we had a rule in Florida if a player missed a final exam, he was ineligible for any bowl game. So he was out for the Sugar Bowl game.

Our second quarterback was injured and out for the season, so he could not play in the Sugar Bowl. We had to play our third-team quarterback in the bowl game. The only time he had played at all that year was when we were way ahead, or the game was about over and he got in for a few plays. We had about two weeks to get that quarterback ready for the Sugar Bowl.

We went to New Orleans to play the game. We got a turnover, kicked a field goal, and led 3-0 the first quarter. We had told our quarterback if he could play without making mistakes, we had a chance. We could play defense, and we were hoping for a few breaks in the game. That first quarter, the third quarterback did not play bad. He did okay.

Early in the second quarter, he threw a pass to the flat, it was picked off, and Georgia ran it back for a 76-yard touchdown. On the next series, he threw another interception. Georgia kicked a field goal soon after that interception.

We were on a drive near the end of the third quarter, and he threw his third interception. Again, Georgia added another field goal.

To start the fourth quarter, he threw his fourth interception. As he was coming off the field, I saw our best receiver walking off the field with the quarterback. I wanted to hear what they were going to have to say to each other. As I walked up to them, I heard our best receiver say to the quarterback, "John, if you will tell me which one of the defensive safeties you are throwing the ball to, I will try to intercept it."

In the last 10 years or so, I have never been asked to speak much more than one hour. Here I am listed to speak for an hour-and-a-half. I am going to tell you a few stories, if I have to talk that long.

I do tell this story when I am in certain areas of the country. It may not be fitting in all areas, and it is not intended to belittle any one group. It is just as it is in our multicultural society.

This man went into a store to purchase one single item. He found the item and went to the checkout line. He got in a short line, hoping to get out of the store in short time to get on his way. He stood in the line behind one man for several minutes. After five minutes, he stepped up closer to the clerk to see if he could figure out what the problem was. As he came up close to the checkout clerk, he could hear the customer talking in Japanese. After a few minutes of hearing the clerk trying to communicate with the man from Japan, he finally stepped in. "Hey, pal, you are in the United States of America. Speak Spanish." You can tell that story if you are from Miami.

Recently, I spoke to the Florida Football Coaches Association. I have spoken there for the last 34 years. I have to be cautious in that I do not want to repeat myself over and over. So, each year I look over all of my notes to see what I have said in the last few years. I am always looking for something that I think will be helpful to the coaches.

When I first started as the head coach at West Virginia in 1970, I started keeping a notebook of quotes from coaches that I had heard at different clinics and meetings, or from other coaches that I thought were motivational information that would help a young coach.

I want you to know that I do not speak on X's and O's at clinics anymore. I let the assistants do that part of the game. I meet with the coaches, and I know what they are doing, but I do not talk about the X's and O's.

If you are a head coach at the college level or at a big high school, you are nothing more than a "problem solver." The coaches are going to do the coaching. As a head coach, you have to keep things running. You have to solve the problems to keep things on track. You are a problem solver, and the assistant coaches do the coaching.

The big guys with all of the money are the guys who can solve all of those problems. So, if you are one of those coaches who can solve problems, be thankful that you have a job. Be thankful that you have an opportunity to solve problems. We say that a crisis brings on "opportunity." This is where heroes are made. This is where you can rise to the top.

Here is where I am coming from. Next year will be my 56th year of college coaching. There is another coach still coaching college football that is in his 61st year. But he is an old man. You know who I am talking about. He is old! For an old man, he has not done bad at all. He is a great coach. But, after 50 or more years in coaching, you can learn a great deal. I am going to talk with you about some of the things I have learned over the years.

Football is a priority to me. It is a priority, but it is not the priority. If I were talking to a group of young guys just getting into coaching, I would advise you on this subject. Do not make football your "god." You will be miserable if you make football your highest priority. I must put my faith above football. I must put my family above football. Then football comes next.

I can assure you that you will not win all of your games. I wish I could win all of our games. You just cannot do it. So you must not make football your top priority. When I first started coaching, football was first. As I got older, I realized that I needed a higher priority in my life, and that is where my faith and family come in my life today.

The number-one quality you want in a coaching staff is loyalty. Without loyalty, you will not be able to reach the goals you want for your program. This has been true throughout my coaching career.

It is difficult to have loyalty when you cannot hire your own coaching staff. It is difficult if you do not have the authority to demand loyalty from your staff. The coaches must know they must be loyal to the head coach and the rest of the staff.

I have studied, and I have read a great deal on leadership. Most everyone who gets into coaching wants to be a great leader, or they want to be a head coach and lead the program they way they think it should be to be the best. That is very realistic, and it is a good thing in coaching. Most coaches know they may have to work their way up the ladder to get to the top as a leader. One coach may be a great leader and do things different than

what some of you think he should do. A second coach may be a great leader and do things entirely different than the other coach. A lot goes into to leadership.

I have been fortunate to study some great military leaders of our times. I have been to Europe and visited some of our great battlefields. It is very interesting to study famous leaders in that there are certain qualities in all leaders. I want to talk about a few of these leaders.

The number-one quality of a great leader is that the leader must be a person of integrity. If coaches and players are not true to you, you will have problems. I tell our coaches and our players that I am not going to lie to them. I let them know I do not expect them to lie to me. That is integrity.

The second leadership quality is compassion. They are compassionate toward the men that serve under them. As I visit with high school coaches when I am out recruiting and visiting schools, I can tell how the coach handles his players to see if they love them or not. You can get the feel for how coaches treat their players and how they have compassion for them.

As we look at the great military leaders, we see compassion in their leadership. Generals MacArthur, Eisenhower, Bradley, and Patton had compassion for their troops. Civil War Generals Lee, Grant, and Stonewall Jackson had compassion for their troops. They all wanted to be up on the frontline with their men. His own men shot Stonewall Jackson. He came up to the frontline during the night. He was mistaken for the enemy, was shot, and later died.

The third trait of all great leaders is to have courage of your convictions. You must have courage of your convictions. If you believe in something, you must have courage to carry out your ideas. "This is what we must do to win." You have to believe in what you think will work for you in your situation. Set your plan, and then have the courage to stay with that play. You are going to be tested. You are going to be questioned about your play. "Coach, you cannot do that." People will tell you, "Coach, that will not work." You must have a plan and have the courage and conviction to stick with the plan.

One word that I have used over and over with our players and coaches is "enthusiasm." When I first went to Florida State, I was high on the word enthusiasm. If your team can play enthusiastically, you might win the game. We talk to our kids about enthusiasm all the time. Enthusiasm is spirit! Spirit means "full of God." That is God in you. We all have physical ability. Now, we have to find something in that physical ability to make you explode.

I wanted the word enthusiasm to mean something. We have an indoor workout room that is about 200 feet long. The walls in the room are very high. I had the word "Enthusiasm" painted from the ceiling to the floor. It was just the word "Enthusiasm." I got the word enthusiasm from one of Woody Hayes' stories. He told us at a clinic that the word enthusiasm comes from the Greek work *enthios*, which means "full of spirit, God in you, full of God." Do not be afraid to say that, men. You are just trying to get these people to be the best they can be. Then, over our practice field, we have a big sign that has the word "Enthusiasm" on it. I talk about the word all of the time to my players and coaches.

The other word I use is "persistence." That probably is more important than anything else I could stress. It means, simply, a player who will not quit. He will not give up. It may be the most important thing in that we do. It means: "I will not quit." On our field on our tower, I have the word "Persistence." It is something to remind the players of what we stand for.

About two years ago, I got a big sign and put if over the gate at our practice field. On the sign was the words, "I am the boss!" It was a sign about six feet long, and it was very impressive. However, it only lasted about two days because my wife came over to the practice field and took it down. She told the team that was her sign, and it was going back in her kitchen where it belonged. That was the end of that sign.

Next year will be my 35th year of meeting with my team the night before a game. We go over some thoughts related to the game the next day. I call this meeting to make sure we know what we expect from our players the next day in the game. It is what I call "The Six Commandments to Victory." Men, everything I cover here is what I got from somebody else. The only thing is some of these points are older than you all.

We have a special meeting either in Tallahassee or on the road. We have supper at 6:00 p.m., and then at 6:30 p.m. I talk to them for about 15 minutes and give them my last little pep talk. I build those talks around six points. I do it for every game. I take six points and try to use different thoughts to motivate them for the ball game. The six points I build my talk around will win us the ball game.

"Boys, if we do these things, we will win." As a football coach, there is not much you can do to control the outcome of the game. You have already done your coaching and preparation during the week. Once they kicked off, all you can hope for is for your boys to carry out what you practiced.

The six commandments that I am giving you, as coaches we can control them. I use six commandments but some other coaches may have more and some coaches may have less. These commandments are basic to the game of football.

1. No Breakdowns In The Kicking Game

When everything else is equal, this is probably where you are going to win or lose. We have a good offense, and our opponents have a good defense. We have big kids, and they have big kids. The kicking game is where you are going to win or lose the game

Be sure you have your punt team perfect, your punt rush perfect, your punt-return team perfect, your kickoff coverage and kickoff-return teams perfect, and your field-goal and extra-point teams perfect. Be sure you start with that. We start out every practice with special teams at Florida State. That is the first thing we tell our kids; "We must have no breakdowns, and we must win the kicking game."

2. No Missed Assignments

The second commandment is: "No missed assignments." Now, men, these commandments I am giving you are things you can do something about. You can train, practice, and prepare your kids to handle these things. You need to practice daily by stressing "no missed assignments."

When we put in a play, we put it on the blackboard first, where we can see it. Then, we explain it to the players so they can hear it. We have a walk-through, and then we walk through it versus dummies. We try to simulate it the best we can. We do not scrimmage all the time. We cannot afford to get people hurt. Yet we need to go full speed somehow without getting people hurt.

During the season, we practice at three speeds. One is at full speed. In the early part of the season, we get a scrimmage in when we can without jeopardizing our football team. Once the season starts, we are afraid to scrimmage. We do not want to beat our players up. When we do scrimmage, we can go full speed. Full speed is full speed.

3. Play Great Goal-Line Offense and Defense

We always practice for a while at the goal line. We go full speed a lot of time because we do not get many players hurt practicing on the goal line. No one gets a long running start at anybody. By goal line, we mean from the three-yard line to the goal line. Every day in spring practice, we finish with goal-line situations for five minutes.

We put the ball on the three-yard line, on the left hash, and tell them it is third-and-goal. They get three attempts at running the ball. They may run a play-action pass, a sweep, or another play. If they do not make it, they can still kick a field goal. After that, we put the ball on the one-yard line on the left hash mark. Now, the situation is fourth-and-one to go for the touchdown. The offense needs to get the ball in the end zone. The defense needs to stop them. In this type of scrimmage, it is a defensive advantage. You can turn 11 people loose on defense.

Then, we go to the right hash mark and repeat the drill. The kids have a lot of fun. The defense may beat them four straight series. If they do, you can bet that next day the offense will score. You need to win on the goal line.

4. No Foolish Penalties

This usually occurs in the kicking game. "You would have won that game if you had not roughed the kicker. When you roughed the kicker, you gave them a first down, and they went on to score."

Another situation may occur when your opponent is fixing to kick a field goal. One of the defensive players lines up offside. Now, they score seven points instead of three, and you lose the ball game. Those mistakes will get you beat. We say, "No foolish penalties."

This is the way I view penalties. We are the most penalized team we play. When we play, we always get more penalties. We try to prevent this, but we have not been very successful. Here is the thing about that situation. If you want to stop penalties, cut out your aggressiveness, quit hitting people. Is that what you want? You check the conferences; the most victorious teams are the most penalized. If you are an aggressive team, you will get penalties called on your team. We tell our players, "Just don't get the foolish penalties." Foolish penalties include lining up offside, jumping offside, hitting the opponents in the mouth—those are the foolish penalties.

5. Allow No Long Touchdowns

Men, you can coach that aspect of the game. You ask how we can prevent the long touchdowns. Back up. Do not let anybody get behind you. The first thing I learned, as a player was: if you do not know where the ball is, back up. They are probably trying to fool you, so get deeper.

If I am playing defense, if you cannot get a long pass against us, and you cannot get a long run on us, how are you going to score? If I play great goal-line defense, how are you going to score? You are going to have to kick to score on us.

6. Keep Fumbles and Interceptions to a Minimum

How do you keep kids from fumbling? We do a good job on this aspect of the game. We teach them how to hold a football. The fingers go over the end of the ball. At the other end, the ball is under the arm, and the elbows are down. There should be no daylight in the cavities. We stress both hands over the ball when the runner is going down. Most fumbles occur as you are being tackled. As you are going down, the second guy comes in and knocks that thing out of the arms of the ballcarrier. We stress: once you are going down, get both hands on the ball.

Something we have used to hold fumbles down is this: when we go skeletal offense or running plays, we line up all of our extra people at 10 yards. We tell our ballcarrier that the subs are going to try to knock the ball out. That way, we keep their attention to let them know when they get through the line of scrimmage, this "thing" is not over.

Every time we do 11-on-11 or skeleton drills, we tell the defense to knock the ball out of the arms of the ballcarrier. When they go for a touchdown, we keep trailing them until they slow down, and then knock the ball out. Invariably, when we have skeleton drills, a player will catch a ball and start running for a touchdown. Before he scores, he will get the ball knocked out of his hands because he relaxes too soon. We tell him do not let up on that ball until he scores. If he does let up, we will have someone knock the ball out of his hands.

I do not talk a lot about interceptions. I am afraid I will scare off our quarterbacks and they will not throw the ball. I had a quarterback who threw an interception against Miami. I told him we could not have interceptions. The next week, he kept throwing the ball one yard beyond the receivers reach. I asked him why he was throwing the ball so far over the head of our receivers. He said, "Because I want to keep it away from the defender." I told him not to worry about it. You can talk too much about interceptions. You just coach them to use their heads.

Let me add a point or two about fumbles. When we meet in spring training, we will show our players how to hold a football. Everybody will get a ball, and we will check each other. Then, we will teach them how to recover a fumble. If you do not cover this aspect, you are making a mistake. There is a bad way to recover a fumble. If you do not cover it with

them and they try to recover the fumble, they will not do it right. There is a right way to recover it. We roll it out there and have them recover it. We tell them not to hit the ball, but land beside it. We teach them to pull the knees up to the chin. We teach this all the first day when we are in shorts.

Another sign we have in our workout room is this:

> Do It Right!
>
> Do It Hard!
>
> Do It Again!

We tell the kids this over and over. We tell them to do it right over and over. It makes you sick telling them this over and over. They get the message. We like that slogan.

Question: Do you favor a playoff system in college?

I do not favor a playoff system in college. Now, if we are voted number one in the polls, we will take it. If someone else is voted number one, we are going to be upset. That is the way it goes in college circles. Some coaches want a playoff system. The presidents do not want it. The ADs want it because of the money. But football is not like basketball. There are a lot of factors involved in this question. I do not think it will happen in my tenure.

This guy was driving home late at night. He hit a tree and crushed his car. He could not get out of the car. A patrol officer came by, saw the wreck, and came to assist the man pinned in the car. The police officer shined a light in the car, saw the man, and asked, "Are you hurt?" The man replied, "I do not know. I am not a lawyer."

Next I want to go over some slogans that I have used over the years. I have saved these for years. We may hang these signs in the locker room:

> *You do not win games; you lose them!*

You have to keep from losing before you start winning. It goes back to the points I covered in the Six Commandments.

Get mentally tough, or get out of coaching.

I do not know of anyone who has been criticized more than I have. I know my family has heard it all. I like the saying about listening to fans. If you listen to them enough, you are going to be sitting with them soon.

Don't lose your convictions!

Don't lose your guts!

Carry out your play regardless of the criticism!

You may be wrong, but you are the boss!

The greatest mistake is making the same mistake over and over again!

If you can't stand the heat, keep out of the kitchen!

Great leaders have had great losses and have had a hard time gaining success. We could name Churchill, Lincoln, Lombardi, Nixon, Edison, and several others. They had setbacks, but they overcame them and shook them off to go on to greatness.

Moving on, I have a few more points I want to cover.

Team rights supersede individual rights. The way kids are now-a-days, this is important. Today, it is a me world.

Responsibility without authority will get you beat. This is important in coaching. If you are on my staff, and I give you a job to do, I expect you to do the job, and I will give you the authority to carry out the responsibility. If I give them a job and have to tell them how they must do the job, if I want to give them a task and tell them how to do it, then it is not giving them the authority.

If two partners always agree all of the time, it means one of them is not necessary. Say what you think, and do not be afraid to differ with the head coach. After you go outside, you all must be together on the field.

The best steel must go through the hottest fire! "We had the game won, and we blew it!" Then, when you start looking for a friend after that happens, it is tough to find people who'll support you. We all must go through tough times. It will make you a better coach.

If a dog can't do what I am teaching him, I will teach him what he can do! This is very similar to coaching football. Let the players do what they do best and what we can teach him to do. If you get a lemon, make it into lemonade.

I could go on and on, but I want to allow you to answer questions.

Question: What is the greatest thing that has happened to you in all of your years of coach?

There have been so many individual stories that I could not pick just one thing that has happened to me in coaching. But, to be very honest, I am proud of the fact that I have never been fired as a coach. In today's world, I think that is something to be grateful for. However, it ain't over yet.

Question: Has any player had an impact on your life?

Yes, I do have several players that have impacted my life. One that comes to mind is Charlie Ward. He was a great athlete and a better person.

Question: How do the athletes of today compare to the athletes when you first started coaching?

When I first started coaching, we did not have as many good athletes as we have today. Today, the size of the players is larger, they are faster, and they work at the game almost year-round. This has been a big factor in the athletes we have today.

When I started playing football, if we had two players who weighed 215 pounds, you would think they were giants. If you had a player that weighed 240 pounds, you would say he is a giant, and he will never play. The skill level of the players today and the size of the players today is amazing.

You could take a Division III school today, and they could beat the national championship teams from 50 to 60 years ago. There is that much difference in football today. However, I do not think kids are as tough today, but there's so much more skill in the athletes. And, I do not think the athletes today are as disciplined as they were several years ago.

I think the decline in discipline and the problems we have in our high schools today, such as the incident at Columbine High School where we had several students killed, all started when we kicked God out of our schools. In 1960, our government said we could not pray in school, we could not have the Bible in the schools, and we could not have any religious signs in the schools. That is where our troubles started. When I went to school, we had prayer over the loudspeakers. They had prayer at our ball games. Now, we can't do that.

Question: Do you have a prayer with the team before a game?

Yes! Before we go out on the field, we pray. I tell them they do not have to stay for the prayer. Our prayer is related to two things. First, we pray for our team to stay healthy. Second, we pray for our team to do our best. We do not pray to win!

We must watch our heritage in this country today. We are going to have to fight to keep our freedom very soon. You do realize we are at war! It is "freedom versus terrorist." We are in the war, and we must stand on our basic principles that built this country. The battle is on.

Question: In the movie [We Are Marshall] about Marshall University and the airplane crash, how accurate was that movie?

Coach Red Dawson had played at Florida State, and I was his coach. I was an assistant at Florida State at that time. Red was coaching at Marshall, but he did not get on the plane that crashed. Rick Talley was the head coach who was killed in the airplane crash. He had played at Virginia Tech.

Jack Lyngel became the new coach at Marshall. I was the head coach at West Virginia, and Red Dawson called and asked if he and Jack could come to see us. They asked if they could study our veer offense. I told them I would help them as much as we could because they had been through a great deal to get the program back up and going at Marshall. They came up and watched our films and practice and visited with our coaches. The picture was very accurate. They did a good job in the movie.

Today, we have so many distractions that it is very difficult to coach the players. Can you imagine when I first started coaching? There were no distractions for the players. They had just invented beer; but they did know about sex! So we did not have a lot of distractions. There was not much a player could get into back then. It is tough to motivate players today with all of the distractions.

Men, I have enjoyed sharing some thoughts with you. I wish you the best for next year. Thank you!

DEFENDING THE SHOTGUN PASSING GAME

University of Kansas

I want to talk about our base defense and coverage. I hope to get to some zone reads and blitzes later. Our base front is a four-man front with some version of quarter coverage behind it. When we started to put in our scheme, we got bogged down with the terminology of what to call things. If you get too elaborate, you make the defense hard to understand and remember. We decided to make it simple and call it what it was.

Two years ago, when I got this job, the first thing I changed was the defensive techniques played on the tight end. They made no sense to me and confused the players. We teach those things to our players because that is something we know. Who cares what we know; the players are the ones who have to know how to line up. Teach them something that makes sense.

When we set our front, we use the terms open/closed or field/bench (Diagram #1). However, we flip our front by using directions. If we call left, the Sam, nose, and end go to the left side of the defense. The tackle, Leo, and Will go to the other side. Those groups travel together in our base defense. The tackle is our 3-technique defender. The Sam, nose, and end go to the callside of the defense. The Leo aligns on the tight end. He has an inside shoulder alignment on the tight end. The nose aligns in a shade technique on the center opposite the 3-technique defender. The end plays on the outside shoulder of the offensive tackle into the openside of the formation. The Mike linebacker aligns to the formation side on the outside shoulder of the center.

The Sam and Will linebackers could be interchangeable. They are the same body types and same type of players. This simplifies the defense in

regard to these two players. They see the same technique every time, and their blitz package becomes simple. This helps with your practice time because you are teaching one technique to each linebacker.

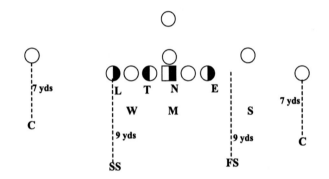

Diagram #1. Base Defense

With our base defense, we run a cover-4 scheme in the secondary. This is our read scheme. We call "open cover 4." That means the Sam linebacker, nose, and end go the openside of the set. The type of formation will determine what the defensive backs call on that side of the field. They have to know if they have a tight end, two receivers, or a 3x1 formation. If we have a tight end and wide receiver, we play a true quarter mentality to that side. The strong safety and free safety are at nine yards in their alignment and playing a vertical man technique. In the diagram, the offense aligns in a wide slot to the left and a tight end/wide receiver to the right. That is a 2x2 set with one back, and we apply our two-gap rules for the linebacker fits. This also allows us to get the strong safety out of a run fit to his side.

The corner lines up with inside leverage on the wide receiver at the depth of seven yards, playing a vertical man technique. If the wide receiver runs a hitch or anything vertical to the outside, the corner plays man coverage on him. If the receiver goes under with his pattern, the corner releases him and passes him off to the next defender.

The strong safety reads the tight end and reacts off his movement. There are only three things the tight end can do. If it is run, the tight end will reach, base, or scoop block. That tells the safety his run fit. In the passing game, the tight end can run the flat, go under, or run vertical.

We wanted to take some pressure off the safety in the run scheme. Last year, we saw 66 percent of passing in our conference from the 2x2 formation. In a 2x2 formation in a normal set, the linebackers have two gaps (Diagram #2). In a 3x1, they have one-gap spacing. On this formation, the Will linebacker to the tight-end side has the hardest job on the field. His run fit to the tight-end side is A gap to D gap. On flow to him, he has the D gap. On flow away from him, he has the A gap.

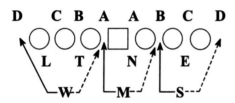

Diagram #2. Linebacker Run Fits

The Mike linebacker on flow his way fits into the A gap, and on flow away fits into the openside B gap. The Sam linebacker on flow to him fits into the D gap, and on flow away he fits into the B gap. We try to keep the strong safety out of the immediate support. He does not have containment on run to his side. It slows his play, so he can play the play-action pass better.

In the pass coverage, the Sam and Will linebacker's rule is to match the pattern of the #2 receiver. We number the receivers from the outside in (Diagram #3). When you use terms like curl/flat and hook/curl, that refers to areas on the field. In quarter coverage, you talk about receivers. Their rule is to match the pattern of the #2 receiver or whoever becomes the #2 receiver. If the #2

receiver goes inside and the #3 receiver comes outside, the receiver running out becomes the new #2 receiver.

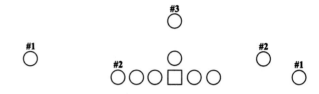

Diagram #3. Numbers Rule

In this set, the tight end is the #2 receiver. The Will linebacker has to match his pattern. If the tight end goes to the flat, the Will linebacker has that coverage, even thought he is outflanked slightly. If the tight end goes vertical, the Will linebacker reroutes, sits, and finds a new #2 receiver. We do not want the Will linebacker to think on flow away he is a curl-to-flat player. The #3 receiver is coming from the backfield most of the time. In the 3x1 set, the #3 receiver is in a receiver position.

In a cover-4 scheme, the first part of that responsibility is a four-vertical route by the offense. The worst thing that can happen to a defensive back is to get beat deep. That is their primary key and where their eyes should be. The safeties have to see those vertical routes by the #2 receivers. That does not mean they do not see the entire field, but that is their primary concern.

If the tight end goes vertical, the strong safety has that coverage, and the Will linebacker carries him to the curl area and zones off the short area of the field. If the tight end curls or runs out, the Will linebacker has the coverage. Once the tight end passes 10 yards, the strong safety picks up the coverage in almost a man situation. If the tight end runs to the flat, the Will linebacker has coverage on him. The strong safety plays under the #1 receiver and plays for the curl, dig, or post pattern. If the Will linebacker makes a bad read, the strong safety makes him right by playing in the curl, and the corner is over the top with the #1 receiver.

The Mike linebacker has to match the pattern of the #3 receiver. If the running back comes out on a pattern, the Mike linebacker has coverage on him.

He has #3 or whoever becomes #3. If the tight end comes inside and the running back goes to the flat, the Mike linebacker picks up the new #3, which is the tight end. The Will linebacker releases the tight end and picks up the new #2, which is the running back. When the tight end does not run vertical, the strong safety releases him and helps anything that is not vertical. His first read is the #1 receiver. He plays him for a post, dig, or curl.

The next situation we get from this formation is into the two-receiver side. This situation makes it almost impossible to play half in and half out of the box with the Sam linebacker. The Sam linebacker has to play the B gap on flow away from him. If he has to match the route of the #2 receiver, it is an impossible job. To handle that situation, we call "mix" (Diagram #4). The mix call protects the Sam linebacker with his run fit. The corner and free safety key the #2 receiver. If he releases to the flat, we get a solid corner concept into the flat, with the free safety playing over the top of the corner. The corner plays through the #2 receiver into the flat. That keeps the Sam linebacker from responding to the flat immediately. Now, he can protect his B gap and is protected if anything goes to the flat.

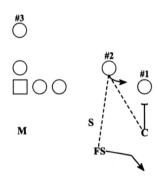

Diagram #4. Mix

If the #2 receiver does not go to the flat, the Sam linebacker matches #2 and plays football. If #2 comes up the field, he can get to the backside B gap from that position. He aligns, splitting the distance from the offensive tackle to the wide receiver on that side. The Mike linebacker stays on the #3 receiver. If the #3 receiver goes to the flat, he releases him and plays the new #3 coming inside.

Mix is simple for the linebackers. The problem comes with the free safety and the corner. There is a lot of gray area in this adjustment. They both read the #2 receiver. It is simple to say, but when does it become a roll-up situation for the corner? If the flat by the #2 or #3 receiver comes within the first five yards and is fast, the corner rolls down. If the release is slow or a pivot release, the corner stays on his inside leverage with the #1 receiver, and the free safety drives on those routes.

The technique the corner plays on the roll is important. His alignment is seven yards off the #1 receiver with tight inside leverage. The corner sees the #2 receiver. If the #2 receiver does anything inside or vertical past the five-yard area, the corner is man-to-man on the #1 receiver. If flat happens fast, he cannot go to the #2 receiver. He has to run through the #1 receiver and reroute or widen his pattern before he can get into the flat.

The technique for the Sam and Will linebacker is the same, as they read the vertical release by the #2 receiver. We want them to stay relatively flat to the line of scrimmage as they work outside. We want them to collision and reroute the #2 receivers as they go vertical. After the reroute, they settle and find the next #2 receiver or help the corner on short inside routes by the #1 receiver.

The bad situation in this coverage is the deep out cut by the #2 receiver. If the quarterback can throw those types of patterns, they will complete them. The Sam linebacker cannot get into those areas, and they are too deep for him to stop. The safeties are heavy on the inside, protecting the middle of the field. If your quarterback can make those types of throws, you will get some completions.

Another part of the gray area in this coverage is whether the #2 receiver goes inside or not. If he comes up the seam past the five-yard area, we treat that as a vertical, and the safety covers him. If he goes inside and pivots back to the outside, the safety covers that route. The corner has read the inside route and is gone in man coverage on #1. The safety has to cover that pattern. If we get a naked bootleg, the linebacker to that side has to go as the secondary containment, and the other two linebackers have to find the wheel route and crosser from the inside.

If we get a 3x1 situation, we play a "lock" coverage adjustment (Diagram #5). To the single-receiver side, we play lock man-to-man on that receiver. On the three-receiver side, we play vertical man technique. The corner has inside leverage on the #1 receiver. If he goes under, the corner releases him. The strong safety has the #3 receiver on all vertical routes. Since this is a triple formation, the linebackers' run fits become a single gap. The Will has the B gap to the backside, Sam linebacker has the D gaps to the trips side, and the Mike linebacker has the A gap to the trips side.

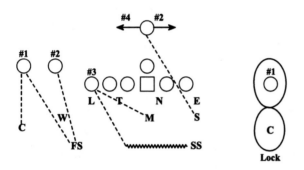

Diagram #5. 3x1 Adjustment

In a 2x2 set with no tight end, you can go to a single-gap spacing for the linebacker's run fits; however, that commits the strong safety to a B-gap fit. That puts the corner on an island, and we do not want to do that to happen to many times.

The Mike linebacker has coverage on the #3 receiver. In the trips set, it puts him in a run/pass conflict (Diagram #6). He has a run fit in the A gap but must get under #3 vertical. It becomes a double problem if the #3 receiver is a wide receiver. To help him, we move the tackle from a 3 technique into an A-gap alignment. That allows the Mike linebacker to step out into the B gap, where he can cover the #3 receiver and fit into the B gap.

If there is a tight end on the backside of a trips set, the strong safety has to get involved with the run fits to the trips side of the formation. He has the #3 receiver on a vertical, but we have a linebacker removed from the front and the linebacker will not

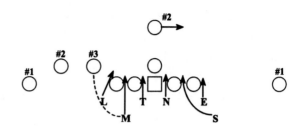

Diagram #6. Mike Adjustment

be a factor on a run into the B gap. The play that can possibly hurt is the tackle pull from the backside turning up in the B gap. He can see the tackle, and it is a very obvious and fast read. Anytime he lines up in that position, he should say, "Lock-spill" to the linebacker. If the tackle pulls, he heads to the B gap for the spill. The linebacker fills the hole and spills the ball to the strong safety. The other adjustment is to call "lock box." In that case, the linebacker turns the play back inside, and the strong safety fits inside.

If we get a twins set and two backs with a tight end to the backside, we play "cloud" to that side (Diagram #7). The corner rolls to the flat to that side. The strong safety is over the top of the corner and has the tight end running the corner route. We play mix to the twins side of the formation.

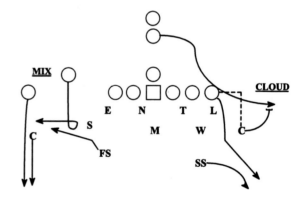

Diagram #7. Cloud

The empty set gives us a 3x2 formation. When you defend the empty set, you base the coverage on what type of quarterback you are facing. The #1 receiver to the three-receiver side is the least-used receiver in the pattern. The quarterback cannot get the ball to him, and most of the time they do not want to throw to him. Last season, we saw 22 percent empty sets. We see more of the empty set now than ever before. It is better if you put a nickel back into the game if a team shows a lot of empty set.

To the two-receiver side, we play mix, and nothing changes for that side. To the trips side, we play combination coverage (Diagram #8). The free safety plays the set, keying the #3 receiver to the #2 receiver. If the #3 receiver is vertical past 10 yards, the free safety jumps it. We fit the Mike linebacker under the #3 receiver, but that leads to another problem. That goes back to the quarterback. Does he run the ball? The Mike linebacker walls the #3 receiver to the outside, up to 10 yards. The free safety plays on the inside of the #3 receiver as he comes up the field. If the #3 receiver does not come up the field, the free safety looks to the #2 receiver.

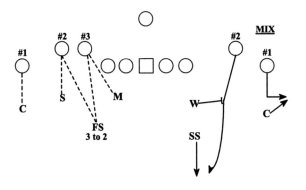

Diagram #8. Empty

The corner has a deep-third mentality on this scheme. The Sam linebacker has to run his butt off to stay inside the #2 receiver. He needs the safety to talk to him as he runs inside-out on the #2 receiver. He tries to see the #1 receiver. The safety has to tell the Sam linebacker whether he has a #3 receiver vertical. The corner has to keep inside leverage on the #1 if he goes vertical. He favors the #2 receiver if he comes vertical. He cannot break across the #1 receiver to help on a post route by #2. He must be inside with the ability to break inside on a pattern thrown to the #2 receiver.

If the #3 receiver runs to the flat, the free safety yells to the Sam linebacker, "I got him." He takes the #2 receiver vertical. That releases the Sam linebacker to settle in the flat and play football.

I want to show you the option that you are better off playing. We play a mix to the two-receiver side, which is our standard cover 4. To the three-receiver side, we play "mini" coverage (Diagram #9). All we do is ignore the outside receiver to the trips side. The corner plays him man-to-man, and the free safety and the nickel back or a third corner play mix on the two remaining receivers.

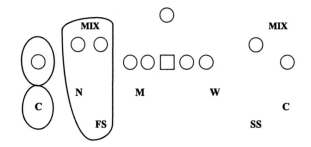

Diagram #9. Mini

The Mike linebacker plays the inside the #3 receiver to the trips side as he always did. If the inside receiver goes under, the free safety helps the corner with the #2 receiver or looks to the backside for something coming through the secondary.

If the #3 receiver goes to the flat, the nickel back rolls to the flat, and the free safety plays over the top. The Mike linebacker works outside to the curl area inside the #2 receiver. The Will linebacker, corner, and strong safety play the same scheme to the two-receiver side.

The thing you do not want to do is press with the corner in mini coverage on the #1 receiver. He plays off and looks inside. He does not perceive the #1 receiver to be a threat. He has him man-to-man. However, if the ball is thrown quickly, he can be a factor on the tackle. Teams like to put the running back at the inside-receiver position and bubble him. The corner can be a factor on that type of play. You cannot play this with a linebacker instead of a nickel back. The linebacker would have to cover the vertical post cut by that receiver, and we do not feel he can do it.

The Mike linebacker has a 10-yard rule. His maximum drop is 10 yards deep. Some of the quarterbacks we play against are tailbacks. Colt

McCoy is that type of player. We do not want him in the middle because everyone else is outside. The Mike linebacker does not let anyone inside of him.

In our front against the empty, we want to run line games in that situation. The end rushes up the field and has a two-way go. We call that "eyes." He can rush inside or outside the offensive tackle. The nose bull rushes and tries to make the defensive end right. If the end takes an inside path to get to the quarterback, the nose works outside on his rush for contain. To the other side, we give both the tackle and the Leo a two-way go. These are natural game plans and simple to teach.

I want to show you our run fits with a two-tight-end set (Diagram #10). We use single-gap spacing to control the line of scrimmage. We use the strong safety as the run support and take the free safety out of the run-support scheme.

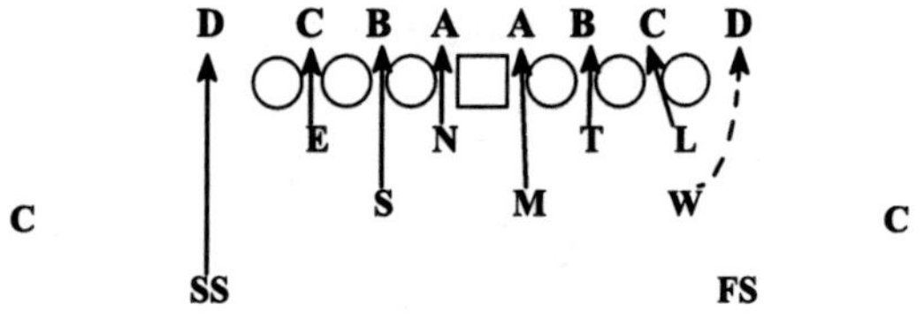

Diagram #10. Two-Tight-End Run Fits

When we run cover 2, we call it in a third-down passing situation or a second-and-long situation (Diagram #11). It is not built to play the run from this coverage. We try to teach the coverage as a match-up cover 2. We play people and have gotten away from the zone terms that people talk about. We do not play curl/flat; we play people. We play two-deep and five-under pass defense and match up to receivers.

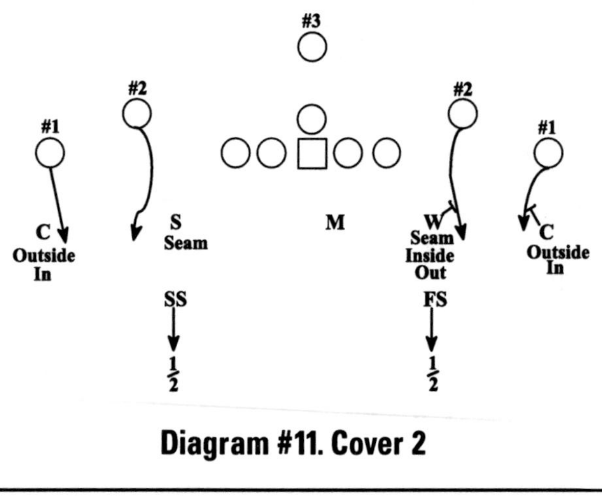

Diagram #11. Cover 2

The corners play at a depth of five yards. They play a tight outside shade on the #1 receiver. They try to reroute the receivers to the inside. We deny any outside release. The defender takes as many outside shuffles as he needs to get the receiver to the inside. When he gets the receiver rerouted to the inside, he opens his hips to the quarterback. If the receiver releases to the inside, we do not chase that release as far. After he takes two shuffles to the inside, he gets back to the outside zone.

The outside linebackers are the seam players to their side. They want to force the receiver outside. If they get a true vertical, the seam defenders run with the receiver to the goal line. He does not try to stay in front of the receiver. If he gets one yard inside and two yards behind in a trail position, that is all we ask. The linebacker is looking and listening. The corner or the safety will tell him if the #2 receiver is trying to get vertical. Once he hears or sees the #2 not going vertical, he stops and zones up. He does not drive on the hitch by the receiver because they will throw the curl behind him.

The Mike linebacker will cancel the #2 receiver coming to the inside. Patterns that cross are passed off. We are not playing man-to-man; we are zoning off all switch patterns. If the #2 receiver runs to the outside, the linebacker retreats and gets under the next pattern coming to the inside.

If the #3 back runs a checkdown pattern to the flat, the Mike linebacker has to play him. The corner and outside linebacker are too deep in their coverage to react back up to that delayed pattern. If the #3 receiver goes to the flat immediately, the Mike lets him go, and the corner or outside linebacker will pick him up. He calls "push, push" and drops at a 45-degree angle to the outside to replace the outside linebacker because he pushed him off his coverage.

The safeties in cover 2 are 12 to 14 yards deep one yard outside the hash marks. They key the #1 receiver. If the outside receiver gets an outside release, he pushes outside an additional two yards and squares back into his pedal. If the receiver takes an inside release, he stays down the hash mark.

In a trips formation, we play somewhat different. The linebacker opposite the three-receiver side is the low-hole player. He is the #2 weak defender. If the offense runs the #2 and #3 receiver vertical, the backside linebacker is the only player left in the middle of the field. He cannot let anything cross into the middle. He has to cancel all crossing patterns. His rule is to cover the #2 receiver to the first crosser.

On a sprint-out pass, we have rules for the defenders. The curl defender drives on the intermediate route. The flat defender drives the flat route. The high defender drives the corner route. The Mike linebacker runs to the curl. We played this coverage last year, and it was about 72 percent effective.

The zone package that we use has been very helpful with our cover-4 scheme. The mentality of dropping defensive linemen in the zone-blitz scheme is getting outdated with modern football. If you are getting empty or quad sets, you cannot zone blitz with defensive linemen.

If we give a field call, the zone blitz is "field smash" (Diagram #12). The field call sets the end, nose, and Sam linebacker into the field. In our blitz terminology, we use words that start with S, W, or M. When the defensive backs hear those words, they know we are in three-deep coverage. On an S word, the strong safety follows the Sam linebacker. Any W word means the free safety follows the Will linebacker. We bring this blitz from the field. In the blitz package, we play three-deep and three-underneath in our coverage.

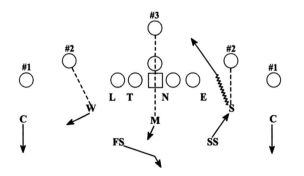

Diagram #12. Field Smash

On the field smash, the Sam linebacker is blitzing off the edge. The corners drop to the outside thirds, and the free safety goes to the middle of the field. The strong safety drops hot to the #2 receiver to the Sam linebacker's side. The Will linebacker is in the outside zone to his side, and the Mike linebacker has coverage in the middle. The Mike linebacker drops to #2 hot, and the Will linebacker drops to #3 hot.

If we call a W word, the free safety is hot to the #2 receiver to that side of the formation. On the M word, the strong safety drops hot to the #3 receiver in the middle. By setting the front the way we do, it makes it simple for the defensive backs. They know who is blitzing and where they are going regardless of the formation.

That is how we get into our zone blitzes. It is a very simple concept that gives you many options. You can make up the ones you want and have no confusion at all with their installation.

There is a major difference in the way we play our three-under defenders. You have to match people up in the zones. The offense does not send receivers into zone where defenders are playing. When we blitz the Sam linebacker, the sight adjustment says to throw to the receiver that the Sam linebacker was covering. We roll the strong safety to the hot receiver. The Will linebacker takes the hot #3 receiver, who is the tailback. The Mike linebacker the jumps the tight end. That is the quarterback's quickest hot reads.

When the strong safety drops down to take the Sam linebacker place, his leverage depends on the alignment of the #3 defender. If the #3 receiver has no threat to get into the flat to his side, he drops, maintaining inside-out leverage on the receiver. He knows the hot-to-three defender is on the other side because of the #3 receiver's alignment. He cannot give up the inside spot routes and must reroute him outside.

If the #3 receiver is close to him and can get into the flat, he drops down into outside leverage on the #2 receiver. He is still rerouting the #2 receiver, but he is doing it from a different leverage. With the #3 receiver going to the flat, the strong safety and Mike linebacker exchange receivers. The Mike picks up the #2 hot route, and the strong safety plays hot on #3.

We play a box mentality with our three underneath defenders. The Mike, Will, and strong safety are concerned with the three receivers in the box. The #1 receivers do not matter. We are concerned with the #2 receivers and the #3 receiver. We want to make sure none of the receivers in the box can get outside.

The corners have to key the #1 and #2 receivers. If they come vertical, the corners have to midpoint the receivers and get into a position to play both of them. The free safety must do the same thing with the #2 receivers. The deep defenders are looking for something that will tell them the offense is not running four-verticals. If one of the patterns drops off into some other route, the three-deep defenders go to the receivers running in their zone and play them man-to-man.

That is the way we teach it. Defensive linemen cannot play those types of techniques. Everyone in America runs the zone blitz by bringing the Sam linebacker off the edge and slanting the defensive line away from his blitz. They drop the defensive end away from the blitz. The problem is the contain player on the openside of the formation. You take the 3-technique tackle and make him the outside contain. It is a good blitz if that defender can contain.

We have started to double call our zone-blitz package. We do not like to call A-gap and B-gap blitzes to the tight-end side. It forces the end into a 9 technique to contain. We do not play a lot of 9 technique, and it compromises our C-gap coverage on a running play. It also gives the stunt away. We call "smoke-smash" as a double call. We run the smoke from the two-man side, and the smash from the three-man side. That way, your end does not have containment when the tight end is toward him. You can make up any blitz you want. The W blitzes are the same as the S blitzes, except the Will linebacker runs them and the free safety follows him.

The rules on the zone blitz are important. Whoever is the edge contain rusher has the quarterback. If it is option, the hot-two defender always has the pitch on the option. If we ran a field smash into the field, the Sam linebacker has the quarterback, and the strong safety has the pitch, provided they ran the ball that way. If we drop a defensive lineman, he can never drop to a wide receiver.

We can run a "mass" stunt. That is a two-linebacker stunt between the Mike and Sam linebackers. If we call "open sass" (Diagram #13), the Sam comes off the edge, and the Mike linebacker blows the B gap. The end plays run first, then drops for the hot-2. The strong safety drops down and takes the hot-3. The Will linebacker to the other side has the hot-2 to his side.

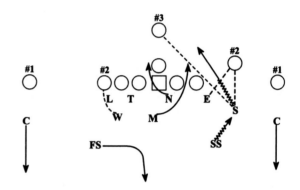

Diagram #13. Open Mass

We have a stunt where we bring both the Mike and Sam linebackers into the A gaps and drop the nose. We call "mass-A," which is Mike and Sam into the A gap.

To me, zone blitzes are good first-and-10 change-ups. We try to find out their best third-down call and fit the blitz to that play. Third down and long yardage is not a good time to call these types of blitzes. It is not really a blitz but a pressure scheme. The coverage is simple, and running the blitz is simple.

I appreciate you staying for the lecture. I hope I said something that will help you. Thanks for your time.

THE INSIDE A-GAP POWER PLAY

University of Minnesota

Thank you. It is great to be home. It is exciting for me to come back to the state of New Jersey. It does not surprise me to come back to my home state and speak to a packed room. Football is important to the state of New Jersey. The greatest high school football is played right here in this state.

I have been given a special opportunity at the University of Minnesota. At Minnesota, we have six national championships in football. Only four other schools have won as many national championships as the University of Minnesota. We have won 18 Big Ten championships. It has been awhile since we have done it.

We are opening up a new stadium on campus. It is an amazing stadium and it is gorgeous. It will hold 57,000 and the inner structure of the stadium can go to 80,000 very quickly. We open on the road at Syracuse on September 5, and later in the season, we come back east to play that team in Pennsylvania with the old coach. We come back to play Penn State. It is special for me to be here. I want to give the guys who run this clinic a round of applause.

It gives me goose bumps to listen to the Marines talk about the things they stand for. They stand for courage, commitment, and teamwork. We, as football coaches, are working for that same type of commitment. If there was ever a branch of the armed services I would want playing for me, it would be the Marines. They are a demanding group of men.

I have only been a head coach in college for two years. I spent 23 years as an assistant coach. For 23 years, I worked for the opportunity to be a head football coach. I wanted to be at a place that had a chance to win and play in a prestigious conference. I am very blessed to be the head football coach at the University of Minnesota. If you have a dream of moving on and up in your profession, you must remember anything is possible. If it can happen for me, it can happen for any coach in this room. You have to believe in your vision.

You are here today because you want to learn something about winning and to grow as a coach. You want to get better at being a football coach, which is meaningful to me. I am not going to give you a lot of philosophical junk which a lot of head coaches do. I am going to try and teach some football. I am going to teach you a play that I think is the best play in football.

The greatest play in football is the *A-gap power play*. I am going to teach you everything from A to Z about this play. I promise you, it will get you four yards a carry. The New York Giants are a great power running football team. They run it for four, five, and six yards at a time. Against the Panthers, the first play in the overtime game was a power play. It went for 70 yards and won the game.

I believe in this play and I think it fits the game of football. You must have a physical approach to play this game. Everyone is into the spread offense and what it can do for you. My first two years at Minnesota, we were a spread football team. I was extremely disappointed with our ability to run the football from the spread formation. There was too much east-west running for me. The football running game has to be run downhill in a north-south direction. We are going to be a spread team with our passing game, but the running game is going back to the kind of football that I know.

I believe in a physical brand of football. I believe you have to hit the defense in the mouth. If you hit them in the mouth enough, in the fourth quarter the big runs will come. Early in the game, five-yard runs are enough, but late in the game, the 60- and 70-yard runs will start to happen.

We run this play in the A gap. It is a downhill running play. You will see it hit into the B gap and the C gap on occasion. When people think of a power play, they think it is run off-tackle in the six-hole gap. It is not a C-gap play. It is run to the hole the defense gives you. The philosophy behind this play is sound.

PHILOSOPHY

- Sets the mentality of the team
- Downhill running play
- Gap blocking scheme
- Forces defense to be assignment sound
- Can be creative with formations and variations

This play takes care of anything the defense can do. It can be run against the bear front, linebackers running through, and linebackers walking up into the front. It is gap-scheme blocking. We block down, pull the backside guard, and kick out at the point of attack. It is a great football play against any front. We change formations, bunch differently, and use shifts, but it is the same play.

We call the play 20 power (Diagram #1). The defense in the diagram is an "over 4-3 stack" defense. The tight end's block is one of the most critical blocks in the power game. If the playside tackle is covered, the tight end is working with the tackle in what we call a trey block. If the tackle is uncovered, the tight end blocks a man-on rule. The tight end blocks any 6-technique, 7-technique, or 9-technique defender.

The playside guard and tackle block a combination double-team on the 3-technique defender with one of them slipping to the Will linebacker. We call that combination block deuce. The center blocks man-on or blocks back for the pulling guard. The backside guard pulls and turns up in the C gap looking for the Mike linebacker. The backside tackle hinges on a backside cutoff.

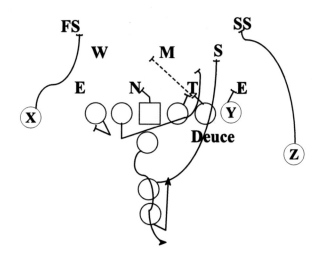

Diagram #1. 20 Power

The tailback's heels are aligned at seven yards from the line of scrimmage. The depth of the tailback is absolutely critical to the play. When we snap the ball, the tailback takes a drop-step to assure the timing is right for the pulling guard.

Mike Shanahan was with the Denver Broncos for a number of years. They were known for running the football. The number one determining factor between winning and losing football games is no longer the turnover margin. Today, the difference between winning and losing is explosive plays. Explosive plays are runs over 12 yards and passes over 18 yards.

Who is responsible for explosive runs? Is it the offensive line or the wide receivers? We think it is the wide receivers. We grind on our wide receivers to block. The wide receivers at Minnesota are going to be great blockers for us. We have taken the model of the Denver Broncos, and we grind after our wide receivers. The wide receivers have to understand the importance of their contributions to the success of the play. In the diagram, the Z has to block the SS for this play to be a real success.

We run the power, and we will run it against an eight-man front. We will block the line of scrimmage and safeties and make sure the corners have to tackle someone. Running football teams force the defense's corner to make tackles. We want to scheme our blocking to force those little corners to make tackles. We call the play *26*, but it is actually

20 power. We do not want this play hitting inside the tight end. We want it hitting in the A gap.

The tight end in the diagram is taking the 9 technique outside. He drives off with his outside foot and drops his inside foot inside. He works his head for the outside number of the defender to make him widen outside. He takes his inside hand and drives the defender to the outside.

The guard and tackle are working a combination block, which we call a deuce block, on the 3 technique and the backside linebacker. The guard takes a set step with his inside foot. He stabs the outside half of the tackle with his outside hand as he comes off. His eyes focus to the inside. He is responsible for any run through by the Mike or Will linebacker. The tackle takes a gap step with his inside foot and puts his face and hand on the outside hip of the 3 technique. We call that "tenderizing the hip" of the defensive tackle. The tackle knocks the 3 technique across the face of the guard. That secures the guard's block on the 3 technique and allows the tackle to get backside for the linebacker.

Most of the defensive tackles in the Big Ten are 300 pounds. You will not be able to knock them too far to the inside with the tackle's block, but we want movement off the line of scrimmage. That is a critical block at the point of attack.

The run is designed to go inside the deuce block. The center blocks back on the nose guard. The center steps with the backside foot into the gap to prevent penetration by the nose.

The backside tackle has a *funnel-and-hinge technique*. If there is a 3 technique on the pulling guard, the tackle has to step down and push the defender to the center. He has to keep the defender off the pulling guard and deliver him to the center's block. After he funnels the defender to the center, he hinges back and cuts off the backside. In the diagram, he does not have to funnel the nose. He gap steps into the inside gap and hinges back on the defensive end.

The most critical point of the play is the pulling guard. We use an option pull. He drops his inside foot, gets his shoulder and hip open, and gets downhill to the other side as quickly as he can. In the diagram, he pulls for the Mike linebacker—that might not be the case. We want him to pull and clean up anything that is causing problems. We teach him to block the first opposite-colored jersey in his path.

The Mike linebacker on this play so many times takes himself out of the play and we do not block him. They have a tendency to overrun this play. The problem occurs with a 7-technique defensive end playing on the tight end. Usually the 7-technique defender is a big, physical player that the tight end has trouble handling. We tell the pulling guard as he pulls, if there is anything hanging off the tight end, he blocks it. He helps the tight end and takes the pressure off the tight end to succeed with his block.

The fullback has the Sam linebacker. He has him whether he is on or off the ball. An important thing to remember has to do with the quarterback. He cannot force the tailback wide. He reverses out and brings the ball to the tailback. However, he cannot force him into the B gap. The tailback can take the ball into the B gap, but he must be able to get into the A gap if necessary.

If the strong safety cheats down into the box, the quarterback may have to put the flanker in motion so he can block the strong safety. That is the case, particularly in a short-yardage or goal-line situation. In those situations, the strong safety is tighter to the line of scrimmage. You should not expect your flanker to block the strong safety rolling down into the B gap from his wideout position. We put him in motion back to the formation and let him crack on the safety.

I was with the San Diego Chargers working for Marty Schottenheimer. We played a game at Oakland and ran this play 21 times in the game. In one stretch in the fourth quarter, we ran it nine consecutive plays. We ran the play right at them and absolutely killed them. You can run this play regardless of the look from the defense. This play gets better as the game goes on. On the play, all you are looking for is four yards. In the late quarters you get much more.

We move the fullback into position by alignments or motion to get a better angle on the Sam linebacker. We align him in the halfback slot or use step motion to get him to that position. The fullbacks we see today are not big enough to take on Sam linebackers. The fullback is becoming an extinct football player. The fullbacks in the NFL are 5'10", 250 pounds, no neck, a big butt, and most of them can catch the football on the arrow route. We use tight ends in those positions to block linebackers.

If the defense goes to an even look with the Sam linebacker on the line of scrimmage, the fullback's block does not change (Diagram #2). There are two basic changes in this defense. The Sam linebacker is on the line of scrimmage outside the tight end and the defensive end is in a 7 technique on the tight end.

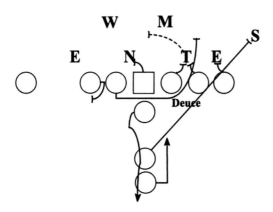

Diagram #2. Power Sam Linebacker

It is critical for the tight end to use proper technique because he has a hard block. He has to take on a 285-pound defensive end. He steps with his inside foot and attacks the inside number of the defender. The worst thing that can happen is the defender getting across his face. He gets his helmet on the inside number and works for his inside armpit. He is not trying to wash him down the line of scrimmage. He wants to drive block him back off the ball. We want vertical movement on all our blocks. However, he can never get beat inside. That is the cardinal sin for the tight end.

If the defensive end whips the tight end, the pulling guard helps on the defender. We coach him to block any opposite color as he pulls for the Mike

linebacker. He takes on the defensive end and blocks him. He does not worry about getting to the Mike linebacker because this is a more important block in the scheme.

People do not think they can run this play because they do not have a strong tight end. You can take the pressure off the tight end's block in two ways. We use the guard to clean up on the 7 technique and the play hits inside.

The next defensive look is the *3-4 under defense*. The defensive end aligns in a 5 technique on the offensive tackle and the nose is in a strongside shade on the center. The Sam linebacker aligns in a 9 technique on the tight end. In our blocking scheme we have three combination blocks. We have an ace, deuce, and trey. The *ace* block occurs between the center and guard. The *deuce* takes place between the guard and tackle. The trey block is between the tackle and end.

In the 3-4 defense, we use a trey combination between the tight end and tackle on the 5-technique defensive end (Diagram #3). The tight end and tackle double-team the 5 technique to the backside linebacker. If the Mike linebacker walks up into the B gap, the tackle makes a gap call to the tight end. A gap call means the tackle blocks his inside gap and the tight end has to single block the big defensive end.

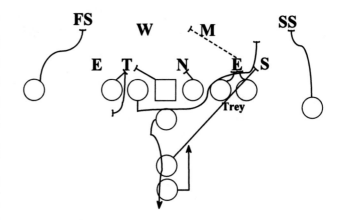

Diagram #3. Power vs. 3-4

The technique the tackle uses is important. He does not fire inside. He post steps with his inside foot and stabs the outside half of the 5 technique to help the tight end. His eyes are inside on the linebacker, but he prevents the 5-technique end from getting immediate penetration. The tight end gap steps to the inside and gets his face and hands on the hip of the 5-technique defensive end. It is amazing the movement you can get when you get control of the hip.

The playside guard blocks back on the shade nose guard in his inside gap. The center blocks back on the 3-technique defensive tackle over the backside guard. If the 3-technique defender is a hard penetrator upfield, there is no way the center can block him. The backside tackle uses his funnel technique to deliver the 3 technique to the center. He gap steps inside and prevents the 3 technique from penetrating or grabbing the pulling guard. He delivers him to the center and hinges back for the defensive end.

The fullback blocks the Sam linebacker outside the trey block. The pulling guard pulls outside the trey block and turns up for the Mike linebacker. We never want the pulling guard inside the trey or deuce block. The quarterback exchange and tailback path are the same on every one of these plays. The tailback is hitting in the A gap first and finding the crease.

On the combination blocks, the post blocker has to use a post step and stab with his outside hand. He has to keep his eyes to the inside for any linebacker blitz. He works the inside half of the defender until the double-team knocks the defender across his face. If he has no penetration coming from the inside, he takes over the block and allows the outside blocker to slip to the next level.

If the 3-4 front has the nose head up the center in a 0 technique, we have an ace-and-trey combination (Diagram #4). The center and playside guard use an ace combination for the 0 technique and Will linebacker. The techniques are the same for all combination blocks. The center gap steps into the A gap and stabs the 0 technique. He protects the backside A gap. The guard gap steps to the 0 technique and comes off for the Will linebacker.

The fullback's block does not need to be a killer block. All he has to do is get his helmet into the

proper position and shield the Sam linebacker from getting to the inside.

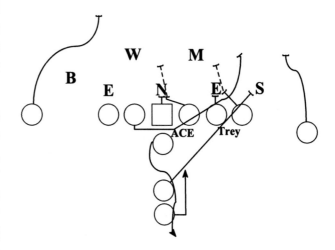

Diagram #4. Ace and Trey

We have a one-back power play called plant (Diagram #5). This is the most popular nickel run in college and pro football today. All the elements of the play remain the same except there is only one back in the backfield. If you go to a one-back set, you will get a six defender box with nickel coverage in the secondary. The tight end gives us six blockers. The Will linebacker is not in the box because of the extra receiver to his side.

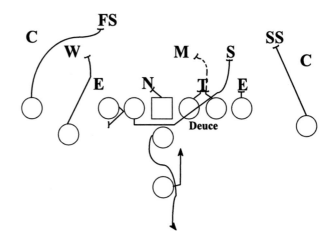

Diagram #5. Plant

The pulling guard has the Sam linebacker. We run the deuce block for the Mike linebacker and everything else on the play is the same. The flanker to the playside takes the safety, and the H-back in the slot to the formationside blocks the Will linebacker. Everything else with the play remains the same. However, the play has a tendency to hit wider in the one-back formation. If the Will linebacker cheats back into the box, we change the play and throw the ball. We package the power play with a pass and an automatic out of the run.

We have a short-yardage package called load power. We use a 22-personnel grouping with two tight ends and two backs (Diagram #6). The load power is a wider play. We do not start the play in the A gap. The play starts in the B gap. We have a third tight end in the wing set. We have two combination blocks on this play. We have a deuce block between the guard and tackle on the 3-technique defender, and we have a quad combination between the tight end and wing back.

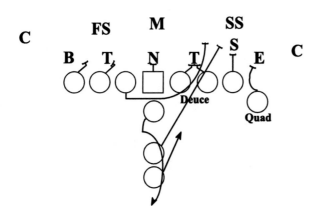

Diagram #6. Load Scheme

I think this is a hell of a football play. It can be run against all defensive fronts. It gives your football team a physical mentality. It makes your team tougher on both sides of the ball. When your defense practices against this scheme, they get tougher with their mental outlook to the running game. I love the play. I want to thank you for being here. I love what you guys do for the kids you coach. Who has some questions?

The question is about the inside post block on the combination block. The post blocker takes an inside step with his post foot. He stabs the outside number of the defender aligned on him. His eyes are to the inside for any type of penetration or blitz. If you get the threat of a blitz to the inside, he gives a gap call and gets his head inside on the blitz.

The key to the play is the back. He has to set up the play. He takes his drop-step to let the guard clear before he attacks the A gap. The play is designed to hit the playside A gap, but on occasion, the back gets the ball in the backside A gap.

If there are no more questions, I want to thank you for having me here. Come see us at Minnesota.

THE SHOTGUN SHOVEL PASS AND ZONE OPTIONS

United States Air Force Academy

I appreciate you being here. I know you really love football to be here tonight. Coming back to Pittsburgh is an exciting experience. I recruited here when I was at Ohio University and I absolutely loved it. The impact you coaches have on lives is sensational. The high school coach has a chance to have more influence on a high school kid than anyone else. The things you teach and the character traits are remarkable. When you think about gut, unselfishness, toughness, courage, competitive spirit, and all the good traits we want to ingrain in kids, they all come from football coaches.

The young men that come to the United States Air Force Academy have a tremendous responsibility down the road. They learn leadership and all the traits it takes to be leader.

I am going to talk about a couple of topics that I know are of some interest to you. When you think of the Air Force Academy, you think of triple-option football. I am going to show you a couple of options, which I think you will find are extremely simple.

At the Academy, we never practice more than 90 minutes. Our team comes in at 2:00, and we begin with special teams meetings for 15 minutes, followed by positions team meetings for 30 minutes. From there, we go to the weight room. To get stronger as the season goes along, we feel we need to lift before practice. It gets our bodies warm so that when we hit the practice field, we go straight to work. We work for 90 minutes at the longest. On Mondays and Thursdays, the length of practice is 70 minutes.

They get to the dining hall, and, from there, they go to study groups, the library, or to a tutor. That is a requirement at the Academy. Because of the requirements it takes to get into the Air Force

Academy, our recruiting pool is small. To get things done, we have to be extremely organized and do some things that are different. They are sound, but it takes discipline, great unity, and precision to get it done.

Our starting center this year was 246 pounds. The left tackle was 249 pounds. Size-wise, we are a very small football team. If you watch us play, you will be impressed with our movement. When it comes to the service academies, something thumps very loudly in your chest.

We run the option because we think it gives the offense an additional ballcarrier. It gives an athletic quarterback more angles to operate in space. The offense makes the defense package shrink in the number of fronts and coverages they play against you. For us, we want to see zone-blitz schemes. We also get the extra blocker into the scheme. We think this offense stretches the defense and makes them cover the entire field. It forces the defense to be sound in their assignments and slows them down.

We run the option, but I wanted to find ways that did not get the quarterback pounded all the time. We added the midline to help with that thought. We want him to carry the ball 12 to 14 times a game instead of 22 to 24 times. One of the ways we improved on that was to add the shovel option.

When we run the shovel option, there are a couple of key principles. The first key is in the offensive line. We want to get as many defenders on the ground as possible. We do that by getting tremendous angles in our blocking scheme. You do not have to block as many defenders with an option. We try to create a 2-on-1 offense.

There are two defenders on the option that we are not going to block. We are going to read one defender and pitch off the other one. We have three players that can carry the ball on the shovel option. When we run the shovel option, we will be in some kind of 20 personnel—that is two backs, no tight ends, and three wide receivers.

On the shovel option, the quarterback aligns in the shotgun with his toes five yards from the front tip of the football (Diagram #1). The two backs will be on the same plane as the quarterback, directly behind the offensive tackles. The play can be run from a number of different formations. By using motion, we can run the play from empty or a one-back set.

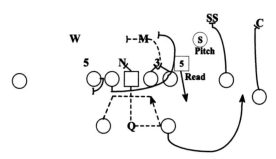

Diagram #1. Shovel Option

The 5-technique defender on the outside shoulder of the offensive tackle is going to be unblocked. The next man to the outside is also unblocked. We read the 5 technique and pitch off the next man outside. The inside slot receiver knows the read and pitch keys and avoids them. He blocks the strong safety. The wide receiver to that side stalk blocks the man who covers him.

We block this play exactly like the gap power play we run. The playside tackle has an inside block. If there is a 3 technique aligned on the guard, they double-team the 3 technique. We want the tackle to stay on the 3-technique defender as long as he can and work for vertical push. The tackle does not have to come off the block until the backside linebacker shows. We leave the playside linebacker alone. When the tackle comes off for the backside linebacker, he has a great angle to make the block. We can cut inside the box, and we try to get people on the ground. We try to cut the backside tackle if we can.

If there is an extremely wide 3-technique defender, the playside guard can release for the

backside linebacker, and the tackle single blocks on the 3 technique. That would be a rare occasion for us to get a wide 3 technique. Defenses play their 3 techniques tight because of the midline option we run on the inside. Anytime the guard is covered, we double-team with the guard and tackle. That is because of the size of our offensive linemen.

The only time we do not double when the guard is covered is when a linebacker walks up in the A gap (Diagram #2). If that occurs, we give a green or gap call and we block down. The center blocks back for the pulling guard. The backside tackle does what we call an anchor hinge. He steps into his gap and hinges back for the backside defensive end.

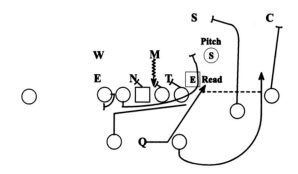

Diagram #2. Linebacker Walk-Up

The backside guard pulls and is responsible for the frontside linebacker. He gets to the frontside linebacker off the 5-technique defender. If the defender gets up the field, the guard turns up in the space of the tight end. If the defender is heavy-handed on the offensive tackle and the linebacker starts to move, the guard has to get to him.

If the 5-technique tackle is tight to the line of scrimmage, the pulling guard goes to his outside and turns up on the playside linebacker. Initially, this technique takes time to get the timing worked out. The only thing the guard has to do is get his body in front of the linebacker. If he can tie the linebacker up in some way, we will have a positive play.

The playside back has to create a pitch relationship with the quarterback. He wants to get two yards deep and five yards in front of the quarterback. If the quarterback is under the center, the relationship is reversed. The back is five yards deep and two yards in front of him. He does not delay in his movement. He takes a drop-step to lose the two yards and gets out on his option path. After the first two steps, he gets his head around to the quarterback and gets into his pitch phase.

The ball rarely comes to the pitchback immediately. The only way that would happen is a double crash by the read and pitch keys. The pitchback understands the play and has run it enough to know who the keys are. He should anticipate the pitch because he knows the reads. If he sees the 9 technique on the crash, he should expect the pitch on his second step.

The backside back takes three steps forward and comes into the line under control. He steps with his outside foot first. As soon as he plants to go to the frontside, his eyes go to the quarterback. On the plant step, we want the back to come at 90 degrees, parallel to the line of scrimmage. If he comes too fast down the line of scrimmage, the 5 technique can force the quarterback and turn around and make the play on the shovel. If the 5 technique closes on the quarterback immediately, the ball has to be pitched. A big coaching point for the backside back is to be under control as he comes across the set.

The quarterback wants to be five yards in front of the underneath pitchback. If the ball is pitched to him, he will be in the vicinity of the playside guard. We want him to turn up immediately. When he turns up, he should turn up and run over the offensive tackle's shoes. We want to turn up and not carry the ball outside. If he gets too wide, the pitch key will make the play on him.

The quarterback is in the shotgun set. He catches the ball and has a short pause before he starts to run. That gives him a chance to catch the ball and the frontside back to get started on his path. If the 5 technique is up the field, the quarterback pitches the ball inside to the backside running back. We tell the quarterback he has to go laterally with the ball. If the 5 technique stays up on the line of scrimmage, the quarterback brings the ball outside and works off the 9-technique defender.

If the defense plays the 3 technique to the backside of the formation with the nose to the frontside, this is a dream kill-shot for the playside tackle (Diagram #3). If the defense loosens the 5 technique, we leave our offensive tackle in a two-point stance. This is a great third-and-six yards for the first down. It neutralizes the pass rush. If the Mike linebacker runs through the B gap, the tackle blocks him. However, if the Mike linebacker goes over the top, the tackle gets an absolute earhole blast on the backside linebacker.

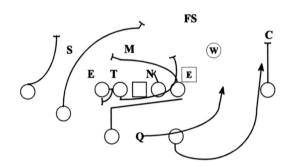

Diagram #3. Backside Shovel Option

The center blocks back on the 3 technique and the backside tackle hinges off the backside. We always read the man over the tackle. We read the first man head-up to the outside our offensive tackle. The quarterback takes three lateral steps before he starts to go downhill. That gives the quarterback separation between him and the shovel back. If he starts going downhill at the 5 technique, the shovel back and the quarterback are too close together and the 5 technique can play both backs. By going three steps laterally, the quarterback has a chance to get on the perimeter if the 5 technique squeezes inside.

If the 5 technique puts his hands on the offensive tackle and squeezes, the quarterback takes the ball outside immediately. As soon as the quarterback gets around the 5 technique, the play becomes a double option.

Against the 3-3 stack defense, we read the defensive end over the tackle and the stack linebacker behind the read key is the pitch key (Diagram #4). The playside tackle has an inside block into his inside gap. He blocks anything that shows up in the gap. The playside guard has a man-on, inside block. He blocks down on the shade nose. The center post-steps with his playside foot on the nose and works backside for the backside linebacker.

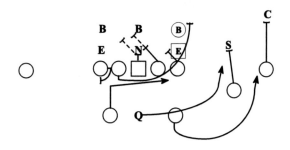

Diagram #4. Shovel vs. 3-3 Stack

We can also run a combination block with the center and guard with one of them coming off for the backside linebacker. If we can get the guard off on the backside linebacker, that is what we want to do. The backside tackle anchors in the B gap and hinges back for the defensive end.

The slot receiver has the block on the strong safety to that side, and the wide receiver blocks on the corner over him.

If the offensive tackle gets in a two-point stance, we feel the 5 technique will loosen to the outside. If the nose is to his side, the offensive tackle can make a jab-step to the outside as if he were going to pass set. That makes the 5 technique start to widen more. The longer the yardage, the looser he gets. He cannot do that if he has a 3 technique to his inside.

The backside hinge tackle anchors into the B gap on the backside and hinges back for the defensive end. The thing he must watch is getting in the way of the shovel back. The shovel back aligns behind the tackle and takes three steps forward toward the line of scrimmage. He has to make sure he does not force the back off his path. When he hinges, he hinges for width and not depth.

The coaching point for the pulling guard is to watch the 5 technique. If he is in no-man's-land and squatting, we want the pulling guard to go outside the 5-technique defender. The good thing about the

shovel pass is the pitch. A bad pitch is an incomplete pass.

We can put the shovel back in the slot and run the play from that position. He is positioned at the line and has to only work on the timing of being in the right place on the pitch. He still has to be under control as he runs behind the line of scrimmage.

If the read defender starts out in a 5 technique and slants into a 3 technique, the quarterback knows the read is done and he runs the double option off the 9-technique defender. We do not try to read and redirect our paths.

The pitchback, on the option, tries to cheat his position to get wider at the start of the play. He drop steps, crosses over, and loses ground on the first two steps. If we get the pitch, we have the playside linebacker outflanked. There should not be any other pursuit coming from the backside.

We run some companion plays with the shovel pass. We can run the shovel play but, instead of pitching it to the shovel back, we throw the ball to a bubble pattern by the slot receiver to that side. That takes a lot more time to practice and get the timing of the play.

The good thing about the shovel is that there is no mesh involved with the exchange of the ball. This gives the defense something else to work and spend practice time on to cover the play. We have gap rules for our linemen to handle the linebacker walk-ups into those gaps. If the nose is to the playside and the 3 technique to the backside, the B gap is open. The playside tackle rule is to block the B gap. If the Mike linebacker walks up into that gap, the tackle comes down and blocks him. If the Mike linebacker stays in his base alignment, the tackle comes through the B gap to the Mike linebacker and blocks the Mike linebacker.

When I first got to the Academy, the first spring was interesting. We decided to put the play in that spring. We knew the play was not that hard to install, but we decided to wait and put it in after we got back from spring break. The first days we put it in, we had two problems. The quarterback did not pause and did not take his lateral steps before he started the play, and the shovel back was too fast. The next day we were almost perfect with the play. This is a play that is easy to install and you can get good at executing the play.

If we get seven defenders in the box and the strong safety creeping down, we can run this play (Diagram #5). If there is a seven-man box with the free safety in the middle of the field, there is probably some kind of man-coverage scheme in the secondary. The playside blocks down or follows their rules. We want the playside tackle to get all the way to the backside Sam linebacker. The pulling guard pulls for the Mike linebacker. The quarterback reads the defensive end and pitches off the Will linebacker. The wide receivers run off the man coverage and stalk blocks them once the defenders realize it is run.

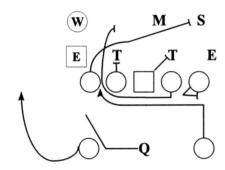

Diagram #5. Seven in the Box

The Will linebacker is not going to let the pitchback outflank him and will go hard to the outside. Against the seven-man box, we attack the backside of the defense because the angles are so good. We can work on all the techniques that go into this play and we can get good at what we do. The guards do not have trouble recognizing what the 5 technique is doing. When the guard turns up for the playside linebacker, he does not have to destroy the linebacker. All he has to do is get a hat on a hat and we will have a positive play. The guard reads his first technique. He knows if he can turn inside the 5-technique defender, the shovel back is going to get the ball.

The next play is the zone option. We run the zone option because it ties into the way we run the

outside-zone play. We can run the play from a one-back set, shotgun set, two-back set, or any number of combinations. The backside of this play is exactly like the outside-zone play. We are eliminating the number of blocks our offensive line has to make. The last thing it does is give us a chance to get a lot of defenders on the ground.

I will show you this from two looks. The first is the shotgun look with a tight end to the playside (Diagram #6). The defense to the playside is a shade nose, a 5 technique on the tackle, and a 9 technique on the tight end. The tight end and playside tackle work a combination block on the 5 technique up to the playside linebacker.

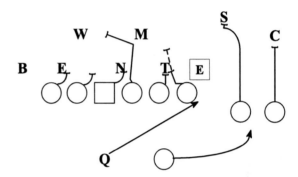

Diagram #6. Zone Option vs. 5 Technique

The tight end steps with his near foot to the 5-technique defender and punches the near hip over the top of his hip pads. If he does it right you can see the hip move and soften it enough for the tackle to get control of the reach block. When we run this play, we have 18-inch splits. We want to restrict the defense. We do not want to move a great distance to get into the blocks. We do not want to open gaps with large splits. The tackle reaches using a jump-hook technique, and the tight end punches out the back hip of the defender and moves up to the Mike linebacker.

The guard has B-gap responsibility. If there is no threat to the B gap, he helps the center on the nose and widens his path as he comes off for the backside linebacker. The reason we have him widen is to push the Mike linebacker over the top of the block. He continues and blocks the Will linebacker.

The quarterback pitches off the 9 technique. The inside receiver climbs to the safety, and the outside receiver stalks on the corner.

If we get the 3 technique on the guard and a 7 technique or 6 technique on the tight end, we use a pull-and-overtake technique on the 6 or 7 technique (Diagram #7). The tight end steps with his outside foot and takes his inside hand through the outside armpit of the defender. He has to hang to that block until the tackle can overtake the block. The tackle takes a pull-step and loses some ground. He gets into the 6 technique and overtakes the outside shoulder. Once the tackle has secured the reach, the tight end comes off for the inside linebacker.

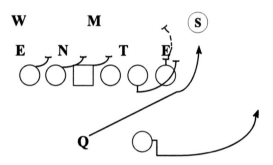

Diagram #7. Zone Option vs. 6 Technique

Those are the two techniques we have to perfect. The good thing is we still pitch the ball off the Sam linebacker. We love this play from a 3x1 set.

The quarterback runs the hump and works inside on the 9 technique. We do not run out to the inside or outside shoulders. We want him running in space to the pitch key.

The good thing about these options is that they do not take an immense amount of time to install and rep. If you start meshing in the midlines, triples, and zone-read plays out of the shotgun, those mechanics take time to rep and teach. These plays are simple and do not take time to teach and to execute. If you have a young quarterback and want to get the ball out of his hands but still make the defense play an option, this is the scheme you need.

If we get the eight- and nine-man box, we call crack (Diagram #8). We use the jump-hook technique by the offensive tackle on the 5-technique defender. The tight end comes down on the defender and knocks out the back hip. He works up for the Mike linebacker. The guard helps the center get his reach on the noseguard. He comes off the nose and widens his angle going up to the second level. He cuts off the Will linebacker.

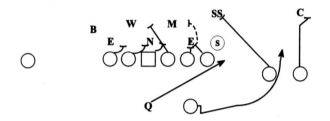

Diagram #8. Crack

The strong safety walks down into the box area. The inside slot receiver crack blocks on the strong safety in the box, and the outside receiver stalks the corner. The quarterback options the 9-technique linebacker and pitches off him. These plays are good plays against the blitz and zone-blitz schemes. They are adaptable to any offense. They are simple to run and simple to teach.

The Air Force Academy is a phenomenal place. When the players graduate, they have a five-year obligation to go serve their country as officers. They play football because they have an absolute passion for the game. We do not have a single player on athletic scholarship. These are special young people. The caliber of students at the Academy is unbelievable. The mission of the Academy makes it an extraordinary place. The surrounding of the Academy is outstanding. Everything there is about teamwork and toughness. You will never be around any people that are as classy as these players are. Gentlemen, it is an honor to be here. Come out to the Air Force Academy and see us. Thank you very much.

THE QUICK PASSING GAME PACKAGE

Indiana University

I want to get right into the lecture today. I am going to talk about our quick passing game. Our general balanced game plan package is based on 70 plays in a game, which means we are going to have 35 plays passing and 35 plays running. That is very balanced. In that balance, we want to have 18 quick game passes or empty passes. We want to have seven dropback passes and six screens (bubble, touchback/wide receiver screens). We want to have four different types of passes such as the naked plays, sprints, and play-action passes. That is a general estimate of how we set up our passing game. Again, this is based on calling 35 pass plays in a game.

WHY THE QUICK GAME IS SO IMPORTANT

- It keeps you from having to protect very long.
- It gets the ball in your playmaker's hands quickly.
- It has a high completion-percentage rate with low risk.
- It is a great answer to blitz.

THE BASIC PRINCIPLES OF THE QUICK PASSING GAME

- We have an answer to each coverage built in.
- We use the concept of center field open: two safeties (cover 2/4); center field closed: safety (cover 1/3).
- This allows the quarterback to pick a side and throw quickly.
- We have an answer to blitz.
- We keep it simple—we don't do too much.

We strive for 70 percent completion in our quick game. This last year, we were successful 68 percent of the time in the quick game.

There are a lot of different pass patterns that work with this approach to the passing game. You have to pick the routes that work best for you. You must make sure you are not trying to run every pass route possible so the receivers and the quarterback can be on the same page.

I want to show you a simple *two-safeties alignment* to show you how we read the defense (Diagram #1). This could be cover 2 or cover 4.

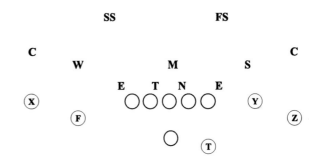

Diagram #1. Two-Safety Set, Center Field Open

The safeties are 16 yards deep. The quarterback looks at the contour of the coverage. The quarterback must decide if he is going to throw the ball to the left or to the right.

The next look is the *one-safety set* with the center field closed. The quarterback recognizes the safety in the middle of the field and knows the center of the field is closed.

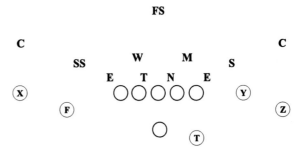

Diagram #2. One-Safety Set, Center Field Closed

The two corners are playing man-up on the outside, with the strong safety and the Sam linebacker covering the #2 receivers in the slot. It could be a cover 1 or cover 3 look with four defenders underneath.

We have seven basic quick game routes. We have four to beat center field open and three to beat center field closed. We can run each of these routes out of a number of formations. Each of these routes has an answer to blitz. Here is how we list the routes.

- Center-field-open routes
  - ✓ Drive
  - ✓ Snap
  - ✓ Harry
  - ✓ Dodge/Chevy
- Center-field-closed routes
  - ✓ Gator
  - ✓ Spacing
  - ✓ Stutter

All of the concepts we use can be used against different formations, so there is carryover on the routes. As I mentioned before, all of these routes have a built-in hot route we can go to if we have to throw quick.

Let me get to the center-field-open routes, which is against cover 2 and cover 4. The drive route is our variation of the slant route. The snap route complements our drive route. Harry is a concept where we are picking on an outside linebacker. The Dodge and Chevy are smash combination routes that we use.

The center-field-closed routes are used against the cover 1 or cover 3 looks. The Gator route is a smash concept. The spacing route is similar to a double-hitch route.

We run the 2x2 quick game with two receivers on each side.

Diagram #3. 2x2 Quick Game

This is our first route (Diagram #4). It is our bread-and-butter route.

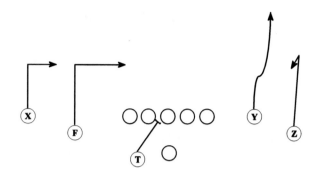

Diagram #4. Rob 50 Drive/Gator

The formation call is *Rob*, which tells the Z and Y receivers to go to the right. The 50 is the pass protection. On our 2x2 plays, we always read our plays from the left to the right. The Z and Y are on the right, and the X and F are on the left.

Rec.	Route	Description
X	Drive	Push vertical five yards. Break straight down the line. Get under the linebackers.
F	Drive	Push vertical five yards. Break straight down the line. Get under the linebackers.
Y	Taper	Push vertical. Must go outside linebackers.
Z	Smash	Push vertical six yards. Sit down.

Get your numbers back to the quarterback. Do not drift.

We like this play into the boundary more than into the field. This is because of the throw for the quarterback.

Next, is our *Rob 50 snap/Gator* (Diagram #5). The snap is the complement off the drive route. We run this route after we have run the drive route.

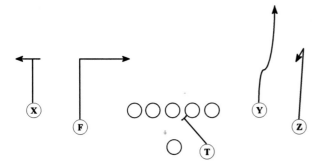

Diagram #5. Rob 50 Snap/Gator

Rec.	Route	Description
X	Snap	Push to five yards and make square cut to the drive for two steps. Snap back out flat. Do not drift up the field.
F	Drive	Push vertical five yards. Break straight down the line. Get under the linebackers.
Y	Taper	Push vertical. Must go outside linebackers.
Z	Smash	Push vertical six yards. Sit down. Get your numbers back to the quarterback. Do not drift.

Our next pass is the *Rob 50 drive/spacing* (Diagram #6). If the center field is open, we are going to the left, and if it is closed, we are going to our right. Again, we are reading from our left to our right.

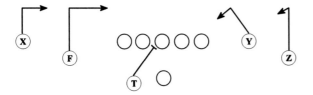

Diagram #6. Rob 50 Drive/Spacing

The spacing is a double-hitch route. On the right side, the slot man is trying to hold the defender to his inside so we can throw the ball outside on the hitch route. This is a good route against teams that play man coverage.

Rec.	Route	Description
X	Drive	Push vertical five yards. Break straight down the line. Get under the linebackers.
F	Drive	Push vertical five yards. Break straight down the line. Get under the linebackers.
Y	Spacing	Release to the inside shoulder of the defender over you at six yards and sit down.
Z	Smash	Push vertical six yards. Sit down. Get your numbers back to the quarterback. Do not drift.

The reason spacing has been good for us is because we run so much Gator with the hitch and taper routes. When the ball is snapped, the Sam linebacker turns his back, turns, and runs to get underneath the hitch route. When he does that, we have to run the spacing routes and get the ball to the outside man.

Our next route is our *Rob 50 Chevy/Gator* (Diagram #7). Chevy is a smash route concept that we use against the teams that play with the middle of the field open. We have a snap route on the outside by the X-receiver. His route is the same as what he ran on the 2x2 snap route.

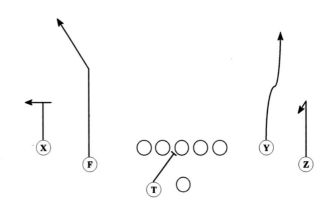

Diagram #7. Rob 50 Chevy/Gator

Rec.	Route	Description
X	Snap	Push to five yards and make square cut to the drive for two steps. Snap back out flat. Do not drift up the field.
F	Corner	Push vertical to breaking point at 12 yards. Come out at 25 yards. Ball will be thrown at 22 yards.
Y	Taper	Push vertical. Must go outside linebackers.
Z	Smash	Push vertical six yards. Sit down. Get your numbers back to the quarterback. Do not drift.

Rec.	Route	Description
X	Drive	Push vertical five yards. Break straight down the line. Get under the linebackers.
F	Corner	Push vertical to breaking point at 12 yards. Come out at 25 yards. Ball will be thrown at 22 yards.
Y	Stutter	Release to the inside shoulder of the defender over you at six yards. Chop it down and get up the field. Avoid the collision of the defender.
Z	Stutter	Push vertical six yards. Chop it down and get up the field. Avoid the collision by the Cornerback to the outside.

We can mix and match these concepts each week. We can pick the routes we feel will be effective against the team we are playing that week.

We can run Rob 50 Dodge/stutter. (Diagram #8). On middle field open, we use Dodge, and on middle field closed, we use stutter. Dodge is the same read as Chevy. We are reading the corner trying to get him to drive on the drag route so we can throw the corner over the top.

You can see a lot of the routes we have run, from drive, snap, Chevy, to Dodge, are the same routes. Everything carries over for our wideouts. For example, the #1 receiver on the Dodge uses the same technique as he does on drive. On the Chevy, the outside receiver runs a snap route, which is the same as what he runs on the 2x2 snap route. All of the routes carry over, and it is easy for our receivers to learn the routes and to be precise in their routes. The quarterback knows where they are going to be and they are on the same page.

All of those routes are used in our 2x2 formations. Now, we will move on to our 3x1 formations (Diagram #9). Let me show you the routes in this formation.

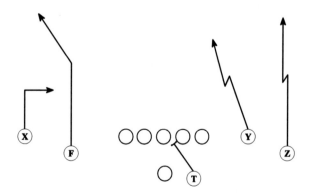

Diagram #8. Rob 50 Dodge/Stutter

Diagram #9. 3x1 Formation

Robbie is the formation, 50 pass pro is the protection, and then, we add the route Gator. This has been our bread-and-butter play for a couple of years. The two outside receivers are doing the same thing they would do on a 2x2 Gator (Diagram #10). They run a smash route with a taper. The F or #2 receiver has to learn to run the smash route at six yards. Our backside receiver is running a hitch/fade conversion route.

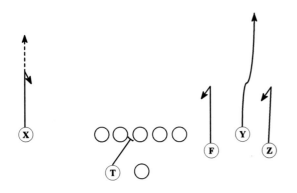

Diagram #10. Robbie 50/Gator

Rec.	Route	Description
X	Hitch	Push vertical six yards. Sit down. Versus press coverage, convert to fade.
F	Smash	Push vertical six yards. Sit down. Get your numbers back to the quarterback. Do not drift.
Y	Taper	Push vertical. Must go outside the linebackers.
Z	Smash	Push vertical six yards. Sit down. Get your numbers back to the quarterback. Do not drift.

The X-receiver runs a hitch route. If the defense plays a press, he is going to convert the route into the fade route. In our system, we can convert the hitch route into the fade route.

In any of our 3x1 sets, if the X-receiver looks the quarterback in the face, the quarterback can throw the ball to him quickly. The X runs a hitch or fade route. The big play would be to get the fade route. The routes are the same as we run in our 2x2. That is our 3x1 Gator. The only difference is the backside X-receiver.

Our next route is our drive route. The call is Robbie 50 drive (Diagram #11). The two outside receivers run the same routes as they run on the 2x2 drive. The #3 man or the F-back has to learn to run the middle route. He is running toward the goalpost. Again, on the backside, we run the hitch/conversion fade route.

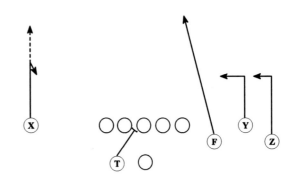

Diagram #11. Robbie 50/Drive

Rec.	Route	Description
X	Hitch	Push vertical six yards. Sit down. Versus press coverage, convert to fade.
F	Middle	Get to your landmark, which is the middle of the goalpost. Look for the ball once you clear the linebacker. Stay on the move.
Y	Spacing	Release to the inside shoulder of the defender over you at six yards and sit down.
Z	Smash	Push vertical six yards. Sit down. Get your numbers back to the quarterback. Do not drift.

Our next route in the 3x1 is our Robbie 50 spacing (Diagram #12). The two outside receivers run the same routes as they did in our 2x2 spacing. The #3 receiver runs through the chute in the middle of the field.

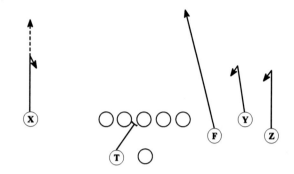

Diagram #12. Robbie 50 Spacing

Rec.	Route	Description
X	Hitch	Push vertical six yards. Sit down. Versus press coverage, convert to fade.
F	Middle	Get to your landmark, which is the middle of the goalpost. Look for the ball once you clear the linebacker. Stay on the move.
Y	Spacing	Release to the inside shoulder of the defender over you at six yards and sit down.
Z	Smash	Push vertical six yards. Sit down. Get your numbers back to the quarterback. Do not drift.

We threw the ball to the X-receiver so much that teams played us in quarter-quarter-half. They played cover 2 to the boundary and cover 4 to the field. When they played cover 4 to the field, they cheated the corner, and the Y-receiver was wide open on the space route all day long. The defense is saying we do not have the patience. They do not think we can throw the ball to that man four times in a row.

Our defense did a study with 92 plays from our opponents. They found the opponents only threw the ball outside to the inside man eight times. In a game against Iowa, we threw the ball out there nine times because we made a bunch of yards on the play. You must be patient to do that.

The middle route must be tight enough to hold the Sam linebacker. The key for the quarterback is the defender over our #2 receiver. To run spacing, you must be sure of the coverage the defense will be playing. We call this play when we see the defense playing quarter-quarter-half.

You can see as we go through this passing concept, the best routes for us have been Gator, spacing, and drive. We have been able to marry into the offense those passing routes into our empty sets (Diagram #13). Our empty is our 3x2 passing game. We read from left to right in the formation.

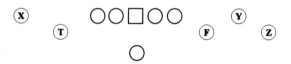

Diagram #13. Empty Formation

This is how we put the same concepts into the empty formation. We run empty right Gator/drive (Diagram #14). The Gator/drive are the route combinations. For us, Gator is to the left and drive is to the right side of the set.

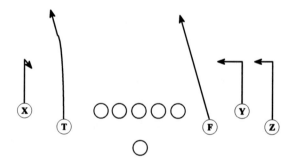

Diagram #14. Empty Right 90 Gator/Drive

In our empty offense, the concepts *middle of the field open* and *middle of the field closed* come back into play. The quarterback comes up to the line, and if the middle of the field is open, he is going to the field right now. He is running the drive part of the play. If the middle of the field is closed, he is coming to the Gator side. The same rules apply for the quarterback. He is still reading the defender over our #2 receiver. On the three-man side, he is still reading the corner to see if they are playing free or man free. The route technique is the same.

One play we have not talked about is our empty right 90 Harry/Gator (Diagram #15). Harry is the middle-of-the-field-open route concept. The reason we like it so much is because we run a zone play with our quarterback from our empty set. If the linebackers on our receivers nearest the quarterback start to play the run, we have both inside receivers run a hitch route.

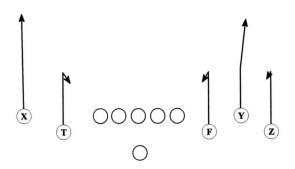

Diagram #15. Empty Right 90 Harry/Gator

Harry is a good boundary route in 2x2 as well. You could bring one of the slot receivers back into the backfield as a running back. After we throw the pass a few times, the Will linebacker starts to play outside on the slot and, as a result, we can run the ball better. Now, the slot can block the Will much easier. It is the same thing on empty right 90 Harry/Gator. All of our empty sets are about match-ups. We want to get our inside receiver matched up on the Mike linebacker.

The hip alignment of the Mike linebacker is on the 5 technique. We can stand up and hit the smash route on Gator. We can do different things with him in our tag package. In empty, we try to get one of our athletic players matched up on a linebacker.

We can add to the formation and run a different route. We make an adjustment where we need it. We run empty right 90 Gator/Gator F slide (Diagram #16). We want a 1-on-1 situation with the Mike backer so we can make a play of the Mike backer.

Moving on, we run the empty right 90 Chevy/Gator (Diagram #17). It is the same as our 2x2 Gator. The quarterback must read the middle of

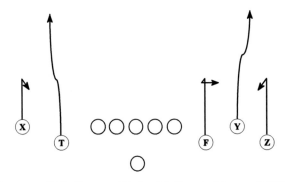

Diagram #16. Empty Right 90 Gator/Gator F Slide

the field. If the middle of the field is open, we are working the Chevy side, reading the cornerback. We want the corner to come down on the snap route so we can throw the ball over him on the corner route. If the middle of the field is closed, he is going to work the frontside.

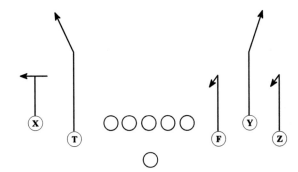

Diagram #17. Empty Right 90 Chevy/Gator

Do you have any questions on the routes up to this point?

Question: How would you practice the routes on routes-on-air?

On routes-on-air, we just practice individual routes.

All of our skilled players look to someone on the sideline when we signal in the plays. When the quarterback gets the signal, he will make a code-word call to the linemen to tell them the protection and if the call is a zone play right or left. It is all codes for the guys up front. All the skilled players get their calls from the sideline. All the linemen get their calls from the quarterback.

I want to start the video and show the different formations along with the routes. You should get a better idea what we are doing by seeing the game films. Thank you for your attention.

QUARTER COVERAGE MADE SIMPLE

Michigan State University

Thank you gentlemen. It is a pleasure to be here today. I am going to talk about quarter coverage and some philosophy. If you are a coach, you are a teacher. If I stood up here and talked a bunch of nonsense laced with a lot of terminology, you would not have any idea what I was talking about.

COMMUNICATE

- Simplify your message.
- Know your audience.
- Tell the truth.
- Seek a response.

When you want to communicate with someone, the first thing you have to do is *simplify your message*. The next thing you want to do is *know your audience*. If I gave this talk to a group of alumni, it would not make much sense to them. If you talk to a defensive back, you want to talk coverage. If you talk to an offensive or defensive lineman, you need to talk in simple terms.

When you talk to any audience, tell the truth. That is tremendously important. There are strengths and weaknesses to everything you do on the football field. That is why you stress the weaknesses and tell the truth to your players and coaches. Always be truthful in every communication you have with them.

Always *seek a response* from the people you talk to. I do not want anyone to walk out of this meeting and not know what went on.

DEFENSIVE PHILOSOPHY

- Simple; comprehensive; complex
- Pressure; affect the quarterback
- Stop the run

- Red-zone defense; adversity
- Turnovers
- Tackling 90 percent
- Explosive gains
- Mental errors (physical, mental, structural)

Any defense has to be simple to learn. It has to be comprehensive so that it covers everything that could possibly happen, and it must appear complex. If you can do that, you have a chance to be successful. You have to play fast to be successful. That goes back to keeping everything very simple.

Our whole philosophy of defense is about pressuring the quarterback. Fifty percent of the time we use zone pressure on the quarterback. We try to hit the quarterback 18 to 20 times a game. If we can do that, we will probably win the game. You have to get in the quarterback's face. That is when the ball comes out funny and not on target. Pressure causes the ball to not be thrown on time and makes the quarterback get out of the pocket. Pressure is extremely important, and we start every defensive meeting with how we are going to pressure the quarterback. If we can hold the passing yardage to five yards per attempt, we have played well.

I have never heard a defensive lecture that did not stress stopping the run. If your defense can stop the run, you will win the football game. Our goal in the running game is to not give up more than three yards per carry.

When we talk about red-zone defense, we have to learn how to handle adversity. In the NFL, they talk about red efficiency. They base their figures on the number of touchdowns scored. Teams that get into the red zone but settle for field goals are not that efficient. We are not as good in red-zone efficiency as we should be.

College football began to compile turnover statistics in 1987. If a team can have a turnover margin of plus two, they will win 95 percent of the games. An interception leads to an average 25-yard change in field position.

We grade our tackling every game. We record the tackles and assists for each player. We record the missed tackles in a game. We total the missed tackles and the made tackles and come up with a percentage of made tackles. We want that figure to be 90 percent or greater.

When we tackle, we always want to hit with the near leg and near shoulder. That generates the power in a tackle. When we teach tackling, we fit the tackler into the ballcarrier. We want him to explode and shoot his arms, head, and shoulders up and through the ballcarrier. It is like going up for a jump ball in basketball—everything comes in one movement.

We go from the fit position to backing up one step and repeating the drill. The tackler takes a short six-inch step and repeats the action in the fit position. Then, we put the tackler in a backpedal, plant, come back to the ballcarrier, and repeat the steps. If they do the drill right, the ballcarrier goes backward. The tackling drills we do in practice are the tackles we perform in a game. We try to make the drills game-type tackles.

Our goal is to have no explosive gains. That is very difficult in the Big Ten because of the athletes in the league. An explosive gain is a run of 15 yards and a pass of 20 yards. It is easier to stop the explosive runs than it is the passes.

To be successful as a defense, you must eliminate the mental errors. We want to know if breakdowns are mental, physical, or structural errors. This is the computer age. We have our film broken down quickly and accurately. If there is a problem, we want to know why that problem occurred. We want to know if it was a mental mistake made by the player. Did he make a mistake because we asked him to do something he cannot?

If that is the problem, it could lead back to a teaching progression error from practice. The third thing is the structure error. That occurs when we do not have the right defense called. When a problem occurs, we have to solve it.

QUARTER COVERAGE

Definition: Tight man in a zone coverage concept with good run support that self-adjusts to various formations and routes.

- Can be played with a variety of defensive fronts
- Can game plan versus certain formations; look to get best advantage (or as a change-up) ("tag" coverage)
- Allows linebackers to get back into box for run support (one-back-gun runs)
- Relatively simple in initial stages but can be built to be comprehensive
- Split safety look allows for various coverage concepts to be played (disguises well)
- Box/cloud/area/zeke/midpoint coverage concept names
- Can be double called versus slot or played out (e.g., 7/3, 7/5, 7/1)
- Good run support—nine-man front
- Run/pass conflicts—safety/no-cover zone 10 yards

Quarter coverage allows the defense to play *man* coverage with zone principles. The defensive back does not know who he covers until the receiver makes his initial move. Quarter coverage allows the defense to handle all the gaps in the front. The terms *box, cloud, area, zeke,* and *midpoint* are concept names which fit into the coverage. The box term defines quarter coverage. We build a box around the receiver. We have a deep third player on the outside of the receiver. We have a short flat defender on the outside of the receiver. We have a short hook defender inside the receiver and a deep defender on the inside of the receiver. We have the receiver in a box with four defenders.

We can double call the secondary coverage. If we call 7/3, the 7 means the outside linebackers walk out into coverage on a slot receiver and the 3 means cover 3. This coverage lets the safeties become involved in run support quicker. It gives us a nine-defender box very quickly. Because of the alignment of the safeties, they become part of the box.

The safety has a no-cover zone—he has to stay out of it. He does not want to cover any pattern that is less than 10 yards. He is a deep cover defender. He should be able to cover one-third of the distance that the ball is in the air. A bootleg puts the safety in a run/pass conflict. Does he come up and stop the quarterback or hang with the receiver? When we talk about run/pass conflict, we refer to the linebacker as an example. If he has a pass coverage responsibility in the hook zone but the offense runs a play-action fake into the B gap, that is his run gap responsibility. He has a conflict about what to do.

CORNERS

- Press coverage shadow on #1 receiver (box) (meg/mod); first outside deep
- "Meg" come off #1 if short (sneak/hitch); first five yards—smash rule
- "Mod" stay on all routes
- Can "area" short Z splits (in/out); first outside deep
- Can "cloud" short Z splits
- Stay base provides good run support versus cracks

The corner gets into tight press coverage on the #1 receiver to his side. You can play the corner off, but the press coverage discourages the three-step game. In reality, it takes a better player to play off the receiver than in press coverage. If the corner can run and has good balance, he will be a better press player than an off-player.

The corner has two ways to cover the receiver. He plays him with a *meg* or *mod* technique. The meg technique means he comes off the receiver if he runs a short pattern in the first five yards. That is the smash rule. If the outside receiver runs a hitch pattern in front of the corner, the #2 receiver can run the smash into the flag behind him. He generally

has to cover that pattern. The mod technique keeps the corner on all routes. The technique the corner plays comes from alignment or a scouting report. We play more meg than mod.

If the split between two receivers gets too tight, the defenders play *in-out* or area coverage. That means the inside defender takes all moves coming to the inside and the outside defender takes all moves coming to the outside. That keeps them from naturally rubbing each other off the coverage. If we try to press, we get picked off immediately. We can also play cloud against that situation. We roll the corner and play the coverage like a cover 2 scheme.

When we get into press coverage on the outside receiver, it keeps that receiver from cracking on the outside linebacker. If we are off the receiver, we have to get involved with run support on a crackback block.

CORNER TECHNIQUE

- Alignment based on divider
- Eye control
- Offhand jam (elbow); stay on balance/shadow
- Get wide receiver off red line (6 1/2 yards from sideline)
- Read through move area 18 yards
- Phase (in/out/runback/short throw)
- Read through V of the neck
- Never offer up outside hand
- Never drop your butt
- Never trail an outside release with the wide receiver's shoulders parallel to the line of scrimmage
- Play upfield shoulder on inside releases (offhand jam)
- Club #1 on line of scrimmage; can change up technique

The alignment is based on the divider, which I will explain later. Eye control is so important because the eyes control the hips. Eye control is the key for any linebacker or defensive back technique that deals with stance and alignment. If there is a problem, it can be traced back to eye control. If we play the right technique in any defense we have, we will be successful. If we are not technique sound, we will not be successful no matter what scheme we play.

In our press coverage, we want the outside foot back in the stance. The corner has no help on the 9 route, which is the takeoff. We number everything. All odd numbers are outside routes by the receivers. The 3 route is a speed-out, 5 route is a comeback, and the 7 route is a corner. Any even number is an inside route. We jam the elbow with the offhand. There are many ways to teach this technique. The bottom line is to redirect the route of the receiver.

After we get the jam on the receiver, we want to shadow him up the field. We want to force the receiver off his line. If we can get his shoulders turned to the line of scrimmage, we have done a good job. If he keeps his shoulders square with the line, we will have problems. If the receiver shakes the defender down and gets inside, that is where the help is. Playing this technique is like boxing. We have to stay on balance every time we punch or jam. If the defender gets off balance or overextended, he cannot play. He cannot drop his butt. If he does that, he locks out his legs.

The defender wants to force the receiver off the red line. Our field numbers are seven yards from the sideline to the bottom of the number. The top of the number is nine yards from the sideline. The red line is six-and-a-half yards from the sideline. We want to close the window into the sideline. If you give the quarterback six-and-a-half yards to throw the ball, that is a big window. We want to give him a two-yard window by forcing the receiver off the red line.

The defender reads the move of the receiver up to 18 yards. If the receiver's hips drop at 18 yards, he is running a comeback pattern. If the pattern gets beyond 18 yards it is a go route. If the defender can get his shoulder in front of the receiver's shoulder, we can control his speed. We react to the ball with the inside arm, up and through the receiver's hands.

We jam with the inside hand and never offer the outside hand. If the defender extends the outside hand, the receiver grabs it or knocks him off

balance. If the defender gets off balance, he cannot play press. If the wide receiver is on the line of scrimmage, we use a club technique to keep him from getting off the line. If a receiver gets an inside release, we want to play on his upfield shoulder. We want to run him upfield so any move to the outside comes into the defender's body.

DIVIDERS/CORNER'S PLAY

The specific landmark for each corner that tells him where the midpoint 1/3 is located. They remain constant throughout the play. In general, corners should play on their divider. This will allow them to always maintain proper leverage throughout a football play.

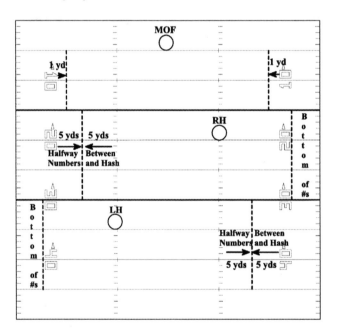

Diagram #1. Dividers

With the ball in the middle of the field, the corner's divider is one yard from the top of the numbers—that converts to the middle of the outside third. If the receiver aligns on that line, the corner aligns outside on the receiver. If the receiver gets an outside release, the defender wants to be on the inside of the receiver. If the defender tries to stay outside, it opens up the entire field for the post route.

If the ball is on the far hash mark, the divider is five yards from the top of the numbers or five yards outside the near hash mark. That is for the college hash marks. The high school hash marks are two yards wider than the college marks. That translates to seven yards for the high school hash marks. If the receiver aligns inside that point, the defender is outside him in alignment. We never want the receiver to split the defender outside his divider. With the ball on the near hash mark, the divider is the bottom of the numbers.

On the mod coverage into the boundary, we cover the smash route with the strong safety (Diagram #2). Since the corner is playing all routes by the receiver, the strong safety has to play the tight end running the corner route behind the corner.

To the field, we play the meg rule. The outside receiver, at five yards, runs a hitch route. The corner comes off the hitch and gets back on the smash behind him. The Will linebacker reacts to the pattern of the slot receiver and comes back for the hitch. The free safety plays down the inside seam of the zone and helps the corner on any inside move by the receiver.

the box and outside of the box. The second receiver from the boundary to the formation is the #2 receiver. The Sam and Will linebackers match and mirror the patterns of those receivers. The stance and alignment is based on the defense called. If the #2 receiver goes to the flat, the linebacker's shoulders turn perpendicular to the line of scrimmage and he has the coverage on all the way.

If the #2 receiver goes vertical up the field, the linebacker has to reroute him and make him restart his pattern (Diagram #3). The problem occurs when the #2 receiver gets on the safety carrying all his speed. The linebacker wants to reroute the receiver off the seam and to the outside. If the linebacker collisions the #2 receiver, it takes him longer to get into his pattern. That gives the rush more time on the quarterback and disrupts the timing of the route. The strong safety reads the #2 receiver and knows what he is trying to do. We want to keep the receiver to his frontside and not let him get behind him into the middle.

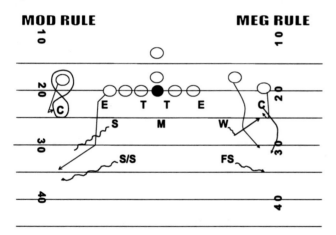

Diagram #2. Meg/Mod Smash Rule

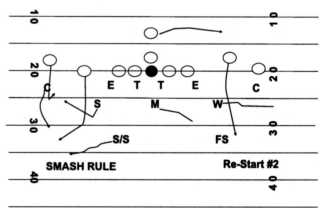

Diagram #3. #2 Vertical

SAM AND WILL LINEBACKERS

- Box: Mirrored positions versus pass; #2 match (stance/alignment based on front)
- #2 to the flat: First to flat; wheel on shoulders
- #2 vertical: Reroute #2 (restart him); final #2 match sail (smash route)
- #2 drag or inside slant: Deliver to Mike

The linebackers have a particular assignment in

We never want that receiver into the middle of the field. The linebacker has to take the speed off the wide receiver.

If the #2 receiver runs a drag or slant, the outside linebacker delivers him to the Mike linebacker. If the #2 receiver runs a double cross to the inside, the Sam, Mike, and Will linebackers pass off the route (Diagram #4). As the Will linebacker reads the route of the #2 receiver, he communicates to the Mike linebacker and settles looking to help inside or outside on the next receiver coming into his zone. If there is a drag pattern coming from the other side, he picks it up. The Sam linebacker plays the same technique.

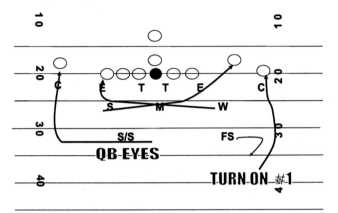

Diagram #4. #2 Drag

MIKE LINEBACKER

- Box: Play front; #3 match (stance/alignment based on front)
- First inside player off #3 match
- Versus three-step: Read quarterback's eyes when hot on throw
- Versus 3x1: Mike/Will load/split rules

The Mike linebacker is a box linebacker and plays the front. He has the #3 receiver who is normally in the backfield. He has to respect the play-action pass, but generally the fake goes to his pass responsibility. If the back comes through for a checkdown route, he has him in coverage. In a 3x1 set, the Mike linebacker has the #3 receiver to the strongside of the set.

We define his responsibility as the first inside receiver. He has to be aware of the three-step hot pattern to that receiver. Formations are just like rats—you cannot get rid of them and they keep multiplying. On a three-step protection by the back, we do not want the Mike linebacker to react to that move. We want him to read the quarterback's eyes. He works to the side the quarterback looks. He looks for the quick slant and inside release by the receivers.

SAFETIES

- Align: 2x10 inside edge of skill; 1x10 outside edge of box

- Stance: Outside foot back
- Sky support/cutback but can be changed up
- Key: End man on line of scrimmage (uncovered offensive lineman); #2 openside receiver
- Responsibility: Flat foot #2 to #1 (first inside deep); box
- #2 to flat: Turn on #1; read quarterback's eyes
- #2 vertical: Carry; first inside deep linebacker should restart #2
- #2 short: Turn on #1; read quarterback's eyes
- Versus 3x1: Backside safety zeke to #3
- #3 flat: Read quarterback's eyes; turn on #1
- #3 vertical: Carry him
- #3 shallow z: Read quarterback's eyes; turn on #1; punch

The safeties in a quarter coverage have to make the most adjustments. If the #2 receiver to his side is a tight end, the safety aligns 10 yards deep and one yard outside the tight end. If the #2 receiver is a slot receiver, he is two yards inside the edge of the slot at a depth of 10 yards. He aligns with his outside foot back in this stance. He uses the quarterback to get direction and the offensive line to verify what he sees. If he reads run, he makes sure the linemen are coming downfield. If he is to the openside of the formation and reads an aggressive down block by the tackle, he thinks run.

On run away from him, he is the cutback defender. On run toward him, he is sky support on the run. If he is to the openside of the formation, he has a run fit inside the force defender.

If the #2 receiver goes to the flat, he does what we call flatfoot. That means he holds his position and turns his eyes to the #1 receiver to the outside. His responsibility becomes help on the #1 receiver or the next deep threat. The Sam linebacker takes #2 going to the flat.

If the #2 receiver comes vertical, the strong safety has him (Diagram #5). If we have a 3x1 formation, the backside safety has the #3 receiver on a vertical route, which is the zeke call. On any inside release by the #2 receiver, the safety plays that like the outside release.

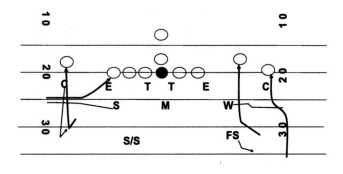

Diagram #5. Safety Reaction on #2

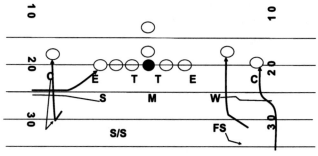

Diagram #6. 3x1 Load

The safety to the flatside runs through the curl pattern of the #1 receiver. The safety on the vertical side has to carry the #2 receiver for the post or corner route.

In a 3x1 formation, there is the possibility of four receivers to the trips side. We call that a load situation (Diagram #6). The Mike linebacker is responsible for the first inside receiver. If the tight end comes to the Mike linebacker on a drag route, he can pass him back to the Will linebacker. That takes some work in practice to do that. The Will linebacker reads the single back. When he goes away, he looks for someone coming back to his side, which is generally the inside receiver to the trips side.

To the trips side, if the #2 receiver comes up the field, the strong safety has to take that move. The corner has a stem route and has to buy 15 yards for the strong safety. He has to hold that route out of the middle. The free safety has the #3 receiver going vertical. Since the receiver did not go vertical, the free safety plays the middle of the field. He helps on the vertical by the #3 receiver from the trips side, the #1 receiver from the single-receiver side, or deep cross by the #2 receiver into the middle.

If the #4 receiver goes to the single-receiver side, the Will linebacker has the coverage on him (Diagram #7). However, he does not rush up the field to cover him. He is in a no-cover zone. To the three-receiver side, the patterns are a vertical route by the #3 receiver, and a flat/curl combination by the wide receiver and slot. The free safety has a zeke technique on the #3 receiver. The Sam linebacker takes the flat route by the slot receiver. The strong

safety drives the curl route of the wide receiver. The Mike linebacker reroutes the #3 receiver and buys time for the free safety to get over the top.

3 X 1 SETS

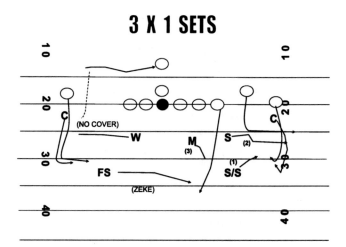

Diagram #7. 3x1 Weak

Before I close, I want to show you how we cover an empty 3x2 set (Diagram #8). We play a combination midpoint scheme to the three-receiver side and an area scheme to the two-receiver side. On the two-receiver side, the free safety and corner play an area concept on the split receivers.

The Will linebacker plays his #2 read and takes the flat or short routes by the receivers. The free safety and corner play their coverage the same. If both receivers come up the field and run a deep cross, the free safety takes all patterns to the inside and the corner takes all patterns coming into the outside area.

To the three-receiver side, the corner reads from the #1 receiver to the #2 receiver. The strong safety reads the #3 receiver to the #2 receiver. The Sam linebacker reads #2, and the Mike linebacker reads #3. If the #2 receiver goes to the flat, the Sam linebacker takes that route. If the #3 receiver comes vertical, the strong safety has him. If the #3 receiver drags to the inside, the Mike linebacker picks him up. Since the #3 receiver went inside, the strong safety looks to the #2 receiver.

Gentlemen, I know I went fast. I hope you got something from this presentation. Come see us at Michigan State. Thank you.

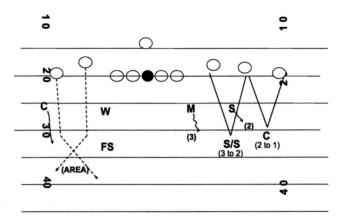

Diagram #8. 3x2 Adjustment

DEVELOPING DEFENSIVE LINEMEN

University of North Carolina

I want to give you a brief history about myself. I grew up as a gym rat. My father was a high school football and basketball coach and later became an administrator. My first six years of coaching was spent in the high school ranks. I started out at a small school in Sand Springs, Oklahoma. I got a break in 1979 and was hired on Jimmy Johnson's first staff at Oklahoma State.

Throughout my career, I have coached a variety of different positions. At Oklahoma State, the first year on Coach Johnson's staff, I was a receiver and tight ends coach. I switched to the defensive line in 1983, when we went to Miami. I coached the defensive line at Miami from 1983 to 1989. In 1989, we went to the Dallas Cowboys and I coached the defensive line. I coached the defensive line there until the last two years when I became the defensive coordinator and coached the linebackers.

I have a passion for coaching the defensive line. In all the places I have coached, I had 25 players make it to the National Football League and nine of them were first-round draft picks. When you have the opportunity to speak at clinics, you need to talk about things that are applicable to the coaches to whom you are speaking. You want to talk about things that are going to help high school coaches. I started out as a high school coach, and I never wanted to go to a clinic and hear a coach talk about a scheme which was not applicable to the players I was coaching.

I will give you some drills, ideas, and mind-sets about coaching defensive linemen. I want to give you the role of the defensive line. I want to share what we expected of the defensive line when I was at Miami, the Cowboys, and North Carolina today.

GENERAL OVERVIEW

- Defensive line role
- Developing mentality
- Progressive teaching
- Basic fundamentals
- Practice time
- Video
- Q & A

The overview is an outline of what I am going to do today. Notice I want to save a little time at the end for questions and answers.

When you talk to your players, you must make them understand that no matter how talented or good they are, the defensive line sets the tempo for the entire football team. I have believed that all my life, and a lot of that belief is a byproduct of the things I learned from Jimmy Johnson. He coached the defensive line at Oklahoma when they had the Selman brothers. He coached Hugh Green and Rickey Jackson, who were great defensive linemen at the University of Pittsburgh. Every great team I have ever been around, the defensive line set the tempo for the mentality of the entire practice. That includes the national championship teams at Miami and the Super Bowl teams at Dallas.

If you cannot stop the run and pressure the quarterback, you will not win many football games. Go back and think about the history of football. There are reasons the defensive line groups are the ones that get legendary nicknames. You remember names like Doomsday, Purple People Eaters, Fearsome Foursome, and The Steel Curtain. Two years ago, the New York Giants were not given a chance to win the Super Bowl. Their defensive line totally dominated the entire playoffs.

If you look at the trends in college football, you will see defensive linemen flying off the board on NFL draft day. Exceptional defensive linemen can change the complexion of the game. The influence on developing the mentality of what your defensive linemen can do has become extremely important. The physical impact of your practices is controlled by the defensive line. They set the tempo for the entire defense.

We know it is a team game, and we need to have 11 players with great attitudes for practice. However, you cannot coach each player exactly the same. Some things are universal in coaching the defensive linemen. You coach the get-off and pursuit the same way with each player. However, there are some things that are fundamentally and uniquely different with each player.

At the Cowboys, we had Ed "Too-Tall" Jones who was 6'9". We later drafted Russell Maryland, who was 6'0". You cannot coach those two players to do the same thing from a pass rush or leverage standpoint. You may not have that extreme difference with the player you coach, but you may have a 5'10" noseguard and a 6'4" tackle. You must structure the way you teach those players.

At North Carolina, we have a defensive line role that we teach each player.

DEFENSIVE LINE ROLE

Your role with the team concept:

- Football is a team game—be a team player. You must be willing to make sacrifices to help the team. In doing so, you are ultimately helping yourself.
- Approach each phase with a positive attitude. Attitudes are contagious. A positive attitude will help the team win.
- Every player on the team has a role to play. As the season goes along, your role becomes clearer. It is your job to do everything mentally and physically to be successful within your role and the team concept.
- Applaud the accomplishments of your teammates.

- Each drill and practice is designed to *help you* improve. Practice with a purpose. There is a definite correlation between the way you practice and the way you perform in games. Practice at top speed.
- Always look for ways to improve.
- You must make a commitment to all areas: practice, weight room, film study, meetings, off-season conditioning, as well as games.
- Ask yourself:
  - ✓ Am I committed?
  - ✓ Am I sincere?
  - ✓ Can I be trusted?

Every place I have been, we always ask the players the last three questions. We want to know if they are committed, sincere, and willing to make sacrifices to be special.

I believe the off-season is critical to the development of your entire football team. We have started to develop some role models for our players. In the past month, our coaching staff has downloaded 193 film clips of players we have seen in the NFL that looked like somebody on our football team. I did not say *play* like someone on our football team. We look for body type similarities. We have a running back on our team that looks like Brandon Jacobs of the Giants and one who looks like Adrian Peterson of the Vikings.

We put those clips on a computer and let our players come in and watch them. We hope that by watching these stars from the NFL play, it will give them a mind-set about how to make themselves better.

When we talk about developing the mentality of the defensive line, the first thing they must possess is great *desire*. They must have a willingness and burning passion to excel. I look at video tapes all the time. I have seen tapes of players in practice who make play after play. However, on the game tape they are making two or three of those types of plays. That is not good enough. You have to sell your young players on the fact they must have the desire and passion to get to the ballcarrier or passer on every single play.

They must obtain *physical toughness* by practicing tough and hard. This is a hard thing to do. I know none of us have enough players. However, I know if you do not practice physical, you will not play physical. That sounds stupid, but we won three Super Bowls in Dallas.

In practice, we actually tackled Emmitt Smith. Every Wednesday, we had a live inside drill. If he carried the ball, we knocked him to the ground. His plays were limited, and we never hit him low or took cheap shots, but we hit him like it was a game situation. Because we practiced physically and put an emphasis on being tough, we developed a tough mentality at Miami, Dallas, and North Carolina.

To play defensive football, you must know *assignments* so you can play confident, fast, and aggressive. You have to keep things simple for your players. When I listen to people talk at other clinics, I am amazed at how much they try to teach. They have hundreds of techniques and assignments. How can anyone master all that? I could not, and I do not know many players I have coached that could.

If you keep it simple for your players and let them know exactly what you expect out of them, they will have the confidence to play fast, cut loose, and become playmakers for you. If you are overcomplicated, they will overthink what they are supposed to do.

I know from experience and I'm guilty of trying to teach too many things. We taught pre-snap reads. We looked at the offensive linemen's alignment, splits, depth off the ball, pressure on the fingers, and running back positions. If you give the defensive lineman too many things to remember, the offense will snap the ball and the defensive line will be brain locked. Keeping everything simple allows the defense to be as aggressive as they possibly can be. Desire is the most important intangible in winning—desire will overcome some physical limitations.

The next point takes precedence over everything we do. We believe *conditioning precedes everything*. We lost five games this year and finished 8-5. We had a lead in the fourth quarter in four of those games. When the game is on the line, you have to stop the run and rush the quarterback in the last two minutes. You cannot have your best players tapping themselves out. You cannot have your best players standing on the sideline during that critical part of the game.

As part of our philosophy, we try to play seven or eight defensive linemen a game. However, it does not matter how many plays they play in a ball game, they must play every play as hard as they can. They have to fly around, make plays, and compete as hard as they can. If they cannot, they have to come out of the game.

This off-season is a crusade at Chapel Hill. We got away from the fast explosive defensive linemen we had with Dallas and Miami. We got bigger. We had a defensive lineman this year who was arguably the best defensive linemen in the nation. He did not get fat, but he got stronger and bigger. He was up to 328 pounds. We evaluated his performance during a drive which lasted eight or nine plays. In the first three or four plays, he was a monster. However, in the last three or four, he looked like just another defender on the team.

We are trying to get leaner and faster and make the entire defensive line better. If a player is in condition, it gives him a chance to play hard every play. It is necessary for mental toughness and maximizes his speed and quickness.

When I talk about keeping it simple, you have to make sure it is built into the packages you play on defense. It is important to not ask too much of your players. If you are too complicated players cannot be aggressive.

I want to use an example of two players we had at the University of Miami. In 1987, both these players were left defensive ends. The starter was almost robotic in everything he did. In his mind, he went through the checklist of steps for every technique he performed. In 25 plays, he might have one tackle, two assists, and maybe a quarterback pressure.

In 25 plays, the other player would jump offside one time, but would have two sacks, a forced fumble, a strip, and made plays all over the field. He was the backup player at left defensive end. We kept it simple for him so he could get into the game. We overcoached the other player so much he could not play. That is when the light came on for us. We want to make sure we are not overcoaching these players. Let their natural instincts and skills show.

Most of you will be able to appreciate this. I coached at Miami in two generations—once as an assistant coach under Jimmy Johnson and once as a head coach. College and high school coaches came to us and wanted to look at our cut-ups. We had 16mm film at that time. We had six cans of cut-ups and all of them were a 4-3 front and cover 2 in the secondary. We had two cans of stunts that we had run in our 12-game season and the other four cans were straight defense.

Our players could line up and know exactly how to play everything we ran. That allowed the coaches to focus on fundamentals. The players learned techniques, tackling, hustle, and effort. It eliminated confusion and thinking, and created reaction. People would look at us and would know what we were going to play on every down. Of course, our players knew what we were going to play on every down and that was the important thing.

We have a teaching progression for defensive linemen.

DEFENSIVE LINE TEACHING PROGRESSION

- Mental
  - ✓ Assignment
  - ✓ Alignment
  - ✓ Stance
- Technique
  - ✓ Get off
  - ✓ Head/hand placement
  - ✓ Read/react
  - ✓ Escape/rush
- Effort
  - ✓ Pursuit/chase
  - ✓ Tackle

The first part is somewhat technical. There is no compromise on the mental part of the progression. Every player on our team, regardless of his talent, speed, size, or who he is, has to learn his alignment, assignment, and stance. The third part is a no-compromise area also. Pursuing the football takes nothing but effort. Everyone must play with great effort regardless of his talent, speed, or size.

The second part of the progression separates the coaching aspect and the athletic ability of the players you have. We are a team that attacks the line of scrimmage when the offense snaps the ball. We want to play football on their side of the line of scrimmage. In this part of the progression, we teach hand pressure and leverage points. They must know the contact point and be able to dominate and control their visual key. The visual key for the 3-technique defender is the guard. The key for the 5-technique player is the tackle and the 9-technique defender's key is the tight end.

The read-and-react part is what is covered in the individual periods in coaching. That is where the player learns how to play defensive schemes. I believe consistency in what the defensive line coach calls "certain techniques" is extraordinarily important. The coach and player have to be on the same page. The player has to know what a reach block is. He has to know the difference between a reach block aimed at the outside armpit and a reach block that tries to gain control of two gaps.

The coach has to delineate what he is telling the player so they can converse when they come to the sideline. That allows the players and coach to accomplish something and make adjustments. It gives them a common language to describe what is happening on the field.

The last thing in the technique list is escape and rush. The biggest mistake I see players make is trying to escape from a block before they have control of the blocker. When we teach this, we put our linemen in a disadvantaged position and make them recover before they try to escape. It teaches them not to run behind the blocker and lets the linebacker exchange leverage opportunities.

Our ends and tackles use a three-point stance. We teach two types of stances at North Carolina. We play recognition or situational downs. In a running situation, we align in a basic stance. We want our players to be comfortable in their stance. You have to adjust the stance for the body differences of certain players. You cannot expect a tall player to align in the same stance as the shorter player. They have to make adjustments to become comfortable.

NORMAL STANCE

- Feet spread width of armpits with very little stagger
- Right hand down, right foot back, left hand down, left foot back
- Slight weight on hand, legs up under body
- Knees flexed no greater than 90 percent
- Heels slightly off ground
- Back parallel to ground (tail may be slightly higher than shoulders)
- Head and eyes up, weight equally distributed to balls of feet

This stance must permit powerful, explosive first steps. We use this stance primarily for rundown situations. There are so many players that cannot succeed because they cannot get into a proper stance.

The second variation is the *sprinter* stance. We use this stance in passing situations when we need to rush the passer.

SPRINTER STANCE

- Feet spread slightly tighter than armpits, exaggerated heal-to-toe stagger
- Hands and feet the same as above, more weight on hand
- Tail higher, legs cocked
- Free hand leading
- Eyes locked on the ball

In this stance, we are not worried about the control. We want to be aggressive and get up the field and into the guard and tackle as quickly as we can. A high percentage of effectiveness in defeating the blocker is who get their hands on the other player first. Getting the hands inside has a lot to do with who wins the battle.

The first couple of years I coached the defensive line, I fell into a bad habit of using verbal commands in teaching drills. You do not want the defensive line to listen to hard counts and cadence. The defense wants to read and react triggered by the movement of the ball. Movement triggers all the drills we do. We have a scout team player moving or a ball on the stick moving. When we do off-season conditioning drills, we have a coach using some type of movement to begin the repetition.

Moving on movement is the essence of the get-off. In our defensive alignments, the players on the right side of the defensive line will be in a left-handed stance. If they play on the left side of the line, they are in a right-handed stance. We teach both stances to everyone because you never know who will be injured. I know there are coaches that think it does not matter, however, after 35 years of doing this, I think it does.

Looking at the types of pass-rush moves and schemes you have to play, it is infinitely better to be in those kinds of stances. It goes back to the footwork. On the right side of the defensive line, the left foot is the power step and the first to move. If that foot is taken away by the charge of the offensive linemen, you must have the right foot free to recover your charge and keep the shoulders parallel to the line of scrimmage.

CHARGE AND GET OFF

- Explode on first movement of the ball or offensive linemen
- Explosion step (first step)—roll off ball of foot, bringing up rear for balance
- Balance step (second step)—bring parallel up to rear, parallel base as you charge, eyes forward on key for reach
- Read must be completed during balance step
- Next step will be reaction step

When we teach this part of the get-off drill, we back up the players. There is nothing more intimidating or confusing for a defensive lineman than to get multiple reads. We compensate for their mistakes by backing them up and giving them more time to read. The more experience they gain, the closer they play to the ball. What we are striving for is to take as much of the ball as we can get. We want to crowd the line of scrimmage and get as close to the offensive blocker as we can. We want to be into his face before he can react.

REACTION STEP

- The third step will be your reaction to your read.
- The better you become at reading and reacting, the closer you should crowd the ball.
- Make all steps as short and quick as possible. *Never* be so intent on "reading" that your charge is delayed or soft. Be aggressive, attack the line of scrimmage. Penetration is vital!

I want to talk a little about practice. The time allotted to the position coaches changes from day to day and week to week. The amount of time allotted is relative to the team you are playing. Passing teams require a different time allotment than running teams. If the opponent is a passing team, more time has to be spent on rush techniques than run assignments. However, I think you are making a tragic mistake if you do not devote a certain amount of individual time every day to certain things.

I believe that every position coach can improve the athletic ability of the players he coaches. If the coach will focus on that aspect of the skills required to play the position, the players will become better at those skills. You cannot coach defensive backs and not spend a significant amount of time on backpedaling drills. You must have drills that assimilate game situations. A certain amount of time in our drill is spent improving the athletic ability of our players.

DEFENSIVE LINE INDIVIDUAL PRACTICE

- Always have drills that reinforce fundamentals and technique.

- Have drills that emphasize execution of the game plan defensive scheme.
- Drills should build confidence through repetition.
- Do not make drills too elaborate (one or two aspects per drill). If they are easy to explain and set-up, the players get more reps.
- Only use drills that help you master your position.
- Incorporate conditioning and stamina into drills.

I have some pet peeves with drills. Do not try to teach too many things at one time. The players must see and know that the drill will make them become a better player. The second peeve is a drill that is too complicated. If it takes too long to set up the drill, by the time you finish the drill, the players only get one rep apiece. In our coaches meetings, I continually tell our coaches to keep their drills simple, have some application to the game plan for that day, and do not make it too complicated.

When you do drills, one or two concepts are all you need. If you are doing a bag drill, having the players explode off the last bag into a finish is awesome. That is what the game looks like on Saturday. They are working on a fundamental drill and finishing with an explosion.

Do the drills that help your players master their position. If you use a fire zone blitz scheme, you have to practice tackles and end dropping off the line of scrimmage. However, if you are going to use the scheme twice in the game, do not spend 15 minutes doing something that will only occur once or twice. Make sure the things you practice are going to show up proportionally as to what your players are going to do in the game.

The last thing is for defensive line coaches to incorporate conditioning into their drills. If you come to our spring practices at North Carolina, you will find our drill periods extremely hard. We will go 30 minutes in our drill period. We will push them and they will be wringing wet because of the difficulty of the drills.

I have a script of drills that we do in our defensive line. There is a different emphasis placed on each set of drills. The first group of drills is devoted to developing athleticism.

- Bag
  - ✓ One foot in the hole
  - ✓ Two feet in the hole
  - ✓ Shuffle and redirect
  - ✓ Lateral
  - ✓ Redirect
- Ladder
  - ✓ Quick feet
  - ✓ Lateral run
- Change of direction drills
  - ✓ L drill
  - ✓ Pro agility
- Stance
  - ✓ Takeoff
  - ✓ Mat drill

During the stance period, we work on the two variations of the stance. In the normal stance, we have the ability to go sideways as well as straight ahead. In the sprint stance, we are not worried about sideways movement. The emphasis is on speed and penetration to the quarterback.

When we do the mat drill, we use a tumbling mat to break the fall of the players. They get into their stance and explode out onto the mat. They turn everything loose, explode off the ball, and dive into the mat. This teaches explosion without worrying about injury from the ground.

The second group of drills is classified as run drills. Emphasize head and hand placement in these drills.

- Versus
  - ✓ Sleds
- Run reads
  - ✓ 1-on-1 basic blocks
  - ✓ 2-on-1 basic blocks
  - ✓ Torque drill
  - ✓ Torque drill from reached position
- Run escapes

- ✓ Tackling
- ✓ Bag tackle
- ✓ Bag redirect
- ✓ Tackle

The torque drills are used to make the defensive linemen work from a blocked situation. We put him in a disadvantaged situation and make him reestablish control of the blocker. We fit the defender in a position where he is reached and must recover from the block. That teaches him to recover control of the blocker before he tries to escape from the block.

We do all kinds of tackling drills. We tackle sleds, bags, dummies, and people. To become good tacklers you must tackle every day.

The third group of drills is devoted to pass rushing. In these drills, players should work on the technique that fits their body style.

- Pass rush 101
  - ✓ Run curve
  - ✓ Run curve with ball
- Pop-ups
  - ✓ Gauntlet
  - ✓ Tight gauntlet
  - ✓ Clup rip dip
  - ✓ Counter drill
- Hoops
  - ✓ Touch drill
  - ✓ Chase
  - ✓ Leverage drill
  - ✓ Two hands
  - ✓ Speed rip
  - ✓ Rip
  - ✓ Wipe
  - ✓ Counter club
  - ✓ Spin

PASS RUSH ESCAPES

You have to develop drills that fit your defensive scheme. I want to do drills to help my players become better athletes. Defensive linemen will always be playing in trash. There will always be bodies under their feet or someone trying to trip them. Develop drills that will help them develop the skills they need to play the game. Coaches should make a master list of the drills that will accomplish what they want to cover. From the master list of drills, they should develop a checklist of the drills they do.

I ask my coaches to make a list of all the things they plan to teach during the course of the season. I want them to list the drills they will use to teach those skills. As they go through the season, they should put check marks by the drills they do. That will tell you a tremendous amount about what you emphasize.

We like to emphasize creating turnovers. We did a tremendous job of running drills that promoted turnover production during the pre-season practices. However, as the season went along, we found we were doing less scoop-and-score, tomahawk, and ball-stripping drills. If you get away from the things you are supposed to emphasizing, the less effective you will be at that skill. You can find that out from your drill checklist.

When I was with the Cowboys, we finished number one in total defense twice. We went back and did a study of those two years. I would be willing to bet you, if they did the same type of study of the 2008 season, the results would be the same. The longest runs in the national football league always came in the second half of the season. Teams started off doing well through the first four or five games. We considered runs over 15 yards to be long runs. In that year, 60 percent of the runs over 15 yards occurred in the second half of the season.

The reason for that happening is very simple. During pre-season training camp, that was the emphasis. Everyone tackled and got off blocks every day of training camp. As the season wore on, those things were not the emphasis of the drill work. With the use of the checklist, you are constantly aware of what you are teaching your players.

In our pass-rush drills, the first drill listed is a run curve drill (Diagram #1). I started doing this drill back

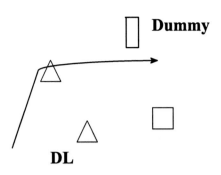

Diagram #1. Run Curve

in the late 1980s. There is nothing outstanding about this drill except it teaches your defensive linemen to get off the ball. In doing this drill, we time the defensive linemen and try to plant the seed in his mind of speed. We set up a cone for the takeoff point of the defender. There is no movement key in this part of the drill. The defender takes off when he is ready. We set a stand-up bag at the depth of seven yards. That is the depth of the front foot of the quarterback in a five-step drop.

We set a cone at a point which represents the set point of the offensive tackle's outside foot. The defensive lineman has to get off the ball, curve around the cone, and cross the face of the dummy. The whole thing we are trying to teach is how fast the defender can do it.

If it takes the defender 1.2 seconds to perform that move, he has 1.8 seconds to make the tackle. We assume the ball will be thrown in three seconds.

The next part of the drill is run curve with the ball. Reacting to the movement of the ball took 1.7 seconds. They lost five-tenths of a second in their reaction time. That lets them know what they have to do to get to the quarterback.

Right now we have 60 film clips of defensive linemen from the NFL. We have films of Julius Peppers, Dwight Freeney, and many others. Our players come in and watch those clips to help them become better players. It helps our players develop their own pass-rush moves.

We do the gauntlet drill to help players understand there is generally more than one blocker to defeat (Diagram #2). If the tackle defeats the guard, he may have to take on the center or running back to get to the quarterback. The gauntlet is a series of stand-up dummies, staggered so as the player weaves through them he has to use both hands to attack each dummy. On the first dummy, he may use a right-handed club move and a left-handed move on the second dummy. In those drills, they run the club, rip, and dip moves. We have a dummy at the finish with a ball attached so the defender can strip the ball.

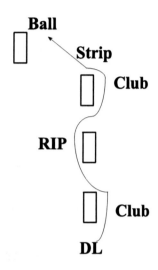

Diagram #2. Gauntlet Drill

We use all kinds of variations of drills with the hoops. You can make the hoops very inexpensively, and they will pay great benefits in the pass-rush game (Diagram #3). The more competitive you can make the drill, the more you will gain from it. We play chase and tag on them. If the first player can catch and touch the second player, the second player has to go again. Make the drills as much fun and as competitive as you can. You have to use your own imagination and creativity to come up with different ways to incorporate the skills.

The thing you want to watch is how tight the players stay to the hoop. The tighter they can stay to the hoop, the more flexible they are in their hips. The players that run the tightest to the hoop are probably going to be your best pass rushers. If you put a dummy holder in the middle of the hoop, it

helps them to be more physical as they run. Have them perform rips on the dummy as they go around the hoop. We do the drill with the linebackers and defensive backs that we plan on using in a pressure scheme. When you watch your game films, you can see the skills from the practice field taken to the game field.

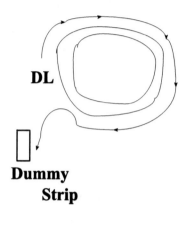

Diagram #3. Hoops

I have great respect for the fact that you coaches are here today. I got into coaching 35 years ago. I taught high school biology and coached boys and girls track in addition to coaching football. I rode on many school buses just like all of you in this room. However, the main reason I became a coach was to make a difference in the lives of the kids I was involved with. There is no greater calling today. The future of our country relies on the coaches in this country. You are the ones that can truly make a difference in the lives of the kids. You can help kids. You can help them stay out of trouble, and you can become a role model for them.

I believe that 95 percent of you in this room are a father figure for some player in your program. Those kids do not have the father figure in their lives that they so desperately need.

It was a pleasure to be with you today. Come see us in Chapel Hill, and thank you very much.

DEFENSIVE TACKLE TECHNIQUES

Former Auburn University Assistant

My topic today is "Defensive Tackle Play versus Blocking Schemes." The blocks I will talk about include the following: drive, cutoff, reach, down, double, G-fold, influence trap, veer trap, power scoop, and the draw play. The techniques of the defensive tackles that I will talk about include: the zero, shade-G, 3 technique, and the 4 technique. I will talk about stance, reads, keys, responsibilities, and coaching points of the defensive tackles.

OUR DEFENSIVE GOALS

- Have passion for the game.
- Give effort.
- Win.
- Stop the run.
- Be physical.
- Be smart.
- Be great tacklers.
- Be great on third down.

We always talk about three-and-out and getting off the field. We stress three-and-out principles. Everything we do in practice requires three perfect repetitions before we leave the field or drill. If we do not get the three plays perfect, we repeat the downs until we get three perfect plays. When you conduct practice that way, it gets the defense thinking "three-and-out" on each play. We want to be great on the first down, second down, and off the field on the third down. We never go on snap count, or the quarterback cadence in our drills. It is always on movement for us.

We are a ball-key defense. When the ball moves, we move. When the center touches the ball, we yell, "Ball, ball!" This alerts us to be ready for the snap.

I want to start with the front alignments, the noseguard position, and the zero technique (Diagram #1).

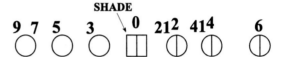

Diagram #1. Front Alignments

Zero technique: Head-up on the center, either hand down. Key the ball to the center.

Shade: Shade outside of the center, inside foot aligns down the middle of the center. Key the ball to the center.

2i (G): Shade inside of the guard, outside foot down the middle of the guard. Key the ball to guard.

2 technique: Head-up on the guard, either hand down. Key the ball to guard.

3 technique: Shade outside the offensive guard, inside foot aligns down the middle of the offensive guard. Key the ball to guard.

Loose 3 technique: Shade outside of the offensive guard with the inside foot aligned on the outside foot of the offensive guard. Key the ball to the guard.

4 shade: Shade both feet of the offensive tackle slightly inside. Key the ball to the tackle

4i technique: Only played on a down call. Shade inside the offensive tackle with the outside foot aligned down the middle of the offensive tackle. Key the ball to the tackle.

Following are the alignments for the different calls.

ZERO TECHNIQUE

N

Diagram #2. Zero Technique

Stance:

- Head-up on the offensive center, foot to foot.
- Three-point stance, either hand down.
- Back is flat, with tail slightly up and head up so you can see.
- Knees bent and ready to uncoil. Explode out of both hips. Attack center with eyes and hands.

Alignment:

- Zero technique, head-up on offensive guard.
- Get as tight to the football as possible.

Key: Movement of the football

Read: Center

Responsibility: Backdoor, 2 gap

Coaching Points:

- You must attack with your eyes on the V of the neck of the center. Explode out of both hips.
- Shoot both of your hands to the center's breastplate with thumbs up, gaining control of the breastplate.
- Grab cloth and fully extend your elbows, keeping the center sway from your body.
- Attack and keep accelerating feet, press and 2 gap, play the backdoor of the block (defensive call)
- Always gain ground; never lose ground
- Release off block, backdoor.
- Relentless pursuit to the football.

Zero Technique's Block Reactions (Key: Football)

All Blocks:

- Attack the V middle of the center with eyes and hands. Explode out of both hips.

- Get good lockout, pressing the center straight back and squeezing the hips.
- Press and keep accelerating your feet, remain square and down the middle of the center. Force the center back.
- Your are responsible for the backside A gap (defensive call).
- Hold on to the center for as long as possible, and flatten to the center and play backdoor to the football (defensive call).

SHADE TECHNIQUE

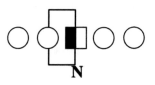

Diagram #3. Shade Technique

Stance:

- Split crotch of center
- Three-point stance. Shade hand down. Free hand in front, ready to strike, never resting on thigh or hip.
- Feet shoulder-width apart, with a slight toe-to-heel stagger.
- Back flat with tail slightly up and head up so you can see the center and the football out of your peripheral vision.
- Knees bent and ready to uncoil. Explode out of both hips.
- Free hand out in front, ready to attack. Do not rest elbow or hand on thigh.

Read: Center

Responsibility: A gap

Coaching Points:

- You must attack with your eyes on the V of the neck of the center. Explode out of both hips.
- Shoot both hands to the center's breastplate with the thumbs up, gaining control of the breastplate.
- Grab cloth and fully extend your elbows, keeping the center away from your body.

- Attack and keep accelerating feet, penetrate through the shoulder of the center.
- Use eyes to recognize blocking scheme and locate the football.
- Always gain ground; never lose ground.
- Release off the block violently using your hands.
- Relentless pursuit to the football.

Shade Technique's Block Reactions (Key: Football)

Drive Block:

- Attack the V of the neck of the center with your eyes.
- Get a good lockout, pressing the center backwards.
- Keep accelerating the feet, and fight to remain square to the line of scrimmage.
- Peek through your gap responsibility. You are responsible for the A gap.
- Squeeze the block, and shed the blocker violently and quickly away from your gap.
- Pursue the ball.

Diagram #4. Drive Block

Cutoff Block:

- Attack the V of the neck of the center with your eyes.
- Peek through your gap. You are responsible for the A gap.
- Flatten the center, and backdoor him to the football.
- Shed the blocker violently, and pursue the ball.

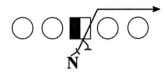

Diagram #5. Cutoff Block

Reach Block:

- Attack the V of the neck of the center with your eyes.
- Work to regain leverage in the A gap,
- Create a new line of scrimmage. Press hard with your outside hand and push-pull.
- Shed the blocker violently, and rip and pursue the ball with intensity.

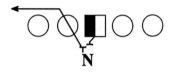

Diagram #6. Reach Block

C-Block:

- Attack the V of the neck of the center with your eyes.
- Flatten and squeeze the center with both hands, peeking through your A gap.
- Once you recognize the guard pulling, squeeze the center.
- We can cross the center in front, according to our game plan.

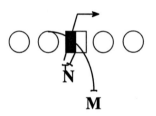

Diagram #7. C-Block

Down Block:

- Attack the V of the neck of the center with your eyes.
- Once you feel no pressure from the center and your hands are on his back numbers, redirect and attack the guard with both hands.
- Squeeze the guard to the outside, and don't get washed.
- Flip your hips without giving ground, and backdoor the guard, closing all gaps.

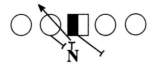

Diagram #8. Down Block

Influence Draw Block:

- React to the pass, get off the spot, and begin your rush.
- Always look inside when rushing the passer.
- Once you feel pressure from the center, plant and retrace your steps, squeezing the hole. Keep shoulders square.
- Locate the ball and release from the blocker violently.
- Pursue the ball.

Diagram #9. Influence Draw Block

Fold Block:

- Attack the V of the neck of the center with your eyes.
- If the center pulls, you step toward the offensive guard and squeeze.
- Squeeze the guard, and do not get washed. Hold your gap.
- Game plan: wipe or backdoor?
- Pursue the ball.

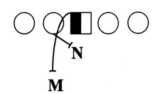

Diagram #10. Fold Block

Double Block:

- Attack the V of the neck of the center with your eyes.
- Defeat the drive block.

- When you feel pressure from the guard, hip into it and drop your outside knee. Sit on stool.
- Apply pressure into the gap, and split it.
- Key to defeating the double-team is to defeat the drive block of the center.
- Use your hands to turn the center and maintain leverage. Explode through the seam.

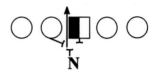

Diagram #11. Double Block

Power Scoop Block:

- Attack the V of the neck of the center with your eyes.
- Flatten the center, and press him backward.
- Peek through your A gap, and keep pressing your seam.
- Split the center and guard by turning your shoulders and ripping with your outside arm, pursue down the heel line, closing all seams.
- The key is to explode into the seam. Don't lose ground. Split the blockers once you recognize the power scoop.

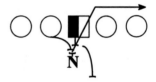

Diagram #12. Power Scoop Block

Smoke Draw Block:

- Attack center or guard. Recognize play and scheme. Read the hip. Attack the front of the man.
- Step into center or guard, squeezing the block and keeping shoulders square to the line of scrimmage. Do not get upfield or out of the A gap.
- Sit on the line of scrimmage, buzzing your feet, and hold your gap for cutback in the A gap.

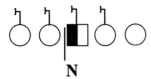

Diagram #13. Smoke Draw Block, Left

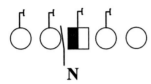

Diagram #14. Smoke Draw Block, Right

G TECHNIQUE

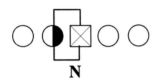

Diagram #15. G Technique

Stance:

- Take a three-point stance. The shade hand is down. Free hand is in front ready to strike, never resting on the thigh or hip.
- Feet are shoulder-width apart with a slight toe-to-heel stagger.
- Back is flat, with tail slightly up and head up so you can see the center and the football out of your peripheral vision.
- Knees bent and ready to uncoil. Explode out of both hips.
- Free hand out in front, ready to attack. Do not rest elbow or hand on the thigh.

Alignment:

- Split the crotch of the offensive guard.
- Get as tight to the football as possible.

Key: Movement of the football

Read: Guard

Responsibility: A gap

Coaching Points:

- You must attack with your eyes on the V of the neck of the defender. Explode out of both hips.

- Shoot both of your hands to the guard's breastplate with thumbs up, gaining control of the breastplate.
- Back is flat, with tail slightly up and head up so you can see the center and the football out of your peripheral vision.
- Knees are bent and ready to uncoil. Explode out of both hips.
- Free hand out in front, ready to attack. Do not rest elbow or hand on the thigh.

G Technique's Block Reactions (Key: Football)

Drive Block:

- Explode into the guard with good eye and hand placement.
- Lock out, pressing the guard backwards.
- Keep accelerating the feet and fight to remain square at the line of scrimmage.
- Peek through your gap responsibility. You are responsible for the A gap.
- Squeeze the block; shed the blocker violently and quickly away from your gap.
- Pursue the ball.

Diagram #16. Drive Block

Cutoff Block:

- Explode into the guard with good eye and hand placement.
- Adjust to attack the guard square, and work to regain leverage in your A gap.
- Press hard with your inside hand. Push-pull!
- Shed the blocker violently, close all seams and pursue the ball.

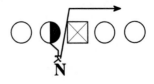

Diagram #17. Cutoff Block

Reach Block:

- Explode into the guard with good eye and hand placement.
- Attack the guard square, and flatten down the line.
- Create a new line of scrimmage, keeping a good lockout.
- Shed the blocker violently, backdoor the guard, and pursue the ball with intensity.

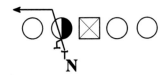

Diagram #18. Reach Block

Down Block:

- Explode into the guard with good eye and hand placement.
- Attack the guard, and squeeze him to the outside with both hands. Recognize the down scheme.
- Flip your hips without losing ground, and backdoor the guard. Shed the blocker violently, and pursue the ball.

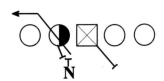

Diagram #19. Down Block

Double Block:

- Explode into the guard with good eye and hand placement.
- Attack the guard square, and defeat the drive block.
- When you feel the pressure from the center, hip into it and drop your inside knee. "Sit down on a stool."
- Apply pressure into your seam and split it.
- Key to defeating the double-team block is to defeat the drive block of the guard.
- Use your hands to turn the guard, and explode back into your seam.

Diagram #20. Double Block

Power Scoop Block:

- Explode into the guard with good eye and hand placement.
- Get a good lockout, pressing the guard backwards.
- Keep your feet moving, and fight to remain square to the line of scrimmage.
- The key is to whip the drive block and keeping your hat in the A gap. Hold on to the guard as long as possible.
- Shed the blocker violently, turn your shoulders, splitting the guard and center, and rip with your inside arm. Pursue down the heel line, closing all seams.

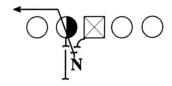

Diagram #21. Power Scoop Block

Double Block:

- Attack the V of the neck of the guard with your eyes.
- Defeat the drive block.
- When you feel pressure from the center, hip into it and drop your outside knee. "Sit on the stool."
- Apply pressure into the gap and split it.
- Key to defeating the double-team is to defeat the drive block of the guard.
- Use your hands to turn the guard and maintain your leverage. Explode through the seam.

Diagram #22. Double Block

Power Scoop Block:

- Attack the V of the neck of the guard with your eyes.
- Flatten the guard, and press him backward.
- Peek through your A gap and keep pressing your seam.
- Split the center and guard by turning your shoulders and ripping with your outside arm. Pursue down the heel line, closing all seams.
- The key is to explore into the seam. Don't lose ground and split the blockers once you recognize the power scoop A gap.

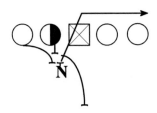

Diagram #23. Power Scoop Block

Fold Block:

- As you attack the guard, feel the fold and attack the center.
- Flatten and squeeze the center with both hands, peeking though your A gap.
- Squeeze the center.
- We can cross the center in front, according to game plan.

Diagram #24. Fold Block

Influence Draw Block:

- Always play the pass first. Get off the spot, and rush the passer.
- Once you feel pressure from the center, plant and retrace your steps, squeezing the hole. Keep the shoulders square.
- Locate the ball, and release from the blocker violently.
- Pursue the ball.

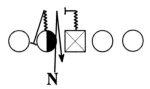

Diagram #25. Influence Draw Block

Smoke Draw Block:

- Attack the center or guard, depending on blocking scheme. Recognize play and scheme. Read the hip. Attack the front of the man.
- Step into the center or guard, attacking with the hands, squeezing the block, and keeping the shoulders square to the line of scrimmage. Do not get upfield or out of the A gap.
- Sit on the line of scrimmage, buzzing your feet and holding your gap for the cutback in your A gap.

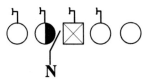

Diagram #26. Smoke Draw Block, Left

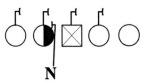

Diagram #27. Smoke Draw Block, Right

3 TECHNIQUE

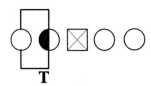

Diagram #28. 3 Technique

Stance:

- Get in a three-point stance with the shade hand down. The free hand should be in front, ready to strike, never resting on the thigh or hip.
- Feet are shoulders-width apart, with a slight toe-to-heel stagger.

- Back is flat, with tail slightly up and head up so you can see the offensive guard and the football out of your peripheral vision.
- Knees bent and ready to uncoil. Explode out of both hips.
- Free hand out in front, ready to attack. Do not rest elbow or hand on the thigh.

Alignment:

- Split the crotch of the offensive guard, hand to the man.
- Get as tight to the football as possible.

Key: Movement of the football

Read: Guard

Responsibility: B gap

Coaching Points:

- You must attack with your eyes on the V of the neck of the offensive guard. Explode out of both hips.
- Shoot both of your hands to the guard's breastplate with the thumbs up, gaining control of the breastplate.
- Grab cloth and fully extend your elbows, keeping the guard away from your body.
- Attack and keep accelerating feet, penetrate through the shoulder of the guard.
- Use your eyes to recognize blocking scheme and locate the football. Never look over the guard's shoulder pads. Peek through your gap.
- Always gain ground; never lose ground.
- Release off the block, violently using your hands.
- Relentless pursuit to the football.

3 Technique's Block Reactions (Key: Football)

Drive Block:

- Explode into the guard with good eye and hand placement.
- Get a good lockout, pressing the defender backward.
- Keep accelerating the feet, and fight to remain square to the line of scrimmage.

- Peek through your gap responsibility. You are responsible for the B gap.
- Squeeze the block; shed the blocker away from your gap.
- Pursue the ball.

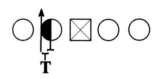

Diagram #29. Drive Block

Cutoff Block:

- Explode into the guard with good eye and hand placement.
- Adjust to attack the guard square and peek through your gap. You are responsible for the B gap.
- Flatten the guard, and backdoor him to the football. Keep your head in your seam.
- Shed the blocker violently.

Diagram #30. Cutoff Block

Reach Block:

- Explode into the guard with good eye and hand placement.
- Attack the guard square, and work to regain leverage in your B gap.
- Create a new line of scrimmage, keeping a good lockout. Press hard with your outside hand. Push, pull, and rip off.
- Shed the blocker violently.

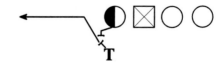

Diagram #31. Reach Block

Double Block:

- Explode into the guard with good eye and hand placement.
- Attack the guard square, and defeat the drive block.
- When you feel pressure from the tackle, hip into it and drop your outside knee. Sit on the stool.
- Apply pressure into the seam and split it.
- Key to defeating the double-team block is to defeat the drive block first.
- Use your hands to turn the guard and maintain leverage. Do not go to the ground unless you are losing your gap.

Diagram #32. Double Block

G-Fold Block:

- Step into the guard and recognize the pull. Lean toward the tackle.
- Attack the tackle and squeeze him, looking inside.
- Once the ball bounces outside, cross the block. If the tackle goes in front, use the pull-cross technique. If he is behind, flip the hips, and use the club-and-rip technique, and backdoor the block (game plan).
- Shed the blocker violently.

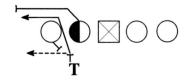

Diagram #33. G-Fold Block

Influence Trap Block:

- React to the pass, get off the spot, and begin your rush.
- Always look inside when rushing the passer.
- When guard disappears and center blocks back, look for trapper.
- Step inside with shoulders square, and box the trap.
- If you get caught upfield, attack the trapper, and squeeze him as hard as you can.

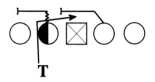

Diagram #34. Influence Trap Block

Down Block:

- Explode into the guard with good eye and hand placement.
- Once you feel no pressure and you feel the back numbers of the guard, recognize the down scheme.
- With your outside hand, feel the back numbers of the guard, and recognize the down scheme. If in front, use a pull-cross technique. If behind, flip your hips, use the club-and-rip technique, and backdoor the block (game plan).
- Shed the blocker violently.

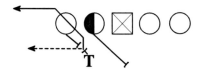

Diagram #35. Down Block

Veer Block:

- Explode into the guard with good eye and hand placement. Squeeze the guard to the inside and off his hip, staying square and looking inside for any pulling lineman.
- If a pulling lineman appears, turn your shoulders, wrong-arm him, and split the block. If you get caught upfield, attack the guard, and squeeze him as much as you can.

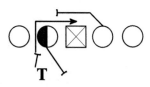

Diagram #36. Veer Block

Power Scoop Block:

- Explode into the guard with good eye and hand placement.
- Get a good lockout, pressing the guard backwards.
- Keep your feet moving, and fight to remain square to the line of scrimmage.
- The key is to whip the drive block and keep your hat in the B gap.
- Shed the blocker violently, turn your shoulders, splitting the guard and tackle, and pursue down the heel line.

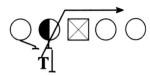

Diagram #37. Power Scoop Block

Influence Draw Block:

- Always play the pass first, get off the spot, and rush the passer.
- Once you feel pressure from the guard, plant and retrace your steps, squeezing the hole. Keep your shoulders square.
- Locate the ball, and release from the blocker violently.
- Pursue the ball.

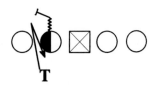

Diagram #38. Influence Draw Block

Smoke Draw Block:

- Attack the guard or tackle, depending on the blocking scheme. Recognize the play and scheme. Read the hip.
- Step into the guard or tackle, attacking with hands, squeezing the block, and keeping the shoulders square to the line of scrimmage. Do not get upfield or out of the B gap.
- Sit on the line of scrimmage, buzzing your feet, and hold your gap for the cutback in your B gap.

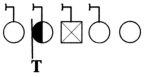

Diagram #39. Smoke Draw Block, Left

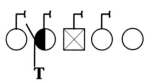

Diagram #40. Smoke Draw Block, Right

4 TECHNIQUE

Diagram #41. 4 Technique

Stance:

- Balance your feet. Align on the tackle, and shade your feet inside on the tackle.
- Take a three-point stance. Hand to man is down.
- Back is flat, with tail slightly up and head up so you can see.
- Keep knees bent and ready to uncoil. Explode out of both hips.
- Attack with the eyes and hands.

Alignment:

- 4 technique, shade feet of tackle
- Get as tight to the football as possible.

Key: Football to man

Read: Tackle to guard

Responsibility: Backdoor, 2 gap (defensive call)

Coaching Points:

- You must attack with your eyes on the V of the neck of the tackle. Explode out of both hips.
- Shoot both of your hands to the tackle's breastplate with the thumbs up, gaining control of the breastplate.
- Grab cloth, and fully extend your elbows, keeping the tackle away from your body.

- Attack and keep accelerating feet, press and hold inside, and maintain leverage on the tackle (B gap)
- Press B gap, and play backdoor on the tackle versus run.
- Game plan: defensive call for pass.
- Relentless pursuit to the football.

4 Technique's Block Reactions (Key: Football)

Drive Block:

- Explode out of both hips.
- Explode into the tackle with good eye and hand placement.
- Get good lockout, pressing the tackle, and holding inside leverage.
- Squeeze the block, and hold the B gap.
- Pursue the ball.

Diagram #42. Drive Block

Cutoff Block:

- Explode out of both hips into the tackle with good eye and hand placement.
- Adjust to attack the tackle. You must fight to not get cut off.

- If cut off, squeeze the block and backdoor him to the football. Keep your head in the seam.
- Shed and pursue to the ball.

Diagram #43. Cutoff Block

Reach Block:

- Explode out of both hips into the tackle with good eye and hand placement.
- Attack the tackle, and hold inside leverage in B gap.
- Play backdoor.
- Shed and pursue to the ball.

Diagram #44. Reach Block

Thank you for your time, and thank you for what you do, for coaching our young people. Football is the greatest game, and we need great people like you coaching football.

SPREAD OFFENSE: THREE- AND FIVE-STEP TIMING

University of Southern Mississippi

I want to tell you my background so you will know where I am coming from. I was born and raised in College Station, Texas. I played high school and college football in Texas. I started coaching at the high school level just outside of Dallas. From there, I became a G.A. at Baylor University in Waco, Texas, under Grant Teaff. I spent two years there and Coach Teaff retired. When he retired, Chuck Reedy, who was the offensive coordinator, became the head coach. He hired me and I worked there for the next four years.

From there, I had the opportunity to go to the United States Air Force Academy with Fisher DeBerry. Fisher was a tremendous coach, and I learned a lot of football there. We were teaching and coaching great players at the Air Force Academy. It was a great opportunity and I spent two years there.

I got a call from Middle Tennessee State University wanting me to become their offensive coordinator. That was a big move for me. I had a lot of things in my head that I wanted to see work. While I was at Air Force, Coach DeBerry let us travel around and visit with other coaches and programs to get ideas about coaching. To my knowledge, there was only one program in the country at that time running a no-huddle offense. That is what I wanted to do, so I took the job at Middle Tennessee.

I felt that type of offense put the most stress on a defense. When I went to football games in the early 70s with my father, I started to think about this type of offense. Teams would play all afternoon going three yards and a cloud of dust. They played like that until they got desperate or at the end of the half. In those situations, they opened up the offense and made some big plays. I wondered why they did not do that the whole game.

I was told early on that I could not run an offense like that. As I started to build my philosophy, I visited with Rich Rodriguez who was at Tulane University. They were the only team in the country doing it. They were also the only team running a multiple-tempo offense.

When I went to Middle Tennessee, we needed an edge. They were a 1-AA school that was getting ready to make the jump into the 1-A division. We were going to play 1-A competition with 1-AA players. I had to figure out what type of offense to run. The first thought was to run the option like we had at Air Force. At Air Force, we ran every type of option there was. In the two years I was there we won 23 games. We averaged over 40 points a game and were very successful.

Going to Middle Tennessee, I felt we had to run the option or spread it out and throw the ball. We needed some type of edge. We needed something to be different. We did not have the same talent as the people we were going to play. We were going to get our butts beat if we tried to do what everybody else was doing.

When we got there, we did not have a quarterback to run the option. We decided to spread the field and throw the football. The first year we threw the ball, but we could not run the ball. That was probably my fault because I was not sold on running the ball. We won three games and ended up 32nd in the country in offense. That was when I decided that to be successful you have to run the ball out of the spread offense.

In the spread offense, you have to be balanced and be able to run the ball as well as throw it. From

Middle Tennessee, I went with Ron Zook at Florida. After that, I went to Oklahoma State with Mike Gundy for three years and, finally, to Southern Miss as head coach.

The reason I am telling you all this background is I want you to understand that this offense is time-tested. This offense has been at four different schools in four different conferences. Over that 10-year period we have averaged about 200 yards rushing and 240 yards passing. It did not matter what school or conference we played in, the offense was successful. It has not been the same offense the entire time. You have to adjust to the personnel you have at each school.

BALANCED OFFENSE

In 2005, I went to Oklahoma State. The first year was terrible. We tried to do exactly the same things we had done at Florida without their personnel. It was a bad year. They wanted to run me out of town. Mike Gundy was a two-back coach and wanted to run the ball. He brought me into OSU to run the spread, and the way we played that first year was terrible. We stuck with what we were doing and adjusted to the personnel we had at Oklahoma State.

If you look at what we did at Middle Tennessee the first year and what we did at Southern Miss last year, you will see the same system. However, there are some changes in the offense. The offense changes with personnel.

In this offense, we want to take what the defense gives. I believe if you can run and throw, the defense cannot stop it all. The defense will tell you they are going to stop the run first. They will put eight or nine defenders in the box if the offense allows them to do it.

I cannot allow them to do that. First of all, I am not smart enough to block all those bodies. We spread the field horizontally and create vertical seams in the defense—that is the key to our success. If the running back gets the ball, there is never going to be more than six defenders in the box. We have five offensive linemen to block five defenders. The quarterback handles one of the defenders and the running back has a chance to move the ball.

If the defense puts more defenders in the box, we are going to throw the ball. I am not the kind of coach who goes into any game with a determination to run the ball for 200 yards. If the defense loads the box, we will throw every down. I go into a football game and take what the defense gives me. If they allow me to rush the football, I will run it.

Balance to me does not mean we go into a game and run the ball 40 times and throw it 40 times. One week, we may rush the ball for 100 yards and throw for 300 yards. The following week, we may rush it for 300 yards and throw it for 100 yards. I do not care how we move the ball, but I want to be able to do both. I do not believe a defense can take both the pass and the run away from you. If they do, they are that much better than you are.

Our base running game consists of the inside zone, outside zone, power, counter, and option. We will always run the inside zone in every game. We may not run all five of those running plays in a game. We may go two games and not run all five of them. However, we have the ability to run them in a game. We work on them every week. These are the plays we hang our hat on. However, the inside zone play has to go for us to be successful. It is the most important run in our offense.

We have to get the ball outside with the outside zone and option. We run the power so we have that smashmouth mentality. Do not get me wrong—we spread it out, but we are going to hammer the football. If you can average 200 yards a game running the football, you are doing something right. You always need some kind of counter. On the play we run, we pull only one blocker.

I am going to talk about one running play before we get into the passes. We run the zone option and it is one of the staples in our running game. This play will be in every game plan we have. The quarterback does not have to be a burner to run this play. We ran this play about four times a game. I like to run this play on first or second downs and third-and-medium. Last year, this play averaged 10 yards a carry. We have used this play over time, and we feel we have answers for anything the defense does. This play is also good against the zone blitz, which we are seeing a lot.

When I talk about the play, I talk about the middle of the field being open or closed (Diagram #1). If the defense has two safeties, we talk about the middle of the field being open. If there is a single safety, the middle of the field is closed. The middle of the field is the quarterback's first read. The first defense is an *over 4-3 alignment*.

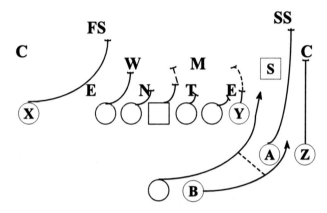

Diagram #1. Zone Option vs. Over

ZONE OPTION BLOCKING RULES

- TE: Full zone work with PST to second level
- PST: Covered reach; uncovered trail; overtake DE or climb
- PSG: Covered reach; uncovered trail; overtake DL or climb
- Center: Reach A gap; uncovered trail; overtake DT or climb
- BSG: Scoop
- BST: Scoop; B-gap threat; possible shift

The blocking rule for the *tight end* is a full zone scheme with the playside tackle. He is working with the tackle and getting up to the second level of the defense. The tight end is at the point of attack and has to set the edge. He has the most critical block. He has to handle the C-gap defender up to the playside linebacker. He works with the playside tackle depending on the technique of the defender playing on him.

He steps with his near foot. If he has a 9 technique on his outside shoulder, he has to step wide. If he has a 6 technique head-up on him, he steps to the outside shoulder and tries to get his head outside the shoulder using his inside arm. We do not have to get both hands on the defender because we have help from the tackle coming from the inside. He must have his eyes on the linebacker. He comes off the block when the linebacker makes him come off. He stays on the combination block until the linebacker threatens the line of scrimmage. If the linebacker never shows up, he stays on the defensive end.

The blocking scheme on this play is the exact blocking scheme for the outside zone. If the *playside tackle* is covered, he reaches the defender. If he is uncovered, he is going to trail and overtake the defensive end block from the tight end. He is working with the tight end and is responsible for the C-gap defender. The ideal situation is the tackle taking over the defensive end and the tight end getting off on the linebacker coming over the top.

The tackle and tight end's eyes are on the linebacker. We have two sets of eyes on the linebacker. If the linebacker does not move, the tackle and tight end double-team the C-gap defender as long as they have to. If the linebacker tries to run underneath the play, the tackle comes off on the linebacker and the tight end blocks the defensive end. We work on this block because it is the block we use on the inside zone, outside zone, and option.

The *guard* has the same rule as the tackle. If he is covered, he reaches the defender. If he is uncovered, he trails the next defender outside or climbs to the second level. I want defenders on the ground. We cut them as much as we can. A defender cannot make a tackle if he is on the ground.

If the *center* is covered, he reaches the playside A gap. If he is uncovered, he is trailing the guard and overtaking the defensive tackle or climbing to the second-level linebacker.

The backside guard is scooping to the center. The backside tackle scoops his B gap for any threat into that gap. He checks for a possible shift by the linebacker. If the defense brings the safety down to the line of scrimmage, the tackle will shift up and cut him off like he did on the linebacker. If there is a tight end on the backside, he runs a scoop scheme.

The second defense is an *under 4-3* with the middle of the field open (Diagram #2). Nothing has changed for the tight end and playside tackle. They are working a zone scheme on the defensive end coming off for the inside linebacker.

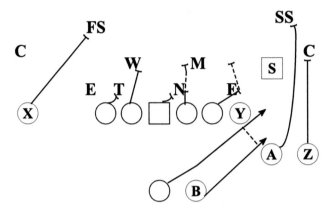

Diagram #2. Zone Option vs. Under

The guard does not run through the nose to get up on the linebacker. He is zone stepping as the center is coming hard into the A gap. We do not feel like we have to get up on the backside linebacker. We want to get the A-gap defender blocked.

We keep track of knockdown blocks. We take pride in that. We keep a chart of that for the players. We talk about it every day and they have a goal of how many knockdowns we are shooting for. We have goals within the separate units and team goals.

If we do not get many knockdowns, we are looking for "loafs." We chart loafs and knockdowns. If we have a lot of knockdowns, we probably do not have many loafs. However, if we do not have a lot of knockdowns, we are probably loafing in the offensive line. A loaf for us is a lineman not busting his butt all the way to the end of the play. It does not matter if he is on the playside or backside. If he is not going full speed from the beginning to the end, that is a loaf.

After the games, we have Sunday practices. After practice on Sunday, we handle the loafs from Saturday's game. At the end of practice, the team circles up. We call it the "Eagle circle." The coach is in the middle. He calls out a player's name. The player sprints his butt to the middle of the circle. The coach tells him how many loafs he had in the game. If he had three loafs, he yells his name and announces, "My name is John Smith and I let the team down three times." The whole team does three up-downs. The player sprints back to his position and the next player's name is called. We handle all loafs this way. I have been in situations in spring football where we have done 150 up-downs. However, we have done as few as 12 for a game. Everyone on the team is graded including the quarterback. If he does not carry out his fakes all the way to the line of scrimmage, he gets a loaf.

The first thing the quarterback has to do is identify the pitch key. He has to make sure the receiver to that side and the back know who the pitch key is. We have used a thousand different ways to identify him. It does not matter how you do it but everyone has to be on the same page. One thing I would not do is call out the jersey number of the key defender.

The way we do it now is to point at the pitch key. The receiver points to him also. That is the simplest way to do it. It is not a giveaway because we point out blitzes, linebackers, and many other things. In this diagram, the pitch key is the Sam linebacker.

After the quarterback points out the pitch key, his next big job is to secure the snap. That is something we never take for granted. We work with our centers and quarterbacks every day on the snap. The centers snap and move on every play in practice. You cannot take the snap for granted. It does not matter who the pitch key is if the quarterback puts the ball on the ground.

The quarterback secures the snap and attacks the outside cheek of the pitch key. We do not run at the inside shoulder or hip. I never want the quarterback in a situation where he has to run the ball and not pitch it. If he attacks the inside shoulder of the pitch key, the defender can cut off the pitch and make the quarterback run the ball.

We do not want to pitch the ball backward. When I was at Air Force, the pitches were downhill. We did that this year in our pitch scheme. This year, we had a bad pitch that was called an incomplete pass. That is the type of pitch I am looking for. I want the back to catch the ball going downhill. I do not want the back catching the ball on the pitch and have to run five yards to get to the line of scrimmage.

In practice, every day we do a five-minute option and screen drill. We run two huddles is this drill. The first huddle calls the play and runs it. As they are coming back, the second huddle is running their play. In that five-minute drill, we are running 16 to 18 repetitions. We are going hard and fast for the entire five minutes. The players do not like the drill because we are going so fast.

It is hard for the scout team to get lined up because we are going so fast. The coaches are yelling at everyone because they are not getting to coach their players. If you want to make a correction, it has to be done on the run. We do not stop the drill for correction or coaching. It is as rapid as we can go. The players that are going to get the work are the slot receiver, the running back, and the quarterback. The defense is doing something different every time. The quarterback has to be thinking all the time.

I want the quarterback to pitch the ball every time. It does not happen that way. Defenses will design their coverage to make the quarterback carry the ball. That is one reason we do not run it more than four times a game. I do not want the quarterback running a lot. He has to run the ball enough with the normal things that happen in a game. He has to pull the ball down on a pass and run on occasion. On a busted play, he sometimes gets stuck with the ball and has to run. We do not like him to run that much. I will run the quarterback as much as we need to.

When we pitch the ball, the quarterback delivers it with a thumb motion. We have tried others, but the best pitch for us is made with the thumb snapped down.

The quarterback has to identify the D-gap player. He looks for the first defender outside the

tight end. That is the pitch key. He could be on the line of scrimmage, on the second level, or in the secondary. If the defense has disguised the alignment and moved, that is fine. Once we identify the pitch key, we run the play.

ZONE OPTION RECEIVER RULES

- TB: Open crossover footwork; run and gain; maintain pitch phase 4 X 2
- Z-back: Block man on
- A-back: Block next defender beyond the point
- X-end: Block man on

The Z-back's rule is to block the man that aligns on him. It does not matter what the coverage may be. If he recognizes the defense as man coverage, he can run off the defender. The only thing I do not want him to do is cut the defender. You cannot cut a defender at the point of attack on an option. If they cut the defender, he will get off the ground and make the tackle because it takes some time for the ball to get to him.

The A-receiver is the slot receiver. He has to know who the pitch key is and block the next defender. The X-receiver is backside and he cuts off. If he was on the playside, he blocks the man on him.

If we are going to spread the field and be in a one-back set, our receivers must be great blockers. They are the reason we run for 200 yards a game. Our receivers understand that fact. They may not understand it when they arrive on campus, but they do before they play. I do not believe in the *prima donna* receiver that thinks he is just a pass catcher. I want our receivers to have a linebacker mentality. That is the way we coach them. We work them hard and challenge them. If one of them backs down, we challenge his heart. We call them out in front of everyone and challenge their pride. We get after them and expect them to block.

The frontside blocks are basic stalk blocks. My two years at the Air Force Academy, I coached the wide receivers. With as much option as we ran at Air Force, we did a lot of stalk blocking. In our stalk block, we attack the outside number of the defender unless he is within five yards of the receiver.

If he is within five yards of the receiver, he is in the "danger zone." In the danger zone, we must protect the inside first. That keeps the rolled-up corner from hitting the tailback before he gets the ball. If the defender is within the danger zone, the receiver comes off and attacks his inside number. If the defender squats, the receiver works to his outside numbers. The reason we work the outside number is to get the ball pitched and on the sideline away from all the defenders.

The pursuit drills that the defense runs in practice is exactly what I want the play to do. I want to be on the sideline with everyone chasing from the inside. I want the backside corner to have to make the tackle. By using a multiple tempo offense, the defense does not get to rest as they usually do. This type of offense fatigues the defense.

I do not want to show the defense whether it is run or pass by the release of the receivers. If the defender can read run in the first two or three steps, the receiver is giving him the advantage. We want to push hard off the ball and sell the pass. As he gets into the danger zone, he begins to break down. At that point, the receiver becomes an offensive lineman. We take short, choppy steps so we can be balanced. We want to drop our tail, get in a good football position, and climb up the defender.

We want to close the distance, get the hands inside, and grab cloth. When he gets in that position, he takes him wherever he wants to go. If the receiver can get his hands on the defender, it is over with. If the defender widens to keep outside leverage, the receiver drives him out-of-bounds. He tries to take him over the water cooler and the cheerleaders.

We take the defender wherever he wants to go and the back cuts off his block. If the defender gets off the block, the receiver has to let go of the jersey. If we pull the jersey, the referee will call holding. However, most defensive backs cannot make a tackle if the wide receiver is pressing on them. The thing we cannot do is let the defensive back control us and make the tackle. We have to move him somewhere. You cannot let him hold his position.

We are in the shotgun and the quarterback is five yards from the line of scrimmage. The tailback's toes are aligned on the heels of the quarterback. That puts the tailback at five-and-a-half yards from the line of scrimmage. I am not as concerned with his depth as I am his width. We want him splitting the playside tackle's inside leg. If he can widen a little more and not give the play away, that is great. We want to outflank the pitch key as quickly as possible. The tailback works to get four yards in front of the quarterback and no deeper than two yards. If the quarterback has to adjust, the tailback adjusts with him.

I told you, I want the quarterback to attack the outside cheek of the pitch key. However, I do not want him to hold the ball until the last minute before he pitches it. I do not want the quarterback taking a hit because he is trying to pitch at the last second. We pitch the ball when the tailback outflanks the key.

On the backside, we expect the tackle to cut off the 3-technique tackle. We expect the backside guard to get the Will linebacker cutoff. If he does not, the frontside guard or center will cut off the Will linebacker. In that case, the backside guard keeps working up the levels trying to get to the free safety.

The next defense is a 3-4 look with seven defenders in the box (Diagram #3). The Sam linebacker is on the line of scrimmage in a 9 technique on the tight end. The defensive end is aligned in a 5 technique with the nose shaded to the tight end. We are still going to pitch off the D-gap player. That is the Sam linebacker because he is the first man outside the tight end.

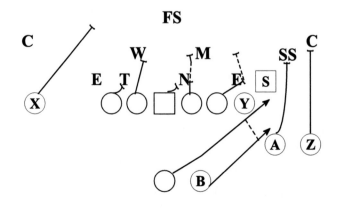

Diagram #3. Zone Option vs. 3-4

The slot receiver knows he has the next man who is the strong safety. The difference is the tight end. He still handles the C-gap player with the tackle. However, the defensive end is now a 5 technique. I do not want the tight end to step down on the defensive end. If he does, the linebacker will be over-the-top before he can get up the field. We want the tight end to come off the ball and get his inside hand on the 5 technique with his eyes on the Mike linebacker.

He steps with his inside foot up the field. He has his hands on the defensive end, but he watches the linebacker. As soon as the linebacker starts to come over the top, the tight end comes off and blocks him. The tackle zone steps for the defensive end, but he is aware of the linebacker. He knows if the linebacker is running fast, he has no help from the tight end. He has to block the defensive end by himself. Everything else is the same on this play.

The next diagram shows the option against the *3-3 stack* defense (Diagram #4). We identify the pitch key as the rover in this diagram. The tight end and tackle have the C-gap defender up to the playside linebacker. The playside linebacker is stacked right over the C gap. The tackle knows he has almost no help on the defensive end.

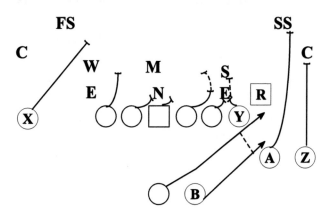

Diagram #4. Zone Option vs. 3-3

On occasion, the Sam linebacker will widen from his stack position. The tight end and tackle know they still have to get their blocks. If the tight end gets to the backside hip of the linebacker, we can still block him. The tight end drives the backside hip as far as he can. The quarterback can always cut the ball up inside.

If the defensive end jumps outside into a 9 technique, the tight end does the same thing. He knows if the end is on his outside shoulder, the linebacker will be inside. The tackle can block the linebacker and the tight end reaches the defensive end. If he cannot get him reached, he stays on him and pushes him outside. If the quarterback cannot get the edge, he runs it inside. It is just like the outside zone play except the quarterback is carrying the ball.

In the passing game, I am always looking for a simple pass. I want the type of pass where the offensive line does not have to block anybody and the quarterback knows where to throw the ball. I went with my wife on a vacation to Pawleys Island, South Carolina. I went to the golf course to play some golf and saw Tom Moore, the offensive coordinator for the Indianapolis Colts, on the practice tee. I introduced myself and asked if he was going to play. He was and I asked him if I could ride the round with him. I rode 18 holes with Tom Moore.

The only thing I asked him that day about football was his best play in a situation where you had to make the yardage needed for a first down. He told me the play was so simple that I would not believe him. He said this was Peyton Manning's favorite play (Diagram #5). The formation was a tight end trips set with a split end to the backside. The split end runs a 10-yard hook and the back flares to that side. The tight end expands outside for two yards, drives upfield for 15 yards, and comes across the middle. The slot receiver and outside receiver push up the field five yards and run hard to the inside.

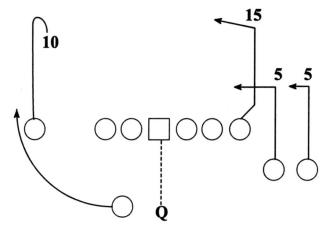

Diagram #5. Cowboy

We tell the quarterback to throw the ball to one of the two receivers coming inside. We tell the quarterback to look at the inside linebacker. If he runs with the tight end, throw to the slot receiver. If the linebacker does not run with the tight end, throw to the outside receiver. They never throw the ball to the tight end, backside receiver, or the swing back.

We put that play in at Florida and it became a great play for us. It is still in our arsenal and we use it. We call it "cowboy." It is simple. In the passing game, you can make the plays as complicated as you want or as simple as you want. The Colts have the best quarterback in the game and they throw this simple pass. Being simple and executing what you do is what the passing game is all about.

We run a five-step drop with three-step timing. I believe a sack is the quarterback's fault. I can show you on film where the defensive end is turned loose on the quarterback and he still gets the ball off for a completion. That is the type of passing game I want.

The play I want to talk about is *double scat*. We have run this play for a long time. The success rate of this pass is 83 percent. We average 7.7 yards per completion. Thirty-three percent of the time, we throw this pass on third down. If you play against me, you will see this play. It is a blind call. When you get into a game and do not know what to call, this is the play. It does not matter what the defense or coverage is. It is a time-tested pattern.

I like to run this in some type of 3x1 formation (Diagram #6). The double scat takes the slot receiver to the trips side and the single receiver to the backside.

People know I am going to run this play, so we put some window dressing on it. We use some motion and set adjustments, but it does not really matter. Our players believe in it and it works. Our players do not care if the defenders know it is coming because they believe they can execute the play.

I do not want the scat receiver to be more than six yards from the offensive tackles. If the ball is on the hash marks, the receiver into the boundary is one yard from the top of the numbers. Landmarks on the field are critical in the passing game. One yard

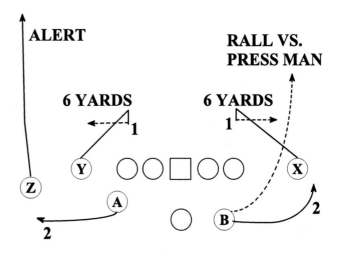

Diagram #6. Double Scat

from the top of the numbers is a critical distance. They can be closer than six yards from the tackle, but no wider.

DOUBLE SCAT RULES

- Scat X-end and Y-end: Stem inside to a depth of six yards; sit versus zone, bounce out versus man; if blitz, look for the ball (hot read)
- Fade Z-end: Run fade; get over top of defender; work to catch ball over outside shoulder
- Bubble A-back: Run a bubble route; settle at numbers
- Swing route B-back: Free release; run swing route; settle at numbers; versus press man, run a rail route

The scat receiver to the single receiver side takes his alignment six yards from the tackle and locates the playside linebacker. I want the linebacker that is aligned in the box on the single receiver side. He wants to look at his inside foot. That is his aiming point. He runs directly to that spot at six-yards deep. If the linebacker drops to zone, the receiver sticks his foot in the ground, turns around, and catches the football.

We tell the receiver to take a picture as he runs to the spot. If the linebacker drops wide, the quarterback throws the ball on his inside number. If he drops straight back, the ball comes on the outside number. Where the quarterback delivers the ball tells the receiver which way to turn and get upfield. The quarterback takes the receiver away from the defender.

If the receiver goes to the inside and the linebacker sits and walls the receiver off, the receiver bounces off the linebacker and takes the pattern to the outside. We want to keep the pattern flat and not up the field. If you push up the field, the linebacker undercuts the pattern.

The next situation is the linebacker running a blitz. When the receiver sees the blitz, his eyes go straight to the quarterback. He is the hot read for the quarterback. If the quarterback throws the ball, he catches it and goes up the field. If the quarterback does not throw the ball he continues to the spot, sticks the foot in the ground, and bounces back outside.

The last situation is the pressed corner. As the receiver runs inside to get to the spot, the linebacker is running at him. The linebacker has the running back man-to-man or is running over-the-top of the coverage. The receiver gets to his spot, sticks his foot in the ground, opens his shoulders, and gets back to the outside.

The Z-receiver to the trips side runs a fade route. This is not a dummy route. We throw the ball to the fade receiver. If the defense comes up on the receiver and we feel we have the right match-up, we throw this pattern. We do not throw the ball to see if we can catch it. We throw the ball expecting to catch it. The quarterback throws the ball 18 to 22 yards down the field, five yards from the sideline. That is where we want the receiver. We drill those patterns five minutes every day. We want the ball caught over the outside shoulder.

The A-back is the inside slot receiver. He runs his pattern for width and not depth. The B-back has a free release with no blocking assignment. He runs a swing route to his side. When the bubble and swing routes get into the numbers they begin to settle. If we throw the ball to the back, I want him to catch it no deeper than two yards from the line of scrimmage. I do not want him catching it five-yards deep in the backfield.

The only thing the B-back looks for is press coverage on the split end. If he sees press coverage on the split end, his swing becomes a rail route. He is going to beat the linebacker in man coverage down the field. If he cannot get open, the quarterback knows he has the scat route coming back outside.

The quarterback reads the middle of the field. If he reads middle of the field closed, he is throwing the scat/swing into the weakside of the formation. If he reads the middle of the field open, he throws the scat/swing to the strongside of the formation. If he reads man coverage, he throws the ball to the scat/wheel to the weakside.

We run five-man protection with this pattern. If we get press-man coverage, the back will run a rail route. With the quarterback I have now, he can read the Mike Linebacker. If he works weak, we throw strong, and if he works strong, we throw weak. He can handle that because he understands the pattern.

I have enjoyed this. If you have questions about anything, give us a call. You can come by and talk ball anytime you like. Thank you very much.

THE WINNING EDGE IN THE KICKING GAME

Portland State University

It is a real pleasure to be here. Thanks for having me. Is there anyone in the room attending their first clinic? I was coaching in Ohio, and this clinic was the second clinic I ever attended. They held it at the Brown Hotel at that time. I was a high school football coach at the time. Roy Kidd was the coach at Eastern Kentucky University. He had an opening on his staff and was going to interview me that night at 8:00.

I was sitting on a couch in the hotel lobby talking football with some other coaches. Nick Dennis, the head coach at Western Kentucky University, walked up. He told me he wanted to interview me for a job. I told him I was supposed to interview with Eastern Kentucky. He told me he wanted to hire me right then and there. I was so excited because at the second clinic I had ever attended, I got a college coaching job.

In Cincinnati, I was making $4,800 a year and got a college job at Western Kentucky making $125 a month. It was great to step up to a big college job (laughs). Western Kentucky was always very good to me. They changed who I was, and we had all kinds of success.

While I was at Western, we never lost a game. We had one tie but no losses. Bud Carson, who was the head coach at Georgia Tech, called me. He told me he wanted to interview me at the national coaches conference for a job with them. We set the interview up for a Wednesday. I did not know where the national clinic was being held. As it turned out, it was in New York City. That was in 1966. My roommate at Western was Joe Bugel. We made $125 a month and were paid on the 30th of each month. By the 5th of the next month, we were broke. We had all this money, so we both got dates and tried to act like a big shot.

When I found out the conference was in New York, I did not know how I was going to get there. I did not have a car, so I hitchhiked from Bowling Green to New York for the interview. I did the interview, but did not get the job.

Just about the time you go to a clinic and think you did not learn anything, something good happens to you. Today, this lecture is going to change where you coach, how you coach, and how your team plays.

Every coach that you know talks about special teams. Most of them pay lip service to special teams and do not give a damn about it. I was at Georgia Tech under Pepper Rogers for six years. I recruited Louisville in those days. We beat Notre Dame, back when they could beat somebody, with Louisville players. I remember when Notre Dame could play. My goal when I took the Portland State job was to win more games than Notre Dame. If I can win two or three a year, I will be okay. The bottom line on special team is a lot of lip service.

While I was at Georgia Tech, a coach named George Allen called. He wanted me to interview for a job as the first special teams coach in the NFL. I went in and talked to Coach Rogers. I told him I had to go for an interview with the Washington Redskins. He jumped up, pounded the table, and said I better get the job. He told me if I went to Washington for the interview, I was fired from this job. He was the new coach, and we had only had just finished spring practice. That was all I needed anyway. I told him I would rather sell shoes than work for him, and I went for the interview.

Little did I know, George Allen was a bigger joke than Pepper Rogers. When I got there, he interviewed me on the practice field. He asked me if I saw the small stand of woods by the practice field.

He told me we started work at 6:00, but before I came to work, he wanted me to chop down two trees. I told him if he had my airline ticket, I would be on my way back home.

I left and went home. Pepper was not kidding, and I was fired at Georgia Tech. Every time you get fired, the best thing that could happen to you is right around the corner. I was sitting home without a job when the phone rang. It was the Detroit Lions. I went for an interview. Two days after the interview, the coach dropped dead of a heart attack while cutting the grass. They named Rick Forzano as head coach. He called and told me he wanted to hire me, but did not know how to deal with Georgia Tech. I told him not to worry, and I would handle that situation. He did not know I did not have a job. I told him I was on the way to the Lions.

Do not worry about not having a job. The way you coach and the way you present yourself will take care of those kinds of situations. Just keep doing what you believe in, and do it the way it has to be done.

Special teams are not given the attention by any coach in America the way it should be. I have had many special teams coaches. The first special teams coach I ever hired was Bill Belichick. I paid him $15,000. He is making $6 million now. People asked me what I thought when I hired him for $15,000. I told them I overpaid him. He was not worth it because he did not know the special teams. I hired Nick Saban, and the list goes on and on. Bobby April, the special teams coach for the Buffalo Bills, worked for me. My special teams coach at Portland State is Bobby April, Jr. He started with me when he was nine years old. He knows the important of the kicking game.

I interviewed a coach for a special teams job. I wanted to know what his overall goal was. He told me eventually he would like to become the offensive line coach. Do you think he had a snowball's chance in hell to be my special teams coach? I ask him why he wanted to take a demotion. Why would he come in as a special teams coach and become an offensive line coach? Special teams have to be the priority for the special teams coach.

The way to become a dominant team is stop paying lip service to special teams and become dominant in that part of the game. Every day in practice, we go over two phases in the kicking game. It may be kickoff and kickoff return on one day, and two other phases on the next day. Write this next statement down, and you will become a different football team. When we have two-a-days, the morning practice has an hour-and-a-half of kicking drills. After the kicking session of practice, we have 30 minutes remaining. That is not lip service. I have done that everywhere I have been. I have been at the Falcons, Lions, Bills, Oilers, Georgia Tech, and countless other places. That is getting it done and teaching it.

When you put in an offensive play, you do not go to practice and run the play in a team drill first. You break the play down in its separate units and teach the individual skills involved in the play. You have to do the same thing in the kicking game. We break down all segments of the game and work on them individually.

If you come to our practices, you will see players working on individual blocks on the kickoff. You will see the wedge blockers working 3-on-3, sifting out the twists and turns of the coverage. We do those things for weeks before we bring it together as a team. You have to commit the time to be what you want to be, not the lip service.

The last 30 minutes of the morning practice is devoted to the freshmen. I just sat in 30 living rooms with 30 moms and dads and signed 30 new freshmen. I would do this if I went back to high school coaching. In the last 30 minutes of that practice, every freshmen on our team moves to first string. If I signed a center, he is the starting center. What does that cause? This year, Portland State started 17 freshmen. You cannot do that if you set them on the sideline and hope they grow up. If you are hoping they will get better and do not work with them, you will soon forget them. You will find yourself looking at a player who has been with you for three years and still cannot play.

I always wear all black. That is an attitude. Special teams are all about attitude. Black is not even a color. It is the absence of all color. At Portland, we wear all black even though our colors are green. It is all about attitude. There is a third-string center who can be a star on special teams. I have a player by the name of Matt Ford, a chicken has bigger legs, but he wants to play. You have to get the third-stringer to change. We are going to change it to the point where he wins game for you. His mother came down from the stands, doing what I call an "O.W." She was "openly weeping" because her son helped us win a game. It was like Dick Vermeil the night he retired. He was weeping like a baby.

There is a way to get those third-stringers to play well enough to help you win. One day a week, we pull power sleds. Those are the sleds you load with weight and pull them around. I make every starter on the team play one special team. I have done that since the Detroit Lions in 1974. That makes your starting offense and defense part of the special teams. It becomes a team concept. We do not have an indoor facility, but we have sleds.

One day a week, we make them pull 14 percent of their body weight on the sleds. If you get too much weight on the sled, they lose their running form. We have found that 14 percent is about the right ratio. I stood there two days ago and watched Matt, my third-stringer, pull that sled. I know who will not quit in a ball game, and I am sure his mother will cry again because this kid will help us.

One day a week, we do plyometrics for our third-string special-team members. One day a week, we do the stadium steps for the third-string special-teamers. At our stadium, you cannot see the top. If those special-teamers have to crawl on all fours to get to the top, they will do it. Those players will not let you down on the kickoff against your big rival. The fourth day, we do hurdle exercises to work the hip-flexor muscles. We work them four days a week.

We do those things because these players have to come to balance before contact. I did not say break down. We want full-speed contact, and it is no fair to dodge. They do not break down, but they come to balance. There is a thin line between those two items. The point is: they have to be killers and love contact.

Our team votes each year for the MVP on special teams. At Portland State, we have two fullbacks who could not play for you coaches in high school. I lied. They could play for a good high school football team. They battled it out for the MVP of our special teams. We have the best field-goal kicker in the history of the school. He did not get one vote. Our kickoff-return player was fourth in the nation and was voted the MVP in the Big Sky Conference on special teams. He did not get a vote.

Why did that happen? Special teams are about kicking someone's butt. It is not about running around and looking good. When we score a touchdown on special teams, we replay it three times to show the blocks, not the runner. That is the attitude of a special-team member. Our two fullbacks who cannot play dead battled it out for special-team player of the year. We gave each one of them one carry at the fullback position, and that was probably too many.

These players are not on scholarship, but they help you win. I have sat in 30 living rooms this year and guaranteed moms and dads that their sons were going to start in the opening game of the season against the Rose Bowl champions. At the time, I thought Oregon State was going to win the PAC-10 championship. We open up with them next year. The players on the kickoff or kickoff-return teams are the starters. Only in scrimmages do the offensive or defensive teams get to start.

In our weight room, we do not allow any harassment for not being strong. There is no crime for being weak. The crime is if that player does not try to improve. I got Matt Ford up to a 140-pound bench press, and he is winning game for us. A player in your school right now can help you. People ignore them and do not know they are on the team.

Look around on Monday, when you get back to school. You will find some player who has been there for every activity you have had in football. But he has never been in a game. I guarantee you if you get him on the sled, stadium steps, and plyometrics, he will help you.

If you are a 5.4 runner and do these three things, you will improve to 5.2. If you are 4.9, it will get you to 4.7. In the state of Texas, they still run Jerry Glanville's program and have been running it since 1970. This program gets players faster and makes them more powerful. Everybody on your team will get faster.

Do any of you know Bobby Dodd, or is everyone here too young to know him? When you win the coach of the year award, it is named for Bobby Dodd. I coached for Bobby Dodd before I went on to coach on my own. Bobby called me one day and told me I was the luckiest coach he had ever seen in football. He told me in the last three years, we won 17 games at Houston on the last drive of the game. I told him I loved him and he was a great coach, but I was not lucky. We were fast. There are no lucky plays for a short, fat, dumpy guy.

To play football, your players have to run. Get your players going, and get the attitude right. Those third-stringers know you care about them and recognize what they are doing. I promise you these are players who cannot play but overachieve every day. These players who play on your special teams have an assignment. The assignment for every player is to be very physical. We want them to come after the opponent and set the stage for the game. You cannot set the stage on offense or defense as quickly as you can in the kicking game. In the kicking game, you can set the stage about who you are and what you want to be. This is our identity, and it is very important to me.

I am going to start off with the kickoff team. I watch high school films every day. There is a kickoff return on every film. The reason for the returns is the coverage team is defending the entire field. The field is too wide to defend. When we cover a kickoff, we cover only from the goalpost to the boundary. The most important thing in that theory is to have a good kicker. To cover only half the field, the football must be placed from the numbers to the boundary. We want to pin the return team into the corner of the field and blow them up.

Coach the kicker to place the ball where you want it on the field. The approach run to the ball is six steps, not 10 yards. The only time we allow a kicker to take a 10-yard run to the ball is with the wind at his

back. With the wind at his back, we think we can kick the ball through the end zone. We only take a 10-step approach when we kick the ball down the middle. If they take the 10-step run-up, trying to kick the ball outside the numbers, they will kick it out-of-bounds more times than not. We do not kick the ball down the middle unless there is a penalty. If they move the ball up 15 yards, we will kick it down the middle.

I have coached for 42 years, and I have done this all my life. This coverage will work in high school, college, or pros. When we huddle before the kickoff, we call "corner left, wiggle right." Wiggle is an important term in the coverage scheme. As the coverage team comes down the field, all the players have to wiggle around the blocks to the same side. If one player wiggles around the block to the right and the next player goes around to the left, there is a big hole in the coverage. Wiggle means all the coverage team is avoiding blocks the same way. We practice that individually. The players use the same leg, rip arm, and dip as they come down the field.

When I first got into football, we had wedge busters. The rules do not let you bust the wedge any more. We have two players attacking the wedge. We call the technique "high yucca." Whichever player gets to the wedge first, goes up and over the wedge. That is an attitude for your coverage team. They go airborne into the wedge. We do it every time there is a wedge. Players who cannot play are taking two and three blockers out of the return scheme. Those players cannot play a lick. But, never tell the player that.

There are two things I am coaching these players who cannot play. "False praise cheapens plays." There is no false praise, but there is coaching and teaching. The only jobs I get are bad jobs; the colleges come to me. I do not go to them looking for that job. I have never had a good job in my life. Do not go looking for a good job. The good jobs are all taken. You have to get a bad job and change it. I told the president of the college, I will be the best teacher on campus. Coach means teacher.

If you coach with me, it will be different. If a player swears on the practice field, he is done for the day. I send them home. When I walked in to

Portland State, the hair on my arms stood up. Everything was M.F. If you swear on a practice field where Jerry Glanville coaches, you are done for the day. If you are an assistant coach and get after a player and curse him, you are fired. Our job is not browbeating, harassing, and cursing; it is teaching. You teach it and teach it and teach it some more. If you do that, it will change your entire team and how you coach your players.

Your players did not get false praise, but they did not get cursed either. When the player does a good job, you tell him. However, do not give him five "'atta boys" when he deserves one.

On kickoff-coverage team, we align five coverage defenders from the hash mark to the sideline of the side we intend to kick the ball (Diagram #1). We number the player on either side of the ball 1 through 5. We align both the #1 runners on either side of the same hash mark. They are our "high yucca" players. Whichever one of them gets to the wedge first gets airborne and goes over the top of the wedge. In Hawaii, they would show it on the JumboTron® about four times. The entire stadium would get excited and on their feet by the time the player got to the sideline.

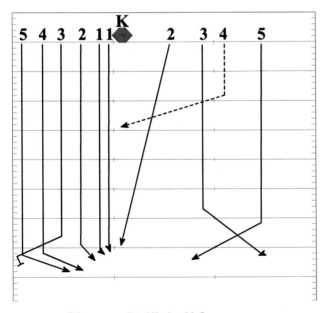

Diagram #1. Kickoff Coverage

The #3 defender on either side is the outside contain man. We designate the safety man. In the diagram, the safety is the wideside #4 defender. To confuse the return, we may use defenders running from one side of the coverage line and looping to the other side on their run up to the ball.

In 1970, we ran this coverage against the San Francisco 49ers. We call it the "West Coast twist," and it still works (Diagram #2). The #1 runners coming down the middle of the coverage twist their paths when they get 20 yards into their runs. We run an X-cross between the #4 and #5 runners on the outside. When you cover kickoffs, you cannot stay in lanes because the lanes are moving. You have to converge and kill people. On this coverage, we kick the ball down the middle. If we kick it down the middle, we have a penalty to move the ball up, or we have the wind at our backs.

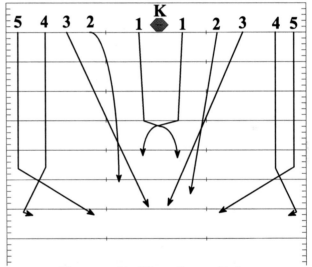

Diagram #2. West Coast Twist

If you want to be a better coach tomorrow, pay attention to these points about the kickoff return. This will win you one more game next season (Diagram #3). The number-one rule about the kickoff return has to do with playing on the road. When we play on the road, we will accept no penalties on the kickoff return. If you get a penalty on a kickoff return on the road, you get your butt kicked and lose the game. Every player on my team knows if it happens, I may go crazy. You cannot have a penalty on the road because if the offense cannot move the ball, they will give the ball up in a position where the opponent will score. We were fourth in the nation and led the league in kickoff returns.

We emphasize the double-team block between the outside blocker on the front line to the side of the return and the outside blocker at the 35-yard line. We double-team the best coverage player on the opponent's team. One player on the opponent's kickoff team makes 80 percent of the tackles. When that player plays us, he does not make tackles.

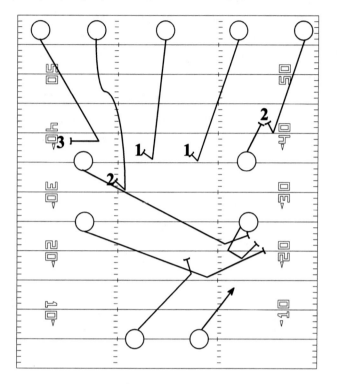

Diagram #3. Kickoff Return Side

The second thing that makes you successful on the kickoff return is to play the play longer than the opponent. The officials will be spotting the ball, and the offense will be coming on the field, and we are still double-teaming their stud out-of-bounds. Play the play longer, and you will be a good football team.

We have three players in our wedge. They have to sift the defenders and block the #3 coverage runner. They end up blocking two in most cases. We usually end up with a 2-on-1 block in the wedge.

On the kickoff, the return player who does not get the ball is extremely important. He enters the wedge area first. The rule for the non-ballcarrier is to block the defender that could tackle him. If the defender cannot tackle him, he does not block him. It is that simple. We watch for that in the team meeting and emphasize that point. We stand up in the chair and cheer when he does it right.

His second rule is never chase a missed block. If the off back misses his block, he cannot turn and chase him into the pile or the wedge. If he turns and chases, he makes it worse and ends up hitting the defender in the back. He needs to block someone else.

If the ball is kicked away from the callside, the return man takes it up that sideline. The three-man wedge tries to get to that side and help.

If a team kicks the ball down the middle of the field, we run a return with a cross blocks in the middle. I have run this return since I was at Western Kentucky. We cross block on the #1 runners coming down the middle. We use the guard positions on the front line to perform the cross block.

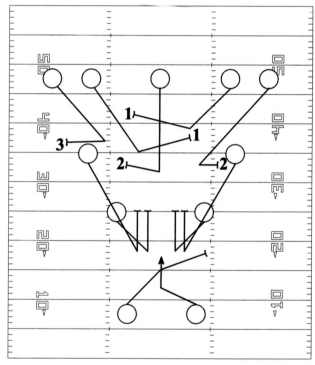

Diagram #4. Kickoff Cross Block

The next thing I want to talk about is extra-point and field-goal block. We hold every record with every team I coached in blocking points and field goals. The coaching staff from Bucknell University in Pennsylvania told me they showed all my field-goal blocks to their team. They said they had never seen anything like it. That was astounding to me.

The extra-point and field-goal block is the only play in my coaching career that I do not grade. If you ask any of my players about that situation, they will tell you it is between the player and God.

Montana in the Big Sky Conference is the team to beat. They have won the championship the last 10 years. They kick the crap out of everyone. We played them and were ahead by the score 9-5. They average 42 points a game. The only reason we could lose this game was because our goalie dies. They had a 14-play drive and scored and went ahead 11-9. They line up for the extra point. We blocked the point and ran it back for a two-point conversion.

The reason we blocked the point is inside the players. That effort is totally individual within the player. It defines who their parents were. It defines how the player grew up. Extra points are huge in a football game. There are more games lost by one point than won by 50. This type of effort is what the game of football is about and what is inside of you. If you want to go to a field-goal-block meeting, here is the New Testament.

When you talk about Solomon and the Proverbs, God told him he could have anything he wanted. He did not choose gold or silver; he chose wisdom. Proverbs is all about what is inside of men. They ask who you are and how important it is. People ask me how we practice this. It is not about schemes. We block kicks better than anyone in football.

This type of effort will win you games. We have won games we had no right to win. I will show you some of the things we do. When we come off the edge, the corner is the "skinner" (Diagram #5). The strong safety is the "jumper." The skinner dips his shoulder, stays on his feet, and comes around the horn of the wing man. The jumper comes between the end and wing player. He puts his hands on the backs of the tight end and the wingback. He jumps through the crease between the end and wing and pulls his legs through with his hands.

When we tell one of our secondary players they have to be in coverage, it kills them. They feel they have nothing to do with the play and want to rush the kick.

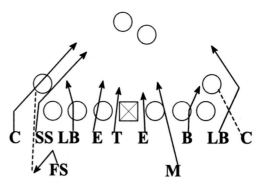

Diagram #5. X-Point Block Edge

On a field-goal block, if the ball crosses the line of scrimmage, get away from it. I have a young team. I have 46 freshmen, and 17 of them play. That is like having a carload of hemorrhoids. If we block an extra point, pick it up and try to score.

The next block is "4-on-2." We load the middle of the formation with two linemen on each guard (Diagram #6). They get shoulder-to-shoulder, look for penetration, and get the hands up. The get-off is the important thing in this block. It is nothing great as far as a scheme, but it is the effort that is the emphasis. I started doing this with the Detroit Lions, and I have done it ever since.

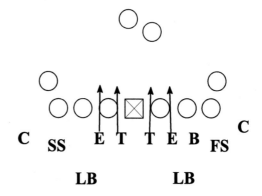

Diagram #6. Load Block

You cannot cover the punt if the punter cannot directional punt. You do that so one end has an outside release. The defense is taught not to let outside coverage people inside. We punt the ball to the outside. That means we have a free runner going to the ball (Diagram #7). When we punt the ball, we punt from a spread alignment with three big people as the personal protector for the punter. The middle man in the wall allows the ball to come through the wall and hinges back to fill the hole.

The punter reads the outside defender into the boundary side. If he does not come and peels back for a return, the punter can run the ball to that side. The punter has the right to run the football out of punt formation if he sees the contain player peel back to block.

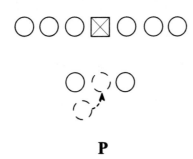

P

Diagram #7. Punt Formation

We do not allow anything but successful fakes, and we do not call any of them. This is a good rule to write down. Anything that you invent after midnight, throw it out. Do not put that in your offense. I invented the fake punt at about one o'clock in the morning. It was a stupid idea, but I thought you'd get a kick out of it. The snap goes to the middle man in the protection wall. He runs to the outside with an option to pitch the ball to the punter.

There are no punt returns in this lecture. Why would you let a punter feel good about one play? After the punt, we want punter to be glad he got the punt off. We come after every punt. We may never get close to blocking a punt, but we are coming. We played Green Bay in Atlanta. They had the game won, and all they had to do was get the punt off. They had punted the ball eight times already. This was their ninth punt. We did not block the punt; the punter dropped the ball. He dropped the ball because the pressure keeps coming on every punt.

We do have a punt return. The record holder in the NFL for punt returns for a year is Dick Jauron. He averaged 17 yards per punt return when I was with Detroit. He may be the only guy I can beat in a race. He went to the Pro Bowl when Mike Ditka was coaching the game. Mike called me and wanted to know who the player I sent to the game was. He told me he could not play. He led the entire league in the punt return, and we did not call one return the entire season. That was in 1974. We tried to block every punt. People did not cover the kicks; they protected the punter.

On special teams, find the player who sets the other team's tempo. You want to take their tempo away from them. Everyone said when we played defense, we got penalized a lot. Jerry Glanville's team on defense never got penalized on third down with two minutes to go. On first and second downs, we went after you. Never get penalized on the kickoff return when you are on the road. That backs you up and the crowd becomes a factor. You end up punting the ball from deep in your own end. That gives the offense the ball well inside your territory. The offense generally gets a score from that field position.

Thanks for having me. Win some games, and let me hear from you.

THE THREE- AND FIVE-STEP PASSING GAME CONCEPTS

East Carolina University

Thank you. It is good to be in Chicago this morning. Before the advent of the spread offense, you had to maintain a two-back offense and the power running game. You played with two tight ends, motioned a tight end, offset the fullback, or made some other adjustment to get into a power run game. You should not lose that, if that is the key to your success. I am going to talk about five quick-game passes. This will not replace your running game, but it can complement it.

I want to start with the way we number our patterns. When we name our routes, we use double digits. It is not so much how we call the play as it is what we do. We also name the patterns. We also hand signal. We have three different ways to call the plays. Our numbers in the passing game are designed to be used with the no-huddle offense. We do not go no-huddle all the time, but we have the capacity to do it.

People who call a play one thing in the huddle and something else at the line when they go to the no-huddle scheme baffle me. We use our no-huddle terminology and put it into the huddle. That keeps us from trying to teach two offensive terms for the same thing. Everything we do has a name and a number. If we call "Chicago 10," the protection is the name and the pattern the number.

When we call "rocket 10 (or 11)," rocket is a five-man protection with both backs in the pattern. The 10 tells us the one-back aligns to the right, and that is the strongside of the protection. The pattern is all hitches by the receivers, and the numbers 10 and 11 only give direction to the running back and the protection scheme.

If we call 10 or 11, the pattern is hitches for all receivers. We also hand signal because we run a zero personnel empty package. If we call 10, that designates hitch patterns for the three-receiver side. On the weakside, we have a hot call, which means the quarterback can hand signal whatever he wants to that side. We can call it simple and call "rocket 10," and everyone runs a hitch pattern. We can also call "rocket 10 hot." On that call, the three-receiver side runs hitch patterns and the single-receiver side runs what the quarterback hand signals.

If the quarterback comes to the line and reads press coverage across the board, he can change the call. If he wants a slant/flat to one side, he can hand signal that because he has called "hot." We get all hitches to one side and slant/flat to the other side. We can run the smash route to one side and the three-step to the other side. That way, we can run a two-man combination against zone and on the other side incorporate a three-step drop.

In our quick game, the steps in the patterns are numbered. The wide receivers start with their inside foot up and the outside foot back. The reason we do that is because of the quick and five-step passing game. The hitch is a five-step pattern. The slants are three-step patterns. The shave slant is a one-step pattern. The out is a four-step speed-out.

When we organize the patterns, we use single, outside, middle, and thirds to designate the receivers. This is how we label it in our playbook:

	S	O	M	3rd
10-11	H	H	H	H
12-13	R	R	F	SI
14-15	SI	SI	A	SI
16-17	SI	SI	S	B
18-19	F	F	O	O

On 10-11, everyone hitches, and we read the pattern from the inside out. If you play a team like Virginia Tech, who likes to stop the run, we cannot line up and run power at them all day. We get into zero personnel, spread the field, and run 10.

On 12-13, it is a read play. The outside receivers are the read patterns. In the chart, the single receiver and the outside are the read routes. If we are in a 2x2 set, the outside receivers run the read patterns. In a 3x1 set, the single receiver is the outside receiver.

The outside receiver explodes off the line of scrimmage. If the corner bails out, he runs a hitch route (Diagram #1). If the corner squats in his coverage, the receiver runs at the defender. He runs a replace mode route, coming back underneath the fade pattern going to the outside. It is a great red-zone package. The middle receiver runs a fade route. In a double-wide slot, the slot receivers both run fades. In the red zone, the slot receivers are running a fade route on a safety. In this area, we invert our receivers and put our best receivers in the slot. That gives them a chance to work a fade on a safety that does not usually play that route. We used to do this out of 21 personnel. We took the tight end, split him wide, and brought the Z-receiver into the slot.

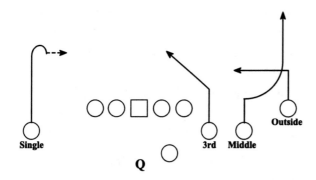

Diagram #1. 12-13

If the corner sinks on the outside pattern, the quarterback and read receiver look at the movement of the inside linebacker. If the corner sits on the outside pattern, the quarterback looks to throw the fade over the top to the inside receiver.

We do not throw many fades to the outside receivers. That is a difficult throw. We want to throw the fade to the inside receiver against a mismatch. If we are in a trips set, the third receiver to the trips side runs a slant. That gets him out of the way and draws some coverage.

The 14-15 pattern has a slant by the outside receivers and an angle by the inside receivers (Diagram #2). The angle route is a flat-type pattern. In a double slot, the outside receivers run slants to the inside, and the slots run an angle into the flat, or they can run a bubble route. We probably run more bubbles than angles. We have done both, but I think the angle clears patterns better.

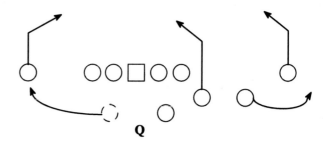

Diagram #2. 14-15

If you throw the bubble for width, that draws the safety and opens the windows for the slants. The third receiver on this pattern runs a slant pattern over the middle. We do not run a lot of this play. We use it as the backside patterns of the trips set bringing the back from the backfield to run the angle or flat route with the slant combination. We can run another combination to the field and the 14-15 into the boundary.

We decide pre-snap which side we want to work. Into the boundary, if the Will linebacker takes the back coming out of the backfield, we throw the slant behind him. To the field, if the flat defender goes with the bubble route, we throw the middle receiver on the slant. If the linebacker does not widen to the bubble, we throw the ball to the bubble in the flat.

The two-deep beaters are 16-17 (Diagram #3). On this pattern the outside receiver run a slant, the middle runs a slant, and the third receiver runs the bubble. Everyone runs a slant pattern except the third receiver. The inside receiver is running a slant, but we call it a "shave" route because of the way he runs the pattern. He runs one step downfield and slants through the inside shoulder of the inside defender. He takes one step to widen the inside window of the outside receiver. If they both go the same distance, the inside receiver covers up the outside receiver in the quarterback's vision.

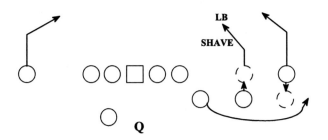

Diagram #3. 16-17

If the linebacker hangs on the inside receiver, the quarterback goes immediately to the outside receiver. There will be a huge window created. The wide receiver gets in the hole between the corner and linebacker and catches the ball. The reason this is a good play for us is we throw a lot of bubble screen and bubble patterns. The third receiver runs the bubble to that side.

The H-receiver in our offensive is our most athletic receiver. He is our tailback. He is 6'1", 205 pounds, and is lightning in a bottle. We try to get him the ball as much as we can. That is the position that Raghib "The Rocket" Ismail played when I was at Notre Dame. If you bubble the back and hit the seam to the outside receiver, there is no one left in the middle of the field. It becomes a foot race because the receiver is between the two safeties.

With no backs in the backfield and the 3x2 set, you can run the combination routes. To the three-man side, we run slant, shave, and bubble routes. To the two-receiver side, you run slant and angle. It is 16 to the three-receiver side and 15 to the two-receiver side. When you run this pattern, it is a better pattern if the outside receiver is off the line of scrimmage. The inside receiver has to be on the line. If you run it that way, it creates a natural seam between the two receivers.

In our normal set, the H-back is off the line of scrimmage, the Z-receiver is off, and the A-receiver is on the line of scrimmage. When we put the H-back to the X-receiver side, he is off the line of scrimmage, and the X-receiver is on the line of scrimmage.

On the 18-19, the outside receivers run fade routes (Diagram #4). If we have a big, tall receiver, we may go to this pattern. We get into a 12-personnel grouping with two tight ends and one back with two wide receivers. That encourages the defense to load the box. That is probably the only way we throw the fade routes. The middle and third routes are the patterns we look for on this pattern. They are running out routes. When I show you these patterns, I am showing you them out of the empty set. That lets you see the three-receiver side and the two-receiver side.

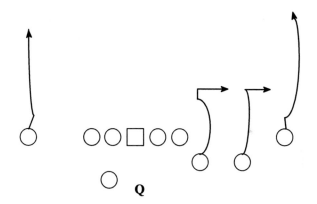

Diagram #4. 18-19

The out is a four-step speed-out. On his fourth step, the receiver rips the right shoulder around to open his hips to the quarterback. The inside receivers run the double outs, and the outside receivers run the fade route. If we run the pattern from a trips formation, the middle and third receivers run the out cuts. We work the out cuts off the flat defender. The quarterback reads from the outside to the inside. We run both patterns away from the inside defenders. If the corner sets on the middle pattern, we throw the third receiver out. The third receiver cannot get in a hurry to run out. It is almost like a turnout pattern. He wants to get in the seam between the linebacker and corner on a cover-2 look.

We like to run this pattern from the empty set and look at the two-man side. The Will linebacker to that side does not like to vacate the box and sets up an easy throw to the inside receiver running the out cut. The pre-snap read tells the quarterback which side to work. If the Will is inside, we work the two-man side. If he walks out on the slot receiver to that side, we work the fieldside. If it is man coverage, we run the speed-outs away from defenders. If it is zone coverage, we look for windows between the defenders. The middle receiver against a press or bail technique runs the pattern to the boundary.

You can run a five-man protection and have five receivers in the pattern, or you can include the back in the protection scheme and get into a six-man protection (Diagram #5). When we use the back, we can use turnback protection by the line. The five-man protection is man protection. We use this with the quick game and cut at the line of scrimmage many times. In the turnback or slide protection, we do not cut as much.

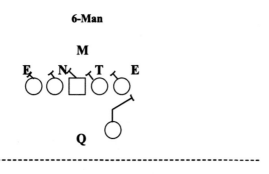

6-Man

5-Man

Diagram #5. Protection Scheme

The one thing you have to be careful of in the slide protection is not to overslide the gap. The blocker wants to jump over into another gap because there is no one in his immediate gap. If he has someone on his inside gap and no one outside, he has to step with his inside foot and bang the defender in that gap with his eyes on his outside

gap. We want to keep the protection scheme tight and understand the weakness of the protection. The thing that can hurt this protection is a defender running the hump to the outside. However, it is a three-step pass and should be gone by the time the defender gets to his rush.

This type of offense does not require tremendous speed or rocket-armed quarterbacks. We have to read and understand coverage and be good route runners. It does not take phenomenal players. It takes disciplined players that can work within the system. We can also run the speed and zone option from these sets. The entire object of the quick game is to make the linebacker get out of the box. If they stay in the box, we throw the quick game all day. The only way to stop the quick game is to play a three-down front. I do not think you can close the windows in a four-down front.

To get our automatic calls into the offense, we double call in the huddle. The huddle call is "14 hot." That means we will run 14 to the right and to the left we will hand signal whatever pattern we want. The left side goes to the line of scrimmage but do not know the route. The quarterback goes to the line of scrimmage and reads a three-deep shell. That fits the 14 called to the right. He signals a route to the topside and throws the 14 to the field. If he reads two-deep coverage, he signals a 16 route into the boundary and throws that side.

The quarterback uses hand signals for each combination we have. He pats his helmet, touches his cheek, or uses any kind of signal we have designated. The receiver gives a return signal so the quarterback knows the receiver is on the same page.

We throw a lot of quick-game patterns in our offense. It is a high-percentage throw and puts the ball in your better player's hands. It has given us an opportunity to line up and compete with many teams who have more talent than we do. I am a huge believer in the quick game. It can be applied to any offensive scheme. It does not matter whether you are an option team, zone power team, or a two-back team with two wide receivers. I believe it is a great equalizer. If you can line up and run power football at someone, run it.

I can rant and rave about the quick game, but if you can run it, that is what you want to do. Last year, at the end of the season we played UTEP. We scored 57 points. We lined up in the two-back set and ran isolation, power, toss sweep, and play-action pass. When you have to play Virginia Tech, N.C. State, and West Virginia, you may not have the same talent level as those teams. If you are not as big and physical as they are, this gives you a chance. It becomes a great equalizer. You can utilize the offense from a two-back alignment.

The next part of the scheme is our five-step game. It ties into what we do because it is our timing game. It involves many horizontal stretches on the defense. We also do many vertical stretch things in our passing game. We do them out of our play-action game. I do not believe in the seven-step drop. That requires you to hold the ball too long and leads to sacks and backward movement. In the three-step and the five-step drops, the quarterback hits his last step, hitches his feet, and the ball has to come out. This part of the game is like the quick game only deeper. I will give you five of the passes we run. We run 20-21, 22-23, 24-25, 26-27, and 28-29.

The 20 route is a six-yard hook over the ball by the tight end (Diagram #6). The outside patterns to each side are curl/swing combinations. On the pattern, the tight end runs to a spot six yards over the ball and hooks up. He bangs into the linebackers and works his pattern off of them. It does not matter what type of set you run. The outside receivers run the curl routes, and the inside receivers run the swing routes to the outside.

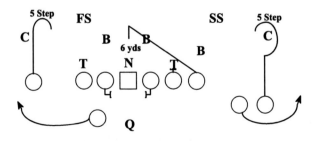

Diagram #6. 20-21

We read the pattern from the inside to the outside. The first thing the quarterback sees is the inside linebacker. The tight end bangs off the linebackers and sits down over the ball. This is a good second-and-long call when you are trying to get some lost yardage back. If a team is playing a two-linebacker set, this play is great against that. Against a three-linebacker set, it gets gray because the tight end has to bang off the Mike linebacker all the time. The tight end is looking for a hole six yards over the ball. The quarterback takes his drop and gets the ball to him. It is good in short-yardage and ball-control situations.

If you cannot get the tight end, we turn and read the play to the outside. Against a Tampa-2 defense, when the Mike linebacker runs to the middle, the tight end replaces his position, and you get quick yards.

If the quarterback does not feel he has the curl pattern, he can still throw to the back on the swing pattern. There are three options for the quarterback. The 22, 24, and 26 routes are complementary routes. The 22 route is the speed-out cut, the 24 pattern is the arrow route, and the 26 is the corner route. The outside receivers run these patterns. On a 22, the outside receivers run a speed-out cut. The 26 route is an arrow route for the outside receivers. It is my favorite route and almost impossible to stop. On the 26 pattern, the outside receivers run the corner route. There are complementary patterns that go with these routes.

When we run a 2x2 set, the complementary routes are a shallow package by the inside receivers (Diagram #7). On 22, 24, and 26, we run the H-back in the slot on the shallow cross. The A-back in the backfield runs what we call a "hot climb." He tries to get over the top of the linebacker, looking for the ball. If the linebacker jumps the shallow route of the slotback, the ball goes right behind his ear to the back running into that window going vertical.

If we get into a 3x1 set, the third receiver runs the hot climb and the middle slot receiver runs the shallow cross. That is the same two receivers that ran the pattern from the 2x2 set and the same read for the quarterback. The first thing we look for are the outside patterns by the wide receivers. From there, he goes to the shallow cross and then the checkdown on the hot-climb pattern.

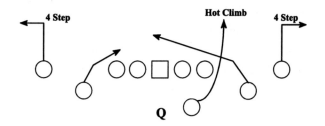

Diagram #7. 22-23

We decide the pattern to run on the outside by the alignment of the defensive back. If the leverage of the defensive back is to the inside, we run 22, which is a speed-out. If the defensive back plays the receiver in a head-up position, we run 24 or the arrow route. The patterns are predicated on the leverage of the defensive backs.

We have tags with the routes. We can tag the route with the term "China." If we call "24 China," the outside receivers run their arrow routes (Diagram #8). The arrow route is a slant route run at four steps. The middle pattern is a shallow cross, the H-back runs an "in" pattern up the field, and the A-back runs a redirect pattern behind the shallow cross. The redirect starts out as a flat pattern, which comes back to the inside into the linebacker area. China becomes the three-man game that overrules the high-low patterns the receivers typically run.

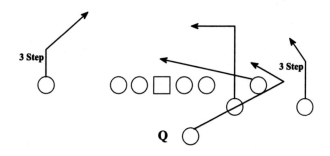

Diagram #8. 24-25 China

The outside receiver runs the arrow route on the fourth step. The wide receiver aligns with his outside foot back. He takes four steps off the ball. On the fourth step, he plants and runs the slant pattern to the inside. The timing works out perfectly with the break on the fourth step. The 20 series is the same as the quick game except it is thrown farther down the field. The quarterback

takes three steps hitches up, and gets rid of the ball.

The 26 pattern can be run with a tag also (Diagram #9). If we want to use the China package with the 26, we run the pattern the same way. The only basic difference is the outside receivers run a corner route instead of the arrow. The shallow package comes off, and we replace it with the China package.

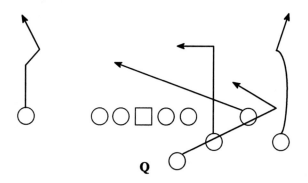

Diagram #9. 26-27 China

The short shots into the flat area are good patterns to throw. It is a simple pattern; however, we generally throw the ball to one of the best athletes we have. If we get the H-back on the swing or bubble, he becomes a load for the defense. If we get him the ball with his shoulders turned downfield, he is difficult to tackle. Those patterns are thrown at 10 yards but net many more yards.

The 28 pattern is our four-vertical game. We run four-verticals a number of different ways. We can send the outside receiver down the sidelines and the slot receivers down the seams. We can tag the vertical routes and run two-man games within the pattern. We run 28 stop. Everyone takes off on the four-vertical routes. We tag the pattern so one or two of the receivers stop their patterns down the field and come back to the quarterback.

We can run two-man games with two receivers crossing their patterns. The outside receiver will run a post to the inside, and the inside receiver will run a corner going into the outside. With a tight end in the game, we can run the 28 pattern with the tight end running a deep cross to one side.

When we run the four-verticals, the quarterback is reading for the outside receivers, and if they come open, he can throw the ball in that area. However, he wants to throw the ball to the inside receivers. We want to bring the running back down the middle into the short zone. If the Mike linebacker runs out to the deep hole in the middle of the field, the running back sits in the void area.

We try to bring one of the wide receivers across the face of the two-deep safety to try to bring him to the inside so we can throw the ball on the boundary. All those adjustments are tag patterns. If we get into a 3x1 formation, the inside receiver to the formation side has to get across the field to the opposite hash mark when we run the 28 route.

We run this 28 play more than any other four-vertical pattern. We call 28 bench (Diagram #10). This play is a deeper version of the 18 pattern. The outside receivers are clearing the coverage, and the inside receivers run 22-yard speed-outs.

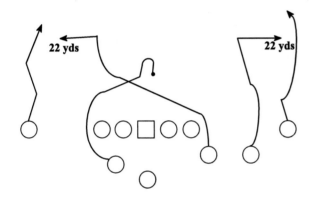

Diagram #10. 28-29 Bench

Even though I talk about the passing game today, I still believe you have to run the ball to win. That is where it all starts. However, what I talked about today are tried-and-true patterns that will benefit any running game. I was fortunate because I worked at Florida State, where I learned a lot of this game. I took this package to Notre Dame, when I was the coordinator there. I took it to Connecticut and used it at South Carolina when I was there. I am now at East Carolina, and it is a big part of our passing game.

It works and is simple. It is easy for a quarterback to read. It is a high completion passing game with a low sack ratio. That is what you are looking for in the passing game. I am not a big supporter of routes that run receivers all over the place. I want to get the ball out of the quarterback's hand and into the athlete's hands. The routes that take a long time to throw fit into our play-action scheme. They do not fit into our dropback game.

You may not think you have a dropback quarterback, but most quarterbacks who can throw the ball can throw these passes.

I appreciate your time. If you have any questions, I will be happy to answer them. I appreciate the Nike Coach of the Year Clinic having me here in Chicago. Thank you.

COACHING QUARTERBACKS IN THE QUICK PASSING GAME

Princeton University

Thank you for having me speak at this clinic. It is fun to start talking football again. It is interesting when you become a head coach. All the things you did to become a head coach, you do not get to do after you become a head coach. Recruiting in our league is unique because we recruit nationwide. I think there are 30 states represented on our team.

What I have tried to do is put together a passing clinic for a high school or small college program in getting your quarterback ready to play. Like in your situation, we do not always get to recruit the player who has all the talent.

What we have to do is turn quarterbacks who are athletic with average arms into players who can perform at our level. We have to coach the players we have. What I have tried to do is put together some things that work well at our level and can work for you at your level. I am going to talk about the three-step passing game. I will also talk about something to make your quarterback with an average arm throw with more velocity.

What we try to do at Princeton is get the quarterback to use the torque in his hips. It is like how karate teaches their students to use their hips when they punch or throw kicks. We try to do the same thing in the throwing motion of the quarterback. The first thing I will show you is the passing concept I am trying to teach. After that, I will go back and break the concept down individually with the drills we use to teach the skills.

The first thing I want to do is talk about the quarterback's stance under the center. We are primarily a shotgun team. Two years ago, we were under the center quite a bit. I will include some of that because I do not know which type of stance you are interested in.

If we are under the center, I want the quarterback's feet a little inside the shoulders. We are a zone team, and I do not want the center to zone step and step on the quarterback's foot. When I talk about the quarterback, I want to talk about the dominant and non-dominant hand. In my career, I have had many left-handed quarterbacks. That is how I eliminate the terms right-handed and left-handed in referring to the quarterback.

With the quarterback under center, the non-dominant foot is slightly back in the stance, but we do not overcoach that point. I do not believe the quarterback can get as much depth from the line of scrimmage on his first step if he has too much stagger in his non-dominant foot. We try to gain our depth with an explosion step off the non-dominant foot. In our three-step drop, all the distance from the line of scrimmage comes from the first step. The second and third steps get the quarterback into the correct throwing position.

We want to stand tall behind the center and not crouch. That allows the quarterback to see everything. The quarterback has to understand the center's problems. He has to ride the center in the direction he has to go. He has to stand tall, but at the same time he must bend his knees so it allows his hands to go forward with the center. Every drop we do and every footwork movement we take is to get us into the correct throwing position.

BASIC FUNDAMENTALS: CORRECT THROWING POSITION

- Non-dominant foot is slightly ahead of the dominant foot (toe to instep).
- Front shoulder is down.

- Shoulders are turned slightly away from the target (slight tension in neck).
- Ball is carried at shoulder level.
- Dominant foot is aligned directly below dominant shoulders.
- Dominant foot is perpendicular to target.

In the correct throwing position, we want the non-dominant foot slightly ahead of the dominant foot in a toe-to-instep relationship. The non-dominant foot is on the midline, and the dominant foot is slightly behind it.

If you keep the front shoulder down, it keeps the ball from sailing. Carrying the ball at shoulder level allows us to be more athletic. We talk about getting the ball over the dominant armpit. An important point to emphasize is to have the dominant foot directly below the dominant shoulder. We want the dominant foot perpendicular to the target when the quarterback throws the ball. We want the quarterback to show a bit of his back jersey number to the target.

That is the correct throwing position. If you are going to use your hips and legs to deliver velocity to the ball, the foot and ball have to be in those positions. If the dominant foot is behind the shoulder, you will lose velocity.

Playing quarterback is not dropping back and delivering the ball without any pressure. That is not reality. Quarterbacks are always getting hit in the pocket. If you watch NFL quarterbacks in the pocket, they want to keep their feet alive as they wait for the receiver to get open. But as they keep their feet alive, the dominant foot gets behind the shoulder. If you watch the ball being thrown, it has to be repositioned. If the dominant foot stays under the shoulder, the ball stays high and the release is better. Everything we do is trying to get the ball out more quickly with more velocity.

THROWING MOTION

- Hand should be slightly above the helmet with the upper arm no less than parallel to ground.
- Dominant foot is slightly left of the target.

- Do not overstride: non-dominant foot should be six to eight inches in front of the original alignment.

We talk about but do not overcoach the position of the ball. We want the ball above the ear hole of the helmet with the upper arm no less than parallel to the ground. When the ball is delivered, it is imperative that the quarterback not over stride with his non-dominant foot (Diagram #1). When quarterbacks have to throw the ball deep, they have a tendency to over stride. There are two things that happen in that case. The front shoulder comes up and the ball sails.

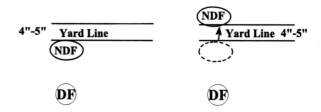

Diagram #1. Stride Length

We want a short, six- to eight-inch stride with the non-dominant foot. The dominant foot is slightly left of the target. That opens up the hips like karate teaches so the quarterback can use the torque in his hips and legs to increase the velocity of the football.

Quarterbacks can practice this in at home. The yard line on a football field is roughly four to five inches in width. You can use a visual example for the quarterback. If the quarterback puts the front side of his non-dominant foot on the back edge of the yard line, after he takes his stride, his heel should contact the front edge of the yard line. That translates into a six- to eight-inch step. The key is to make the quarterback use the same step regardless of the distance he throws the ball. The torque and velocity is the same, and he does not need to overstride to get the ball the distance he wants.

THROWING MOTION (CONTINUED)

- Front arm should be bent and pull down and across the body.
- Should be able to see the cleats of the dominant foot after the throw.

- Flick mud off the finger as you release the ball.
- Eyes should remain on the target, not follow the ball.

The front arm in the throwing motion should be bent. If you use physics, a longer lever takes longer and a shorter lever moves more quickly. Everything the quarterback does is geared to getting the ball out fast to help the offensive linemen. By ripping the front arm down and across the body, it keeps the front shoulder down. That keeps the ball from sailing.

Some of our players have trouble understanding the transfer of the weight. That is getting the weight of the body from one foot to the other. When the quarterback releases the ball, the coach should see the cleats on the dominant foot. That means he has released the weight to the non-dominant foot.

In the chart, I use the term flicking mud off the finger. As the quarterback releases the ball he should flick his index finger as if he were flipping mud off that finger. Another thought would be flipping a booger off your finger. I am sure most of us have done that. However, that is the motion you want to perform.

If the quarterback is throwing the ball behind the receivers on crossing or slant routes, he is following the flight of the ball with his eyes. He has to keep his eyes on the target as the throws the ball and continue to watch the target and not the flight of the ball. It is like shooting the basketball. Good shooters keep their eyes on the rim and not the flight of the ball. The eye is an unbelievable machine and will make the ball go where you are looking.

The best book I have ever seen on mechanics of throwing the football is called It's a Matter of Style by Joe Namath. It is no longer in print. When I was coaching in New Hampshire, I researched the book and found it in a backwoods library in Montpelier, Vermont. It has illustrations and pictures of everything he does. It is by far the best I have ever seen in print.

I want to show you the three-step passing concept we use. I will talk about how we teach the route, and break it down individually the way we teach the quarterback. We call the first route "spacing." Every one of our passing concepts has two components to them. We have an "individual" side, which we call Indy, and a "concept" side in the route. We put our best receiver to the individual side and tell the quarterback that is his "zero read." It is not his first read; it is what he sees in a pre-snap read.

If he throws the ball to the individual side, he makes that decision with a pre-snap read. Generally, defenses try to hide the weakest defensive back as the boundary corner. Many times, defenses—particularly in the two-minute offense—forget to cover or give up the weakside flat. I coach the quarterback to be aware of that weakness or scheme of the defense.

In the route, the individual pattern is a five-yard slant (Diagram #2). However, the quarterback can change the pattern, using hand signals to a quick out, hitch, flat, or slant. If we know we are getting a three-deep scheme into the boundary, we run the hitch. We use a full turnback slide protection and cut off the edge with the remaining back. We have to ability to slide the protection the other way if we see blitz coming.

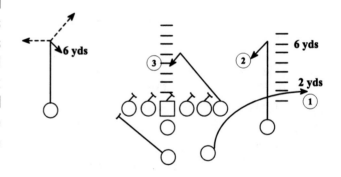

Diagram #2. Spacing Pro Set

The outside receiver to the concept side runs a six-yard hook pattern on or near the hash mark. When he catches the ball, we want him to be one yard inside the hash mark at six yards deep. That puts maximum pressure on the flat defender. By going to six yards, the safety cannot react in time to come down to pick up the receiver. The reason we call the pattern spacing is the spacing of the receivers is absolutely crucial. The tight end takes an inside release and runs a three- to five-yard hook over the ball. The fullback comes out of the backfield and runs the flat pattern. The flat pattern is run at two yards down the field.

This is a 3x1 concept in our three-step game. You will see a number of different formations doing the same thing. In the diagram, we are aligned in a tight-end set with the fullback in an offset I formation in the backfield. The flanker, tight end, and fullback are the three receiver running patterns on the concept side. The split end is the individual receiver into the boundary. The quarterback reads the concept side from the outside. The fullback is the first read, the flanker the second read, and the tight end is the third read.

We can use different formations and use the same concept. If we get into a 2x2 set, we motion into a 3x1 set (Diagram #3). The concept is the same.

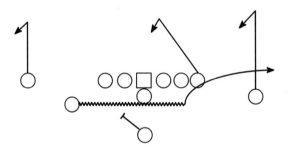

Diagram #3. Spacing Twin Set/Motion

The next set is a 3x1 set with a double flanker (Diagram #4). We motion the outside flanker inside and run him back outside for the flat pattern. Everyone else runs his concept pattern.

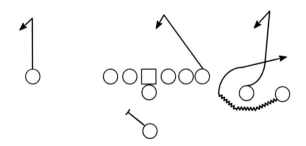

Diagram #4. Spacing Trips Set

The next set is a double slot set (Diagram #5). We use motion to get to the 3x1 set and run the pattern like Diagram #3.

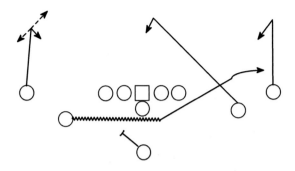

Diagram #5. Spacing Double-Slot

The footwork for the quarterback is slightly different as he throws to the individual side than the concept side. I got this concept from the Green Bay Packers. We can throw the Indy side against press coverage.

We have two different types of drops in the three-step passing game. If we throw a hitch or quick out, we use three quick steps.

STEP 1

- Get as much depth as you can. All distance is gained on this step.
- Explode off of the non-dominant foot. Dominant foot is on the midline, and the front shoulder is down (Diagram #6).

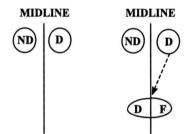

Diagram #6. Foot Position

When we practice this drop, we practice with a yard line running through the crotch of the quarterback. When he explodes back with his first step, his dominant foot should hit right on that yard line. The hard part is keeping the front shoulder down and he steps back. He has to explode and get beyond where he would normally get taking one step. That requires him to drag the non-dominant foot back as he goes. The non-dominant foot will end up on the midline, also.

If the quarterback keeps the front shoulder down, his center of gravity is in the center of his body. We have to change all the momentum going back to a force coming toward the target. The footwork has to stop the force from going back and change it to going forward. With the front shoulder down, the weight of the body is centered and not going back with the dominant foot under the dominant shoulder.

When we talk about three quick steps, you have to consider whether you are throwing to the dominant or the non-dominant side. I will talk about the dominant side first.

STEP 2

- Should be off the midline, toward the target
- Center of gravity is between the feet (Diagram #7).

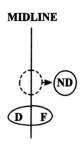

Diagram #7. Foot Position

If he keeps his front shoulder down, as the quarterback steps toward the target, his center of gravity is in the center of his body. The example to explain this movement is a base runner sliding into second base. If he slides into second, as he hits the bag, he pops up to his feet.

STEP 3

- Back foot comes down under the dominant shoulder with the foot perpendicular to the target (pitcher's rubber).
- Come up throwing (Diagram #8).

The third step turns perpendicular to the target. It is like a pitcher throwing the ball from a pitching rubber. In his windup, the pitcher turns his dominant

foot to a perpendicular position so he can push off the rubber as he delivers the ball to home plate. The third step is never behind the second step; it is toward the throw. We want nothing left behind the throw. We want all the velocity going toward the throw.

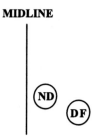

Diagram #8. Foot Position

This is a hard throw. He has to turn his hips and show a little bit of his back jersey number. That is hard for the quarterback to do. This is a very horizontal throw because it is only six yards off the line of scrimmage. When he hits the third step, he comes up throwing. He throws to the receiver or over the head. He is not reading on this throw. He is getting the ball out fast with a lot of velocity.

The next set is throwing to the non-dominant side. The first step to the non-dominant side is the same as throwing the other way. You want to get as much distance as you can from the line of scrimmage.

THREE QUICK STEPS (NON-DOMINANT)

- Step 1: Same first step as to the dominant side.
- Step 2: Throwing to non-dominant side, second step crosses over.
- Step 3: Back foot comes down under the dominant shoulder with foot perpendicular to the target (pitcher rubber).
- Come up throwing (Diagram #9).

The second step to the non-dominant side comes from Bill Walsh. The first step is with the dominant foot, but the second step crosses over the first step. To get into the third step, you have to do what I call a dance step. The second step crosses over the first step to a plant point. The second step hits on the midline. On the third step,

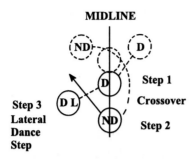

MIDLINE

**Diagram #9. Three Quick Steps
(Non-Dominant Side)**

the dominant foot steps laterally off the midline to the non-dominant side. It is called the dance step because it is almost a backward step made laterally with the dominant foot. That allows the non-dominant foot to move to that side. With the shoulders perpendicular to the line of scrimmage, the quarterback steps laterally right or left with his dominant foot to the non-dominant side.

It keeps the center of gravity in the center of the body. When the center of gravity is in the center of the body, the quarterback can plant again and get rid of the ball. As he replants his foot, it should be a lateral move and not behind the second step. If you put the foot behind the second step, you have the dominant hand behind the shoulder.

I use drills to teach these mechanics. The first on is the one-step drill (Diagram #10). The worst thing a quarterback can do is have a false step. Some coaches teach a punch step, but I do not. In this drill, we align the quarterback with a line running through his crotch. We have contests to see who can get the most depth with one step. When we do this drill, we emphasize getting out fast and getting as much depth as possible.

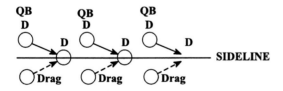

Diagram #10. One-Step Drill

The one point we coach is not stepping in the bucket. That means letting the first step go beyond

the midline. If he does that, he loses depth and tilts his face away from the side, and it is hard to get back without losing your balance. He has to be in balance to get the ball out quickly.

The next progression in drilling the quarterback is to add the second step. He starts off with the drop-step and takes the second step. From there, we add the third step and throw the ball.

I want to cover what we do on the concept side of the pattern (Diagram #11). The first receiver runs a hook route one yard inside the hash mark. The second receiver runs a flat route, aiming for two yards on the sideline. We do that for two reasons. We feel that puts maximum pressure on the flat defender. We feel the read happens faster for the quarterback with the two-yard flat.

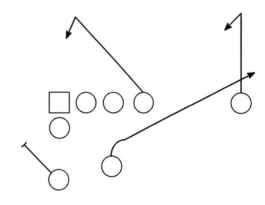

Diagram #11. Concept Routes

We tell the flat receiver, if the ball comes to him, he runs outside the numbers before he attempts to turn up. If the ball is poorly thrown and he cannot catch it in stride, he turns north and south immediately. However, we want him outside the number because we feel there are more missed tackles out there. The tight end uses an inside release and hooks over the ball at three yards. The quarterback reads flat, hash-hook, and ball-hook, in that order.

If the quarterback has to read this pattern, he cannot use quick steps. That requires us to teach the steps to the concept side slightly differently. If you are running this scheme from a shotgun set, a three-step drop becomes one step, and a five-step drop becomes three steps. The receivers do nothing different from the shotgun or the quarterback under the center. The quarterback adjusts the timing with what we call a hop. We feel the flat runner has to run his pattern from inside the outside hook. It is an easier read for the quarterback and maximizes the pressure on the flat defender.

When we throw to the concept side, we use "three long steps." Any time you have to read a flat defender, it takes longer. The footwork of the quarterback has to match the timing of the route. When a quarterback has to sit in the pocket and wait, bad things start to happen. When they have to wait, they start to think too much.

THREE LONG STEPS

- The first step is the same.
- Second step is on the midline gaining distance from the line of scrimmage.
- Third step stops the momentum.
- "Hop" step brings the back foot back under the dominant shoulder and lowers the front shoulder. The hop should not get closer to the line of scrimmage (Diagram #12).

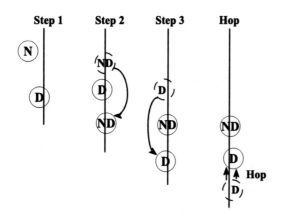

Diagram #12. Three Long Steps

The quarterback on the second step, instead of getting closer to the throw, stays on the midline and gains depth. He uses a crossover step in his second step and continues back on the midline on his third step. The momentum is stopped on the third step, and the hop gets the foot under the shoulder. In the diagram, the first, second, and third steps are on the midline. The hop brings the back foot up under the shoulder of the dominant hand. Notice, however, that the front foot does not move closer to the line of scrimmage.

In our vocabulary, when we say "quick," the ball comes out on the third step. When we say "long," we have an extra hitch in the delivery of the ball. On long drops, the front shoulder can be high on the first step. Because the route takes longer, the quarterback can get deeper. That helps your linemen. The hop step means do not get closer to the line of scrimmage. A hitch step in the quarterback's delivery takes him closer to the line of scrimmage.

We have a 2x2 concept that we call "three-step arrow" (Diagram #13). It has the same principles as the 3x1 scheme. In this case, we divide the field in half. The quarterback reads the number of safeties in the middle of the field. If there are two safeties in the middle, he works one side of the formation. If there is one safety in the middle, he works the other side. If they are a man-free scheme, with one safety in the middle, he works the same side as the two-deep safeties.

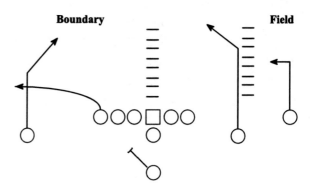

Diagram #13. Three-Step Arrow

In the diagram, we have the tight end and flanker into the boundary side of the field. The split end and slotback are to the wideside of the field. To the boundary side, we run a two-yard flat route by the tight end. The flanker runs a five-yard slant behind that pattern. We usually read this side with a single safety in the middle of the field.

To the wideside of the field, the slot receiver runs a six-yard controlled slant at the inside shoulder of the second-level defender, whoever he is. If the flat defender is to his inside, he has to get inside of him. The outside receiver runs a six-yard hitch and works inside. By the slot receiver attacking the inside shoulder of the flat defender, it widens the throwing lane to the outside receiver. This is a great man-to-man route.

THREE-STEP ARROW

- Use controlled slant to strongside (versus two-deep).
- Use flat slant to weakside (versus three-deep).
- Use three-quick drop to controlled slant, and three-long drop to flat slant.

That sounds like a lot of thinking; however, the footwork will come naturally with the timing of the throws. We teach the fieldside and boundary side concept. The fieldside route is the controlled slant-hitch. The boundary side is the flat-slant route. If we are in the middle of the field, the quarterback decides which side he wants to throw. He signals the receiver so they know which side is the hot side.

Sometimes it is better to throw the controlled slant if you are slightly off the hash into the boundary. The quarterback can also signal the receivers to let them know he is inverting the sides in the concept. In other words, the receivers who normally run the field patterns into the field will now run the patterns into the boundary. Against man-to-man, I want the ball working into the controlled slant-hitch patterns.

It is important for the quarterback to know what coverage he thinks he sees. If he comes to the sideline and I ask him what he saw, he should have an answer because he read the coverage. It may not be right, but he knows what he thought he saw. I can fix or interpret the issue and get him back on track. If he comes off and does not know what he saw, I go bananas. You have to be consistent with your decision-making. You cannot change your

decision on every scenario because you cannot practice them all.

If we get into a two-minute offense and have third down with six to eight yards to go for the first down, we always look at the boundary side flat. All you need is to pick up half of the yardage because you will go for it on fourth down. Defenses forget that area all the time, and it gives you a bailout in that situation. It is uncanny in a two-minute situation the way the boundary flat is open.

I want to leave the three-step concepts and go to the five-step concept. That is the old "West Coast" offense, whatever that term means. It is like the three-step drop because it has two components to the pattern. We have Indy and concept sides (Diagram #14). The individual side is a speed cut out at 12 yards. The wide receiver aligns with his inside foot on the line of scrimmage. He takes three inside steps and makes his break. He breaks off the inside foot at 10 yards and carries it to 12 yards.

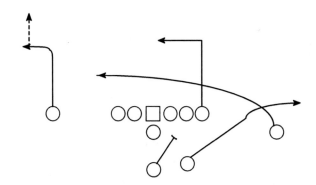

Diagram #14. Five-Step Routes (Trojan)

We can also build in a double move to the individual route, which puts him in an out-and-up route.

FIVE QUICK STEPS

- Same as three quick steps except you add two steps.
- The top three steps of the drop look just like three quick steps.
- Used to throw speed cut outs.

The footwork for the quarterback is the same for the three-step drop. If he is under center the last three steps in the five-step drop is what he has been practicing for the three-step drop. If he is in the shotgun, it is the three-step drop. He has already practiced the mechanics of the five-step drop while doing the three-step.

If the quarterback has decided to throw to the Indy side, we always have a shallow cross pattern coming across the field. If a defender gets under the speed-out, we have the shallow cross coming across into that area. That gives the quarterback a bailout. That is the difference between the three-step and the five-step scheme. In the three-step scheme, he has to throw the ball out-of-bounds if the defense covers the pattern. In the five-step game, he has a bailout.

The concept side of the pattern is a two-yard flat by the inside receiver. The outside receiver runs the shallow cross, and the tight end runs a 10-yard dig route.

I want to talk about some quarterback drills we do. The first is a "carry-and-reach drill." The quarterback aligns on the sideline. He puts the ball in the proper carriage position and retreats, using his crossover drop-steps. He reaches back with his steps, staying on a straight line. This makes them use their arms and not just their legs to get out from under the center.

We use a "parallel stance throw." This is a basic warm-up drill. They stand on a line and secure the ball in both hands. Their stance is a parallel stance with their feet. They keep the feet anchored on the line and rotate the torso of the body back and forth and deliver the ball.

The next drill is an "agility reaction drill" (Diagram #15). It teaches them to keep their feet alive and stay in the correct throwing position. We want them to think to move the back foot first. In this drill, the quarterback drops back. The coach stands in front of him and gives him a movement direction. We want subtle movements with the feet. When he has gone through three to four direction changes, the coach claps his hands. On the handclap, the quarterback gets rid of the ball to a checkdown receiver.

This is probably clinic talk, but we talk about moving the back foot first. However, you cannot throw the ball hard with the dominant foot in the air. If you get your back foot in the ground, you can get something on the throw regardless of what the body position is. If you want to put a bootleg on the end of the drill, you can. That lets you practice throwing on the run. It gives you two skills in one drill.

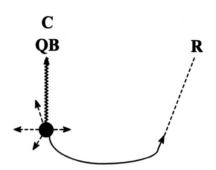

Diagram #15. Agility Reaction Drill

I use dummies to increase the agility of our quarterbacks (Diagram #16). There are a number of things you can do with dummies. The first thing I use is a shuffle through the dummies. I want them to lead with their back foot. They must stay in the correct throwing position at all times. When I clap my hands, they must throw the football to the receivers. The receivers are 8 to 10 yards from the dummies.

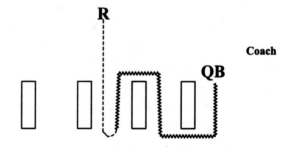

Diagram #16. Dummy Drill

We use variations of the same drill. Instead of shuffling through the dummies, they step over them. When the coach claps his hands, they throw the ball. We do a combination of both drills (Diagram #17). The quarterback stands at one end of the dummies. He steps over the first and second dummies and shuffles through the next group of dummies. We make the quarterback go forward over the dummies and backward over the dummies. Each time the coach claps his hands, the quarterback throws the ball. We emphasize keeping the feet moving at all times and staying in the correct throwing position.

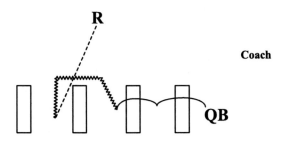

Diagram #17. Dummy Variations

We do not want to turn the ball over at any time. Our quarterbacks keep both hands on the ball at all times. Even when they are watching a drill or practice session, they have both hands on the ball. We want to always carry the ball in a position where he cannot fumble the ball.

We do a distraction drill with a rolled-up towel. I take athletic towels, roll them up, and tape them in a tube shape. I use them to distract the quarterback as he sets up and throws the ball. As the quarterback sets and throws, I throw the towels around his head, shoulder, or anywhere to distract his motion. You can use the towels in any drill and not worry about hurting anyone. The purpose is to make them focus on the target. When the quarterback is in the pocket, there is a lot of crap going on in front of him. I always have two towels, and oftentimes I throw both of them at once.

We do a "strong throw drill" (Diagram #18). The quarterback takes a five-step drop. The coach stands in the area of his fifth step with a blocking shield or hand dummy. The coach hits the quarterback in the upper legs, and he hitches to throw. We emphasize leg strength and concentration during the throw. It is not a violent hit. It is a slap with the dummy to distract his concentration. I always hit them from the non-dominant side. That keeps us from hitting their throwing arm as they deliver the ball.

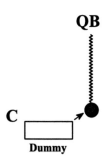

Diagram #18. Strong Throw Drill

The last drill I have to show you is the "deep ball drill" (Diagram #19). Throwing the deep ball is one of the hardest things to teach a young player. This is the best drill I have found to teach players, who have the arm strength, to throw the ball on time with the right trajectory. Have the quarterback stand 15 to 20 yards from the grandstands. Put a receiver in the stands six to eight rows high. Have the quarterback and receiver play catch. The quarterback does not change his techniques of throwing; he just plays catch.

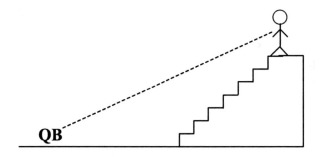

Diagram #19. Deep Ball Drill

After you have played catch for a while, have the receiver not catch the ball and let the quarterback see how far the ball will go. If he throws the ball at the right trajectory and right velocity, the ball will travel far enough. They have the arm and leg strength to get the ball deep. This also a great drill for throwing the inside seam ball in a four-vertical pattern. That ball has to be thrown over the linebackers but underneath the safeties. It also strengthens the arm as well.

I have enjoyed this time with you. Thank you for your time.

Larry Johnson

DEFENSIVE LINEMEN RUN AND PASS-RUSH TECHNIQUES

Penn State

I am glad to be here. Let me set the pace for you. I am going to give you information that will help you as an offensive line coach. This is not just a drill segment. I am very basic. I am a fundamental football coach. Everything I do is based on finding ways to improve my players

That is my philosophy. For the rest of this lecture, you are going to have to bear with me. I am going to make you defensive line coaches by the end of this session. I am a teacher, and this is the new way of getting it done. By believing in something, it will help us get the job done. I am going to tell you some things about football before we get out of here. I am going to trick you. I am going to feed your soul.

I am going to show you my drill tape. It consists of things we have used to make our players better. Some of the drills you may not have seen before. I am going to show you some of our bag drills.

I want you to have this quote to help you understand what we are all about. "Visions without action equals hallucinations." Let me repeat that quotation: "Vision without proper action equals hallucinations." What that simply means is that you have a vision. If you do not do anything to improve that vision, you are just hallucinating. Football coaches get great ideas and decide they are going to do certain things in their program. After some time, they let the ideas go and the ideas fall through. I tell our players all of the time, "If you have a vision, you must follow through. If you do not follow through, you are just hallucinating."

I am going to set a pace. I am looking for a new brand of coaches to join me and the way I coach. Let me tell you a few things. You can tell by my voice that I do not need a microphone. I love what I do. I love coaching the defensive line. I think I have the

best job in the country. I am working for the best coach in the country. I have a great job. I get to do what I love, and that is to coach football. I do not take my job for granted. Every day I walk on the field, I am prepared.

Here are three things I think every coach must do. I do not care how good you are, or how long you have been coaching, you must follow these three principles:

- Make sure you are a good teacher.
- Relate to your players.
- Be organized.

I am lucky in that I came from the classroom as a high school coach. I am very fortunate to be at Penn State. I have just changed chairs from one classroom to another. I feel no different than most of you, and I know what you are going through.

You must be able to relate to your players. If you can relate to your players, you are going to get great things from them.

You must be organized to coach. I have never walked on the field in my drill segment without being prepared to teach. I do not walk out on the field and say, "Let me see, what can we do today?" Kids today will pick up on that. They know if you are just making up drills as you go through practice.

If my drills do not show up in a game video session, I am doing the wrong drills. I will caution you now: if you are doing drills to be doing drills and they do not show up in a game film, you are wasting your time.

We are going to teach our players to play fast in our drills. We are going to teach them how to play full speed. Full speed must be acquired. It is a skill.

When we get the young players, they do not know how to play fast. If you want your players to run to the ball, you must teach that skill. You cannot just assume that is going to happen. You must practice as if it is a game. If you practice as if it is a game, when you get to the game, it is not a surprise to you and your players.

If you come to see us practice, you are going to see we practice fast. We are going to be efficient, but we are going to practice fast. I have two great managers. I could not do without them. They are like assistant coaches to me. I pick all of the drills we are going to use in practice that day and I give it to them along with everything we are going to do in practice that day. I make sure everyone knows what we are going to do. If you have to set up the drills, you are wasting time. We have drills for 12 minutes, and they are set up ready to go when we are ready for them. If you have to set up the drills, you should find a manager or someone on the staff who is not a coach to set up the drills.

I am going to go over some basic things for defense that I think you need to know. I am not a big stat guy, but I am a big run guy. If you cannot stop the run, you cannot play football. I tell my linemen stopping the run gives you the honor to rush the passer.

Everything we do is predicated on stopping the run. I am talking about stopping the run in our base defense. If you cannot stop the run in your base defense, and you have to blitz all of the time to stop the run, then you will not be able to fix the defense. You will not be able to fix it when you need to fix it because you will not know which gap they are going to run into. We play one-gap football. This allows us to play faster because we are only playing in one gap.

I love playing one-gap football because I can fix it fast. The big point that is important to me is the rush defense. Sacks are important, depending on what part of the season we are in. Nevertheless, the rush defense means a great deal to us. We are going to be in the top 10 in the country in rush defense. You look at the last four years, and you will see we were in the top 10 all four years. We have

been seventh in rush defense the last four years. We only had one back to gain over 100 yards against our defense this past year. That was in 13 games.

My first goal going into a game is to stop the run and make the offense one-dimensional. Stopping the run gives the defense the honor to rush the passer. That is something we believe in for everything we do. We are going to stop the run first.

I want to give you the things we do in developing defensive line drills.

DEVELOPING DEFENSIVE LINE DRILLS

As you prepare your defensive line drills, you must keep a certain mentality in mind while conducting the drills. Defensive linemen have one of the most important assignments in football. Their job is predicated on their ability to rush the passer or get to the ballcarrier. The main ingredient for a good defensive lineman is the need for quickness and determination. There are certain areas of consideration when conducting your drills.

Most high school coaches have a tough job because some of you have to coach both the offensive and defensive lines. You must make sure you transition from an offensive line coach to a defensive line coach. You cannot teach the same techniques on offense and defense. It is tough to transition from offense to defense. You cannot assume because they are offensive players, they can pick up the defensive techniques.

Speed is important. I am not a 40-yard-dash coach, but I do look at the 10-yard times. A defensive player must have excellent foot speed. He must always keep his feet alive and moving. If they can run for 10 yards and go from sideline to sideline, they can play for me. I have never had a player who could run a 4.9, or a 4.9 player to play for me. That is not important to me. Can he run, can he hustle, and can he play at full speed? That is important to me.

A defensive lineman must be able to accelerate. Initial quickness must always be emphasized. The desire to accelerate on the movement of the football is the principal athletic trait a defensive lineman needs. Areas of concentration will be to accelerate, react quickly, and develop good physical coordination. If a blocker is quick enough to get his hands inside the framework of the defensive lineman's numbers and get his elbows locked on him, forget it. The defender will not get to the passer.

A defensive lineman must be able to coordinate the action of his hands, feet, and body as he rushes the passer. When rushing the passer or playing the run, a defensive lineman must keep his feet moving. Remember that point with your drills.

A defensive lineman must be competitive. An attitude is one of the most important football qualities defensive linemen should have. He must never give up. He needs to have a mean streak, in wanting to get after people. For that reason, we make our drills demanding and tough. He must want to be a good defensive player.

A defensive lineman must be tough, and he must not be denied. How will he react when playing against a bigger and stronger opponent? He must possess inside power. He must be able to control the line of scrimmage.

Let me move on to the five essentials of a defensive lineman.

THE FIVE ESSENTIALS

- *Stance:* You must not overemphasize the stance parameters of the defensive lineman. What is important is the stance that allows the lineman to take a neutral position. He should be able to move in either direction with an explosive power step.

- *Attack:* We do not teach the big-first-step coaching point that a lot of coaches use in their desire to gain penetration. We feel the big first step puts the defensive lineman at a disadvantage against every type of block, save one. The only blocking scheme a big-first-step technique is effective against is the high-hat read (pass protection). Against all other blocks, the big first step puts the defensive lineman on an edge or in a position where he is unbalanced against a blocker using short power strides. In order for a player to

contact the blocker in a fundamentally sound body position, it is extremely important for the player to utilize short, powerful steps while maintaining a good base.

- *Neutralize:* The effective defensive lineman must neutralize the blocker's impact and stabilize the line of scrimmage. Neutralizing a blocker or a combination-blocking scheme involves several reactions: getting an upfield push on a pass protector, spilling a trap blocker, disrupting a combo block, and so forth. In order to consistently neutralize a blocker or blocking scheme, the productive defensive lineman must be able to move quickly and efficiently in eight different directions.

- *Escape:* This is where the kinship of the defensive line play and wrestling is the strongest. A primary characteristic of an effective defensive player is his ability to quickly and violently shed a blocker. Against the run, escaping predominantly entails lateral movement ability. Against the pass, the defender may have to throw his blocker aside with a club move in order to clear the pass-rushing lane. Good technique and leverage is simply not enough. The escape factor is a critical component to defensive line play, and it should be practiced on a daily basis with specific drills that hone the players' technique in escaping from contact with the blocker.

- *Pursuit:* An effective escape puts the defensive lineman into position to effectively pursue the ballcarrier. No one can outhustle our defense. In addition to outhustling our opponent, our players (through the use of the proper escape technique) will pursue the ballcarrier according to the proper angle and leverage. Hustle and angles are the two components of effective individual pursuit.

We do not overemphasize the base stance, but we do get into the stance. I do believe in the base stance. I do not overcoach it, but I want to make sure it is balanced. I teach stance and start the first day of practice. That is the most important thing we do.

The defensive lineman must neutralize the block before he can get off the block. He may use the swim technique and get by with it one time, but he needs to neutralize the block, because the swim technique will not work all of the time. We talked about escaping the blocks. It is part of coming off the block.

The last point is pursuit. This is something you must teach every day. You must finish every drill. When we show the video in a few minutes, you need to watch us finish every drill. Finishing teaches pursuit. If you do poor drills and do not finish, you can forget about pursuit.

If you do not teach finish when you run the bag drills, you are not teaching pursuit. You are just teaching a bag drill. I want to teach pursuit on every drill.

I want to bring up another point not related to the X's and O's of football. I can do all of the coaching aspects of the game without using profanity. I have been coaching over 30 years, and I have never cursed on the field. I have never cursed in the course of a game. I will tell you why I have never cursed when coaching. My high school coach was a great coach. His name was Herman Boone. Have you see the movie Remember the Titans. That was my high school coach, when he was coaching in North Carolina. He was a great coach, but every third word was a curse word. He did it thinking he was motivating players. He used profanity every other word.

While I was playing for Coach Boone, I would tell myself if I ever became a coach, I would never use that technique. I will tell you why I never wanted to curse in coaching football. When you curse in front of those young athletes, you train another society. They will be using those curse words later in their life. We are supposed to be growing young men, not teaching them bad habits. We do not want to tear down young athletes; we need to build them up.

I assure you that you can coach and not use profanity. I have coached for 30 years, and I know it will work.

I am asking for one coach to join me in changing the society on this matter. One of you needs to come over and join me in this endeavor. Join me and say, "We can do this in the right way." I will guarantee you will get more out of the players if you have passion for them, and you do the right things. I just need one coach to join me. We will create a new society of coaches.

Let me show you these coaching points on the techniques. We want air under the heels on the stance. The free hand is near the line of scrimmage. We want the hips higher than the hat. We want the inside hand down, and the inside foot back.

On attack, I do not want to step on someone's toes here. When we watch high school films, we see a lot of players that do not know how to get off blocks. They will attack, and then they pursue the ballcarrier. They drop their hands and start running to the ball. When they drop the hands, they get blocked downfield, and they do not know why they get blocked downfield. They have not been coached to get off blocks. Getting off blocks is a part of tackling.

On the starts, we use a six-point start. We teach this on day one on how to take off. The reason I teach this is because I am interested in the pad level. I am a "pad-level coach." We want to see if they can come forward out of the six-point stance. I want to know how fast we can get their pads going forward. We run the drill every day.

We want them to get off the ground and get the pads forward. We are going to run through the blocker and attack the line of scrimmage.

Next, we go to a one-leg balance drill. I got this drill from a track sprinter. All of you have seen the sprinters starting blocks in track. Everyone thinks they push off the back foot. Their stance is tight. They are not really pushing off the back foot. They are really pushing off their front foot. They gain ground with the second foot. When we take off, we want to go across the line of scrimmage. We do not want to take off and just get to the line of scrimmage.

We teach the lineman to balance in their stance, and we push off the front foot. By doing this, I can gain ground. I have to balance, and then push. We still are taking a six-inch power step, but we are gaining ground as we cross the line of scrimmage. We are attacking the line of scrimmage.

There are two keys in that drill. It is great take-off practice. We are gaining ground, and we are going across the line of scrimmage.

The next step is to take the drill to the mat and work on hip explosion. We are not swimming, we are not diving, but we are snapping the hips on the get-off.

We do a redirect drill. The reason we do the drill is to make sure we are running to the football. This eliminates seams.

After we teach the steps on the drills, then we go to the chute and work on them. You can build a chute without going out and buying an expensive one. We do all of the moves coming out of the chute.

I want to cover some drills. The first drill is the hop drill (Diagram #1). We do these drills in pre-season and early on. In addition, we do them in our winter workouts. What we are looking for is knee bounce, and high knees, and watching them finish on the drill. We always teach finish. We are developing bounce, foot movement, and finish.

Diagram #1. Hop Drill

Next is our lateral balance step drill (Diagram #2). I love this drill. We are working on balance and finish.

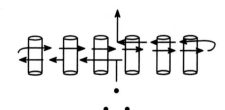

Diagram #2. Lateral Balance Step Drill

We do a ton of bag drills. The first one is the inner drill. We do not use high bags with the defensive line. Get rid of those high bags with the defensive linemen. We want to run over the bags we use. The bags we use are half-moon bags. They are flat on the bottom and round on the top. We do not have to worry about the players getting their knees up high. We want to know if they have the ability to change directions at full speed.

We start in a three-point stance. We go over the bags and move up to the next level (Diagram #3). Then, he goes back down the bags.

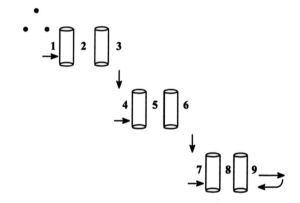

Diagram #3. Up and Back

We add the next phase of the drill and have the lineman finish the drill (Diagram #4). He goes up the bags, turns, and finishes the drill.

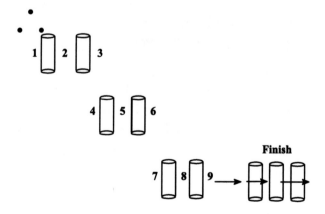

Diagram #4. Up and Finish

Here is another lateral step drill that we like. We have the bags set up at different angles (Diagram #5). We always have the finish aspect of the drills.

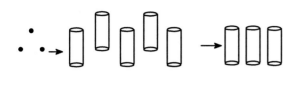

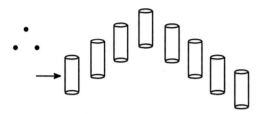

Diagram #5. Lateral Step and Finish

Every drill that we have done over the bags, we can do in the chute. If they bump their head, it is on them. You can use all of these drills.

Here is a four-bag drill that I use (Diagram #6). The drill gives them four sets of bags to go over. It is a great conditioning drill during the pre-season.

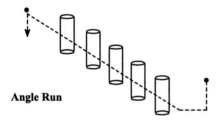

Angle Run

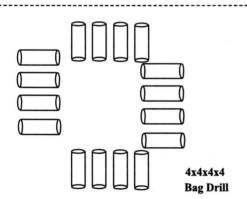

4x4x4x4 Bag Drill

Diagram #6. Four-Bag Drill

I do not like to use pursuit drills with players down on the ground. I do not want to put a player in a position that he should not be in. We keep them up in a two-point stance, or a four-point stance. I point

to a cone and have them run to the cone. Once they get to the cone, they have to come back to the middle and go again. I am trying to simulate a game. It is a start-and-go drill. It is how we play in a game. We make them backpedal, turn, and run. We want to give them moves they will be using in a game. We give them several moves, and then we give them a finish to the drill. We usually go three men in the box to get the drill done in a small amount of time.

We run another drill where they must get back to the middle. They do not care about their shoulder pads; we are teaching them how to run. We make them finish as we do on all drills. We make them think they are doing a drill, but we are really teaching them how to run.

We talked about pursuit. What it takes to pursue is worth mentioning:

- Pursuit is first a mental process.
- Visualize pursuing and making great plays.
- Physical conditioning is necessary so you can have great pursuit on every play.
- Speed: react fast and quickly. You can improve your speed and quickness.

The question comes up how to pursue. This is what we do in terms of pursuit:

- Play technique and gap responsibility first.
- Concentrate on lateral movement when the ball comes your way.
- Take correct course (pursuit angle) to the ball so you are in good position for the cutback.
- You have to want to be the first to the ball.
- Whoever is responsible for contain must turn the ballcarrier inside to the pursuit. Everyone else works inside-out to the ball.

What should you do once you arrive at the ball? This is what we want:

- Come to balance (come under control).
- Good bent-knee striking position.
- Step to and through the ballcarrier (take one extra step).
- Club and wrap-up driving your numbers through their numbers.

What does pursuit do for you?

- Eliminates the long touchdown.
- Discourages opponents.
  - ✓ During the course of a game.
  - ✓ Strikes fear and intimidates future opponents.
- Promotes consistent team performance.
- Creates turnovers all over the field.

Let me talk about tackling. The definition of tackling for us is simple. A tackle is a desired collision between the defensive man and the ballcarrier. *The defensive man must win!*

The objective of tackling is this. It is to stop the ballcarrier in his tracks for little or no gain, and to gang tackle. Tackling is 50 percent determination and 50 percent technique. It takes both aggressiveness and good technique to be a great tackler.

This is what we want on the techniques and fundamentals:

- Meet the ballcarrier in a good hitting position.
- Eyes should be focused on the ballcarrier's numbers.
- Don't give the ballcarrier a two-way cut.
- Keep the butt low; keep the head up. First contact should be made with the chest or numbers. As the chest or numbers make contact, roll the hips.
- Do not leave your feet. Keep a wide base, and take short choppy steps. Drive through the ballcarrier, and take him backward.
- On contact, work the arms from low to high, wrap viciously, and pull the ballcarrier toward you. Squeeze and grab cloth.
- If you get caught in a poor hitting position, somehow make the tackle. Grab arms, legs, or anything you can get hold of, except the facemask.

On open-field tackling, this is what we stress:

- Gather yourself, and come under control three to four yards from the ballcarrier, with feet chopping, and move toward the ballcarrier.

- Keep your eyes on the belt buckle, and get into a good hitting position. Make the tackle.
- Give the ballcarrier only one way to go, and then take that direction away from him.
- Leave your feet only as a last resort.
- Use the sideline whenever possible.
- Force the ballcarrier back into pursuit when possible.

Let me cover a couple of tackling drills. This is the first one we use. It is "Joe Pa" all the way. It is the mat tackle. We are not going to hit the ballcarrier in the center of his chest with our helmet, but we are going to slide it off toward the ball. For drill sake, we are putting the helmet down the middle. We put our arms on his buttocks, and set our hips down. We do not lift! We hit, dip the hips, and come up through the ballcarrier. The reason we use the mat is because we do not want them to hit the ground. What we want to do is to "run the feet," and then make the tackle.

We teach the angle tackle the same way. I do not want to angle tackle and drive the man sideways. We want to get the helmet in front of the man and drive him backward, not sideways. We want to drive the helmet through the man and drive him back. The key is to turn the hips and head and drive the man back.

Here are our pass-rush rules:

- Have a plan.
- Pre-snap read.
- Maintain a consistent stance.
- Pass rush from a shade alignment; be on the edge, same arm, same foot. Trust your hips.
- Create momentum and take it away.
- Use your hands.
- Know the quarterback.
- Run through the sack.

I am not a big spin guy. I do not like my linemen spinning on the pass rush. If they spin and they miss, and the quarterback throws a touchdown pass, they are in trouble with me.

If the quarterback throws a touchdown, I do not want our defensive linemen blaming it on the deep defenders. I tell them they did a lousy job and did not rush the passer fast enough to prevent the touchdown. I want them accountable. I do not want to give them an excuse for not getting to the quarterback. The entire team has a job to do, and we cannot blame one group for a touchdown that everyone on the field was responsible for the score. That is what I believe, and that is what I work on.

We study the quarterback. We want to know the type of passer he is. If he is going to step up in the pocket, we are going to come after him. If he is a quarterback who scrambles, we are going to consider that in our pass-rush game plan.

We do not want to jump and run through a sack. We do not want to leave our feet before the pass is out. We want to run through the sack.

Pass-rush drills include the following. We attack the elbow and then club and rip. We finish with a rip move. Let me give you these drills on the tapes so you can see what I have covered.

TAN STUNT: TACKLE AND NOSEMAN

Tackle: Take a 45-degree step, aiming for the back hip of the center. Pin the hip, and then work out to the quarterback.

Nose: Collision the guard. Once the tackle makes contact with the center, come around to cover.

Diagram #7. Tan Stunt: Tackle and Noseman

NUT STUNT: NOSE AND TACKLE

Nose: Move to a 2i alignment. Take a 45-degree step, aiming for the back hip of the center. Pin the hip, and then work out to the quarterback.

Tackle: Collision the guard. Once the nose makes contact with the center, come around to cover.

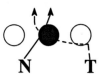

Diagram #8. Nut Stunt: Nose and Tackle

TEX STUNT: NOSE AND END

End: One step upfield. Plant off the foot, turn and drive to pin the hip of the guard. After collision, work to the quarterback.

Nose: Align in a 2i technique. Two steps inside and "flash hands" to hold the guard. When you see the end cross your face, come around tight to contain.

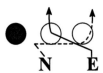

Diagram #9. Tex Stunt: Nose and End

EXIT STUNT: TACKLE AND WILL LINEBACKER

Tackle: Drive hard upfield, aiming for the inside half of the tackle, and then work for containment.

Will: Two steps upfield and "flash hands." Plant on second step, and aim for inside shoulder of the guard.

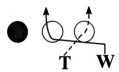

Diagram #10. Exit Stunt: Tackle and Will

WET STUNT: TACKLE AND WILL LINEBACKER

Tackle: Drive hard upfield, aiming for the inside half of the tight end, and then work for containment.

Will: One step upfield and "flash hands." Plant on first step, and aim for the inside shoulder of the tackle.

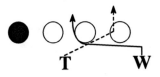

Diagram # 11. Wet Stunt: Tackle and Will

DOUBLE COVER STUNT: TACKLE, WILL AND NOSE, AND END

Tackle: Align in a 3 technique. Hit the guard. Flash hands, and come around tight to contain.

Will: Take two hard steps upfield. Take a reckless inside rush.

Nose: Hit the guard. Flash hands, and come around tight to contain.

End: Take two steps upfield. Fake a reckless inside rush.

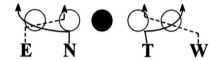

Diagram #12. Double Cover: Tackle, Will and Nose, and End

RAMBO STUNT: TACKLE, WILL AND NOSE, AND END

Tackle: Align in a wide 3 technique. Drive hard upfield, pick the back hip of the tackle, and then work to contain.

Will: Take two hard steps upfield. Step hard for the guard, and pick the guard. Aiming point is the rib cage.

Nose: Hit the guard. Flash hands, and come around tight to contain.

End: Take three steps upfield. Plant the outside foot, and come underneath.

Diagram #13. Rambo Stunt: Tackle, Will and Nose, and End

CONAN STUNT: TACKLE, WILL AND NOSE, AND END

Tackle: Drive for the inside hip of the tackle. Pick the tackle, and work for containment.

Nose: Tex stunt

End: Tex stunt

Will: One step and long stick to the A gap.

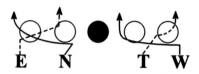

Diagram #14. Conan Stunt: Tackle, Will and Nose, and End

ROCKY STUNT: TACKLE, WILL AND NOSE, END

Tackle: Align in a wide 3 technique. Drive hard upfield, and pick the back hip of the tackle.

Will: Long stick. Read the center. If he turns to you, cross his face. If he turns away, come inside of him.

Nose: Hit into the guard to hold him, then come around tight, working for containment.

End: Contain the rush, and do not take an inside move.

Coaching Point: Versus a tight end, check to Rocky II.

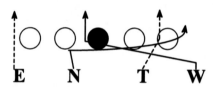

Diagram #15. Rocky Stunt: Tackle, Will and Nose, and End

The NCAA will not let me give you my drill tape, but I have started a youth ministry program at my church. I can sell you the tapes for 10 dollars. I do not make anything from this, as I give it all to the youth program at my church at Penn State. Let me know if you want one. All of the drills are on the tape.

Let me close with this. I have three minutes, and I will be done. I hope I have showed you something in the time I have spent with you that will make you a better defensive line coach, a better man, and that will help you make it a better world.

I want each of you to ask yourself this question: What have been the 10 best years of your life? If you tell me it was when you got married, or when I did this last year, or I did this 10 years ago. I am going to stop you at that point. I am going to tell you the way it must be. The best 10 years better start tonight! It starts this hour, this minute, and this second. You have promised yourself that you are going to make yourself a better football coach.

It is not what you did last year; it is what you are going to do right now. Every morning when I rise, I say this scripture. It is from the Bible, Philippians 4:13. "I can do everything through Christ who strengthens me."

Then I make this comment to myself: "I have to make this a great day." I know we all only have so many years left in this life. If you want to make the next 10 years the best 10 years of your life, if you make up your mind to start now, it will happen. You will be a better football coach. Don't live on yesterday. You cannot live on the last state championship. Live on what you do this moment. If you will live that way, every morning when you get up, you will become a great coach. You will be fired up in everything that you do.

This is natural for me. The enthusiasm I have here today is no fake for me. This is natural. I am like this all of the time.

The only time I calm down is when I walk into my house. I am one of those coaches who has to wear many hats. When I walk into my house, I am a husband, a father, as well as a coach. You have to do that. Do not let your kids not see their father.

I have one story to illustrate this point. My wife and I are the parents of twins, Tony and Teresa. When they were in the early years of school, they played a game at school. It was a game similar to show-and-tell. The teacher asked Tony if he could tell the class his mother's name. He replied, "Christine Johnson." Very good, Tony! Can you tell us your father's name? Tony replied, "Coach Johnson." He did not know my first name, but he knew I was "Coach." That was a reality for me. He said that because that is all he ever heard. He did not know my name was Larry. What is the moral of the story? The kids must know who you are. From that point on, I changed my life. Don't lose sight of that point.

I need one of you to brand yourself with me so we can create a new generation of football coaches. That is all I want. God bless you!

Paul Johnson

THE SPREAD FORMATION OPTION GAME

Georgia Tech

A long time ago when I used to go to clinics, I felt if I could get one or two things from the clinic that was great.

The topic, in general, is the Georgia Tech option offense. We could take four or five days and not cover the topic thoroughly. I will go over our base play from the option package. Our base play is the inside veer or triple option. I will try to break it down into some fundamental techniques and rules.

We call our offense the *spread-option offense* (Diagram #1). Our base formation is the double-slot set. The splits in the offensive line are three feet all the way across the offensive line. We call the slot backs A-backs. The split receiver to the right is the Z-receiver, and the one to the left is the X-receiver. The tailback aligns behind the quarterback and is the B-back. Most every formation we use has a quick motion by one of the slot backs.

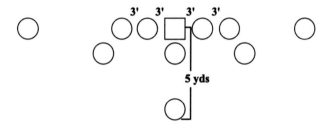

3'   3'   3'   3'

5 yds

Diagram #1. Base Formation

The receivers are interchangeable. The reason we give them names is for the passing game that comes from the formation. We call both the slot backs A-backs. The splits between the guards and the center never change. However, on occasion we may split the tackles wider in their alignment. We have played the tackles as wide as six or seven feet. If the defense will go with us, we take them as wide as they will go.

We are a true option team. We read our way out on this play. We read #1, pitch off #2, and block #3. The backside wide receiver's rule on the triple option is to cut off the backside corner. The backside A-back is the tail motion for the pitch. He is the pitchback. The B-back is the dive aspect of the play. The A-back goes in motion off the cadence. Our cadence is, "Ready, set, hike." The A-back goes in motion on *ready*. We have done it that way for 20 years.

If we call the cadence on two, the quarterback repeats the cadence twice. The A-back comes in motion on the second *ready*. He tries to get a step and a half into the play before the ball is snapped. He comes in motion at full speed and aims at the depth of the B-back. He runs through the butt of the B-back. The B-back aligns with his heels five yards from the front of the football.

The pitch relationship between the quarterback and the A-back is tough to coach. If the slotback is fast, he gets wider than a back that is slower. Once they reach the butt of the B-back, we coach them to take three more steps and turn up with the quarterback. When he catches the pitch, he becomes a football player and runs with the ball. We are not trying to outleverage anyone. If the seam is inside, he takes the ball inside. If it is outside, he takes the ball outside. He reads the blocking on the play and runs accordingly.

The beauty about the offense is from week to week, we do not have to worry what defense we face (Diagram #2). The backside tackle and guard have the same rules. They scoop their inside gap. We call the gap from the tackle's crotch to the guard's crotch. We are not trying to cut off defenders—we try to knock them back. We want to step down at a 45-degree angle. The next step is at 60 degrees, and the third step is up the field. We try to move the line of scrimmage even when we cut off.

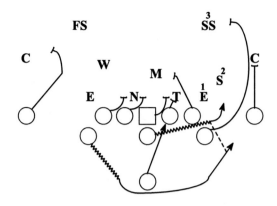

Diagram #2. Base Play

The center has the playside A gap. He scoops into that gap and blocks anything that appears. If he is uncovered, he steps into the A gap and looks for linebackers on a run-through technique. If he is covered by a nose defender, he tries to get through the playside armpit and up to the second level of the defense.

We use the same system of numbering the defensive techniques that Coach Bear Bryant did. If there is a defender head-up the center, he is a 0 technique. If he aligns on the center's shoulder, he is a shade technique or a 1 technique. Moving outside from the center, all the head positions are even numbers. Head-up the guard is 2, the tackle is 4, and the tight end is a 6 technique.

The shoulders of the offensive linemen are the odd-numbered techniques. The outside shoulder of the guard is 3, the outside shoulder of the tackle is 5, and the outside shoulder of the tight end is a 9 technique. The inside shoulder of the tight end is a 7 technique. No one knows why that is the case, but Coach Bryant numbered it that way, and no one has had the guts to change it. There are two special techniques that align a defender on the inside eye of the guard and tackle. They are 2i and 4i.

The playside guard has a base rule. If he is covered, he base blocks the defender trying to get six to eight inches back off the ball. If there is a shade technique on the center, in our base rules, the guard goes straight to the linebacker and the center reaches the shade technique. If the center cannot block the shade, the guard comes down on the shade

and the center and guard block an ace combination for the shade nose and the linebacker. However, as a rule, we want to reach all shade techniques.

I do not think the center can reach the nose and block him by himself. Generally, the nose is a better player than the center. If he was not better than the center, he would be playing center. We know the center will probably not reach the shade, but the way we run the B-back, it does not matter. All the center has to do is get in the way.

The tackle's rule is to block the first inside linebacker to the playside. He uses the best release he can to get off the ball. If he has a 4 technique or a heavy 5-technique defender, his easiest release is an outside release. If the tackle takes an outside release, the guard has to be climbing on the linebacker. If he does not and the linebacker runs through the gap, he drills the B-back.

If the tackle cannot release inside, he goes outside. The guard gives a call that tells the tackle he can keep the linebacker from running through the B gap. He cannot get him if he scrapes, but he can keep him out of the B gap.

It is important to understand how we count for the handoff key and the pitch key. The first defender touching the playside tackle in his alignment is #1 or the read key. The next defender outside is #2. He is the pitch key. The run support defender is #3. The playside A-back blocks the run support. He counts from the tackle going outside. He counts *one, two, three*, and blocks #3. However, we do not ask him to block a rolled-up corner.

The A-back takes an arc release. He takes a drop-step and a crossover step. The A-back aligns with his inside foot back and splitting the outside leg of the offensive tackle. We align them with their inside foot back to keep them from false stepping when they come in tail motion. When he comes in tail motion, he digs his outside foot into the ground and pushes off it.

With his outside foot up, he drops the outside foot, crosses over with the inside foot, and looks for the run support defender. Teams try to change up their run support to confuse the blocking of the A-back. If the A-back reads the corner firing off the edge, that is the man he blocks. The wide receiver sees the corner fire to the inside and knows there is someone coming over the top of the corner. That is his block.

The A-back tries to cut the outside leg of the run support defender. We tell them the aiming point is six inches outside the outside knee. He does not throw on the defender until he can step on his foot. I do not want the A-back taking a dive on the ground. I want him to get in close and throw. I know in high school, you cannot cut. We do not cut all the time. If a defender knows we are going to cut him, he plays it. As a change-up, we block him high on occasion. The playside wide receiver blocks the near defender. He blocks the deep defender. That is how we block the option.

The quarterback's responsibility is to read #1. He opens at 4 o'clock and pushes the ball back as far as he can. He wants to get his second step in the ground, looking at his read key. We get the ball back as far as we can so we can ride the B-back. We put the ball in his pocket and ride him to the line of scrimmage. He rides the B-back until he reaches his front leg. The quarterback has to make the decision to leave the ball with the B-back or pull it by the time the ball reaches his front foot.

My quarterback is 6'3" and his steps are not going to be the same as the quarterback who is 5'11". You have to rep the play so the steps work out. The most important thing the quarterback can do in the ride is get his second step on the ground.

When we coach our quarterbacks, we coach them to give the ball if the defender does not take the B-back. I cannot read the face mask, his head, his numbers, or any other clinic-talk key. If the defender cannot get his head in front of the ballcarrier, we give the ball. A lot of those decisions depend on who you have at quarterback. When I have had good running quarterbacks, we use the phrase, "If in doubt, pull it out." If you have a quarterback that is not a good runner and there is doubt, hand the ball off.

The quarterback reads #1 and options #2. If #1 and #2 are coming hard from the outside, I love that situation (Diagram #3). It turns the option into a toss sweep. That is why the second step is so important. If the quarterback does not have his second step in the ground, he gets killed or has the pitch knocked down. With the second step in the ground, the quarterback can create space away from the defender. He steps straight back and creates more distance between himself and the defender.

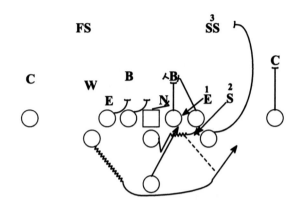

Diagram #3. #2 Crash

If the quarterback sees the #2 defender on a crash, he does not care what the #1 defender is doing. He pitches the ball off of #2 and he is crashing. He disengages from the B-back, steps straight back, and pitches the ball.

The second reason the second foot has to be in the ground is due to the mechanics of pulling the ball. If the read key closes hard to the inside, the quarterback must have his weight on the front foot to pull the ball, seat it, and step around the closing read key. He has his weight on the front foot so he can give some ground and step around the collision.

Once he pulls the ball, he options the ball off of the #2 defender. We tell the quarterback he has the ball, so run with it. We do not care who he options. We do not care if he pitches it or keeps it. We want the option key to come to the quarterback. We are not going to chase him. He does not try to get to his outside shoulder so he can pitch the ball.

The goal line is north and south, and as soon as he gets the chance, that is the way he is going. We do not want him run laterally. As soon as the pitch key turns his shoulder to the quarterback, he pitches the ball. We do not have to be close to the defender. All we want is leverage on the pitchman. When the pitchman has leverage on the support player, we pitch the ball.

If we attack the pitch key, we attack the inside shoulder. That is the shortest distance to the goal line. We teach the quarterback to pitch the ball any way he can. When we teach the pitch, we seat the ball in the chest and pitch it with the thumb down. We pitch the ball from the seat position on the inside with the thumb down. The ball gets there quicker and is less likely to be knocked down.

The quarterback has to deal with stunts trying to confuse his read key. Defenses stack the read and pitch key and exchange their responsibilities (Diagram #4). If you run the option, you will see that stunt. It is not that hard to read. We call that an easy stunt. We rep it enough so that we pull the ball off #2 and pitch it off #1.

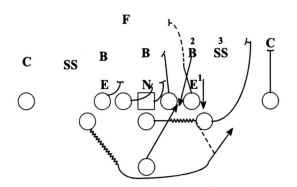

Diagram #4. Easy Stunt

The B-back's aiming point is the inside leg of the playside guard. His technique allows us to block with the scheme we use (Diagram #5). He aims at the inside leg, but he reads the first down lineman inside the read key. If we have a shade nose on the center, that is the center's block. His block is to reach the shade nose. We know he will probably not reach him. If the quarterback has a give key to the B-back, he leaves the ball with him. The B-back reads the nose working toward him. The center continues to drive on the nose and the B-back breaks the ball behind the center's block into the backside.

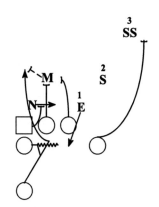

Diagram #5. B-Back Read

The B-back's heels are five yards from the tip of the ball. We have not aligned deeper than five yards. However, we have moved slower backs closer to the line. If you have a good back, that is the right depth for running the ball and pass protecting the quarterback. That depth gives the B-back a chance to read the block of the first down lineman inside the quarterback's read.

The B-back learns the blocking schemes of the offensive line. If the defense is a 50-shade defense, the B-back knows we will load the scheme and double the nose with the center and playside guard (Diagram #6). The read key is the 4-technique tackle, and the pitch key is the rush end. If the quarterback gets a give key, he hands the ball to the B-back. Since we double-team the nose, the B-back does not cut the ball back. He hugs the double-team and keeps the ball to the frontside of the play.

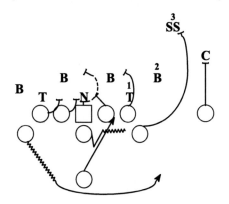

Diagram #6. Load

The B-back will learn the blocking schemes and know what we are going to do in the offensive line. But even if he does not know who is blocking who, he can find the seam. Our B-back this year was the ACC player of the year. He is a good player, but he could not tell you who is blocking anybody. He might not be able to spell the word cat if you gave him the C and the A. That was a joke. He is a good player and will probably be playing on Sundays eventually.

Our B-back aligns in an even stance. He has to go both ways from that stance. He has some weight forward in the stance. If he goes to the right, he curls his left toe into the ground or turf. I want him to curl the toes of the off foot into the ground so he has something to push off and does not false step. We tell him we want him approaching the line of scrimmage like a plane taking off.

We drill him in the chute so he learns to run from low to high. He curls the toes and explodes with his initial step at the inside leg of the guard. We do not want him to overstep, and his first step may be six inches. We want him full speed until he passes the quarterback's front leg. From there, he reacts to the blocks of the linemen.

When you run this play, the defender you must account for is the playside linebacker. He makes most of the tackles on this play. The second defender you have to block is the backside linebacker. However, if he makes too many plays, we will run some counter at him.

When the playside tackle takes his release, he tries to release through the outside armpit of the 4 technique. That is the angle he takes, but he wants to avoid contact with the 4 technique if he can. The tight 5 technique or 4 technique will not allow the tackle to veer release across his face to block the linebacker. That is why we work behind his alignment. If the defensive tackle tries to step with the offensive tackle and slow him down, the read will be a give to the B-back.

Teams have tried to stop the tackle from getting to the inside linebacker by stepping the outside linebacker down on the outside move of the tackle. If they do that, we use the quick toss to the outside and get around the corner.

If we find the #3 defender in the middle of the football field, the tackle and A-back can run a combo

block for the playside linebacker (Diagram #7). The playside linebacker can get over the top quickly and is a hard block for the tackle. In this diagram, the tackle has to combo with the guard on the 3-technique defender before he can block the linebacker. The support player is the single high safety. The A-back takes an inside release and seals the inside linebacker and the tackle chases the safety.

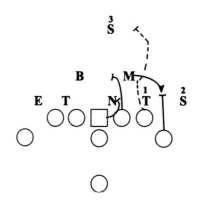

Diagram #7. Tackle/A-Back Combo

We give teams that play that kind of front something a little funky. When they play the eight-man front on defense, they tie the safety and outside linebacker to the release on the playside slot. They tell the linebacker if the slot runs straight up the field, the strong safety takes the quarterback and the free safety runs for the pitch. If the slot arcs, the linebacker stays outside on the slot and the safety runs the alley for the quarterback. That is not a bad way to play and is probably smart. If we find them doing that, we automatic with a safety call. We run the slot on the inside release, but he passes the linebacker and blocks the free safety. The defense has two defenders on the quarterback and no one on the pitch. We did that a bunch against Georgia in our last regular-season game.

If we figure out how the defense is playing us, we have counter and blocking schemes to handle all types of defensive adjustments. But that is a double-edged sword—if they figure out what you are doing, they will get you.

If #3 is in the middle of the field and we are having trouble getting the linebacker blocked with the tackle, we have an adjustment. We release the A-back on the linebacker. However, if the tackle cannot catch up to the safety, we can call a crack scheme. We load the play and call crack. The wide receiver cracks the safety.

If the defense aligns with a four-across look in the secondary, we tell the playside guard and tackle they have the playside linebacker to the backside safety (Diagram #8). People that play four across try to roll the secondary to get the backside safety into the box as the extra alley runner. If the guard has the block on the linebacker and the linebacker scrapes, the tackle blocks him. The guard climbs to the backside safety and cuts him off. If the linebacker blows the B gap, the guard blocks him and the tackle climbs for the safety.

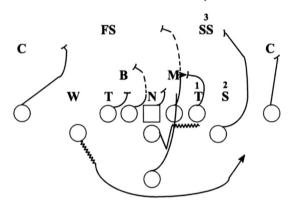

Diagram #8. Safety Adjustment

There are many complementary plays that go with the base option. If the defense loads up to stop the option, we have ways to run the complementary plays to take advantage of what the defense gives up. That is the old argument of who has the chalk last.

If we want to go unbalanced, there are a number of ways we can do it. If we take both wide receivers to the same side, we call over (Diagram #9). Both wide receivers will be on the line of scrimmage and the rules for the play stay the same.

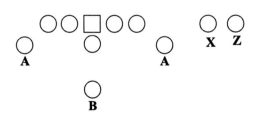

Diagram #9. Over

If we want to change the eligible receivers, we drop the X-receiver off the line and move the A-back on the line of scrimmage. We call that formation *green*. We can get into a trips formation by moving the backside A-back up on the line and dropping the playside A-back off the line. We call that formation *brown*. If we find the defense not covering the ineligible receiver, we huddle call *green to brown* (Diagram #10). We come to the line in a green formation. At the last moment, the backside A-back moves up on the line of scrimmage and the playside A-back moves off and all four of the receivers are eligible.

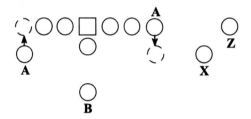

Diagram #10. Green to Brown

If we call a trips set as the huddle call, the A-back is on the same side with the backside wide receiver as the single receiver.

Question: How do you practice and teach the read?

A typical practice is made up of five-minute periods. When we start in the fall, we go 23 periods, which is about an hour and 45 minutes. Later in the year, we practice 14 periods, which is an hour and 10 minutes. Periods 1 through 4 are our fundamental periods—our individual periods where we work on our individual skills. The quarterback and B-back, during the fundamental period, are working on footwork and ball security. They work their steps and mesh with one coach. The coach is the read key in that drill.

Period 5 is a 1-on-1 period with receiver and defensive back, with the quarterback throwing. Periods 6 through 9 are live-option periods. We do this every day. This is a live 11-on-11 period. When we are playing, we go against the scout team. In 20 minutes, we get 45 plays. We script the plays for this session and run two huddles. The coaching is done on the fly. We do not stop the period for individual instruction. During this period is where the quarterbacks get all the live reads. We hit the quarterbacks all year. We do not take them to the ground, but they are hit. If #1 and #2 are coming hard from the outside, we light up the quarterback. Everything has to be above the waist.

You have to practice at the speed you are going to play. If we play Miami, we know they are a 4-3 defense—everything we run is 4-3 blocking. However, we throw some double-Eagle and eight-man fronts into the mix of the periods. We must know how to block all those defenses. That is how you find out if they know the scheme or whether the second-team player is just watching the block of the first-team player. If he blocks the same defender and the defense changed, he is wrong.

After the option period, we take a break because it is 20 minutes going as hard as we can go. After the break, we go to pass skeleton for two periods. The rest of the practice is team time. During that time, we run our entire option package. We run the triple, midline, counter, speed, and belly options. The count system stays the same for all the options and that makes it easier.

Question: How would you attack the 3-3 stack defense?

The first thing I am going to do is move either the slot or the split end to the other side. That makes the defense move a defender to cover the unbalance. That would be the first thing we would do. By using the unbalanced set and motion, we force the defense into a numbers game with the option read. We outnumber the defense to the backside of the formation.

Question: What adjustments did you make to move the ball on Notre Dame when you were at Navy?

When we played Notre Dame the last year I was at Navy, they played a 3-4 defense. The outside linebackers were taking the quarterback. The defensive ends came hard inside and took the B-back. The outside linebackers played the quarterback but were jamming our offensive tackle trying to loop behind the defensive end for the linebacker. The tackle could not get on the linebacker and he was running free in the alley

(Diagram #11). Without changing anything we did with the blocking scheme, I brought the wide receivers down into a flex position, which is a five-yard split.

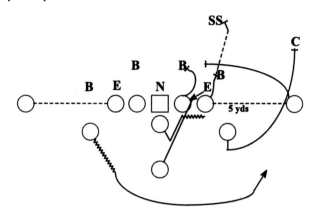

Diagram #11. Double Flex

That put the outside linebacker in a bind. If he stood inside to jam the tackle, we cracked him with the wide receiver and ran the toss sweep. When we went to the double-flex formation, they went from a four-across look to a two-deep look. When we ran the option, we swapped the block of the A-back and Z-receiver. The A-back arced and blocked the corner, the Z-receiver cracked the linebacker, and the tackle went up on the safety.

The double flex has been a good formation for us. We get them tighter and run the toss play. That is a good play because you do not have to block anyone. You pitch the ball and run to the corner.

Question: What is the best defense against this offense?

The best defense against this offense is good players. All the offenses and defenses are similar in concept. The key to any scheme is knowing how to fix what goes wrong. I love playing football teams whose offense is football's best 20 plays. They have a bunch of plays that look good, but none of them mesh together. If you have a system and understand it, you have a chance to fix it. It is like the Notre Dame game. They had a good plan to run against our base offense. However, when we fixed our problems, they could not refix their scheme.

The simpler you can keep it on offense and defense, the better it is. Just rep what you do and get a total understanding of the scheme so when one thing goes wrong, you know how to fix the scheme. When we go into a game, we run six or seven plays. We have many wrinkles off them so people think it is more than that. If you execute what you do, it does not matter what the defense does. If they can get better in three days of stopping it than you can get in 19 weeks of running it, they are going to beat you anyway.

You do not win too many games by surprising people. You win by outexecuting them and playing harder than they do. Too many times we, as coaches, think there is a magic elixir. I see it at our level all the time. Each week, we play against the defense of the week. When you do not play the option week after week, you have to make adjustments in your scheme. We played North Carolina in Chapel Hill and they beat us. We had 440 yards of total offense but only scored seven points. For the next three weeks, we saw what North Carolina played against us on defense. In the Miami game, they lined up exactly like North Carolina. We played better and they did not play as good and we beat them.

The play-action pass in this offense is designed to get the #3 defender (Diagram #12). The backside A-back runs tail motion and blocks or is involved in the pattern depending on the blocking scheme. The backside tackle has a base block as his assignment. He blocks the technique down and the guard will pull outside for the edge rush. We can use a white scheme. That is gap protection. If the tackle has a 4i technique aligned on him, he makes a white call to the guard. The guard fans back for the 4i and the tackle fans for the defensive end. We do not do that too much because it does not look like run. The center's rule is onside gap. The playside guard's rule is base to down. The tackle has a base block.

The quarterback opens, meshes with the B-back, and comes straight back. We used to go two steps down the line of scrimmage before we dropped. The quarterback cannot see as well so we changed it. The B-back runs his track and has the playside linebacker in the B gap. The A-back in tail motion has the C gap.

The patterns are combination routes. If we call vertical or seam, the playside A-back runs his arc

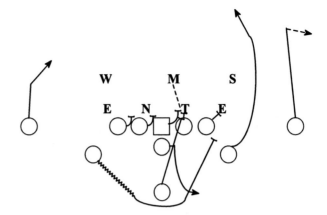

Diagram #12. Play-Action Protection

track and tries to run by the safety. The Z-receiver runs a take-off and tries to run by the corner. If he cannot get deep, he breaks his pattern off to the sideline at 14 to 15 yards. We can tag routes for the backside receiver. We can call 312 X post. We get the same patterns on the playside and an X-post on the backside. If we tag the pattern, the quarterback comes back to him. We can throw the ball on a hitch to the X-receiver because most defenses roll their secondary with the tail motion of the A-back. That leaves the wide receiver 1-on-1 on the corner.

We try to give the defense the same look on the pass as we do on the run. If we had been cracking with the wide receiver, we run the switch call (Diagram #13). We try to give the defense the same look. The wide receiver runs the post, and the A-back runs a wheel route on the corner.

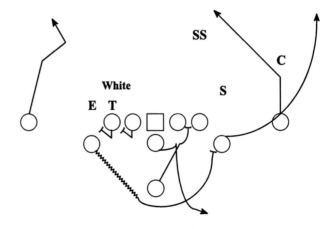

Diagram #13. Switch

We are not a big midline team but we do run it. We call it 10-lead (Diagram #14). If we run it to the 3 technique, we read him. The B-back runs up the center's butt. The backside tackle cuts off inside as he does on the option. The center and backside guard block an ace combination on the shade nose. The playside tackle turns out on the defensive end. The playside A-back blocks the Sam linebacker the best way he can get him. The tail motion comes up into the B gap and leads the quarterback. The playside guard seals inside on the Mike linebacker.

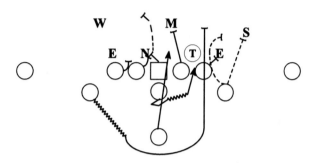

Diagram #14. Midline to 3 Technique

The quarterback digs his toe into the ground and swings his playside foot back without moving his backside foot. The backside foot is on the ground and is the same technique as the second step on the option. The quarterback reads the 3 technique and gives or keeps the ball. If he keeps the ball, he follows the A-back on the lead block.

We can run the midline to the shade-nose side (Diagram #15). We double the shade nose back to the Mike linebacker. We read the first defender outside the 2i technique. Everything else on the play is the same.

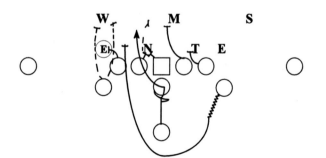

Diagram #15. Midline to Shade

If we call 10, it is the triple option from the midline read. The blocking is the same except the tail motion is the pitchback and not the lead back. We run trap, toss, and all the option plays, but we do not run much midline.

If a team runs a double-Eagle defense, they have effectively canceled the dive back (Diagram #16). We still run the triple option, but we do not read the dive back. We run a two-way option. We base block with the playside guard and tackle and run the B-back in on the linebacker. The A-back arc blocks on the corner and the wide receiver cracks inside. The quarterback pulls the ball and runs an option on the safety.

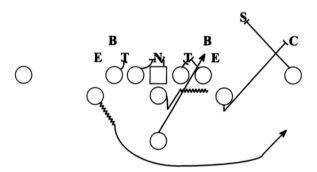

Diagram #16. Triple vs. Double-Eagle

We run *28-option* and area read the play. If there is a stud at the 3 technique, we double-team him with the guard and tackle. That leaves the linebacker and defensive end to take the B-back. If the defensive end comes down to take the dive, the quarterback pulls the ball and pitches off the linebacker. If the defensive end squats and the linebacker is running, we hand the ball off. Somebody has to take the dive. When they do, they run out of people on the outside.

I enjoyed sharing some of what we do with you. Thank you.

RECUITING/LEADERSHIP/BIG-CHUNK PLAYS

University of Cincinnati

It is great for me to be back in Michigan, where I started coaching. I have been a head coach for 16 years. For me, this is home. I cer-tainly remember coming to the clin-ics. My offensive coordinator, Jeff Quinn, has been with me for 18 years. That is longer than the time my wife and I have been married. Now, I do not know what that means, but it is a fact. He was with me at Grand Valley State. My quarterback coach, Greg Forrest, was with me at Grand Valley State. I remember my roots.

I want to talk about a couple of things going on in college football as they relate to high schools. I want to address the recruiting process in college and the relationship to high school coaches. I am very interested in getting this message out to the high school coaches and others who are involved. It is first and foremost relative to our profession.

We are so fortunate in football in that we have not become involved as much as basketball has with the AAU situation. Specifically, I am talking about taking the control out of the coaches' hands. More and more, we are seeing AAU coaches involved in the recruiting process. In basketball, the head coach is not as involved in the basketball recruiting process because of that fact.

Football is different. High school coaches are on the front line in that process. I want to urge you as coaches, relative to the recruiting process, you need to stay involved in it. You are a teacher, and you are an educator. You are someone those kids need in this process. As you know, the recruiting process can become very confusing.

From my end, as a college coach, and from someone who has recruited from the Division II level, I want high school coaches to be involved in the process. You are very import in this process. Because you have contacts, you have the ability to help your kids through the recruiting process. You should be there for the kids when they need you.

It is a two-way street. I only want to ask one thing of the high school coach. I see a problem developing in football related to the commitment. What is a verbal commitment, and what is not a verbal commitment? At the end of the day, I am a parent, as many of you are. Urge your players not to make a commitment until they are ready to hold to that commitment. The process works both ways. If a college coach makes a commitment to a high school player, and the kid is injured before he gets to college, the college coach should hold to that commitment. Again, it works both ways.

The problem we are seeing in the commitment process is the backing out of the commitments. If your players are not ready to commit, they should not make any announcement. They should not make a commitment until they know what a commitment means. At the University of Cincinnati, if we make a commitment to a young player, we stick by that commitment. We are going to sign you. If that player goes out and commits robbery or gets involved in crime, we are not going to sign the player. If it is an injury, we are still going to be there for the player.

In our profession, the integrity of the commitment is what concerns me at this time. We are not asking anything else but for coaches and players to make sure it is a two-way street in this process. If a student-athlete has studied the colleges and has prepared to make his decision, that is fine. The thing that concerns me is the number of commitments that are broken and turn out to be nothing but words.

In addition, the recruiting process has accelerated exponentially relative to the offering. As you may know, most of the commitments at the BCS level are made before the first game of their senior season. In terms of that timetable, and in terms of the schedule, I think it is important to have some carryover here, so when you go back after the season, you have to deal with the mom and dad in this process. They want to know where they are in the process of their son going to college.

This past year, we had 25 scholarships to give. We had 23 of our scholarships committed on August 1, 2008. Relative to the process, the timetable has moved up in the commitment time frame.

I am not in favor of the timetable as it is now. It requires the colleges to put a ton of emphasis on May recruiting. That stinks for us. May recruiting is a noncontact period. That makes a difference in terms of contact and just bumping into another player. The head coaches are off the road. Head coaches cannot be there to see the kids. So when do we get a chance to see them? We get to see them in June at camp. I do not like it, and most of you would say it is not the best way to do it. Those camps in June are very important. Those are the times when they can come to your campus, where you get a chance to eyeball them.

Relative to the process, all I want to do is to get some information across. First, the coaches have a huge impact in the process. It does not require you to tell your player where to go to school. Players rely on the high school coach. The high school coach has been a mentor to the players. They trust the coach, and they want guidance from the coach in that process.

The second point is crucial, and that is the verbal commitment. When your players are ready to commit, ask them to write down what verbal commitment means. I am not trying to lecture you; I am telling you this as I see the system from my end of things. We all have seen so many verbal commitments where the players back out, and then they give another verbal commitment to someone else.

The final concern is the process. It has moved up so quickly; it happens right now. For example, we already have nine commitments for our 2010 class. Those are juniors today. This is how fast this process is moving, relative to junior evaluation. I am not sure that changes anything that you have been doing. At my end, from an informational standpoint, where do we move from here?

Next, I want to talk about leadership. Specifically, I want to discus building leadership within your ranks. I think I am qualified to talk on this subject. For the last two coaching jobs I have had, I did not recruit any of the players I had to play in my first year at those two schools. I had to deal with the players who were already on campus. It is similar to what the high school coach has to do. That is true at 9 out of 10 of the high schools. You have to deal with the kids who are there. You have to develop the players you have on your campus

Leadership to me is what we are all searching to find. We are trying to build leadership from coaches to every player within our ranks.

We have seven steps in building leadership. The first thing it starts with is character. I think everyone in this room would like their best player to be their captains. That is easy. When your best player has the character necessary to be captain, then you are in a very good situation. However, I want to prepare you for the situation when your best player does not have the necessary leadership skills, and you need to develop those skills. If we assume he has a God-given gift athletically and can be your best player, the high school coach can develop the leadership qualities necessary for that player.

It all starts with character. If he is the player you want to put out front as your captain, and you want to model him as your guy, think about his character. If he is a player who does not want to go to class, and does not make good decisions off the field, and he is a player who runs to the cone, but not through the cone and doing the little things right, it is going to be hard for him to handle things when they go wrong.

You can lead without character. However, it is hard for people to follow a person who does not have character. When it comes time for people to follow that person in tough situations, it is going to be tough for them if he does not have character. You can spin it any way you want, but they will not follow that type of person in tough times. To get the other people to follow, you start with character. It is: "walk the walk."

This all starts at the top. It starts with the head coach, then the assistant coaches, and it works its way through the entire football team. When we are talking about the foundation of leadership, it starts with character and developing those leadership traits.

The best way I can put it, relative to character, is just to picture your son in the locker room. Picture your son in the locker room, sitting next to the player we are discussing. What would you want your son to hear about expectations of character on a day-to-day basis? That is the best measuring stick for me. I have 11-, 8-, and 6-year-olds, and I try to remind myself of this. I ask myself this question. What would my son want to hear from me? What do I want my son to hear if he is in that locker room? I think it starts with character in terms of building leadership.

In our locker room, we have placed, in a very prominent area, displays for our players to remind them what character is. We have the traditional character traits that you would want your son to see on placards in our locker room.

The first placard is our "Bearcat Commandments." When you talk about expectations of character, the key is elimination of confusion. What I try to do on a day-to-day basis with 18- to 21-year-old players is to eliminate confusion. I want to be clear with my message. I want to be crystal clear with my message. What a better way to eliminate confusion than to have that model of Bearcat Commandments, than to have it on a placard in your locker room. By doing this, the players know exactly what you mean.

BEARCAT COMMANDMENTS

- *Treat women with respect.* Today, that is the number-one point in regard to how young men handle themselves on a day-to-day basis. The players have a mother, a sister, an aunt, or a grandmother, and they can identify with treating women with respect. If a player breaks one of these rules, they are done. If they break one of these commandments, they are not going to be a part of our program. We do not have a lot of commandments, but we do have some strong codes of conduct.

- *Do not steal.* When you walk into an environment—especially a group of men together, a unit—if you steal, you break trust. I have never found an individual who can overcome the situation if he has been involved in stealing within the group, or from a teammate.

- *Do not cheat.* Cheating is so contrary to what we teach on a day-to-day basis. If they cheat in a football drill, they are cheating themselves, and they are cheating their teammates. That is an area I find difficult to work with.

- *Do not lie.* Be a man about it. If you have made a mistake, be accountable for the mistake, but do not lie.

Those points are in our locker room. When we talk about leadership and character, they know what we are talking about.

I cannot put the best player out front if he has broken any of those commandments. Our players see those commandments in our locker room, and it is a model for them on a day-to-day basis.

Let me talk about our mission statement. This is what we are responsible for as coaches. This is what we do. I realize coaches are fired based on the number of wins and losses they produce. However, we are teachers and educators first. You must love to be around your players. That is the reason we are in this vocation. I have run out on the field as a high coach coach in front of 800 fans, and I have run out on the field in front of over 50,000 fans in the Orange Bowl. What motivates me every day is working with those young men and caring about them. That is what coaching is all about.

What are you responsible for as a coach? I believe I am responsible for these five areas in coaching in terms of developing our players and character:

- *Intellectual development:* They are going to high school and college. You must get them ready intellectually. You must hold them accountable for that.

- *Spiritual development:* You are responsible for their spiritual development in some fashion. They are all young men, trying to find themselves. I am not saying you must put a Bible in front of them every day. I am saying you must make available to them—through either Fellowship of Christian Athletes, or Bible study, or community service, or whatever—something that will allow them to develop spiritually.

- *Social development:* You need to make them accountable. You must make sure they learn right from wrong.

- *Skill development:* You are a football coach. Football coaches are responsible for the development of the players' skills.

- *Physical development:* Today, physical training is not just about weight training. Everyone has a great program when it comes to weight training. Everyone gets the weight training. Schools are on top of this aspect of the game. Players cannot be the best they can be unless they take care of their body. If they are not getting enough rest, or if they are staying up late, they are hurting their physical training. If you open the weight room at 6:00 a.m., and you have a ton of players there to work out, if they are staying up until 2:00 a.m., they are not going to be able to develop physically as they should. If they are eating pizza all of the time, they will not be as physical as they could be. If they are dehydrated, they will have problems as well. If they are drinking beer and smoking dope, they will have problems physically.

A player can only go so far. First, if they do take care of their body, the weight training does not matter. This is what I think you are responsible for, as a coach and as a teacher, with regard to the physical-development aspects. Our players see this as well. They understand this on a day-to-day basis.

We have a creed that we live by. Our guys understand it and rally around the creed. This is our creed:

> *The pride and tradition of Bearcat Football will not be left to the weak, the timid, or the noncommitted.*

I want players who want to win. I want players who want to come to work every day. I want players who are excited about the opportunity to play for the Bearcats.

We have a saying that kids use every day. When they come out to practice, we ask them this question. "What are you selling today?" We ask them if they are selling "tired hang dog"? "Are you selling 'I am not fired up today?'" We want to know what they are selling because I want players around me who are anxious and excited about the opportunity to play.

Our kids see this point every day. If a player comes out to practice, and he has his gloves strapped to his helmet, or has his shirt hanging out, and just mopes around, he is telling me that he is selling the fact that he is not ready to practice. He is unprepared to get better that day. That demeanor is something you can talk about every single day. This goes back to character, as far as I am concerned. You cannot lead until you have character. All of those points go to this topic in particular.

We talk about our culture with our players. We ask them this question: "Do you care?" I want players on our team who are passionate about playing the game. I want players who love the game and care about their teammates. They do not have to love all of their teammates. They do not have to go out with them or hang around them. However, they must care about each other because they are all in the game for the same reason.

They have to be committed at any level to be the best they can be. If they are not committed to football, they need to go play another sport.

There has to be a trust factor that is involved in all of this. That happens by building a relationship over a period. Trust must be there, relative to the coaching staff and the players. This is our Golden Rule: "Treat others the way you would like to be treated." Finally, we have accountability. Do the right thing all of the time.

When players walk into our locker room, they see those points on the placards. We do not have any confusion on these points. We are laying the groundwork for building leadership within your program. We all want our best player to be the leader in all of this. If your best players have character and they are out front leading the team, it creates an atmosphere that is very strong.

How do you get it started? Again, it starts with character. You eliminate confusion relative to character on a day-to-day basis.

The next area is what we call cohesion. Nothing brings cohesion and morale together better than having a "next man in" philosophy. This is what carried us this year at the University of Cincinnati. We played four quarterbacks this year. We played four different quarterbacks on a team that won 11 games. We could not have played those four quarterbacks if we had not had the "next man in" philosophy.

What is the "next man in" philosophy? A player is not starting the game. He has been validated to the level where he has been told he is not going to start the game, but he needs to be ready when his chance comes. He better be ready! Let me give you a great example of this.

There were very few issues in the weight room. In other words, there is no "first team" in the bench press. There is no "second team." Everyone is the same. They are rotating in groups. As a result, in the weight room, you have great morale because it is not about playing time. Everyone gets the same amount of time to do rep work. Everyone puts in the same amount of time.

We want to get that same atmosphere on all of the situations on a day-to-day basis. Very rarely do we tell the first team to do something while the second and third teams do something else. The second-team player knows when his opportunity

comes, he better be ready. As I said, we went through four quarterbacks this year. The only way you can do that is for the second, third, and fourth quarterbacks to get themselves ready. They knew that when their chance came, they were going to get that opportunity. They expected to go into the game and to perform at a high level. This is where we tell them they are a "back-up," but really, they are not a back-up.

This is a difficult scenario. It is tough to build that "next man in" concept. When you get that "next man in" philosophy, the synergy you get with everyone working together is incredible. We did this at the University of Cincinnati with a coaching staff that was all on the same page. I did not do this by myself. It has to be the entire staff, including the strength coach, and all of the assistants, and everyone has to be on the same page. That is how you get collaborative cohesion. That is how you get everyone together.

In high school coaching, you can only work with the players you have. You cannot trade them. You cannot cut them, and you cannot put them on a waiver wire because they are not starting. You must develop the players you have.

The one thing I do not want to hear in a staff meeting is what a player cannot do. I want to know what he can do. We want to get him into a position where he can help us. If he can play, we want to work to get him ready so that when his time comes, he can help us. That is "next man in" philosophy. It is having a positive approach with the players you have, and when they get in the game, they can help us. You must keep a high profile with them. When they get ready to go into the game, let them know it is their time to shine.

In the staff room, the coaches can cry about playing the fourth-team quarterback. However, we are not going to let our players know we are concerned about this fact. Collaborative cohesion is the "next man in" philosophy for us.

The other thing that is important to that cohesion is where we all stumble at times. It is the "weigh-in/buy-in" concept. Think of a staff meeting. To me, it is a limited democracy. I want people to weigh in, but I am going to make the decision. You cannot get everyone to buy in unless you weigh in. They must have some kind of impact and some type of message. You cannot get everyone pulling together unless you can weigh in.

We have a Unity Council, where the freshmen, sophomores, juniors, and seniors can weigh in on some issues. Not on everything, but on some things. To get them to buy into the things we are doing, they know they have a voice in what we are doing. The cohesion gives them a reason to buy into what we are doing.

It is very important to keep things exciting. We do not want things to go stale in our program. We want things to happen in our program that are exciting daily. We want something different to happen and to keep the energy level high.

The new culture, to me, is simply a standard of excellence. I talked about the philosophy of what you are selling. Morale is important. I think this is crucial to your players. If you allow them to dress sloppily, it will carry over to the practices. We do not allow our players to wear hats or jewelry in our meetings, or in any of the football buildings. They must have their shirts tucked in. When we are on the road, I want them to look sharp. Again, I want them to sell championship! I want them to sell success. That is what I am looking for from our players. Morale in terms of building character is very important.

The other point in building leadership is not necessarily based in a player, but in you as the head coach. It is not necessarily your opinion but your ability to get things done through other people. Getting in front of the team and stating, "It is my way or the highway" is not the answer. It is just another way of saying you must do things my way, which is saying there is only one way. Those days are leaving.

Leadership today is, to me, especially with the people at the top, that you better know what you are good at doing. That is first. Whatever you are good at doing, that strength must come out every day. If you are not a great speaker, you need to surround yourself with someone who is good at speaking to get your message across. If you are not good as an organizational type, then you need to hire someone who is good at organizing things. Therefore, in leadership today, at this level, it is important to know what you are good at doing. Again, you need to go to that every day. Another way to put it is this way: if you are a home-run hitter, hit home runs; if you are a singles hitter, stay with singles. Do not try to hit home runs if you are a single hitter.

The second part of the equation is the fact that today you cannot do it all. It is impossible. You need to hire people who can pick up on things that you do not do as well on a day-to-day basis. It is okay to let certain people know that some areas are not your strengths. Jeff Quinn has been with me for 18 years because he is the most organized person I know. That is a part of leadership in my background.

The head coach must be able to get things done through other people. You have to be able to communicate to others to get them to get things done that are important for you. You need someone who can get your ideas out to the troops. You have to send a message through others. To me, I have to get all of my coaches and all of my support staff to be working in the same direction as I am. If you have three different voices going on, you have problems. You need everyone to have a shared message from the one man who is in charge. This goes more to the head coach as a leader than it does to players.

You can go across the country and find that each of the Division I head coaches have different styles. All of them can be successful. Do what you do well! Whatever your strengths are, play to your strengths. You do not have to be like someone else. Their strengths are different from your strengths. Keep playing for those same themes. When that happens, you can develop a higher comfort level, and things will be easier for you.

Today, as a leader and a coach, you better be ready for change. Whatever that is, you better be ready to survive when that changes comes. When I talk to our staff about the book, Who Moved My Cheese? by Spencer Johnson, I ask them how we are going to survive. The book is about two mice and two little men that have to adapt to change in their lives. They have to find a new ways of doing things.

Today, we have to be ready for change at all times. We have to be on our toes, expecting something to happen, and we must be ready to act to change.

We always talk about being change-ready. We want to be ready for the change. We must be ready because it is going to happen. Sometimes, you make the change. Sometimes, it just happens. Just look at our economy today. Has it changed? Was anyone ready for the change in the economy? A very small percentage was ready for the change in the economy. I feel certain the powers-that-be will be ready for this situation the next time. They will have a plan in place to prevent the same situation. So we do need to prepare and be change-ready, especially in our business.

Leaders are no longer commanders, but maestros in visionary. I go back to coaches today. "Hey, this is the word." You must get everyone coming together. Developing your coaches is so crucial. You must bring the young coaches along so they are developing. If they are developing, they are going to do a better job teaching and coaching. Today, coaches are not commanders, and they must bring everyone together.

This does not mean your staff meeting must be eight hours long. I am not that way. However, there has to be a way to bring everyone together. It is not telling everyone to do it this way because I said so.

Today, with text messaging and e-mail, it is unbelievable what can take place. You can get a text message and ask, "What did they mean by that message?" There is so much miscommunication out there. It is important that good leadership have clarity in their messages.

We communicate with our players using the placards in our locker room. I am big on this method. We want them to know what our expectations are for them on a daily basis.

We have four plasma screens in our locker room. They are boards for information. They are not for ESPN. They are for getting information to our players each day. I think this is crucial for conveying what our expectations are each day.

In the last two jobs that I have been involved with, we did not know the guys very well, but we worked on it right away. We started working on all of these traits immediately so our players would know what to expect from us. In addition, this built great leadership and great morale within our organization.

If I could get all of you here today to walk away and be able to say, "I can get my team to play harder, and longer, than your team." How would that be? That would be cool. It would be the best clinic you every attended, right? If I could get my team to play harder and longer than the opponents, I am going to win a lot of football games.

Different playmakers can make a big difference; we all know that. If you can get your players playing harder and longer against the teams you play, you have a good chance of building a good program.

In the time I have left, I want to touch on things I have learned over my 18 years as a head coach. Offensively, you can keep so many different stats. You can keep total rushing yards, third-down conversions, and a lot of other stats. Here is what I know. I think this is universal, relative to offense, especially to the offense we run.

How do you score more points than the other team? As coaches, we often talk about the different systems we run in football. All of those systems are going to work, based upon your knowledge. Nevertheless, it is still about scoring points. How do you track scoring points? What is the measuring stick you use? Is it how many yards you pass for? I can give you a lot of examples that prove that passing yardage has no bearing on how many points you are going to score. Is it how many yards you rushed? I can give you stats that will show that rushing yardage is not going to measure up to winning.

I have only found one goal or stat that, over the last 18 years of coaching, is going to equal scoring more points. That is "big-chunk plays." Big-chunk plays are runs of 15 yards or more, and pass plays of 20 yards or more. The offensive coordinator may want to brag about the team's offensive stats. They may pass for 250 yards and run for 250 yards, but the defense cannot stop anyone. The offensive coordinator is not concerned about that as the offensive stats look like he is doing a great job. It is no big deal to him, but I am the head coach, and it is a big deal to me. I do not care what those stats look like. On offense, I care about scoring points, not stats. The only measuring stick I have for that is big-chunk plays.

When we count big-chunk plays, if we have five or more in a game, we have won 86 percent of our games. We know that five big-chunk plays give us a great chance to win. We also have to look at those big plays against our defense. If we gave up more than five big-chunk plays, our percentages went from 86 percent to 46 percent.

How do you get big-chunk plays? It would be easy if you had the perfect players. If you have better players, you have a chance to get big-chunk plays. So let's assume we are all equal when it comes to players. We know big-chunk plays make a difference. We know we must call plays that give you a chance to make big-chunk plays.

Number one, you have to call big-chunk plays. Second, you must coach it in the running game. Everyone wants to talk about our passing game. We had more of the big-chunk plays in the running game than in the passing game.

This is how we coach it. First, we sustain blocks on the offensive line with no one on the ground. You cannot have linemen on the ground if you expect to have big-chunk runs. We talk about our line sustaining blocks and staying on their feet. If you are on the ground, you cannot sustain a block. This is where we start in coaching the big-chunk plays.

The second element is effort on the perimeter. We need great effort on the perimeter. The wide receivers must block. If they do not give us great effort on the perimeter, we are not going to throw them the football. It has to work both ways. It is all about effort.

If I walked into your practice, I could start coaching your offense. I could tell if the line was staying on their feet on the blocks, and I could tell if the receivers were giving a great effort on the perimeter.

Finally, we want running backs who gain yards—after the first hit. We want backs who will give us great effort after that first hit. We are going to sustain our blocks on the line, we are going to give great effort on the perimeter, and we are going to teach our backs to give great effort after the first hit. He may be hit at the line, but if he can give great effort and get two additional yards, that is great. He is going to get that big-chunk play if he keeps giving great effort after that first hit. We judge our backs on productivity after the first hit.

We do not have to have a 4.3 back to make big plays. If we can do the three things we talked about, the defense better bring the back down at the line of scrimmage every time, or we are going to make some big-chunk plays. We are talking about big-chunk plays in the spread offense. It is really about the run game and getting those big-chunk plays. If you can get those plays into your offense, you can be successful. With the passing game and the running game, big-chunk plays give you a chance to win.

To me, it is less what the schemes are about in the passing game; it is more about getting those big-chunk runs. You can get that in any offensive structure. If you can get receivers to give effort, get linemen to sustain their blocks and stay off the ground, and you play backs who gain yards after the defense first makes contact, you can win football games and have success.

Thank you very much. It has been great being here.

THE ZONE READ OPTION GAME

University of Oregon

I am going to talk about our zone running game. The first part will be about the inside zone play and the second half hour will be on the outside zone play. We had an outstanding year this past year because we had good players. That is the bottom line to the success of our season. I think our coaches do an excellent job of putting those players into situations where they have an opportunity to be successful.

What you are entrusted to do as a coach is to create an environment where your players have a chance to be successful. I have not stepped over the white sideline and played in a game in about 20 years. You cannot play—the players have to be an extension of what you teach them. You have to create the environment and let them play.

I am a huge clinic football coach. I love clinics. I have gone to them all my life. The first clinic I attended, I listened to Joe Bugel talk about the counter trey. He talked about running the counter-trey pass with linemen pulling in both directions. I knew we could not run that play. If both the linemen were not pulling in the same direction, we could not do it.

You have to pick and choose things from a clinic that can fit into what you do. You cannot install schemes. I hope you can find something that I say today that can be adapted to what you do. If you are looking for a cure-all message, you will not find it here today.

I think you can take something out of my talk that you can apply to what you do. I do not think you take an entire offense or defense. I think you can take something that fits what you do and apply it to the players that you have.

This offense fits for us. This past season, we finished second in the country in rushing the football. We average 6.2 yards per carry. We have four running plays. We run the inside zone, outside zone, counter, and draw.

If you give your players something to hang their hats on, they will perform. If they can run the offense with any scenario they may face, you will be successful in running the ball. If they have all the answers to the problems the defense may give them, they will be good.

The best way to beat the team you are going to play is to have your team play with conviction. Are there any basketball coaches in here? The one thing I cannot understand about their sport occurs in the clutch stages of the game. With the game tied and five seconds left in the game, the coach calls a time-out. He picks up a whiteboard and draws a play. I do not know how long I would last in Eugene, Oregon if I did that.

If your players have not run that play in a critical situation over a thousand times in practice, you will not have a chance to be successful. With our inside zone play, we get so much practice time and so many reps that we can handle all the other scenarios that come about. Instead of trying to outscheme your opponent, put your players in an environment where they can be successful because they understand exactly what they have to do.

I am going to talk about the inside zone play. Paul Brown, the father of modern football, said, "If you can get your players to value the football, you will have a better player." If you tell players today to do something because I told you so, you will not reach them. We explain to our players why we do the things we do. That gives them a bit of ownership and they understand much more.

Why do we run the inside zone? The inside zone play is a great equalizer. We are double-teaming a defensive lineman with a mathematical idea behind it. We have four legs and he has two legs, so we win. The zone play can be run against multiple looks by the defense. You can draw this play up and run it against five different defenses.

The inside zone play is our "go to work" play. It has become our signature play. We want to get off the ball and be a physical, downhill-running football team. This is not a finesse play. We teach our offensive linemen a block we call the *bust block*. The idea is to bust their sternums up against their spines on every play. We want to come off the ball, create a double-team, knock the crap out of the defender, and deposit him in the linebacker's lap.

This is physical football. The offensive linemen play with confidence because they know they have help from their teammates in their blocking scheme. This play is great against blitzes and twists because we pick up blocks as they attack gaps.

This is the offense we run and everyone knows that. We have great players but we execute it well. We ran this play 202 times this past season. What I am going to talk about is what we do. We averaged about seven to eight yards per carry with this play.

PHILOSOPHY OF THE PLAY

- Physical, signature play
- Penetrates the front
- Distorts the defense
- Physical play in the double-teams

We tell our offensive guards and tackles or our centers and guards in their combinations, we want them to be butt-to-butt and cheek-to-cheek in their double-team. We want them handling the defender as if they were a bouncer in a bar throwing him out of the bar. They understand what type of force has to be implemented to throw a guy out of a bar.

In the basic concept of the play, the center must ID what we call the point. Our offensive line is going to block five playside defenders. If the defense aligns in a five-man box, it is an easy scheme. If the defense is a six-man box, the quarterback is responsible for the sixth man in the box. He reads the defender and controls him. The quarterback is blocking that defender. He cannot physically block him because that is a mismatch. What he does is run the ball if the defender attacks the running back. He makes the defender respect him as a runner and keeps him out of the play.

When the center IDs the play, he locates the 0 defender in the defensive scheme. People overcomplicate and spend time teaching defenses to the offensive line. We count defenders in our offensive scheme. We want to know if it is a 4-1, 4-2, 3-2, or 3-3 look. We are a spread team. If the defense covers the receiver, they cannot get too many more defenders in the box. If the offensive line can count to six, you have a shot to run this play.

When we coach our offensive line, we do not get into over, under, or stack fronts. You spend all your time in your meeting trying to explain all the fronts. A 4-1 look is a college 4-3 alignment, with the outside linebacker removed from the box. The 4-2 is four down linemen and two linebackers. The 3-2 is three down linemen and two linebackers. The 3-3 look is an odd stack defense with three down linemen and three linebackers. As long as the linemen can count, they do not need to know whether it is an over or under front—our rules will take care of that.

You need to have complementary plays with this play. We run the play-action pass and the naked bootleg. That keeps defenders from ganging up on the running game. That is not a revolutionary concept.

You can play with a tight end or a detached tight end. If he is tight, his rule is to block his playside gap. If the ball is going to the right, he blocks to the right. If we go to the left, he blocks to the left. His rule is to block #3. The tackle blocks the playside gap to #2, the guard has the playside gap to #1, and the center blocks 0, which is the point from where the count starts. The backside guard blocks the backside #1, and the backside tackle has the backside #2. If there is a #3 defender to the backside, the quarterback is responsible for that defender.

The center's rule for identifying the point is the defender assigned as the A-gap player to the side of the play (Diagram #1). With the tight end in the formation against a college 4-3 defense, the center identifies the Mike linebacker as the 0 defender. The 3 technique on the guard is the #1 defender. The rush end in the 7 technique is the #2 defender, and the Sam linebacker is the #3 defender. The nose in the backside A gap is the #1 defender backside. The Will linebacker is the #2 defender. The 5-technique defensive end is #3 and the quarterback's read.

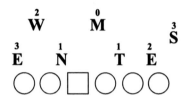

Diagram #1. Line Count vs. 4-3

In a 4-1 alignment with no tight end, the center makes the Mike linebacker the 0 defender and the linemen count from that designation. If we get a stack look, we get combination blocks between two linemen blocking in a zone-blocking scheme. In the odd 3-2 look, the count is simple (Diagram #2). The nose is the 0 point, and we count out with the linebackers as the #1. The defensive ends will be the #2. The outside linebackers will be the #3.

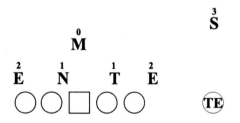

Diagram #2. Line Count vs. 3-2

If we run the zone play to the left, the center designates the nose as the 0 defender (Diagram #3). The Will linebacker is #1 and the guard blocks him. The defensive end is #2 and the offensive tackle blocks him. The Mike linebacker is #1 to the backside, the tackle is #2, and the defensive end is #3. The quarterback reads the defensive end coming off the right side.

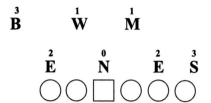

Diagram #3. Zone Play Left vs. 4-2

If we run the zone play to the right, the center designates the Mike linebacker as the 0 defender (Diagram #4). The right guard has the defensive tackle on his outside shoulder. The right tackle has the defensive end on the inside shoulder of the tight end. The backside guard blocks the nose, and the tackle blocks the backside linebacker. The defensive end to the left side is the read defender. If he bends down for the running back, the quarterback pulls the ball and runs out the backside. If the defensive end comes up the field, we run the zone play to the right. The tight end has the Sam linebacker.

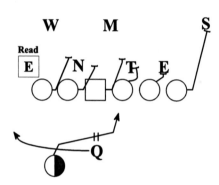

Diagram #4. Inside Zone Right vs. 4-2

If you spread a receiver to the outside, you must have the ability to throw the ball to him. That is the concept and basis of the spread offense. We spread the defense, so they will declare their defensive look for the offensive linemen. That makes it simple for us. The more offensive personnel we put in the box, the more defenders the defense will put in there and it becomes a cluttered mess.

I played quarterback in high school in New Hampshire. My high school coach was a prototypical crusty old football coach. He coached in work boots, Bermuda shorts, and a tank top. We ran an unbalanced, two-tight-end, power I formation. We averaged five passes a game. I threw a lot of touchdowns because there were 90 million defenders within three yards of the ball.

When I got out of college, I went back and coached for him. I told him, in college, we split players and threw the ball to them. He thought that was a bunch of college bull. I finally talked him into splitting a receiver. We ran it in practice. I split the receiver and no one on the defense went out to cover him. Since we had never been out of the power I, the defense thought the receiver was going to get a drink. I was so excited. I ran up to the head coach and told him no one was covering the receiver. He told me, *Good. Now, get him back in the box so he can block somebody.* I learned on that day, you have to throw the ball to the receiver so the defense will honor him.

If the defense walks the #3 defender to the backside out into coverage, the quarterback knows he is going to hand the ball off and there is no read.

If the defense is a 3-3 stack scheme, we designate the nose as the 0 defender (Diagram #5). It is like the 4-2 scheme because there are six defenders in the box. The alignment is not the same but it does not matter. The center and backside guard handle the center stack. The middle linebacker is the backside #1 defender. To the playside, the defensive end is the #1 defender and the stacked linebacker is #2. If the tight end is tight, he blocks the #3 defender who is the force player to his side. If he is detached, he has the same rule.

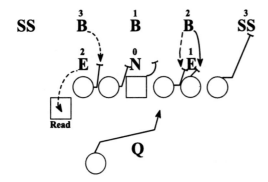

Diagram #5. 3-3 Stack

The backside tackle steps into his playside gap and takes whichever player comes into that gap. The quarterback reads the remaining defender for

his handoff key. This is a very simple concept. That is *what* we are doing in the zone scheme. The next part is the *how*, which is the mechanics of the play.

The depth of the quarterback is five yards from the line of scrimmage. His toes are at five yards. That is the starting point but it is more of a guideline than a rule. You have to adjust the alignment depending on the player. The running back's toes are at six-and-a-half yards. That also depends on the back.

We had Jonathan Stewart a couple of years ago and he played at seven yards. You do not want to slow a good back down. If the back is slower, move him up in his alignment. You can have the quarterback at four-and-a-half to five-and-a-half yards. The running back will be anywhere from five-and-a-half to seven yards off the line of scrimmage.

What you have to do, as the coach, is to figure out when the back is hitting the hole. If he is late to the hole, move his alignment up. If he is getting there too soon, back him up, but never try to slow down his speed to time up the play. Adjust his alignment.

I am a big fundamental coach. You must practice the shotgun snap with your quarterback and center every day. If you are not going to practice that, do not get into this type of set. It is not something you can do on Tuesday, use it in the game on Friday, and expect it to work. You have to spend a lot of time on the snap.

The quarterback has to catch the snap, but he cannot be a hundred percent focused on the ball. He has to see what the defense is doing. We think the right ratio is 75 percent on the ball and 25 percent on the defense. He has to be able to see both the ball and the defense. That is why we work so hard to perfect the skill. When we work on the snaps, I intentionally snap the ball bad to make him concentrate.

The quarterback gets in an athletic stance. I tell him he is like a shortstop in baseball. I have seen quarterbacks take the snap with their feet in a stagger. That looks good but he cannot move to either side as easily. In the square stance, he can move right or left with equal ease.

As he gets the snap, he drops his leg to the side of the ballcarrier. That allows the back to take a path to the attack area. We give the back the opportunity to run the same path every time he receivers the ball. We call it a *J-path*. The step looks like the letter J. The running back takes a slight open step with his playside foot. His second step replaces the spot where the quarterback's foot was. It may not be exactly where it was but it is close. On his third step, he starts to square his shoulders to the line of scrimmage. The running back takes his step and aims at the butt of the frontside guard.

The running back is responsible for the mesh. The quarterback is responsible for the read. If the quarterback is reading the defensive end and the running back is reading linebacker movement, the ball will be on the ground. It does not matter what type of play you run, someone has to be responsible for the mesh every time. If the ball ends up on the ground, it is because the running back and quarterback did not communicate enough.

Our players communicate the handoff mechanics on every single play in the game, in practice, on every down, and every day. They have to talk about the mesh and know what they are doing. The philosophy I have in coaching is: *If you accept it, expect it.* If they do not talk about what is going on with the handoff, expect the ball to be on the ground on Friday night. I will not accept mistakes in the handoff.

We do not always read the backside end. If we have someone to block the backside defensive end, the quarterback is responsible for the mesh. That lets the running back get his eyes up for his read on the defense. If the quarterback is responsible for the mesh, he tells the running back. He says, "Mesh, mesh." You have to get that fundamental down and if you do not, expect turnovers.

The second fundamental on this play is the fake when you do not have the ball. It is not a great play if the quarterback hands off to the running back and watches him run. Everyone in the stadium and on the defense knows who has the ball. The quarterback

has to accelerate off the disconnect in the mesh area. The action has to look the same whether he has the ball or not. That is a hard thing to coach. However, if you do not harp on it in practice, you are accepting what happens at practice and you can expect it to happen on Friday night.

The same rules apply to the running back. He cannot get the ball pulled and stop running. We grade the running back on his fakes. If he does not penetrate the line of scrimmage on his fake, he gets a loaf. It is important for the running back not to cut back in the direction of the quarterback when he is faking without the ball. If he does that, he brings the defense to the quarterback. We want them going the other way. He needs to stay frontside on the play when he does not have the ball. Obviously, when he has the ball, he runs to daylight.

That is the concept of the play. It has to look like it is hitting one way, and it has to go the other. You have to make the defense defend the entire field. You must not let the defense gang up on one aspect of the play.

We tell the running back to read the first down lineman to the playside. If he expands in the gap, the running back hits the gap. The philosophy of the play is a tough running play. If the line can get up two yards on the defense, the back can too. We want him to jam the ball into the hole and be a tough runner. We do not want a jingle-footed back trying to hit a home run. We want him to hit the ball into the line and get the tough yards. We are a blue-collar guy going to work. The line will have a hat on the five defenders in the box. The unblocked defenders on the perimeter are following the ballcarrier. If he gets downhill and runs hard, it is hard for them to make the tackle. However, if he jiggles in the hole, they will make the tackle.

When we talk to the back, we tell him it is speed *through* the hole, not speed to the hole. When the running back receives the ball, he is at 85-percent speed. As he gets the handoff and makes a decision to take the ball frontside or cut it back, he makes one cut. When he makes his cut to the line, he changes speeds and runs through the hole.

Vision is a big part of the success of this play. Our running backs coach, Gary Campbell, does a good job of that. He can paint pictures with words. He told the running backs it is like they are out on a Saturday night and see a good-looking girl. That girl is in the A gap and you are going for her. Before you decide to commit, scan the room and have a look at the girl over there. It is amazing how many cutbacks we got after he gave them that analogy. That is something they can practice in the off-season. They are going to jam the ball into the A gap unless they see something that is prettier.

On our double-team blocks, we tell the linemen to stay on the double-team until someone has control of the defender. We want to take care of the down linemen. Down linemen make tackles for losses. Linebackers dance around the pile and make tackles for two- to three-yard gains. We must secure the down lineman before we think about coming off on the linebacker. If the linebacker is within an arm's length of the block, he can come off. Never disengage from a double-team block and have to run to get to the linebacker.

This may sound like a contradiction, but we do not read anything. When you read, you become uncertain. We want the ball in the running back's hands. We do not want the quarterback carrying the ball. The option can put the ball in his hands, but the defense can force it out of his hands. We want the quarterback to give the ball unless he cannot. When you start to talk about the read player's shoulders or jersey number, you overcomplicate the play.

If the running back is continually getting tackled by the defensive end, the quarterback should be pulling the ball. The analogy is a 2-on-1 fast break. You tell the player with the ball to take it to the basket. If the defender commits, get rid of the ball. When we talk about this play, there are two ways to approach it. At a clinic, we say this is the zone read play. That is not what happens. This is a downhill play and the line is blocking for the running back, so give him the ball.

The outside zone play is a complement to the inside zone play. The inside zone is a hole-to-cutback play. The outside zone is a hole-to-bounce play. The reason we run the outside play is to circle the defense. When you get good at running the inside zone, the defenders begin to tighten their techniques and concentrate on squeezing the inside gaps.

If we feel that happening or we start to get many twists and blitzes on the inside, we run the outside zone play. It gives you speed in space, and the offensive line can play with confidence when you have something to change the focus of the defense. The outside zone is good against multiple looks. We ran the outside zone 122 times last season for 6.8 yards per carry. It is a good complement to the inside zone.

This is a pure zone play. The blocking rules for the offensive line are the same as the inside zone. The difference is the aiming point of the offensive linemen. The who we block is the same, but the how we block is the difference on the outside zone. The linemen take a kick-step to the outside and a karaoke crossover step to get up the field. The backside opens on the playside foot and loses ground. The farther you are from the point of attack, the more ground you can lose.

It is a stretch play, and the running back is the player who must catch up to the blocking scheme. This is not a cutback play. It is a cut-up play. If he can get the ball outside, he takes it to the corner. If he cannot get outside, he plants his foot in the ground and goes at a 90-degree angle running north and south.

This is a great play against two high safeties. The technique we use against the defenders is *rip and run*. We try to get to the outside shoulder. We run off the line of scrimmage and get into the defenders. If we have not reached them by the third step, we run them as far as we can. If the blocker reaches the defender on the third step, it piles up everyone coming behind that block. That creates a seam. It is like elephants on break. The thing we cannot allow is penetration.

We want to run off the ball and be physical. We are flatter to the line of scrimmage as we rip off the ball (Diagram #6). We adjust the path of the running back and the depth of the quarterback. We do not think the back can make the cut from the deep position. In this set, we want the back at about five yards and the quarterback at six yards. That allows the back to run the flat path to the outside. You see two distinct levels on the two plays. However, we run other plays using those depths. The alignment is something you cannot key.

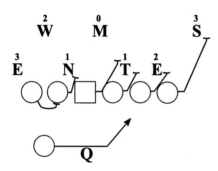

Diagram #6. Outside Zone vs. 4-2

If the defense is looking at the depth of the backs and trying to figure out what play is coming, they are thinking about the wrong thing. If that is the key, you will be fooled. My old high school coach told me a long time ago, "If your head is moving, your feet are not." That means if you are thinking about what to do, you are not doing it as fast. We also move the back and shift to different places in our formations. It is easy to disguise the alignment of the backs.

If the defense stops the play, it will not be because they read the setup of the backs. We have to put our players in the best position to make sure they are successful. The running back has to take at least two steps past the quarterback before we allow him to cut up.

I want to leave you with some things we try to do. Steve Greatwood is an unbelievable offensive line coach. I really believe he is the best offensive line coach in the country. Our offensive line leads the country in yards per carry and rushing touchdowns and we only run four plays in the running game. The offensive line plays with conviction. If you can keep it simple for the players in the offensive line so they have confidence going into a game, you have an opportunity to win the game. The five offensive linemen are the key to your football team.

I do not think anyone on our offensive line was offered a scholarship coming out of high school. I think the system we run helps our offensive linemen. The key is to make sure they know what they are doing. They are an impressive group of guys and they shop at True Value® Hardware for clothes. If you can get those players to play up to their potential, you have a good chance to win.

I know I went fast, but I hope you got something from this talk. Thank you very much.

BASIC TAMPA COVER 2 COACHING POINTS

University of Tennessee

Thank you. I want to briefly talk about some basic football philosophy. The first rule in getting better is to show up. It is the same in school as it is in football. You must go to class, and you must go to practice.

Coaching is teaching. You must be a great teacher to be a great coach. Back when I went to school, things were different. I was not a great student. I do not think we had requirements to get into college when I was in college. My IQ would probably be down low if you tested me. I did get through college. However, when I went to school, if you did not have good teachers and if you were not real smart, you majored in physical education or history. I wanted to play football, I wanted to play sports, and I wanted to be a coach someday.

If your teacher was good and could keep you interested, you may not cut classes as much. It is the same way in football. You have to teach if you are a football coach. Coordinators have to coach coaches. I like to go into their meetings to see what they are teaching. If you are the position coach, you have to teach the players.

You cannot just tell players to go make a tackle. You must teach them to tackle. I ask the coaches how they teach tackling. To play defense and to tackle, you have to bend your knees. You must get the arms up just like a boxer. In the NFL, we tackled once a week in practice. On Wednesdays, the linebackers tackled. On Thursdays, the defensive backs tackled. On Fridays, the defensive line tackled. Coaches have to show them how to tackle.

How do you play onegap football? You start out by getting into your stance. How do you pass rush? How do you get to the football? To accomplish this, we use the pursuit drills. We do this drill on the first day of practice. We start on the 35yard line. We

start out with the first team. We have a back on each sideline. We call, "Set, hike," and the defense must pursue to the sideline where the ball goes. They must pursue all the way to the goal line.

They must cross the line. We give them a thumbs-up or a thumbs-down. If they get a thumbs-down, they must do the drill over. If we give them thumbs-up, the next defense steps up. We run this drill three times. If they do not go full speed, everyone comes back and does it again. Everyone is accountable. It is not a big deal, but it is showing the players how to hustle.

When we grade the film on Monday, we have a session where we can discuss the game. We talk about missed tackles. We talk about turnovers. We break it down to the line, linebackers, and secondary. Everyone is accountable.

The next question is, do you really care about your players? In the NFL, there are a lot of good coaches. However, some coaches are not that good. There are more than you would think. There are a lot of good coaches that could become head coaches. To be a head football coach is an opportunity. Critics say certain assistants cannot become a head coach. I can give you several coaches that were assistants that were given a chance and they turned out great. Look at Woody Hayes, Joe Paterno, Bob Devaney, Bear Bryant, and Tom Osborne. It is all about getting the opportunity to become great. You have to give them a chance.

Do you really care? There are coaches that do not really care about their players. Don't be a phony. Don't think the young players cannot read through you. Players that are 17, 18, and 19 years of age believe in their coach. You must be tough and you must get on them at times. You must let them know you respect them and that you care for them. If you do that, they will respond to you. You must be tough on them, but you must let them know you care about them. If you are faking it and if you are a phony, you do not belong in this business. I cannot stand phony coaches. I get too fired up to be around them.

This is what I am talking about. We need to tell players what they need to hear, and not what they want to hear. You do not have to slap players in their faces, or get up in their faces to get their attention. If you are a good coach, this will come easy for you. You must let the players know you care about them. If you do that, they will do anything for you. They will run through a wall for you.

I have coached a lot of years in college and the NFL. I can tell you, it does not matter how much money they have or how much they are worth. In the NFL, the players make a lot of money and some of them are prima donnas. Not all of them, but there are some that are overpaid. I tell them this. In the NFL, players have a short career. I tell them to make each year count for them for the future. They are not like doctors, and lawyers, and coaches in the NFL. We can coach forever in the NFL. A person can be a doctor forever. However, the players can only play for so long, and then they must move on to something else.

There are so many great NFL players and coaches. I would not favor one over the others, but there are some special guys in the NFL.

Another important coaching point is *don't beat yourselves*. When we put on the game tape, we ask the questions: What are we doing? What are the corners doing? What is the linebacker doing? It is the same in college as in the pros. In all of these years in coaching in college and in the pros, more often than not, it was not that we were not in the right defense or that we did not call the right stunt, it was that the players beat themselves. At times, it was because we tried to put in a little too much for the player to do in a short time.

"On the field" is a very important area of discussion for coaches. When we say, "Take it to the grass," we mean you must be totally organized. Some coaches are great in the classroom. They can do everything nice and neat. They have everyone organized and the meetings are great. However, when they get on the grass, they are different. They do not get their drills going on time, and they just do not get much out of the drills for the players. Coaches cannot waste time on the practice field. They must cover the drills in the classroom, and then, when they get on the grass, they have to key the drills so everyone is moving on time.

In our coaching meeting with the assistants, I want the position coaches to show me how they are going to teach their drills and how they are going to teach the players what we are trying to accomplish. I want them to get up in the meetings and show me how they are going to present the information to the players.

I have a lot of good stories I could tell you, but I want to get back to football. I will tell you this story because I think it is interesting.

I decided to go to Knoxville and be the defensive coordinator at The University of Tennessee in early January. I thought I had been a good defensive coordinator in the NFL. When I told the owners that I was leaving for Tennessee, they asked me who would be a good coach to take my place. I told them Raheem Morris would do a good job. I told him now it was his time and he would do fine. They hired him to replace me as the defensive coordinator for the Bucs.

Two weeks later, Raheem Morris became the head coach of the Tampa Bay Bucs. I can assure you, he was in the right place at the right time. I thought I was a good defensive coach and did a good job. I told Raheem he would go down in history as the greatest defensive coordinator in the history of the NFL because he was unscored upon.

Let me get back to football. Take it too the grass. You need to be organized. You must have energy to coach on the field. Don't waste time on the practice field. Players need reps, so you have to keep them moving to get the reps. Players are going to feed off the coach. They are not going to feed off the opponent.

Every coach is different in this respect. Tony Dungy never raised his voice, but he could coach.

Tom Osborne could coach. I never heard him swear or belittle anyone. He was a great coach. Everyone is different. I have coached with some coaches that would get after their players. Regardless of how the head coach is, everyone must have the energy to keep the practice going at a fast pace. I do not think Tom Osborne slept for the 25 years he coached. You must coach within your personality, but you better have some energy.

I want to talk about quickness. Let's talk about high school players. I am back into that recruiting now. Do you know what I am looking for? I am looking for players that are quick. It is about the feet. The faster the 11 players you get on the field are, the better chance you have of winning. Tackle the player with the football before he gets across the goal line. The game is not that hard to figure out.

You must have commitment. If you have commitment, the fast players can get there quicker than the slow players. I love the big, fat players. However, if I have to make a choice, I will take the faster players. You need quickness to play football.

I love players that hustle. You have to have players that will hustle to the ball. You have to teach them how to hustle to the ball. What is hustle? It is not eight or nine players coming to the football. It is 11 players coming to the football. There are a lot of ways to teach hustle, and there are a lot of ways to get 11 players running to the football.

I will tell you what we do. We watch the films together as a team. We go over each play. If a player loafs on a play, we tell him about it. When we make a good play, we point it out. When the team can identify the good and the bad plays, they all know who is doing a good job. When we can get 11 players to the ball, that is hustle to us. That is what it is all about.

You must treat the second and third-team players the same as you treat the starters. If you do not treat them the same, you will lose those players, and they will not help you when you need them. Team unity is very important.

We have three things that we stress for the players. We say, "Play hard, play fast, and play together." If we can do those three things, we have a good chance to win.

I am going to talk about *Tampa #2 coverage*. I know most of you have played cover 2 before, and most of you understand it. Other teams called this Tampa #2 coverage because of our success in the Super Bowl and with the manner in which we played this defense. Teams have been playing cover 2 for a long time. However, they did not run the Mike linebacker down the middle. This is where teams get out of whack playing this defense. There are five or six ways to play cover 2.

We first started playing cover 2 when Tony Dungy and I were assistant coaches with the Minnesota Vikings. He had played some of this type of coverage in college at Pitt. I give Tony credit for the Tampa #2 coverage. It was the fact that we were coaching at Tampa Bay at the time and won a lot of games. As most everyone knows, Tony Dungy went with the Indianapolis Colts from Tampa.

The whole key is to take the Mike linebacker and tell him to run deep down the middle between the hash marks (Diagram #1). He is down the middle of the field and he is responsible for anything deep in that area. The Mike is no problem. The reason you play Tampa 2 is so the corners can reroute the wide receivers on the seam routes.

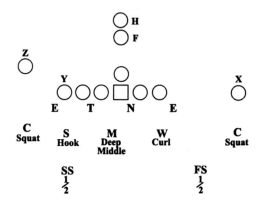

Diagram #1. Tampa Cover 2

The corners are playing up on the wideouts. The safeties are playing minus two yards on the pro numbers. In high school and college, they line up halfway between the numbers and the hash mark. That is approximately five yards. That is the safeties' landmark. He has to stay on the landmark, back up, and read the quarterback. That is the whole key. When the quarterback turns his head toward the receiver, we do not move from that spot until the ball leaves the hand of the quarterback. Some teams will tell you they go by reading the eyes of the quarterback. We get into trouble when we get off our landmark.

The Mike linebacker opens to the field as he gets depth. He does not want to get outside the hash mark. He opens to the field and retreats in the middle of the field.

If the corners do a good job of rerouting, you will be fine deep (Diagram #2). A lot of teams play their corners off and have them look inside for the run block. We look straight at the wide receivers. The corner has his outside leg splitting the feet of the receiver. We are four yards deep. We are going to reroute the receiver as he comes off the line of scrimmage. The receiver is coming at the corner on the snap of the ball. The corner cannot let him get up the boundary.

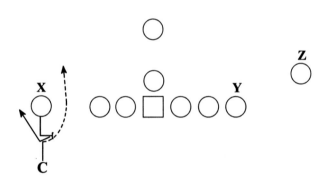

Diagram #2. Corner Redirect

Two things can happen. First, the receiver can flatten to the sideline. We tell the corner, when you sink, sink toward the boundary. There will be a hole between the safety and the sideline. You cannot reroute and sink back inside.

Second, the receiver can come inside and run a 7 route or a corner route. The corner lowers his hips and works back toward the sideline. You want to force the quarterback to put the ball over your head to the receiver. He keeps sinking until the second receiver shows up (Diagram #3). When the corner

sinks, he must be ready to cover the second receiver a little quicker.

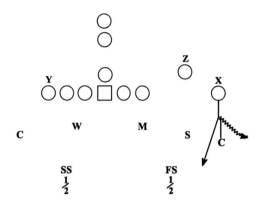

Diagram #3. Cover 2, Corner Sink

The safeties are on their landmarks. They drop 12 yards deep. Underneath players have the same responsibilities. The corner has the flat if the slot receiver goes to the sideline.

The question is how to stop the run with this defense. It is a seven-man front. If you have eight men in the box, you have a good chance of stopping the run. You must know what you are doing to get those eight men in the box. Make sure you have the defense set so you can adjust. I can tell you, cover 2 became a lot better when we had better players. When you are playing the eight-man front, know what you are doing. If you have a free safety coming to fill the slot, make sure he can spill the ball to the unblocked players.

If you are going to play cover 2, someone has to play the two gaps or you must run stunts. I will show you this later on the tape. We play 6, 3, 1, and a 5 technique on the front (Diagram #4).

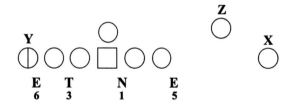

Diagram #4. Front Line Techniques

We play linebackers in techniques as well. The Sam is head-up on the tackle. Mike is head-up on the center. We call that a 10 set. That is against a 1x2 pro set. However, when we see the slot formation, the Sam moves outside on the slot. Now, we have our Mike and Will in our slot rules. They are stacked in stack A and stack B alignment (Diagram #5). The Sam backer is covering the seam area. The corner on the tight end side does not have to play cover 2. There is no need to. They have the slot to the other side. The tight end is not going to beat us on a deep route.

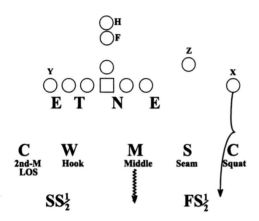

Diagram #5. Adjustment vs. Slot Set

I cannot believe how sophisticated the offenses are in high school today. Back when I was in high school, the quarterback did not run the ball. Now, they start working with the quarterbacks early and have them doing everything by the time they are in high school. High school coaches are doing a great job. Coaches teach the quarterbacks to zone read, and the quarterback can take advantage of the defense. They can run and they can pass. The kids today can do a lot with the ball.

I am going to show you some tape where you can see how the entire team is involved in the seven-man front defense.

One additional point I want to make about the defense. When we run a pirate, we make the ball go outside. We step up inside and force the play outside. Mike and Will spill the ball to the corner. The corners do not have to be physical, but they must be able to tackle. They must be able to reroute and they must be able to get off-tackles. You cannot let a wide receiver block a cornerback.

I have talked about the cover 2—let's see it on the film. I think you will get a better understanding of what we do when you see the film.

Coaching on all levels is all relative. If you are a good coach in high school, you can be a good coach in college or the pros. It is all relative. However, if you do not have a passion for coaching, it will be difficult for you at any level. The hard part about college coaching is the recruiting. Some coaches go from 9 or 10 o'clock in the morning until 10 o'clock at night working on recruiting. I want to work on football, not recruiting. I have an advantage at Tennessee in this because I know the head coach very well. I respect him as the head coach. Nevertheless, I can pick up the phone and tell him I need to work on football and I would rather not go recruiting that day. No, all jokes aside, we are going to have fun at Tennessee.

One point I do want to make. When you move from one school to another or from one job to another, always respect the people that coached there before you arrived. Tennessee has done a great job with their coaches. Phil Fulmer did a great job. They have only had two coaches there in 30 years. John Majors was there before Phil took over. John did a great job as well.

I can tell you that girls basketball is a big deal at Tennessee. They draw 18,000 fans to a girl's game. We had a chance to visit with the team recently. John Majors came back to visit with us and he had not been back to visit Tennessee in 17 years. But he came back and visited with us. I know Lane has a great opportunity to be the head coach at Tennessee and he is only 33 years old. I have a great opportunity to be at Tennessee.

I know there are a lot of good coaches here, and I hope you get an opportunity to coach at the next level. I can tell you that I love coaching. I even want to thank you for giving me the opportunity to speak with you. I thank all of you for coming to hear me talk. I am just happy to be coaching on any level.

I told you I had a lot of stories. I played at Nebraska for Coach Bob Devaney. I was a junior and we were playing Oklahoma on the Friday after Thanksgiving. That was 1962 and we beat Oklahoma, coached by Bud Wilkinson. That night, we went out and celebrated the win. I celebrated a little bit too much that night. I was suspended from playing in the bowl game. I was going into my senior year. Coach Devaney was a player's coach, but he was firm. I went to see him to get back on the team. He allowed me to come back on the team for my senior year. I went back, played my senior year, and had a good year and we went to another bowl game.

After I graduated from Nebraska, I tried out for the Minnesota Vikings. I made it all the way until the last cut. They shipped me to Canada to play in the CFL. For two years, I froze my butt off. We did not wear gloves, long-sleeved jerseys, or other things to keep warm. I cracked one knee playing in the CFL. I went back to Nebraska and became a G.A. for Coach Devaney. He taught me to give a player a second chance and I have tried to make the most of it.

I love you guys. I want to thank you for showing up. Best of luck next year.

SECONDARY COVERAGES AND TECHNIQUES

University of Richmond

I am pleased to be here. I want to start with what we did last year, a week after the national signing date. We had a new head coach, so we had a lot of work to do to get ready for spring ball. During our first two-and-a-half days, we did not meet about football. Our head coach brought in a psychologist, who works with companies to get them to perform better. He talked to us about what our identity was and what our mission statement should be, and it ended up becoming The Richmond Way. After we thought it out, we put it up on signs around the facility and on all of our playbooks. I would like to share that information with you.

THE RICHMOND WAY

It is five principles we thought we stood for. It was what we always went back to. I think it really helped us this year because, as you know, we ended up winning the whole thing. There were some trying moments along the way, but every time there was a trying moment, we just went back to doing what we thought we stood for.

First, the number-one goal of our program—for players, managers, trainers, coaches, and administrators—was for all of our players to graduate. Now, we have a 97 percent graduation rate at the University of Richmond. It is something the school takes a lot of pride in. We have great academic support, but one of the main reasons for that success is that we get kids to come to Richmond who are already motivated to succeed. You know, we take a lot of credit for kids who are already motivated in the classroom. Nevertheless, we are really proud to have a 97 percent graduation rate and a national championship.

Second, we expect all of our kids to be positive contributors to the university community and to the city of Richmond. Richmond is a different place. It is a small private school, and it costs fifty grand a year to go there, so sometimes the football players may feel like they are out of place there. One of the things we asked them to do to offset that was to involve themselves in other aspects of campus life, and they have bought into that. That is important for them, and it is really all about citizenship.

The third thing in The Richmond Way is to be a good teammate. We talked about this one for a long time, but we were all saying essentially the same thing. My father kept a plaque in his office that read: "It is amazing what can be accomplished when nobody cares who get the credit," and I think that sums it all up. That was the story of our football team this past year at Richmond. Be a good teammate.

Next, we want to treat everybody with dignity and respect. That is self-explanatory, so it is all we need to say. In the classroom, the cafeteria, and on the campus, there is a way to speak, act, and dress that shows respect for the dignity of other people.

Last, we will always prepare to win. Since the ball does not always bounce your way, you may not always win even when you have done your best, but you can always prepare to win. Do the thing you need to do to prepare yourself to win, and then you can expect to win realistically.

That may not sound like something that would take two-and-a-half days to come up with, but if you get 10 football coaches, a psychologist, and others associated with the program all together in one room, coming to a consensus takes some time. Actually, it was a productive session, and a great way for our head coach to take over.

We did have trying moments during the season. We started out ranked in the top five, but midway during the season we were 4-3. We lost a big rivalry game to James Madison University by seven points after being ahead by eight with just over a minute to play. That was a real tough loss for us. We are now 4-3, and no one is thinking about a national championship.

What we did was to go back to those five principles. That is what our head coach talked to our kids about. We did not panic. He told them to go to class, prepare to win, be good teammates, treat people with dignity and respect, and do all those other things, and just keep playing. The next week, we beat Massachusetts at their place, where they had won 26 in a row. We got on a roll, and we won nine in a row and the national championship.

I cannot really say how we did it. It was a bunch of kids who stuck to those principles. It was a quarterback who did not turn the ball over. In addition, it was a case of catching a break every time we needed one. It has not completely sunk in even yet, but it is a great feeling, and a great credit to our university, to our program, and especially to our kids.

Everybody has different ways of doing X's and O's, and they are all good. However, if your chemistry is not right, and you cannot keep your kids playing hard, none of it is going to work.

My topic today is on defensive backfield play, with emphasis on fundamentals and man techniques. I have some things here that we believe in about defensive back play and fundamental movements that are not real complicated.

FUNDAMENTALS

Basically, there are four things that happen in defensive back play, four movements that you have to have. You have to be able to backpedal, you have to be able to break out of your backpedal, you have to be able to track the ball in the air, and you have to finish your coverage with man technique.

We do not play a lot of real true man coverage all the time, but we do a lot of 1-on-1s. We feel, even playing zone coverage, you have to be able to relate to your man. A lot of times, man technique is how

you finish your zone coverage, close on your cushion, and break on the ball.

BACKPEDAL

We do not want to make it real complicated. First, you want to have a narrow base, have a steady chin and head, have a tight frame, and we want to have our shoulders leaning forward. Those are the keys to a good backpedal.

I do just about all of my individual drills on the lines of our practice field, and the width of the stripe is a great training tool. I get my guys' toes just outside the line on all the backpedal drills because when they are just straight backpedaling, we want their toes at that width. That is less than shoulder-width. It is a great training tool, and we do that a lot.

A lot of guys have a shoulder-width base when they backpedal, especially the further into the pedal they get, so I tell our guys that when they backpedal, they only need their universal stance base when they are going to strike a blow. Of course, they are not going to be striking a blow when they are backpedaling.

When you backpedal, you have to be able to backpedal at different speeds. We get a lot of young guys in our program who are going to be good players, but they can only backpedal fast. That can be a detriment to your skills because if you backpedal fast all the time and the receiver does not run off the ball fast, you are just creating your own cushion.

To correct that, we do this speed-and-easy drill every day. I start them pedaling on the line while I hold the ball in front of them. When I put the ball up, I want them to pedal with speed, and when I put the ball down, I want them to motor down. It is just those two commands: "Up! Down! Up! Down!."

Here are the things to look for in that drill. The shoulders tend to change when the speed changes. You want to make sure that chin stays on a level plane, so when you push them out fast, make sure the shoulders stay down.

In the change-of-speed drills, we are talking about shoulders and chin, but on the weave drills, we are talking about their base. We are going backwards for a reason. We are not going backwards to engage in any kind of contact, so I just push them off the line and weave them with a command. They will just pedal out and weave all the way from the sideline to the second hash, which is a long way to stay in a pedal. I want to make sure that every time they change direction, their feet come back down under the haunches of their buttocks.

That is why we do this drill for an extended period, because the further you go, the more likely it is that your base will widen where you change on a weave. When you change on a weave and the first foot steps out, you have to replace it with the opposite foot. As you weave, you have to replace your feet. Each time you change direction, that opposite foot has to come back down and get up under your haunches. If not, your feet will be shoulder width-apart when you are down the field and you cannot get out of a break.

We do a hip-flips drill as more of a warm-up. We just get them right on the line, pedal them, and do 180-degree flips. The big thing here in zone turns is to be able to maintain your vision on the quarterback and stay on the line. So, we warm up each day with the hip flips.

BREAK

Obviously, at some point in the play, we have to stop going backwards, and that is what we call a "break." That quick change-of-direction equals two quick steps, which we call plant and jab, and they have to be taken under the framework of the body. We use the command, "Plant! Jab!" with a loud voice inflection.

To stop, you have to get a plant foot down, and it has to land directly under your buttocks—bang! A lot of people talk about that plant a lot of different ways, where you "T it out,," or where you have to land on the ball of your foot, or whatever. I am not much interested in that approach so much as emphasizing that the foot has to come down right here under your butt. If it does not, it is not really a plant foot, and you will have to take another step to stop.

The jab step follows the plant step. It is a six-inch step in the direction you are headed. You stop, and you get going again. It is: "Plant, Bang! Jab, Bang!" We do not talk in terms of various angles coming off the plant foot; we just say to point the jab step where you are going. Again, all of this must be under the framework of the body.

Every day, we do line-cone drills, and I have them on tape for you later, where all we want to do is go 360 degrees around a series of cones for tight feet. As you come off of one cone and go to the next, you have to keep your feet tight. I will show you those drills in a minute, and you will get a better idea.

Here are some of the break drills we work on. The first one, "plant/jab and hold," we do not do it a lot, but we do it in the spring and during pre-season. We get them in a pedal, not fast, and then we just have them plant, jab, and hold it, hold it, hold it. After we check them, we blow a whistle, and they run it on out. They hold it and get it all loaded up. Then, we go the other way.

We will then go to a "box" drill, where we will get two plant-jabs. They just go back, up, and back, up, again, and some call it an M drill. Our kids are real smart, so they think it should be called a W drill.

I want to talk about the "post drive" drills a little bit, because they are huge. Basically, plant-jab refers to where I am coming downhill. I am on top of the receiver, and he is running something in front of me. Now, post drives, speed turns, and 180-degree turns are on deeper stuff. I have kept my cushion, I have pushed out of there, bang, bang, bang, and now he is going somewhere. I have to be able to relate to that route.

We teach the post drive just about like we do a plant-jab. We are in our pedal, he goes to the post, and we put a foot in the ground, jab right here, turn and run with it, stay on top of it, and control it. We work on post drives every day. That is easy.

It is what comes off the post that makes the difference. This is especially true at the corner spot, between a good one and a great one. What comes off the post stem, where a receiver pushes you off the ball and gets to his post takeoff landmark, can be any number of routes, including the curl, the dig, or the double move to the outside.

In route recognition on an inside stem and a push vertical, there is a point where that route is going to either turn into a curl, a dig, a post, or our very favorite, the double move, or post corner. What I am getting at is how to handle each of those routes, because those are the hard ones to cover.

We work three different drills to teach how we finish off of the post drive. They are all on tape, but I want to briefly go through them now. First, we pedal and run over the top of an imaginary post. That is the easy one.

Then, we pedal and go "post to curl." We push him inside, plant, and then it is straight back at him. Now, we do not do these drills on routes, but we do them on air every day. That is called "post to curl."

Next, we go "post to dig." We pedal, do our post drive, stick our foot in the ground, and go get the dig at 90 degrees through the upfield shoulder.

The third drill is called "speed turn," and we work it against the double move. The biggest thing here is where the eyes go coming off the turn. When the receiver tries to sell me on the post, I run with the post, and I am in position to dig out the dig or attack the curl. Then, all of a sudden, he puts his inside foot in the ground and breaks back outside.

The best way out of that is the speed turn, and kids have a tendency on that to look back for the ball. We do not want that. We want them to find the receiver and forget about the ball. We try to put a scout-team player out there for the drill and have him move around. Then, when we come out of our speed turn, we have to locate him. He might be here, he might there, or he might be wherever. But there is no way we will cover the double move if we are trying to locate the ball. The eyes are critical to success.

We are going through route progressions here. We have broken downhill, and we have covered the post and all the inside stuff. Now, I want to cover the outside go routes, which is the outside vertical routes. How do you cover them?

For us, it is a 180-degree turn. I pedal with whatever leverage the coverage calls for, and I realize that the receiver is running an outside go route. Obviously, in man, we are going to teach him to man turn, but how you do that is critical. When he breaks my cushion, I want to turn 180 degrees like I am running a track meet. I want to point my nose at the end zone. Now, I am running with him, and then I can cut him off.

If I turn less than 180 degrees and just point my nose at the receiver, he is already going full speed, and he can go right by me. In my opinion, to stay on top of the go route, I have to pull that arm through 180 degrees, get myself running, and then find him. We do what we call a "180-degree breaks" drill, and we just do it on the sideline.

MAN PROGRESSION

Most of what I have covered so far, except for the man turn on the go route, has been kind of general defensive back movements. They absolutely come into play in man-to-man, but they come into play just as much in zone.

I want to discuss some specific man-to-man concepts that we work on. I have developed these over the years. We do a three-step drill, and we do a stem drill.

This is the three-step drill, and it is the best drill I know of (Diagram #1). Everybody is throwing three steps out of the gun now. It is easier to defend from under center, but it is doable out of the gun. We have a line, we service ourselves with a wide receiver, we have a defensive back, and we have a quarterback. The defensive back is 1x6 yards on the inside, and at seven yards. I have two cones that are about five yards apart. The inside cone represents the slant, and the outside cone represents the speed-out. The coach stands behind the defensive backs.

The quarterback is critical in this drill, and I will talk about it under center first. He is going to be our read. This drill has huge carryover to our quarter zone coverage, but we do it as a man drill. Anyway,

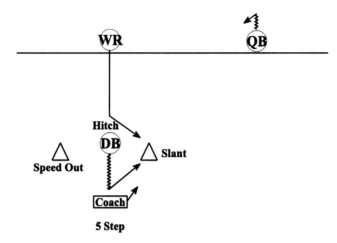

Diagram #1. Three-Step Drill

the ball is never leaving the quarterback's hands, so we get a ton of reps. I will stand back here as a coach, and there are four commands.

First, I will point at the inside cone. I am simulating slant and the quarterback knows that is three-step. Next, I will point at the outside cone, and that represents the out route. On the third command, I will give him a fist, and that means he is going to run in between the two cones, which represents the hitch. So we have the slant, the hitch, and the out, which are all three-step routes. If I give a five sign, the quarterback takes a five-step drop, and the receiver is just going to run straight.

We teach our guys to read the three-step on the quarterback's second step when he is under center. The second step is the difference. If he is throwing a three-step drop, the second step will be shorter because he is loading up to throw to a spot. If it were five steps, the second step would be bigger because the quarterback is trying to separate himself from the line of scrimmage. Anyway, whatever he is doing with his feet, the ball is locked and loaded on the three-step. It will be high and tight. I believe you can see the second step, and I know you can see the ball.

Here is what I want. If I point to the slant, the receiver pushes inside and runs to the outside of the cone. The defensive back has his eyes inside, reading the three-step. He has to see both the receiver and the quarterback, and when the quarterback sits down, he has to beat the receiver to the cone. He goes plant-jab to the inside of the cone to avoid a collision, plus that is the landmark to take on the slant read.

I have a line of defensive backs ready to go and a line of scout-team kids running the routes. We get the next guy in, and I give the next command. In three minutes, we can get 20 reps. The defensive back always goes to the inside of the cone and the wide receivers to the outside of the cones. The ball is never in the air.

Next, I will give a fist command, and the receiver runs a hitch. I see it and drive on it. The coaching point on the hitch is to always drive to the receiver's outside shoulder, in case the route turns into a hitch-and-go. I do work the hitch and go into the drill sometimes. We just collision it and run with it.

The last command is the five sign. This is big because it trains their eyes. If we are playing true man coverage, once the ball transitions to the three-step, we want their eyes to go from the quarterback to the receiver. So, the quarterback gives a five-step read on the five sign, and I want the receiver just trucking. All I want to see is the defensive back to pedal, recognize the five-step, and go from an easy pedal to a speed pedal as he does in those everyday drills. He will only take it about six or seven yards.

Now, we are training their eyes and the speed of their pedal. We play about seven yards off, so we can afford to come out of there easy while we read the three-step. The drill teaches them not to create their own separation by getting to the speed pedal too early. It is a great drill and we try to get it in three or four minutes every day.

The other man-specific drill we do is the "stem" drill (Diagram #2). We are talking about all five-step routes now. This drill also has some zone carryover. Okay, here is my line, and here is my wide receiver. Now, I will take the two cones back from seven yards and put them down here at 12 to 15, depending on what I feel like working on that day. We are down the field with these cones, and they are about 10 yards apart now.

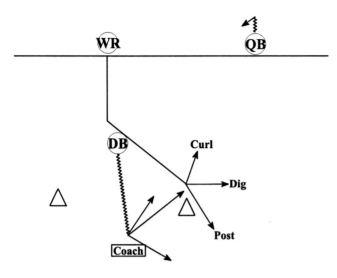

Diagram #2. Stem Drill

We do not need the quarterback anymore. We have already said it is a five-step route, so my eyes are on the receiver now. I have already touched on this, but we are going to push three things on the inside. We will come off straight, then push to the inside cone and either run curl, dig, or post. There is no ball in this drill, either.

We will pedal and maintain inside leverage. We will drive the curl, drive the dig, and get over top of the post. A couple of things can happen on the post. Most of the time, he maintains inside leverage, recognizes post, and fits in on the upfield shoulder as he should. Sometimes, though, if he is doing a real good job of protecting his inside leverage, the post route may actually go behind him. You have to teach that like a zone turn and run with it. We would get as much depth as possible and keep him from topping us and going vertical.

We work on two routes on the outside stem. We will push it, and we work on the deep comeback and the go route. We will push it, maintain inside leverage, and weave. If it is the deep comeback, we will plant-jab and attack the upfield shoulder. If it is the go route, we are big believers that we go 180 degrees, run, and cut him off.

Those are the main two drills we do that are man-specific, but as I said, they have zone carryover. Now, I want to show you some of our ball drills. Then, I want to run some tape for you.

BALL DRILLS

The first drill is the shoulder-to-shoulder combat drill (Diagram #3). We have the coach, and we put two defensive backs out in front who are shoulder to shoulder. We do not use a cone. We just pedal them, pedal them, and then the coach gives a shoulder key to the inside. They will plant-jab 45 degrees downhill. The inside man becomes the receiver, and the outside man becomes the defensive back. The defensive back tries to undercut the route, while the coach tries to stick it in there to the receiver.

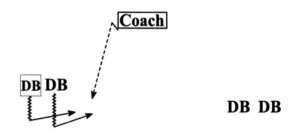

Diagram #3. Shoulder-to-Shoulder Combat Drill

We will have two more kids waiting, and we will go to the other side with the drill. We will do it that way, and we will do it on the out routes. On the out routes, they will break at 90 degrees. We should definitely undercut that. You cannot always undercut the downhill one, so it is fine to secure the upfield shoulder and just hold on. Generally, we will secure and rip inside on the curl and secure and rip outside on the out route.

The zone turn drills can be tough on the corners, particularly the bottom-of-fade drill and the comeback drill. The overhead fish drill is also a tough one.

When we talk about a zone turn against a fade type of route, we are going to pedal, zone turn, try to box the receiver out, and rebound the ball like in basketball. That is what we do in the bottom-of-fade drill.

In the comeback drill, we are pedaling, we zone turn, and that guy sits down outside on us. We have to get a foot in the ground, come back, and try to secure that. It is tough.

Now, the fish drill is the one I really like. This is where we all look silly coaching defensive backs. This is when the ball gets in over our heads on a real good throw. The receiver runs his takeoff, and I am zone turning. If I can go up and rebound the ball, I look like an All-American, but it does not always happen.

The ball is going to get in over my head, and I cannot get it with two hands. The ball is where I cannot rebound it. I have to make a man turn and try to pull his intentions down. I am in trouble, but I am going to try to do something to get the ball out. I will probably end up flopping around like a fish on dry land, but at least I will get the tackle.

Let me see if I can get the video going, and we will look at some of those drills. Thank you for your attention. If we can do anything for you at the University of Richmond, just let me know.

PUNT GAME PROTECTION AND COVER SCHEMES

Northwestern University

I do not know how many of you have seen us play, but we are probably as different as you can imagine. I will go over the reasons we are a spread punt team.

First, we are a four-wide punt team. We have four gunners outside. It mirrors the philosophy of our offense, in that we are trying to spread the defense out. We are trying to create as much space as possible. We are trying to force the punt-return team to show their hand as much as possible.

We are a three-man shield with the four wide. We have a snapper and two guards on the line with the four bullets. We call them the two wings, and the personal protector. Because we use a man-blocking scheme at times, we are going to need that shield to pick up a blocker when the guys up front miss.

We are a man-protecting team. It allows us to be solid on certain players. It allows us to jump them at the line of scrimmage. Also, those protectors can get out into the coverage as well.

We do a traditional punt, which we call zero. This is where the punter kicks the ball down the middle of the field over the center's butt. We will also rugby punt out of that set as well. We can run it either way. We are doing what most teams do on the punt. We are pointing to the defense, and we are counting out loud across the line.

The next thing we do with our punting game is what we call formation variation (Diagram #1). We move players up on the line, take them off the line, and move them around. We will give you between three and four different formations for our punts in a single game. Yet our rules on our blocking scheme stay the same. While we are giving you four different looks, we are only doing one thing with our

kids. You have to practice four or five different things to get ready for us.

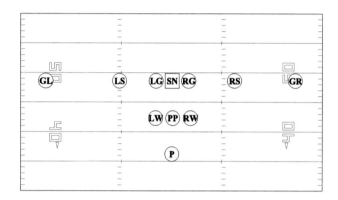

Diagram #1. Basic Spread Punt Formation— Middle of the Field

This is the reason we went to this formation. We see several advantages in using this system.

PRIDE ADVANTAGES

- Four skill players covering
- Multiple formations
- Different for teams to prepare for
- Multiple fake options
- Reduces rush looks
- Spray the ball around
- Creates chances for turnovers
- Sky situations

The fact that we can rugby punt from this formation was a big deal for us. The rugby kick, where the ball rolls on the ground, reduces the chances for returns. Two years ago, our net punt average went up 5.5 yards, and last year it went up another 4.5 yards. It gave us the ability to get the ball down the field to gain better field position.

Let me talk about some of the formation variations we have used. We started with the 2x2 look. Next, we went with the 3x1 look (Diagram #2). We felt if we going to the rugby kick with two gunners, we could rugby kick with three gunners and that would be better. Now, we have three men on the left side as we are trying to directionally kick to our left.

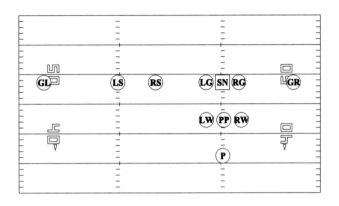

Diagram #2. 3x1 Formation, Right to Left

We called the play lake, and it meant a 3x1 formation, kicking from the right hash to the left side of the field. Next, we went with the formation to the left hash and put the three men to the right side (Diagram #3). Now, we could still rugby to the left side because our kicker was a left-footed kicker. You can kick the ball to either side of the field with this formation.

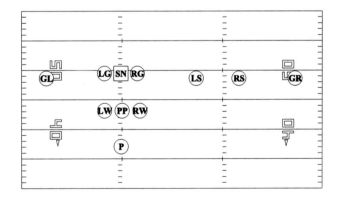

Diagram #3. 3x1 Formation, Left to Right

As we saw that defenses were not respecting us on the pass from the punt formation, we made a few changes to make them respect the pass. We move the right wing up on the line, and moved the right sniper to the slot, and made him eligible for a pass (Diagram #4). We snapped the ball to the personal protector, and he threw the bubble screen to the right sniper.

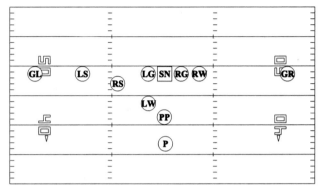

Diagram #4. 3x1 Formation Pass Threat

To change up the coverage, we came up with a new way to cover the punts. We put the right sniper in motion and had him go to the ball (Diagram #5). We had the ability to move our players around to prevent the defenders from pressing our best players on coverage.

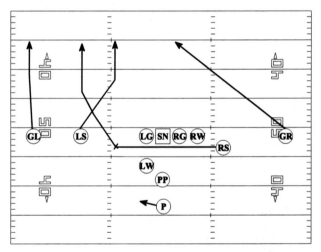

Diagram #5. 2x2 Motion, Left to Right

We wanted to be able to rugby kick even though we were on the left hash. We put our right wing on the line again. We took the left sniper off the ball and stack him on the right side behind the right sniper and the right gunner (Diagram #6). Before the snap, we put the left sniper in motion. We do not have to worry about an inside defender coming off on our gunner. We move them off the line of scrimmage and make them eligible for the pass. We have shown you another formation with motion that you must defend.

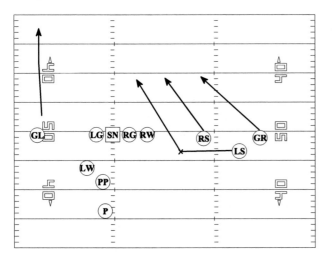

Diagram #6. 1x3 LS Motion Left

One advantage I did not list is the fact we are changing the kick point when we rugby kick. In most regular-type kicks when a team punts, there is a set kick point. In this kick, we are moving the kick point three or four yards. With the rugby punt, we are changing the kick point all of the time.

Let me talk about the players we use on our punt teams. I want big and fast players on the punt teams. For the four gunners, we use our fastest and most skilled players. If I had my choice of who I wanted on this team, I would want an aggressive wide receiver. The reason I say this is because these players work every day getting off the press and getting down the field. Some coaches like defensive backs in these positions because they are used to running people down and making the tackle. I want players who can get off the press.

The three guys up on the line with the ball line up this way. The guards have a one-foot split from the foot of the long snapper. It is not a big split at all. As they get into their stance, we try to cheat them back off the line of scrimmage as much as we can. The rule is that the helmet of the guard must break the hip of the long snapper.

Our wings are back to protect the punter. This is our three-man shield. On the three deep men, we use tight ends and fullbacks. We want the more athletic players in these positions. In addition, we

want those players to be able to catch the ball on the fake punt. They all have eligible numbers.

We want them to be able to square up their base stance as much as possible. We can go out after the man, so we wanted to be as square as possible in case we did want to jump outside. We wanted at least a toe-to-instep relationship with those guards. Inside foot up, with the outside foot at least up to the instep of the other foot.

Our deep wings line up 7.5 yards deep. We did change it up during the year. The inside foot could split the stance of the guard in front of them, or they could stack on the outside foot of the guard.

Here is what we tell our players on their coverage:

- Snipers: Inside to the ball always.
- Gunners/outside squeeze players: Keep the ball two to three yards on the inside shoulder.
- Guards/bracket players: Keep the ball four to five yards to the inside shoulder.
- Long snapper: To the ball.
- Wings/contain players: Outside of widest blocker.
- Personal protector/linebacker player: Mirror at second level, inside/out to the ball.
- Punter: Goes to the area based on the game plan.

The reason we want our deep wings at 7.5 yards is because the kick point for our short-body-type punter was at nine yards. We ask the wings to make contact at seven yards. We put the one half yard in for them so they could step into the rushing defenders. We want them to step up and deliver a blow instead of receiving the blow.

The punter lines up between 13 and 15 yards. It all depends on how big he is, and where his kick point will be. For us, we lined up at 13.5 yards, with the kick point at nine yards. This is for a two-step punter.

We do place the personal protector back behind the left wing. He protects the kicking foot of the kicker on the punt. After the snap is made, he steps up into the opening and protects to the side of the kick foot of the punter. The reason for this is when we rugby punt and go to the left, we want the personal protector to stay square shoulders the entire time of the rugby punt. On the traditional punt, the personal protector steps up into the opening and protects the kick leg of the punter. It is important for the personal protector to step up into the opening and not just hop up half a step. We want him up in the opening so the punt will clear him, and so he can block the man without backing into the punter. We want him to step up into the shield.

If we were punting from the middle of the field, this is how we would line up. The gunners would line up by splitting the difference between the hash mark and the numbers on the field. The outer swingmen split the difference between the offensive guard and the outside gunner. This puts them about two yards inside the hash mark.

If we are on the left hash mark, I have him on the outside top of the numbers. Our inside men split the difference between the two gunners. We put our smart players on the outside because they have to learn the rules. The inside men just have to learn to split the difference. It goes back to the old adage, "The closer you get to the ball, the smarter you have to be."

Let me talk about multiple formation in our punting game. By the time you see our scouting report, you are going to find you have four or five different formations to prepare for. Our punt teams get two days to go over the punt information. They have two days to prepare for five or six formations. It is different for them to prepare for our punt game.

We have eight different players that can be eligible for a pass on a fake punt situation. We know we can only have six eligible players at one time. If you are a punt return coach, how much time are you going to spend on defending the play from a punt formation? You are going to spend your time on defending the fake punt instead of working on the return punt.

We punted the ball 62 times. We had two guards and a snapper in the front group to block, and we have two wings and a personal protector to block. We have six men to protect the punter. We saw a six-man defensive rush five times last year out of those 62 punts. We reduce the rush look with this formation. Most of the time, the opponents want you to kick the ball so they can get their offense on the field.

If a team brings seven on the rush, we can adjust the blocking up front and block them. Since we have shown we can block seven, we never see it now.

We can spread the ball around. We are going to rugby punt, we are going to kick it down the middle, and we are going to directional punt. We are going to give you as few chances as possible to return the punt. You do not want some of the return men in the Big Ten touching the football. We want to keep the ball out of their hands as best as possible.

Of the 62 punts last year, 25 percent were returned against us. That means we eliminated 75 percent of our punts from being returned against us.

Many times when we use the rugby punter, we tell him to hit the ground with the ball 25 yards down the field. We want the ball to hit the ground and roll. He is not trying to boom the ball down the field. However, there are certain situations where he will boom the ball down the field. At times, he is trying to get the ball to roll on the ground after he kicks it 25 to 30 yards. When he kicks toward the short guys on the return, he is kicking ball into four players. At times, the ball has hit the opposing players. Teams want to get away from the ball that is bouncing down the field.

The sky situation is what we call our "pooch" punt. We have four men going down the field to try to down the ball for us. It is a big advantage for us. This year we had 16 "sky" punts, and we downed 12 punts inside the opponent's 15-yard line. We had only one touchback, and we had three shanks of short kicks. When we call "sky," we are going to punt the ball high and straight down the middle.

The first point we must consider is the ability of the punter to rugby kick. Can he do it? It is more difficult than you think. To kick the ball while you are moving takes some hand-and-eye coordination. So we must find out if our punter can make the rugby kick and if he can control where the ball is going. The rugby punt does not stay in the air for 4.5 seconds as a regular punt may stay in the air. The rugby kick stays in the air for about 2.5 seconds. If the kicker pulls the ball back inside, where you do not have coverage, it can end up in a touchdown in a hurry. So it is important to understand if your punter has the ability to rugby kick and place the ball where you want it to go.

When the defense is bringing six rushers, we must be able to block them. The long snapper must be able to block man-to-man. Again, the question is: can he do it?

The third consideration is punting when you are back deep near your own goal line. Another way to put that for us is KTW: kick to win. All you have to do is to get the punt away and the game is pretty much over. What are you go to do if you are backed up kicking from your minus-two-yard line? Are you going to change personnel? Are you going to stay with that same punt formation?

This is how we do it. When we are backed up, we keep our same personnel, but we do change our formation somewhat. When we go KTW, we totally change our personnel groupings and totally change our punt.

Next, I want to talk about our guards' protection techniques. We are going to be in a man-blocking scheme. It allows us to be aggressive and physical with rushers

Next, I want to talk about the inside-three protection mindset. This is the inside three men. We are trying to stop a vertical charge by a head-up or by an inside rusher. We do not want the defender to be able to vertically charge up the field. We want to jump him early, and run our feet, and stop him at the line.

With an outside rusher, we want to physically redirect him off of his original course (Diagram #7). We are trying to stop the vertical charge on the inside rushers, and we are trying to widen the vertical charge on the outside rushers.

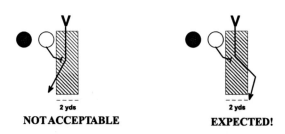

Diagram #7. Physical Redirect Rusher

Their technique against an inside rusher, or a head-up, or tight outside rusher is to jump them right at the line of scrimmage. Obviously, the first thing we want to protect is our inside gap. We are going to jump them at the line of scrimmage and run our feet.

Our technique against the wide outside rush is a vertical set keeping inside relationship to rusher. We want to keep the shoulders square as long as possible. We attack inside numbers with the outside hand, then punch with the inside hand. We run our feet to physically red-direct the rusher.

We tell the blockers up front when they make a redirect block, they need to knock the rusher two yards off his course. If you let him stay in the two-yard rectangle, you have not done a good job of redirecting the rusher. We want to force the rusher outside so we can create width for the punter.

The long snapper's technique is to hold his man up at the line of scrimmage. We have him grab the jersey if he has to, but we do not want him to come free. We hold the rusher if necessary, and seldom do the officials call it.

Let me talk about the personal protector and the wing. These are the shield protection techniques. What are those three players trying to do? What is their mindset? The first thing we must teach those three men is patience. Do not chase a rusher outside. Protect the kick point. Make the rushers go to the outside. Do not let them go over the top. The most important thing they do is to protect the kick point. If their rusher is running crazy up the field, the question is: does he have a chance to get to the kick point? If he does not have a chance to get to the kick point, he does not take that man. That is the most important thing you have to teach those men.

We used to tell the wings to keep the inside foot nailed to the grass. What I wanted was for the blocker to stay at home and not chase the pass rusher outside. I will remove the part about nailing the foot to the grass the next time I cover this technique. He is to attack the inside number with a short jab step. Force the punt rusher outside. Once again, that goes back to the point of protecting the kick point.

The personal protector is to stay square on the inside rush. He must cover the rusher up with his feet. He cannot take a side. He needs to step to contact and do not accept the blow. Against a jumper, he uses the midpoint punch and gets the hands down.

Let me get to the film. If you have questions, let me hear you. We have several examples of each formation.

When we are rugby punting and we are on the hash mark, and we are going to kick in that direction, we tell the punter the ball must be kicked outside the hash mark. If we are in the middle of the field, and we are kicking toward the hash, the ideal position is to split the difference between the hash mark and the numbers on the field. If we are on the near hash and we are rugby kicking in that direction, we tell the kicker it must be outside the numbers or out-of-bounds.

This punting game phase of our special teams has been good for us. It has eliminated a lot of the rush looks, and we have been more productive. We have eliminated a lot of good backs from getting their hands on the ball when we punt.

Thank you.

COACHING POINTS FOR OFFENSIVE LINEMEN

Former NFL Coach

Thank you very much. I want you guys to come on in and sit down because I am going to give you your money's worth. Get up close because everything is going to be demonstration. First, thanks for having me. Everything I know, I learned from someone else. I stole everything, and once in awhile I might have come up with something small.

What I am going to do is spend 45 minutes on run blocking and 45 minutes on pass blocking. When I was a younger coach, I was jealous of some of the other coaches. They would go to the Super Bowl, and I hoped they would lose because I was not there. I have dealt with all of that. My ego is not as big as it used to be. There is more than one way to skin a cat. We are all in this thing together, and I hope you can learn one thing.

STANCE

I am going quickly over some of the things. I have to spend about five minutes on the stance. The thing I have learned about the stance is about the stagger. If you are in a right-handed stance, it is easier to go to the outside than it is to go to the inside. Everyone thinks a parallel stance is good because you can go either way. In a parallel stance, you cannot go either way. In the staggered stance, if the right foot is back, you have no trouble going that way.

If a player spends the majority of his time blocking someone on his outside shoulder, you should have that foot back. That is why coaches put linemen on the left side of the ball in a left-handed stance. People have been doing that for 30 years. The majority of blocks are to a defender on your outside. That is particularly true in pass blocking.

If a lineman is on the right side and has to go inside, he should be in a left-handed stance. The

first thing you will say is: the defense will know he is going that way. That may be true, but they do not know what he is going to do. Just remember that the deeper the foot is back in the stagger, the easier it is to go in that direction.

If the lineman is going to his right, he does not want to put weight on that foot. If you want to take the weight off the right foot, push down on the left knee. That puts more weight on the left side of the body and takes it off the right side. That allows the lineman to move the right foot without shifting his weight to the left side first.

If he wants to make a crossover step, he does the opposite. He drives the right knee down, which allows him to move the left foot and cross over. The bottom line is to drive the knee down the opposite the way he wants to step.

SPLITS

If you are the right guard and you come to the line to line up, you take a normal split. That one is not too tight and not too wide. If you are the frontside guard and have to work with the center, you tighten down the split. You do not want to have a gap. If the center and guard are working together, it is easier to block a defender if the split between the center and guard is tighter. People may read the split, but they do not know whether he is running a frontside isolation play or a backside zone play.

If the backside guard has a 3 technique aligned on him, he moves his split outside toward the tackle. He is almost foot-to-foot with the backside tackle. They can get a better double-team on the 3 technique and a better scoop block going away from that side. If players jump into the inside gap, we have established what we will do when presented with a gap to the inside. Now we call the play to get him in the inside gap and block down on him.

If there is a defender in the gap, do not let him get in the gap. The guard is the split adjustor. You let the guard move in and out and the tackle stay aligned in the same alignment. If both linemen start to move in and out, it screws up the entire concept. The tight end can be a split adjustor also.

LEVELS

The next thing I want to talk about is levels. Levels are the distances the offensive linemen align in relationship to the line of scrimmage. When we talk about lining up *on the ball*, we mean as close to the ball as possible without getting the helmet into the neutral zone. There are a number of reasons to be on the ball. In short-yardage and goal-line situations, we do not want to give any ground at all. If you have a good defender and you want to get into him faster, we get up on the ball. If a rusher is bull rushing, get closer to him so he does not build momentum.

The guard and tackle to the side of a power play need to get up on the ball because of the pulling guard from the backside. If they are back off the ball, the pulling guard cannot see as well. This applies to defenders who are more head-up than those in the gaps.

The second level is aligning with the *fingers on the center's toes*. That is where I tell linemen to line up when they do not know where to line up. That is not too close to the line of scrimmage and not too far off it.

The third level is as far back off the ball as the rules allow. That alignment is with the *helmet on the waist of the center*. The lineman has to be off the ball if he has to make up ground inside or outside of him. If you are the right guard and you are on the ball, it is hard to scoop on the nose or zone block with the tackle. If his job is to go sideways or into the gap, he needs to get off the ball. I am not talking about double-team blocking.

If you are the right guard and his blocking assignment is playing a wide technique outside of

him, he has to use a lateral shuffle step. If the technique is extremely wide after he takes his first step, he is still far away from his block. He has to perform a series of short shuffle steps in a lateral movement.

If the guard is zone-stepping to his tackle and the defender playing on the tackle slants inside, he uses this technique. He stays square to the line and lateral steps outside, using a one-two approach shuffle. He wants to make up ground, but he cannot get there on his first step. You have to do that from an off-the-ball alignment. That way he can make up ground and keep his pads square to the line of scrimmage. The more you are off the ball, the more you can move laterally before you have to turn your pads.

I have been an advocate of this next point ever since I talked to a great offensive line coach named Howard Mudd. That has been 30 years ago. He coaches for the Indianapolis Colts now, and all they do is win games. Here is what he taught me. If you run a play inside the tackle, which is a run-to-daylight type of play, block the defender on the angle he is on. We do not want to try to get square on the defender because the ball is not working to that side. The offensive blocker has to put his helmet to the defender's outside, but his shoulders have to turn to get to him. It is okay on the zone play to move the defender by blocking him on the angle he is on.

In the old days, everyone taught a lead step. I taught it, too. If I had a defender on my outside shoulder and I had to block him, I took a short, six-inch step at the target. What we want to do now is get the lead step out of the way. I do not want to call it a drop-step. All we want to do is see how fast we can get the second step on the ground. If I take a short drop-step, it lowers the center of gravity and gets the first step out of the way so you can turn the hips outside.

It allows the second step to come forward and get back on the ground. That is the important thing. How fast we can get the second step on the ground determines whether we can secure the block. I have trouble calling it a drop-step because the head coach will fire you. They think you have to lead step.

The wider the defender in his alignment, the deeper the first step has to be (Diagram #1). Then we drop off the line of scrimmage and get the body going forward by using a series of two-step movements.

Wrong   **Right**

Diagram #1. Two-Step Approach

When we teach this technique, we have to make sure the first step gets the entire foot on the ground. We do not want to be on the insteps or heels. We want the entire foot in contact with the ground. This technique keeps the lineman from locking his hips. It also keeps him from getting turned on the drive. The wider the defender, the deeper the step until he feels he is going to get turned, and then he shuffles.

The offensive tackle on a lead play to the openside always ends up with his butt in the hole. If he has to turn out on a defensive end, he never seems to clear the hole with his body. We get the tackle to almost pass set for two steps. That creates separation, but we cover up the defensive end with our bodies. The tackles kick and slide to get into that position. It is almost the same technique and makes the hole appear bigger.

If the offensive guard has an inside block and he steps at the defender, he locks his hips. He loses a little ground and comes square on the nose with more power. The angle lets him get into the defender. When we block a defender, we never step at the defender. Everything is a two-step approach. It is a series of one-two steps. It is not one, two, and three: it is one-two, one-two, and one-two in the step sequence.

The offensive linemen want to get their feet out of the hole. If the play is an inside zone play, the offensive linemen get into their blocks. We have taught them the skills in the chutes, over the bags, and on the boards, but that is not what happens in the game. The running back is seven yards deep, and

it takes him forever to get to the line of scrimmage. The offensive linemen come off the ball and give up their blocks before the running back even gets to the line. Everything that happens in the zone play from tackle to tackle is all about sustaining the blocks. The running back is the player that moves everyone.

If the running back starts one way and cuts back too soon, the offensive linemen are in trouble. The linemen have to stay on their blocks until the running back makes his final cut. The linemen have to finish their blocks when the defenders try to disengage from the blocks. If you are a guard, tackle, or tight end, somewhere at the point of attack you have to be two-stepping on that defender all the way through the play. I want to get into the defender, climb him, and get my feet out of the hole so the running back can see the seam.

When I first started coaching, we scramble blocked. The next thing we did was block with our shoulders. Today, everyone is blocking with their hands. I teach run blocking with the hands. I get the hips involved with the shooting of the hands. I call everything in the technique an "under." It is a double under or a single under.

The way we train this technique is by using a 20-pound medicine ball. The partner holds the medicine ball in front of him. The offensive blocker steps, trusts up with his hands, and rolls the hips into the punch. The reason we punch from underneath is a counter to what the defender is going to do. The defender will stick his hands into the blocker's chest. The blocker does not wind up with his hands. He keeps the hands tight and punches upward through the hands of the defender into his chest.

When the blocker's hands go through to the chest, he grabs his jersey or he may get the belt buckle. If the defender is a low target, the hands may go into the armpit. The secret is the hands are coming under the defender's hands.

When the blocker drive blocks, he always wants a strong inside grab hand. When the blocker gets into the block, he may not use his outside hand at all. He wants to take his inside hand and drag the defender to the hole. He is going there anyway. The more the defender moves to the outside, the bigger the cutback lane.

If the blocker gets a strong grab with the inside hand and gets his outside arm locked out, he has the defender hooked. He works to get his outside leg locked, and he is positioned, which is good. We want to get a strong inside hand and a high inside leg. That means the inside leg is always forward. That does not mean it stays that way through every step, but that is what we work for. We are not trying to hook the defender on a zone play. We want to run him, and we do that better with a strong inside hand and a high inside leg. All this goes with sustaining the block in the zone play.

There are different ways to finish the block. If the right guard has a 3 technique aligned on him, he blocks him on the inside zone play. The tight zone play is set up to come on his inside leg. As he gets into the block, he puts his head right down the middle of the defender and gets a strong inside grab hand. If the defender moves at all, the offensive blocker torques him. Once he starts to move, we twist the defender the way he is going. We twist the defender and take him down. If you continue to block him, he can react and make the tackle.

If the zone play is set up to go off the inside leg of the tackle, he blocks that somewhat different. The right guard places his helmet slightly to the frontside on the defender. The head does not have to go to the outside armpit. He puts his hips slightly to the frontside. When the defender starts to move, the blocker can reset his helmet. The blocker has to stay in front of the defender. If the blocker takes a tight landmark on the outside, all he has to do is sustain the block. The way he sustains the block is to throw his outside arm out and reset his hat.

He has to stay on him longer, because the play is not coming up his butt. The play is going outside, and the defender's reaction is in that direction. All he has to do is work the defender down the line of scrimmage. The blocker cannot block the defender up the field or inside. He has to run him the way he is going and sustain his block. The finish to the block is to climb

the defender or torque him and throw him down.

If the ball goes wider at the inside leg of the tight end, the helmet goes to the outside number of the defender (Diagram #2). If he puts his helmet on the outside number, the defender will flatten him out. The defender is coming across the line of scrimmage, and the block is going sideways. The blocker has to work the shuffle two-step movement hard to square up on the defender. He gets the strong inside grab hand, and eventually the ball may break right behind him. There could even be a center helping him on the block. What I am saying is you do not have to get the helmet to the outside armpit or shoulder. You can strike the defender and reset the hat when you get into the block. The important thing is to shuffle with movement and get back square on the blocker. Get the outside arm out of the block. If the defender gets wider than he should, the helmet goes to the outside on an outside zone or stretch play.

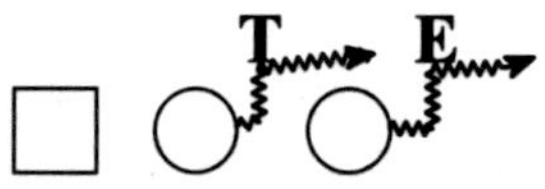

Diagram #2. Inside Zone

If the blocker wants to hook a defender, he uses a strong outside hand and high outside leg. On the zone play, it is just the opposite. We do not want to stop the outside movement of the defenders. We want to drag them outside and create the running lanes.

If all you want to do is reach the defender and do not care about movement, use the crossover step with the inside foot. The blocker takes a deep step off the line of scrimmage with his outside foot and plants his toe. He takes the crossover step with his inside foot and gets up on the outside of the defender. However, the quickest way to get to the crossover step is to pivot on the outside heel and cross over.

Anytime the blocker uses a lead step, the back foot does not move. The fastest want to hook a player is to use the crossover step. The fastest way to move is the crossover step, but you have no power. If you need power, you cannot use the crossover.

When the blocker is running the defender, there is a point where the he has to finish the block. I wish I could tell you where that point is. The blocker has to have a clock in his head where he torques the defender or climbs him to get his feet out of the hole. That comes with repetition of the zone play. It comes back to timing. The lineman has to feel the defender and have the instincts to react.

If the blocker is stalemated, he dips and gets another bite. If the blocker gets too high, the defender has him. His feet can be moving, but he has no power. He must lower his center of gravity, and keep the feet moving. We are starting over on the block.

Sometimes in the offensive blocking scheme, we use the forearm. If the right guard has a nose inside him on the zone play, he has to hit him and come off on the middle linebacker. He steps inside and uses the same foot and same shoulder to hit the nose. If we ever shoulder block, we call it a lazy forearm (Diagram #3). When we shoulder block, the blocker wants to strain and get the defender away from him. He wants to climb, bring his hips with him, and get his feet out of the hole.

Diagram #3. Lazy Forearm

The reason we use the forearm and shoulder is we do not have a lot of control with a one-handed punch. I can buy using a single under punch like the one we talked about early. I do not think you are strong enough to use the hand to get the nose stunned and on the center's block. Using the forearm delivers more power. You want to create separation between the guard and the nose so the center can take over.

The thing that you must prevent in the blocking is walking around the block. The footwork is like the zone play. We want to hit with the same foot and

same shoulder. However, once we strike, we walk through the block. That means we strike with the same foot, shoulder, and high inside leg. We walk the defender back with the inside leg forward on the block. We walk through the defender and not around him.

If the linebacker is further to the backside, the guard may use more of a rip technique on the nose, but he still goes through the nose and not around him. Anytime the blocker can get a piece of the defender, he cannot walk around the block. If the feet of the blocker are parallel, there is no inside pull and no power.

When we are in close quarters, as the line is most of the time, we always have to use the base and the two-step approach. I learned this from a guy by the name of Tiger Johnson. He is 85 years old, and he is one of the greatest coaches who ever coached. The perfect angle for the guard who is coming off on the backside linebacker is just in the inside gap tight to the noseguard. The back is seven yards off the line of scrimmage. That means the guard must slow down and not get in a hurry. When we block, we want to have the feet on the ground.

If the guard has a linebacker block on the Mike linebacker, he can also help the center in the gap (Diagram #4). He does not think the 5 technique is coming down. He steps and hits the nose. The hit on the nose propels him into the block on the linebacker. He does not get in a hurry because it takes the back time to get to the line of scrimmage.

Diagram #4. Mike Linebacker Block

When the guard comes off on the linebacker, he wants the linebacker to think he has outside head position. Once he gets into the block, he blocks him like a down lineman.

The bottom line is, the offensive lineman uses a number of surfaces to hit a defender. He can use his hands. He must use an under punch, a strong grab hand, and a strong outside hook hand. He uses his flipper or lazy forearm and a shoulder rip. When he uses those techniques, he cannot walk around the block. Instead of using the flipper or rip, all he may need is a hand check. The wider the play, the more the blocker has to shuffle to get into position.

The big problem with zone blocking in high school is the running back. He never takes the ball into the line far enough. He always cuts back too soon, and that screws up all the blocking. Here is the thing that coaches do not know how to do. It occurs on all levels. If the right guard and tackle get an angle by the defenders, that is easy for them to play. The problem is the defender who comes straight ahead in his charge. The tackle overleads the defender and misses him completely. The guard cannot get him, and we have penetration. That stops the play.

The offensive line has to be able to block the gray area. You block the gray area by getting foot-to-foot with your buddy. You want to block a moving double-team on that defender. They stay on him until they get to the depth of the linebacker. The wider the first defender goes, the further the inside defender has to go.

The problem with a double-team block is the angle of the drive blocker. If the drive blocker comes down on an angle, he is blocking against the post blocker, and his butt is in the hole (Diagram #5). He has to step inside and get square with the post blocker, so they push in the same direction and use their force together. The drive blocker wants to walk through the block and not around it. He wants to keep a high inside leg as he drives back with the post man.

Diagram #5. Double-Team Block

Another area of concern is the down block. I have tried to block this situation a number of ways.

If the blocker puts his head across the defender, he loops out. If the head is not in front, he rips through the gap. The way I handle the down block is to pass block on the defender. The blocker drops his inside foot and sets. He pushes him with his inside hand and grabs the defender. That pulls the blocker into the defender and eats up the space so he cannot penetrate. If he tries to come back outside, the blocker redirects and blocks that move. It works. If the ball is going off-tackle, the blocker may get pushed back, but if it is going outside or it is a stretch play, he will be fine.

PASS PROTECTION

In pass protection, the footwork is paramount in the success of the blocker. The first thing the blocker must learn is what I call "tight feet." The feet cannot be overspread. If the feet get too wide, there is not chance to redirect and make blocks. You have to learn how to shuffle with tight feet. When we shuffle, the feet do not go more than four or five inches at a time. That is the key to the footwork. The zigzag drill is the drill to work for tight feet. The drill is a simple redirect drill, sliding the feet in four-to five-inch shuffles.

The next fundamental in any pass block is the kick step (Diagram #6). If the defender is on the outside shoulder of the blocker, when he steps back, he does not want his outside foot forward. If the feet stay parallel, the outside foot locks, and the defender can get on the edge of the blocker. When I teach the step, I have the linemen walk out, keeping the outside foot back with the inside foot straight down the field. We must have balance and a good center of gravity in the center of his body.

Diagram #6. Kick Step

The secret is to use the kick-slide technique. It is like the one-two step in run blocking, only applied in the pass block. It is a series of quick kick-slide movements with the feet. We want the weight balanced in the body with good posture. If the second step turns to the outside, the hips start to turn, and the blocker opens the gates to the quarterback. When he kick-slides in his pass drop, he wants the whole foot on the ground in an inside-out fit. He does not want to be on his heels or toes.

What I incorporate is a tilt. If the blocker tries to get in front of the defender, he opens the inside rush. It is a cardinal sin for the blocker to get beat inside. The tilt puts the weight on the inside leg and allows you to move the outside foot in rapid progression.

If the defender is on the outside, as the blocker gets into his kick-slide, he wants to stretch the defender. He wants to work his pass drop to the outside and force the defender wider in his rush. We want to give the rusher the illusion that the blocker has overset on his drop. The blocker wants to keep his outside leg back throughout his drop. If the rusher attacks the inside of the blocker, he shuffles back inside. He cannot bail out by dropping his inside foot back.

If the blocker is getting beat to the outside, it could be because he is punching off his outside foot. If you punch off the outside foot, it makes the blocker reach out for the defender. It puts his weight forward, and he locks the outside leg. If that happens, the rusher can edge the blocker. You do not want the blocker to think too much as he retreats, so make it second nature by doing a simple timing drill in teaching the punch. The punch has to be delivered off the inside foot as the player slides. Players with short arms try to compensate by reaching instead of moving one-step closer.

The tackles have the toughest technique in the pass block set. If the tackle has a wide rusher and the first move is to get back and tilt to the rusher, he has a problem. That gives the rusher the whole ball of wax. The defender can bull rush, go inside, or attack outside. Make the tackle keep toe-to-toe to the line of scrimmage. We want to pigeon-toe the outside foot. Before in the drop, we put the entire foot on the ground. Here, we put the toe on the ground instead of the entire foot so we can retreat faster.

As the blocker retreats, he cannot go straight back. If he goes straight back, the rusher will collapse the pocket. He has to widen the pocket with his vertical set. The blocker turns his head and looks at the rusher, but he does not turn his hips. There is a point, usually on the third step, where things start to happen in the rush. That is where the rusher lets the blocker know what type of move he is facing. We do not want the inside foot to get the weight on the heel. He keeps the entire inside foot on the ground so he has some power.

If the rusher makes the inside move on the blocker, we want to grab him with the inside hand. That pulls the offensive blocker's hips over toward the inside direction. He cannot continue to punch him as he goes inside because nothing will happen. By grabbing him, he hooks the inside movement and pulls his hips in that direction.

On the inside set, the inside foot is higher in the set. With the feet parallel, the inside foot is stronger. If nothing else, I want to trip the rusher. The inside foot is back somewhat. The wider the blocker has to set, the deeper he has to set. On the inside set, we have to keep the shoulders square so we can retrace the sets to the outside. We cannot tilt to the inside for the same reasons you cannot tilt to the outside. If the outside foot gets forward in the drop, you give the rusher the edge.

The latest thing in pass blocking is to jump the defender at the line of scrimmage. If the quarterback goes five steps in the drop, we jump on the defenders at the line of scrimmage. If the right guard has a 3 technique aligned on him, we run block him, but he cannot go as far. He does not want to run block and go all the way to the blocker because he is out of control.

The blocker tries to close the space between himself and the defender. All the head faking and hand play is no good because the offensive blocker has his hands on the defender. The blocker run blocks the defender, but he has to remember the fundamentals of the pass block. He has to stay inside-out and target on the defender. If the blocker only goes part of the way to the defender, he can redirect on an inside move and cover the outside move as well. The move looks like the blocker has fired into the defender, if the defender makes any move toward the blocker.

I do not let the center jump block on the defender. I let the guards and tackles jump defenders. The reason we cannot jump the center is that there is no inside-out for him. The guards and tackles have a clear definition of inside-out. If the guard has a tight 3 technique, the guard jumps him off the inside foot. He uses a two-step movement, keeping his feet moving.

If the defender aligns on the inside of the blocker, he cannot jump him. To jump him, he has to turn his shoulders, and that prohibits him from passing off line stunts. The tackle uses the same technique and rules on the jump technique, but he has to stay under control.

Question: If you use your hands like that, do the officials call holding?

As long as the hands stay inside, there is no holding. If the jersey pulls away from the body, you may get a holding call. When you use your hands, you feel like you are in control.

I am maxed out. Thank you.

ADAPTING THE DEFENSE TO YOUR PERSONNEL

Brigham Young University

I cannot to tell you how glad I am to be here this evening. When I became the head coach at Brigham Young University, I was the youngest head coach in Division I football. Being the head coach at Brigham Young, I was expected to carry on the success that LaVell Edwards had for all the years he coached at the school. Quite frankly, that record is overwhelming.

I want to give you a clear idea of what happens at BYU. I was not the first choice to fill this position. I think I was probably the last resort. When you consider who comes to BYU, it is an unusual situation. The university is owned by the Church of Jesus Christ of Latter-day Saints. It is the largest private religious institution in the world. There are over 30,000 students that attend BYU. Over 90 percent of the students are of one faith.

When you talk about the criteria for us to consider young men to play at BYU, here is how we do it. The first thing we do is recruit Division I football players. When we recruit players, they have to go through the Ecclesiastical Endorsement Council. That means, no matter what faith they belong to, they cannot drink, smoke, or have premarital sex or drugs as part of their lives—they do not have to be Mormon. If the Ecclesiastical leaders do not endorse the recruits, we cannot consider them. They must also have a 3.0 grade point average.

We recruit nationwide and hit every state including American Samoa. We find about 35 athletes a year with 25 scholarships to give. When you consider all those requirements, plus the fact that I am a young head coach, it is a difficult job to maintain the standards they are looking for.

The results have shown that in the last four years, only eleven Division I schools have won more games than BYU. In the past three years, there are only five schools that have won more games. In the past three years, there are eight teams that have been ranked in the top 25 at the end of the season and BYU is one of them.

All those statistics are a matter of perception. Some people in a normal recruiting program would view our situation as a weakness. Once you gather the knowledge to win with those types of players, you are doing a service to the players and the institution. We finished the last three years 11-2, 11-2, and 10-3. Last year, we had 122 players on our team. Eighty-five of them had spent two years serving missions.

These players volunteer to go on their missions at their own expense. After they have been endorsed, they submit their paperwork to the church headquarters. They get a letter back from the church headquarters that gives the location of their mission. It could be any place in the world. For two years, they knock on doors and try to spread the word of the religion. They come back from these missions with incredible strength and maturity.

From a football perspective, a defensive lineman may leave for his mission as a 300-pound lineman. He may come back from his mission as a 200-pound lineman. Not only has he lost size, he has lost strength. Another thing we deal with is married players. Forty-three of our players last year were married. On our charter, we had over 300 people that traveled to our bowl game in Las Vegas. When I looked at our charter, we had enough baby carriages to transport an army.

We do not have a normal program. However, we do not try to make it normal. We want to make the program as distinct and as different as we can.

There is one thing that we are doing that I want to share with you. People do not believe this when I tell them. However, you can ask any assistant coach that works on my staff. We meet after practice every day and go home at 6:30. In addition to that, we do not work on Sundays.

When we started this, I was a young head coach and started the season 1-3. The first home game I coached, I was booed by the home fans. I elected to kick the ball on fourth down rather than go for the first down. The 58,000, which is capacity for our stadium, booed me.

Family is first, and it has to be reflected in our work schedules. I made a decision early on that this would be the way I would approach it.

My background as defensive coordinator was based in playing a 3-3-5 defense and blitzing almost every down. We had tremendous success with this defense everywhere I had coached. We are still running versions of it. I hired an offensive coordinator from Texas Tech. Mike Leach, the head coach at Texas Tech, used to come to BYU to study the game under LaVell Edwards. At Texas Tech, he still uses the same numbering system that was run under Coach Edwards when he coached here.

There are not many defensive backs that can play in the NFL coming to BYU. If that is the case, the question has to be asked, *Why do you play with five defensive backs who cannot cover?* We did not use the personnel we had at BYU the way we needed to use them. By the same comparison, we do not have any receivers from BYU playing in the NFL, and yet, we played with four wide receivers in our offense. However, if you look at quarterbacks, running backs, tight ends, and offensive linemen, we have a bunch playing in the NFL. On the other side of the ball, we are well represented with linebackers and defensive linemen.

At BYU, they expect to win the conference championship and maybe the national championship. When we started 1-3, we had to do something to correct what we were doing. In midstream, we changed our offense and defense. We did that and only worked until 6:30 every night. We changed to the defense we run now and went back to the offensive concepts of LaVell Edwards. We started throwing to the running back and tight end.

From that point, we won five of our last six football games to finish 6-4. We finished second in the league and returned to a bowl game. The bottom line as to the success we have had over the past three years is the personnel we are playing.

If you do not know a particular scheme, it is hard to play it. This defense is not the ideal defense for me. Philosophically, I like to pressure, and I do not like the scheme other than the fact that we are winning. The results are three consecutive 10-win seasons, which has only happened two other times in BYU's history and that was 21 years ago. We have a 32-7 record, back-to-back conference championships, and four consecutive bowl appearances in the past four years.

I am not a big believer in statistics, but we did our own study at BYU. We found that the most valuable statistic in winning and losing in college football is scoring. That sounds obvious. If you score more points, you win. The second criterion to determine whether you win or lose is points allowed. The third factor is turnover margin.

This takes you back to the pioneers coming west. If they could not get the wagon up an incline, they threw things off the wagon. Decisions had to be made about what to take over the top of the mountain. The decision was to take only the essentials. In our thinking, we had only three essentials. We had points scored, points allowed, and turnover margin as our essentials for a successful program.

All the other statistics mattered, but they were not as important as the first three. If you perform well with regard to those statistics, you will probably have a successful season. We thought we had to be in the top 10 in scoring defense and offense to win 10 games. We expanded the study and came up with a number that considered the offense and defense together. We found that if we scored more than 24 points, we won 10 games. If we held the opponent to under 24 points a game, we won 10 games.

When we discovered that, winning became a realistic and tangible goal. This research is specific to BYU. Whether it works in your situation, you have to research to find that out. In our situation, one number joined our program together. Twenty-four points was a realistic number for our offense. We felt we could score 21 on a bad day. To the defense, that number was a truly realistic goal. If all we had to do was hold the opponent under 24 points, that was attainable.

The way we attain that goal is the exact opposite of what I would prefer. However, it is the scheme that best fits our players. The scheme can be about you as the coach or about the players. When we beat Oregon in the Las Vegas Bowl 38-8, we had no scholarship players in the secondary. Our starting defensive secondary were all walk-ons.

We had to figure out how to get the most out of a bunch of smart, hardworking, and mature players. Our whole philosophy is to transfer our knowledge to the players and allow them to make decisions on the field. We make those decisions faster because of the types of players we have. We have given 25 scholarships to walk-on players in the last four years. That is 25 percent of our recruits.

The defense starts with four-man pressure. The change in this package from what we wanted to where we are is extreme. With every defensive package, the easiest thing to do is add. That is particularly true when you are trying to get input from your coaches. Input equals involvement, and involvement equals ownership. You like to have coaches believe in what they are doing. Usually, the only way you can do that is by giving them a say in what you are doing. The easiest thing to do in a staff meeting is to keep adding ideas.

The call sheet got so long we did not have time to practice it. I forgot to mention that our practices are 16 periods long—the periods are five minutes. That is less than an hour and a half. It seems impossible that we have had the statistical success we have had in the past three years and practiced less. Last year, we practiced five times in pads. There are two questions that come from that

statement. *How do you teach fundamentals if you are not in pads?* My question is, *How do you win if you do not have your players healthy?*

The defensive system is not about the volume of things we do. It is about the complementary things we do. I believe you must have a seven-man front with two high safeties. There has to be a place in the package for that. We have to play quarters and half coverage.

BYU 3-4 DEFENSE

- Base zone
  - ✓ Four-man rush with multiple fronts and line stunts
  - ✓ Zone coverage concept with two high safeties and single high safety
- Zone blitz
  - ✓ Five-man pressure with two- and three-deep concepts
- Max coverage
  - ✓ Drop eight and rush three
  - ✓ Secondary cover has the ability to play one or two high safeties

I think you also must have an eight-man front. That means you have to play with a single high safety. Hopefully, both fronts and secondarys look similar in the pre-snap look. You must have some type of zone pressure and a way to drop eight defenders into pass coverage. The scheme must involve dropping eight with a single high safety and dropping eight with two high safeties. The only other thing we could possibly use is man pressure. However, our man package amounts to only three percent of our coverage.

We feel anytime we play man coverage, the risk level goes up. Those risks convert to points on the scoreboard. If you give up points, you are giving up your chance to win. By using a man scheme, statistically you are better, but in our league, we want to control the points.

About 65 percent of our coverage is quarter-quarter-half coverage. We do not give our players a playbook. This might be a teaching philosophy and something you might want to consider with your players. When our players report to fall camp, they get a notebook with blank pages. We present the scheme and they take down what we say. They have an investment in what they are learning.

What you see me using is what I do for clinics, but it is not for our players. Of course, there is a risk of losing something in translation. That is a possibility, but the coach must become an excellent teacher. They have to present the scheme in a way the players can understand it. We want to give them visual pictures and get them involved with written learning. Some players understand one of those mediums better than others. If you present it in a number of ways, they will learn it.

We play a *3-4 defense* (Diagram #1). We have good linebackers. If we had more quality linemen, we might be in the 4-3 defense because the secondary coverage is the same from both packages. There is not a giant difference between the 3-4 and the 4-3 because the coverages are identical. The difference in the scheme is the pass rushers in the scheme. If we play two high safeties, we have the openside linebacker as our fourth rusher. That is no different than having a fourth rusher with his hand on the ground. It is very easy to go back and forth in these two fronts.

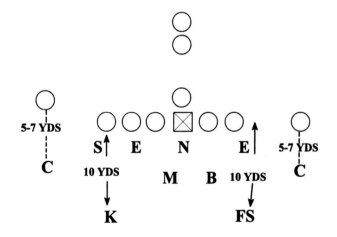

Diagram #1. 3-4 Defense

The Will and Sam linebackers are the defenders that make this defense go. They can be bigger strong safeties or defensive-end-type personnel. If you play defensive ends at those positions, they

must be active, depending on the coverages you play. However, our Will linebacker is the fourth rusher about 65 percent of the time. That is the amount of time we play the seven-man front.

We play the quarter-quarter-half scheme with that defense (Diagram #2). Every coverage you play has a different weakness. You have to understand that when you play a scheme. You do not play pass coverage just to play one. You must understand what the coverage takes away from the offense and what it gives up. In a quarter coverage, we number the receivers on the offense, starting from the sideline and working into the formation. Those numbers appear in our zone drops. We number both sides, and each side works independently in their coverage.

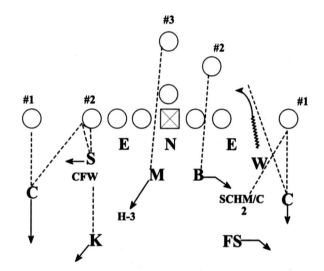

Diagram #2. Quarter-Quarter-Half

We play a field-and-boundary defense. We have a field corner and a boundary corner. The corners in quarter coverage key from the #1 to the #2 receiver. The kat safety and free safety key the #2 receiver to the #1 receiver. The Sam linebacker he has a *CFW* designation. That means curl-flat-wheel. That is his responsibility. He reads the #2 receiver and reacts to what he does. If he runs to the flat, he covers him. If he releases vertical up the field, his eyes go to the #1 and reacts off his pattern. If the back comes out of the backfield into the flat, he becomes the #2 receiver. The Sam linebacker takes him and plays the wheel pattern if he goes up the field. The Mike linebacker has the #3 receiver.

The other side plays exactly the same. The corner keys the #1 receiver, the free safety has #2 and the Buck linebacker has #2 on the seam route. There are many zone-drop teams that use spot drops because they are a man-base team. We are a zone-base team, and most of the words we use have a number and an area. We feel once the defender gets into the zone, he matches up and plays a man within a zone. The offense does not coach their receivers to run to the defender in a zone. They want them to look for the open windows in the defense.

If you spot drop, you open windows in the zone. Our idea is to take away the windows in the zone defense. The Mike linebacker's responsibility is three-hook. That means he retreats to the hook zone and finds the #3 receiver, whoever he may be. The #3 receiver can be the back coming out of the backfield or a tight end working into the hook zone. He rides that receiver through his hook zone until someone else becomes the #3 receiver.

The Buck linebacker to the openside of the formation has a two-seam technique. The seam defender in a cover 2 is an extremely important defender. He has to protect the seam in this defense. If the receiver gets by the seam player, he pressurizes the safety. His receiver is the #2 receiver to that side. If the #2 receiver does not come up the seam, he is a two-hook player.

We try to take the best of the spot drop and man scheme. It is a very effective way to develop the concept. The strength of this coverage is the four underneath zones are covered. The defense has good coverage in the deep areas of the field.

If you play this coverage 65 percent of the time, you must know where the weakness of the defense is. The weakness of this defense is in the flat to the fieldside of the formation. The corner in a quarter coverage is responsible for the #1 receiver running a fade or flag route and reacts back to the out route. The offensive coach has to ask himself how confident he is throwing the out cut into the field. In the past four years, we have had 12 out cuts thrown against this defense. That is now a giant weakness.

Of the 12 passes, one was intercepted for a touchdown. After that interception went for a touchdown, the number of quarterbacks looking in that direction plummeted.

We are getting away with the coverage because we have good linebackers and a good defensive line. We are inviting the offense to throw balls into an area that takes a high level of skill to complete. That allows us to play with a marginal coverage player into the field. That is the philosophy of having a seven-man front and playing this coverage.

When you watch film of us, you will not be amazed at the athleticism or what the players look like on film. That is not what we gauge. We gauge how hard they play and develop a culture of excellence through a test of wills. We go to extreme lengths to do that. When you have players that do not run well but are smart and have a big heart, we can develop that even more.

One of the things we do is called an Eco-Challenge. It is a race. This is a volunteer program that takes place in the summer. It is strongly suggested they participate, but it is voluntary. You have to say that for the NCAA. It starts at 5:00 a.m. with a one-mile swim in a pool on campus. One mile in the pool is 36 laps. If they have to walk, they can always touch the bottom. From there, they ride a bicycle to the stadium and run up and down the stadium steps. That is three miles of stairs. They get back on the bike and ride 38 miles. From there, they take an eight-mile run to the highest peak outside our stadium. The winner usually finishes in five hours or less, and it takes the ones who finish at the end about 13 hours. There has never been a player who started the race that has not finished.

I am coaching a group of players who commit to start the race and will be there at the end—they do not quit. We had one player do this with a broken hand. In the pool, he had a plastic bag around the cast. He did the mile holding the cast out of the water. When he finished 31 laps, the lap counter told him to get out and go on, but he insisted on finishing the entire distance. When you play with players like that, you have a great chance to win.

This coverage is cover 6. The right side in the diagram is the boundaryside (Diagram #3). We have words that tie the defense and the responsibility together. The boundaryside is called the coldside. That defines the entire side. The "cold" term tells us this is the rolled up or cloudside of the defense. The corner to that side rolls down into the flat coverage. They work independently of the left side. The left side is the thiefside.

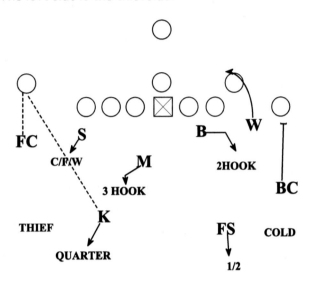

Diagram #3. Cover 6

The Will linebacker has a rush technique off the edge. The Buck linebacker is a two-seam player. He has the slot receiver to that side if he comes up the seam. The Mike linebacker has three-hook coverage. He looks for the third receiver to his side coming into the right-side hook zone. The Sam linebacker has a CFW rule. These are simple adjustments to the defense. The free safeties play the half field. The kat safety runs combination coverage with the field corner.

This is a decent look at how we defend with lesser athletes. With the type of place that BYU is and the players we have, we have to use these schemes. We play against some talented teams.

We can get into an eight-man front by walking the Sam linebacker up to the outside and blitzing him (Diagram #4). We call the stunt "sting." The kat safety walks down and replaces the Sam linebacker and becomes the eighth man in the box. He plays the

Sam linebacker's responsibility. He has the CFW technique in the coverage. This is a simple adjustment, but you have to execute the defense better than the offense. We want our defenders to be masters of what they do in their techniques. Everything in our defense is field-and-boundary adjustments.

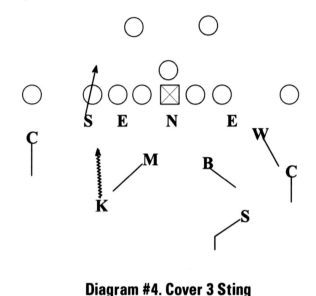

Diagram #4. Cover 3 Sting

The field-and-boundary corners play a quarter-quarter-half coverage. The Will linebacker is the curl-flat defender to the openside. The Mike linebacker is still playing three-hook. The Buck linebacker has the two-seam coverage.

If your seven-man front is good enough to handle the multiple formations and power runs, you do not need the eight-man front. If the front seven are not good enough to handle the power run and multiple formations, we need extra players in the box. We play this front about 20 percent of the time.

We work hard to make sure our pre-snap look always looks the same. We do not want to move too quickly to tip the defense. We want to disguise and move late.

In the last four years, the average scoring drive against BYU was 13 plays. Offensive coordinators are not very patient, they like to score points. How many of them will drive the ball 13 plays over and over again? Not very many of them will do that. At some point, they self-destruct. If you are sound in your execution and are patient enough, you can stop the offense.

You may not think this defense is innovative enough, aggressive enough, or wild enough, but it is productive. At the end of the day, that is what we care about the most. If it takes the offense 13 plays to score points, they will not have many drives. That means we will win the game unless they can score more than 24 points.

We have a blitz package we use. We got this from the Pittsburgh Steelers. We play this package about eight to nine percent of the time. The average yards gained per play against the zone-pressure scheme is 1.3 yards. I think the reason it is so effective is because we play so much zone. The only time we use it is to pressure the quarterback when we know the protection scheme or to take away certain run plays. For us, it is all about being in the right defense against the right kind of play.

The zone blitz is the best way to attack a team's protection scheme. If you do not know what their protection scheme is, you are wasting your time. You will have a hard time covering the underneath zones. Because we play one and two high safeties, you need a zone blitz from both of those schemes.

In this zone blitz, we want to bring two linebackers from the same side. We run this only when the back is blocking that way (Diagram #5). If the slide of the offensive line is to the boundary with the back blocking to the field, we have a chance if we bring two linebackers from the field on the one blocking back. In the diagram, the Sam linebacker is aligned on the slot receiver. He cheats at the last minute and comes off the edge. The defensive end charges inside in the B gap, and the Mike linebacker comes off the outside, inside the Sam linebacker.

The kat safety rolls down and takes the coverage for the Sam linebacker. When we roll the kat safety down, he has to handle the *seam-sail* route. That is the way the offense tries to beat the free safety. If the #2 receiver comes up the seam, the kat safety handles that route. If he runs the sail route or short flag, he handles that as well.

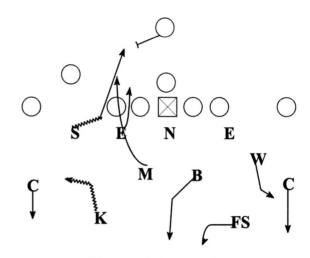

Diagram #5. Zone Blitz

We are not going to call this unless we know where the slide is going and what assignment the back has. Both the Mike and the Sam linebacker come off the edge. The coverage is three under and three deep. If the offense can protect the blitz, they will complete the pass. We can run the blitz against a tight end if we know the protection. It is the same principle.

The reason we zone blitz is that we know we can beat the protection. If you cannot beat the protection, it is a liability for the defense. With a three-under-and-three-deep scheme, there are holes everywhere in the coverage. When we run the scheme, we hope the protection breaks down and we get to the quarterback.

We run this defense in short-yardage and goal-line situations. The number of goal-line plays we have defended over the past four years averages eight a year. That ends up averaging less than one a game. We do not think that is worth the practice time to rep a goal-line defense.

If you do not know why you run a particular stunt, you do not need it. When we run this scheme, we have something in mind and we have a reason to run it. If the offense has a great running back that does not like to block, this is the blitz you bring. If you have an undersized or timid running back, this gets one of your best pass rushers on that blocker. We want to exploit all mismatches. These blitzes account for eight to nine percent of our entire defense. They are effective as a complement to the other schemes.

The opposite of the pressure package is *maximum* coverage. We have the ability to drop eight defenders with a one- and two-safety look. For BYU, this is one reason we are controlling the points scored against us as well as we do. We played six spread offenses this year. Once you commit the fourth rusher, your coverage options go way down. That is especially true if they align with three receivers on one side and two receivers on the other.

If you can disguise the coverage so they do not know you are dropping eight into coverage or they do not know where the fourth rusher is coming from, that is the most effective way to handle the spread. If they can identify where the fourth rusher is coming from, unless you are clearly better than they are, you have some potential issues in your secondary.

When we play spread teams, we align defenders straight across the formation. If the offense cannot identify what coverage you are playing or where the fourth rush is coming from, they do one of two things. They call a time-out or run a play into the wrong defense. If they cannot figure out what we are playing, there is some hope for us.

The fact that we drop eight into the secondary was driven by the fact that we did not have great secondary players. I like the defense because it is basically an eight-man front, which is great against the run (Diagram #6). The safeties and corners are straight across the field in a four across look. We are in an eight-man front, but we drop eight into the secondary. How you play the kat safety is a critical part of this defense.

If we call *thunder*, the kat safety drops down and takes the #2 receiver if he runs a seam or curl route. The free safety can cheat more to the Buck linebacker and give the quarter-cover look to that side. This gives you five underneath-cover defenders and three deep over-the-top. You can also effectively play the run out of this look.

The Sam linebacker pushes to the #1 receiver into the field. The Mike linebacker works the three-

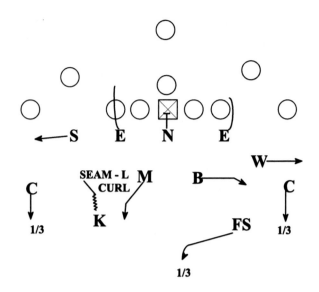

Diagram #6. Max Coverage Three Deep

hook area. The Will linebacker pushes to the outside to the #1 receiver into the boundary. The Buck linebacker drops to the two-hook area. The kat safety hangs in the seam area. If the #2 receiver comes up the seam, the kat safety takes him. He is the two-seam/curl player. If there is no seam runner, he helps the Sam and Mike linebackers. The linebackers can be aggressive and take away receivers on third down because they get help from the kat safety. The free safety goes to the middle third and the corners drop into the outside thirds.

This allows you to play five underneath defenders. That takes the stretch of the offense away. We have defenders in the wide areas of the field. If a team wants to run four verticals, we have that covered. The offense's only answer to that scheme is to go five verticals, which is highly unlikely. If the #2 receiver goes vertical, the kat safety goes with him. That basically gives us a four-deep-and-four-underneath coverage.

The weakness to this coverage is the scrambling quarterback. If he can avoid the rush and buy time, it puts pressure on the secondary to cover the receivers for a long period of time. However, if he scrambles out of the pocket and tries to run the ball, we have five underneath players. We have leverage everywhere he can run the ball.

We can play the coverage with a two-deep scheme as well (Diagram #7). The corners roll into the outside flats and the safeties retreat to the half-field coverage. That gives you six defenders in the underneath windows. The problems occur in the seam area. The seam defenders have to stay with those receivers and carry them to the two deep defenders.

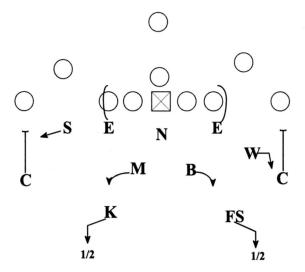

Diagram #7. Max Coverage Two Deep

From this coverage, we can run a four-deep scheme easily. It gives you the flexibility to move your defenders to fit the strengths of the offense. We can also come with the fourth rusher at anytime. When people think about dropping eight defenders into the coverage, it is a prevent defense. You can see we are aggressive and not passive in our coverage. It is a great change-up against spread teams. It has been super effective for us.

The last thing I can share with you that hopefully will add value to this talk is our approach on personnel. The biggest mistake that coaches on our staff make is fearing change. They know this defense. When a different group of athletes comes in, they want to coach the same defensive scheme. We may not have the personnel to run this scheme.

We may be back in the 4-3 defense because we do not have the linebackers to play the 3-4 or we have more quality defensive linemen. We want to make as little change as possible, but at BYU, change is something we live with. With the mission system that goes with this university, we have to expect changes in our personnel pool from year to year. We have to play the defense that our players can execute.

For BYU to finish in the top 25 for three years in a row is difficult. There are only eight teams that have done that. The secret to doing that is to remain consistence with what you do and recruit to your needs. The players who come to BYU each year may not fit our needs. There are critical positions that have to be filled. If we cannot fill those needs, we must play the defense the players we have can execute. If we recruit better defensive backs, we can do more in the secondary.

If there are any questions I can answer, I will be around. Thank you for your time.

DEFENSIVE LINE DRILLS AND TECHNIQUES

University of Kentucky

Thank you. It is a pleasure being here. It is an honor to represent the University of Kentucky, Coach Brooks, and his staff. We have an excellent staff, and we have some good things going on at Kentucky. I have coached for 32 years—31 of them as a defensive line coach, and one as an offensive line coach.

I was sitting downstairs waiting for this session, and I began to wonder if I had ever been in the hotel before. It dawned on me that four years ago I was here in the lobby, waiting for an interview. I had been fired at Ole Miss after six years. I was nervous as hell then, and I am nervous as hell now. I guess it is the hotel.

For a defensive line coach to talk for an hour and 15 minutes is tough. How many defensive linemen are there who can sit around and listen to something for an hour and 15 minutes? Twenty minutes is about all I can stand. If you start to see me drift toward a chair in 20 minutes, you will know it is from the training of being a defensive line coach.

You always hear that defensive linemen are not as smart as offensive linemen. I did have the privilege to coach offensive line for one year, and it helped me tremendously. You get to understand scheme and things on the other side of the ball. I was the assistant offensive line coach. The head offensive line coach told me I was going to work with the nub side of the line. I had been coaching three years, but I was not familiar with what the nub side of the line was. He told me it was the linemen to the openside of the formation. I asked him why they call it the "nub side." He said because the nub tackle plays on that side. The tackle held up his hand and was missing several fingers.

I asked him how that happened. He told me he was cutting grass and the mower got clogged. He reached under the mower to clear the clog without turning it off. That is an example of a smart offensive tackle. I relate the fallacy that defensive linemen are dumb to this story. I do not go for that thought, and I do not coach that way. I expect a lot of my players, both physically and mentally. On the football field, in this day and time, there are so many things that challenge players mentally.

I have been fortunate to work with a lot of good coaches. I worked 10 years for a coach by the name of Larry Lacewell. He was an excellent and demanding football coach. One thing you learned when you worked for him is to be challenged. He challenged you to learn. We played many different concepts. You remember different things from coaches along the way. The thing I learned from him was not to talk too much and spend your time repping what we did.

My players learn through repetition. We do it over and over. To play defense, you have to react. That comes from reps. Offensive linemen can look at a sheet and know they have to block a certain defender. Defensive linemen have to react to what they see. They cannot think what technique they will use until it happens.

At Kentucky, we have three distinct modes of play in the defensive line. We play a *man-key* concept. We are not a ball-key concept. It is different. I have done the two-gap and read concepts. We are a read-and-react team. Before you get in your mind that we play a passive technique, I do not teach it that way. It has a lot of the same principles I taught in the ball attack get-off scheme.

We are reading and mirror stepping, but we are not catching or giving ground. We are extending and working off the ball in attack mode. We work with our hands and gain ground.

The second mode we play is *stunt/blitz* concept with on the ball key. When we do that, we cheat our stance, but I will talk about that later. We move the up foot or back foot, whatever the case may be. It is a gap concept. When we are in this mode, we are penetrating a gap. We have a *pass mode*, which is a ball-key reaction. Many people call it a jet movement. We are expanding and keying the ball when we expect pass.

10 PRINCIPLES OF RUN PLAY

Knowledge

- Stance
- Alignment/assignment
- Pre-snap keys

Technique

- Get-off—play mode called
- Hands, hips, feet
- Separation—vision through separation
- Key progress
  - ✓ Man on
  - ✓ Near back
  - ✓ Off guard

Effort

- Escape—wipe/shrug/rip
- Pursuit
- Tackle

KNOWLEDGE

There some things I want to get across quickly to our players. There are a lot of pre-snap things that the players have to be aware of. Our stance is slightly different than other people. We are slightly wider than shoulders width and the stagger is less than a heel-to-toe relationship.

We want our toes turned in and up the field. Nothing bothers me more than feet that turn out. I am a believer that everything works from the feet up and the head down. If I open my foot, hip, or

shoulder, I am done. I do not know anyone playing the game that wants to have a soft shoulder on the run. If the lineman turns his head, the shoulder, hip, and feet follow. When we get down we want our forearms on our thighs with the hips down. I want the hips balanced between the feet with the down hand in front of the eye. We want to be in as good position to extend off the ball and lead with our hands. If we are moving we may cheat the stance.

Alignment is different for the inside defender than the outside defenders. The inside defender aligns his hand inside the foot of the man on which he is aligned. The 3-technique's hand is inside the outside foot of the offensive guard. He is square and crowding the ball. The shade nose has a little play in his alignment because of the bow in the offensive line. If they have problems with the read, they can back off the ball. The base rule for the defensive end is inside hand outside the foot of the offensive lineman. The end has to see so much more than the tackles. The end has to see the ball on or off the line and whether they have option responsibility.

From there we go to a pre-snap read. I want them to read splits and depth of the offensive linemen. They must know what the backfield set is. I expect them to know whether the back is far or near in their alignment. I want them to know if there are one or two backs, or an offset back. If they do not know the set, the scouting report is no good to them. They have to know what plays come from what set.

We want to know those things so we can address our alignment. If I know the split that the offensive linemen use when they combo block, I want to readjust my stance. I want to take the post man down the middle. I do not want to play a combo block with a blocker on each shoulder. I want to get into the post man and dominate him. If they are trying to power slip him, he wants to get into the post man, press the inside arm, gain ground, and get physical with him. If he is on the edge, they will man up to him and kick his butt.

TECHNIQUE

You have to get off the ball. If I am on a man-key and the man moves, I move as quickly as I can. I am not reading him so I can be slow. If he moves, I explode, get into him, and dominate him. I want to be quick, explosive, and violent.

We lead with our hands. The hands come first and are punched inside on the offensive blocker. The hands come at the level of the block. If the block is from the waist up, we want our elbows in and the thumbs up. I want to play with the hands at eye level. I do not know anyone in the world that plays with their hands at eye level that is playing high. They are playing high when the hands are down. I want my hips behind my pads and my feet behind my hips. Always play with body lean. I used to use the term roll the hips. I want them to extend off the football with a flat back. I want them to shoot their hands into the landmark and extend.

Once we get our hand through we want to get separation. You have to get vision through separation. We can control gaps three ways. You can control gaps with your body, the blocker's body, or with your eyes. If I get reached I work my body into the gap. If the blocker over-reaches, I use his body to fill the gap. If he over-reaches, I strike him in the ear hole, drive him up, and into the gap. I do not know anyone in the world that can generate any power from a high position. I can drive him into the gap with no trouble.

If I get a block and I control my gap, I use my eyes to control another gap. I squeeze my gap knowing the ball is inside. I can see the ball and know where it is. I can help people in other gaps because I can see where the ball is going and fall back to help once the ball gets level to my position. That is using the eyes to control gaps.

The key progression is man-on, near back, and off guard (Diagram #1). I want them to know what their key is. I want to know what their eyes are doing and where they are looking. The defensive end has to see those things and more. He has to read hats and whether the ball is on or off the line of scrimmage. If the ball is on the line of scrimmage, he has a run key. If the ball is off the line of scrimmage, he may play pass.

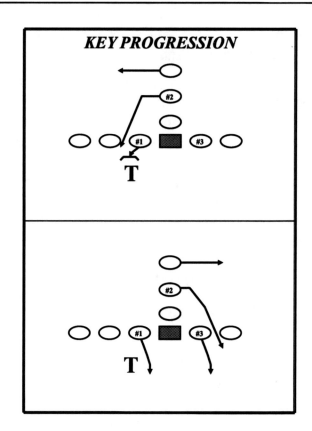

Diagram #1. Key Progression—Read One to Two

The defensive tackle is keying one to two. He keys the reach by the guard and the path of the fullback. He goes #1 to #2. There is no reason to go anywhere else with his read. There is no reason to go to his off-guard read. In the second drawing, he has the guard block with the fullback going opposite. When he has that read, he had better peek and see what is coming back. That happens with the defensive end or 5-technique defender. If he sees the back go away, he has to see what is coming back.

The same thing happens on a pass set (Diagram #2). If the guard sets for a pass, the defensive tackle has to be aware of a draw. He has to see the same thing. He reads the guard and reads the back. He sees the guard in a pass set and the fullback on an isolation path to the other side and must react to what he sees. He has to go to his third progression, which is the offside guard. In the second drawing, you can see the pulling guard coming back. He has to see all those things happening. He has to read his keys and go through the progression.

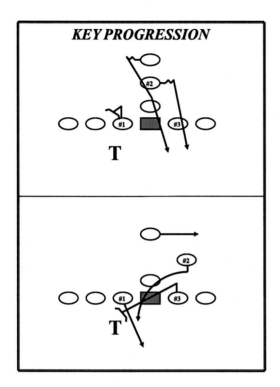

Diagram #2. Key Progression—Draw Play

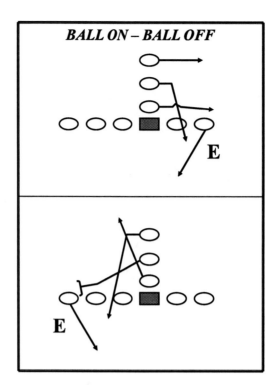

Diagram #3. Ball On, Ball Off

The defensive end has to see ball on or ball off the line of scrimmage. The end squeezes to the inside if he is playing a 5-technique (Diagram #3). As he squeezes to the inside, he wants to splatter the dive back on the dive option. We do not want to come across the tackle because we want to bounce the ball to the outside. The technique terminology is splatter and hammer instead of spill and box.

We used to use the term spill. However, defenders were giving themselves up and not helping on the tackle. They went inside and got logged inside. That is not what we want them to do. We changed the terminology to splatter. We still want to get on the inside half of the blocker, but we get our hands on them and try to get upfield. We are not simply running under the block. If we cannot get up to the ballcarrier, we force him to bubble and go outside. The problem is the defender may get too far outside, and the ball cuts inside of him. That is bad because everyone is fitting outside of him.

If the defender is going to rip inside and splatter the play, he has to get up the field. The last situation is the power-O and the bootleg that comes off of it (Diagram #4). The 9-technique defensive end has to

squeeze and key what is coming inside. His man goes inside; his next key is the near back, who is going to the opposite side. He reads his next key, which is coming down the line of scrimmage. He takes on the inside half of the pulling guard. After the contact, he climbs upfield, trying to pick off the pulling tackle coming behind the guard

On the bootleg, the defensive end reads his man-on as a down block. The near back is coming toward him. He collisions, taking the inside half and looking for the third key. He finds the pulling guard trying to hook him. He sees the ball off the line and gets upfield to contain it.

There is so much in the game that has changed with the blocking scheme. The tight end can be on the other side and is trapping to the other side. If the tight shifts off the line of scrimmage or aligns up off the line of scrimmage, the defensive end yells "Y off." That alerts the defensive end on the other side to be aware of the tight end kick-out on him. The defensive end has to find those blockers. It may be a fullback or the third tight end.

Before I talk about that, I will give you an overview of playing the run.

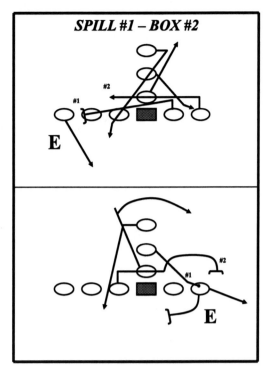

SPILL #1 – BOX #2

Diagram #4. Spill and Box

PLAYING THE RUN

- Three points of contact—hat and hands.
  - ✓ Must have inside hands.
  - ✓ Thumbs up, elbows tight at side.
  - ✓ Speed of hands is critical, not power of stab; hands are merely levers.
- Focus on V of neck.
- Attack with flat back and hands at eye level.
- Hit on the rise; extend hips.
- Run feet.
- Knock blocker back; separate and twist.
  - ✓ Blocker's shoulders to lock out upfield.
  - ✓ Arm (power arm/trail arm, push/pull).
- Keep body lean at all times. Do not run your hips under your shoulders (keep hips behind your pads, feet behind your hips).
- Play on offensive side of line of scrimmage.
- Release and chase ball with full effort and intelligent pursuit angles.

EFFORT

To make plays on defense, you have to get off blocks. In our escape mode, we teach wipe, shrug, and rip. We work the most on wipe and shrug. The shrug is a swim move. We only rip on rare occasions. I do not want them to rip when trying to escape from a block. We rip only if the ball is in a pass-flow scheme. If the blocker is trying to cut the defender off or trying to block him, we want to wipe or shrug. If the defender tries to escape using a rip technique, the offensive blocker latches onto the defender's arm and rides him out of the play. We do pursuit tackling. We have three types of tackling drills we work. We work release tackling, sweep tackling, and roll tackling. I have some film to show those. Two of those three require the defender to release from a block.

In playing a blocker, there are three points of contact. We want to use our hat and hands to contact the blocker. The hands must be inside on the blocker's breastplate or target area. We want the thumbs up and the elbows tight to the side, except when we play a low block. In that case, they must get the hands down and the feet back. The speed of the hands is critical. It is not the power of the stab because the hands are levers to keep the blocker off the defenders body.

We tell them to focus on the V of the neck, but that is a general location and will change. I have players who read feet or the number on the shoulder pad. We do not overcoach that point. It is what works best for the player. We attack with a flat back, and the hands must be at eye level. We want to hit on the rise and extend the hips. The most important thing is to keep the feet moving at all times.

We want to knock the blocker back. As we lock out and go into our separation move, we want to twist the blocker's shoulders. We push or pull the shoulders of the blockers to execute the escape. We want a body lean at all times. We do not want them to run their feet under their pads. The hips should be behind the shoulders and the feet behind the hips. When they snap the ball, we want to play on their side of the line of scrimmage. When we release from the block, we want to chase the ball, using intelligent angles. It takes maximum effort to pursue the football.

I have some tips on pass-rushing techniques.

TEN PRINCIPLES OF PASS RUSH

Knowledge

- Stance and alignment.
- Have a plan. Know your opponent. Predetermine move and counter, if needed.
- Pre-snap keys.

Technique

- Get off—explode on snap. Every step to quarterback.
  - ✓ Have great body lean.
- Rush a half man.
- Be quick and decisive on initial move. Be violent.
- Hands
  - ✓ Quick and hand (vice-like).
  - ✓ Break blocker's arms down.
  - ✓ Coordinate hands with feet.
- Take advantage of blocker's momentum and mistakes.
  - ✓ Power rush soft setter.
  - ✓ Use finesse moves on short setter.
  - ✓ Take advantage of what blocker gives you—counter.

Effort

- Accelerate off moves.
- Get hands up; break on ball. Effort tackles.

If we get a jet or go call, we change our stance and alignment. We narrow and extend our stance. We want to get as close to the ball as possible. If I am a contain rusher, I may be up to three feet outside the offensive tackle. If the rusher is outside a tight end, he gets no wider than one foot. I tell them to widen to ensure an inside release of the tight end. If the defensive end gets any wider, he spreads himself away from their rush lane.

When the defensive lineman comes off the ball, he should have a plan of how to attack the blocker and rise to the occasion. When we have one-on-one pass rush in practice, I want to know their plan. When I ask them and they do not know, it makes no sense to me. If they do not have a plan in practice, what will it be like in a game when it is third-and-10 and they are hot and tired?

You must have a plan, and you must know what the opponent is going to do. You have to predetermine the move you are going to use and have a counter move to break down the blocker. Our tackles this past year did a great job of understanding slide protection. We get a pre-snap read on the blocking back. We define some of our stunts and twists off the alignment of the back.

Question: What moves do you teach?

I teach them a battery of moves, and they develop and perfect the move they do the best. They also develop a counter off that move. If they are not effective with that move, we let the lineman develop an additional move that he feels confidence in doing.

The defensive lineman must have a plan that ties into the back's set. If we get two backs in the backfield either in the I formation or the offset I, we have to know where the protections are going. I tell the tackle, if he reads heavy hands from the offensive blocker, that is probably a run, even though we are in a jet alignment. When we say "heavy hands," that means the offensive lineman has weight on his hand. If the weight is not on his hand, he is going to pass set or pull. We do not want the lineman using a double move where he fakes inside and comes outside because he might be coming out into a double-team block.

The defensive tackles communicate and talk in the pre-snap read. If one defender calls a heavy call and the other gives a light call, it is probably a run with one side pulling. The defensive end needs to know if there are four receivers to the same side. If the defensive end sees trips and a near back his way, it almost guarantees a sprint-out his way or something moving toward him.

The defensive lineman has to get off the ball, and every step he takes has to be toward the quarterback. We may be working a move, but always gain ground toward the quarterback. When you rush the quarterback, always attack half the blocker. We want to get to his shoulder. The only time we rush the full torso is the bull rush. Even with the bull rush, you landmark the outside shoulder initially and go to the bull rush later. The offensive blocker would rather the rush come straight to him and try to bull rush. If he has to move his feet to respect the outside move, it makes it harder for him to get set to take on the bull rush.

When the rusher makes the first move, it has to be quick and decisive. He has to be violent in his approach with his hands. We want to knock the blockers' hands down and get them off our bodies. We use three blocks with the hands as our primary move. We use a sweep move, which is over the top. If I am an outside rusher and the blocker extends his outside arm, I use my outside hand to sweep his hand down and swim over the top. Our defensive ends use a Miyagi move. That comes from the movie The Karate Kid. It is the "wax-on, wax-off" move with the hands. It is a circular-rotation karate move performed with the hands.

When you rush the passer, you have to coordinate the hands with the feet. If he works with his right hand, he has to step with his right foot. We want to take what the offensive blocker gives us. We have to study film to understand the tendencies of the blocker. If he sets soft, we want to use more power on him. If he sets short, we want to shake him and get inside. We want to take advantage of what he gives us.

Whatever move you use, you have to accelerate off the move. That is hard to do in practice because all the emphasis is on "do not hit the quarterback, and stay away from him." When it comes game time, the emphasis is: get the quarterback. You have to find something in practice to teach acceleration off the move to the quarterback.

Do not rush the quarterback with your hands up. We want to get the hands up only when the ball is shown. We do not want to leave the ground unless the ball is out of the hand. After the ball is released, we want the defender to break on the ball and tackle with maximum effort.

If the pass rusher comes off the line and the blocker stays square to the line, the rusher should beat him to the corner. The pass rusher wants the blocker to turn his hips so he can get on the edge and get his hips pass the blocker. If we have a blocker who crowds the line of scrimmage, we can get off on him before he gets his outside foot down on the ground and force him to turn his hips. The defensive end can force the blocker to open his hips by width and alignment. If we can get the shoulders turned, we can use our pass-rush techniques.

I am always teaching our players different moves. The moves they use depend on the type of personnel you have. The defensive tackle has a smaller area to work. We do an "in-out-in" and an "out-in-out" move on the inside. Those stunts are head-and-shoulder movement. I do not want to fake with my feet. I want to move the head and shoulder to the outside, to the inside, and charge back to the outside. He keeps his feet under his pads and fakes with his shoulders.

I give a picture sheet of a particular offensive set to our players every week. I pull it off the computer, and it shows what they do from this particular set. In the example, the set is a gun-near set. From this set, our opponent ran the formation 89 times. Seventy-five percent of the time they threw the ball. On the sheet, I show them the variety of plays they ran and into what areas of the field. They should know when they see this set, they think pass. This chart lists what to expect from this set. It has the common runs and tips of what to look for.

I also give them a pass breakdown chart (Chart #1). It lists the passes for first, second, and third downs and the scrambles of the quarterback. If they play two quarterbacks, I use dotted lines for one of the quarterbacks. You can see in this chart that the quarterback scrambled all over the place. Sometimes, you can find scramble patterns for a particular quarterback. Sometimes, we find a quarterback who only scrambles to his left. If that is the case, we want to plan our blitzes and line movement to match those tendencies.

This chart (Chart #2) is something we started this year, but I did it a long time ago. We have our own goal board. The first goal is to win. The second is to hold teams to 3.2 yards per carry. We want to cause a turnover or recover a fumble. This year, we scored two touchdowns by defensive linemen returning a fumble. We want to sack the quarterback on one out of eight passes. We want to total 24 tackles. We want to pressure the quarterback on one out of three passes. We want hustle tackles where we tackle a wide receiver or running back downfield. That includes hustling out and making a tackle in the screen game. We get a production grade for each lineman. We take the number of plays and divide it by the number of points he amasses for things done in the game. The last thing we post is the production leader.

Across the top of the chart, you put the teams you play and keep a running total of what you did throughout the season. To come up with a production grade, we use a production chart for the defensive team. To find out how productive our team is, we evaluate the player's performance. The production grades come from comparing the points they accumulated to the number of plays they play.

We assign points to plays in a game. We give points for tackles and assisted tackles. We give points for fumbles recovered and caused. We give points for interceptions and scores. We have other categories for which we award positive points. We also give negative points for mistakes and loafs. We add up the total points and divide by the number of plays they participated in to come up with the player's productivity. That goes on the chart. Players who have the highest number of points in the fewest plays are your most productive players.

We want them to produce, have fun, and take pride in what they are doing. Thank you very much.

PASS BREAKDOWN *vs.* U.C.F. *vs.* N.C. STATE *vs.* U.A.B./U.S.M. *vs.* TULANE

P/1st & 10

7-step	SPRINT-OUT: 3X		FAKE JAILBREAK: 1X DBL. REV. PASS: 1X	P17: 3X	SPRINT-OUT: 2X
5-step	BOOT: 7X	P24: 1X P16: 1X	GUN: 19X	P25: 5X P15: 2X	BOOT: 3X
3-step			GUN: 3X UNDER: 3X		

BUBBLE SCREEN: 5X
SLIP SCREEN: 1X

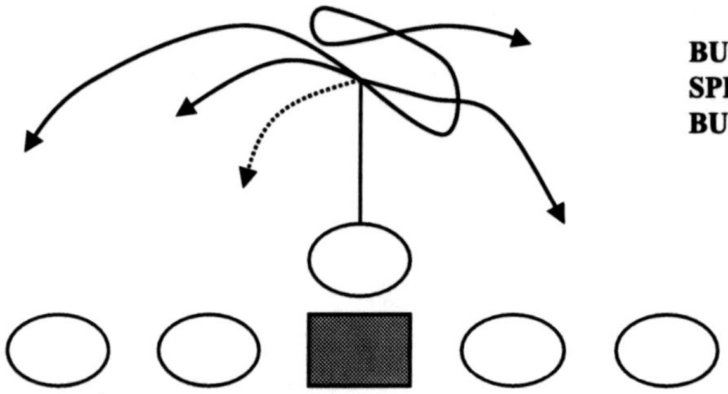

BUBBLE SCREEN: 6X
SPRINT THROWBACK
BUBBLE SCREEN: 1X

2nd & 4+

7-step	SPRINT-OUT: 2X				
5-step	BOOT: 1X	P24: 2X P14: 2X	GUN: 23X	P17: 1X	BOOT: 2X
3-step			GUN: 3X UNDER: 3X		

BUBBLE SCREEN: 2X

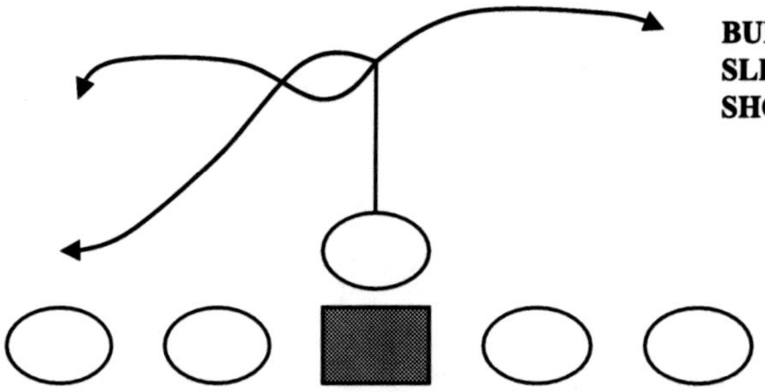

BUBBLE SCREEN: 3X
SLIDE SCREEN: 1X
SHOVEL PASS: 1X

3rd & 3+

7-step	SPRINT-OUT: 3X				SPRINT-OUT: 1X
5-step		P24: 1X	GUN: 31X		
3-step			GUN: 11X UNDER: 1X		

MIDDLE SCREEN: 1X
SLIP SCREEN: 1X

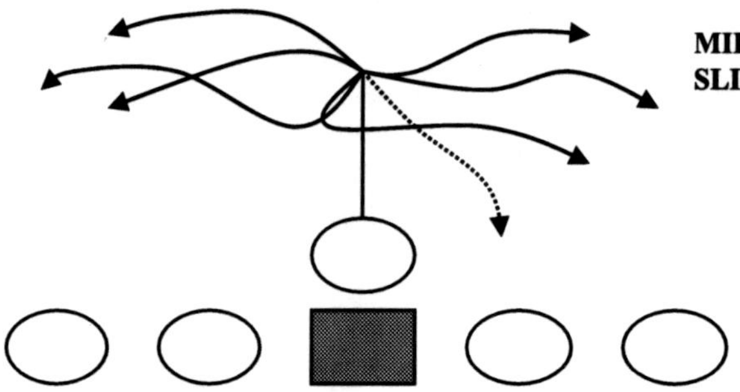

MIDDLE SCREEN: 3X
SLIP SCREEN: 2X

Chart #1. Pass Breakdown

DEFENSIVE LINE GOAL BOARD

OPPONENT											S E C	B O W L
WIN												
RUSH UNDER 3.2 YDS/CARRY												
CAUSE TURNOVER OR RECOVER FUMBLE												
SACK QB 1 OF 8 PASSES												
TOTAL 24 TACKLES												
PRESSURE 1 OF 3 PASSES												
HUSTLE TACKLES (tackles on wr/rb on passes downfield)												
PRODUCTION RATIO 1:6												
PRODUCTION LEADER												

Chart #2. Defensive Line Goal Board

BUILDING A PROGRAM THE RIGHT WAY

University of Missouri

Thank you. I am honored to be the head football coach at the University of Missouri, and I feel very fortunate to have that responsibility. The lifeblood of our football program is Missouri kids. We had about 25 kids on our team from Texas, but 75 percent of our scholarship players are from the state of Missouri, including 16 starters on last year's team. That is our lifeblood and we appreciate that.

It was not like that when we got here eight years ago. When I took the job, I felt we had to win with Missouri kids, and although we do not get all of them now, we do get a majority of them. That is how we are winning. We won 22 games in the last two years, and that is where it starts. That is where the nucleus of our recruiting and winning is, and we knew that when we got here.

I want to share some ideas with you about things we do and things we believe in. We got in here eight years ago, and eight years ago next week, we had our first winter conditioning, which we call the *winning edge program*. We do it at six o'clock in the morning on Tuesdays and Thursdays for three months. It is a tough, intense program. It is 70 minutes long, and it is like a Marine boot camp.

It is done in a way to improve strength, quickness, explosiveness, mental toughness, and change of direction. That is pretty much what we do in that deal. If you ever want to show up at the University of Missouri at six in the morning on Tuesday or Thursday in the next three months, then come by and watch what we do.

A lot of people do it, but I think we do it a little bit differently than everybody else. It is one of the most important things that we do in our football program.

Eight years ago this coming Tuesday, we had our first workout. When it was over, we sat down and had a staff meeting. Now, we had just come from the University of Toledo where we had a pretty good football program. We had just gone 10-1 there. So, we sat down to evaluate what we had just seen, and my coaches all looked like they had been shot.

It is an understatement to say that it did not look good. It was not a pretty picture. We were slow, we were not in shape, the number of players who were athletes was not good, the athletes themselves were not very good, the kids were not disciplined, and they were not very mentally tough. It was everything we might have suspected, but it did not really hit us until we went through it.

I will never ever forget the look on my coaches' faces. They looked like they got shot. They were just like in a daze, and I said, "Well, guys, that is why they hired us. We have a lot of work to do."

Now, fast forward to today. As you know, our entire staff has been together for 12 years—eight at Missouri and four at Toledo. The staff has been featured in *Sports Illustrated* and in *USA Today*, and although all of them have had chances to leave, we have stayed together as a staff. What I am saying is that my staff and myself have formed a nucleus and built a program in which we teach people how to win and do all the right things.

That is what we have done. If you fast forward to today, we are graduating all 22 of our seniors. In the APR ranking, which is an academic rating in the country that measures how well you are doing the right things with your kids, we are number one in the nation among all public schools. Our facilities are all new. Our home attendance has increased from 52,000 per game to 67,000 per game, and we have averaged nine wins over the last four years.

So, we have made this big transformation. Have we arrived? No, we have not arrived, but we are continuing to build and trying to take the next step. There is no question about that.

We had a plan in place that we implemented when we got here, and that is what I am going to talk to you about. I want to talk about what we did and how we did it. We did not just go in there and hope that everything worked out. We had a plan, which we stuck to during the tough times of the first few years. We have a system in place, which is what we do, and that is what I am going to share with you right now. I hope that some of these ideas might apply to you.

You see two things when you walk into our locker room, and the first one is this.

MISSOURI FOOTBALL CORE VALUES

- Honesty
- Treating women with respect
- No drugs
- Respecting the cultural differences within our program

These are the things we talk to our football team about. Number one is honesty, and, as you well know, honesty in our society has become a kind of convenience. Where once there was a clear line between being honest and dishonest, now there is sort of a gray area in between, so we are teaching our kids honesty.

Treating women with respect is something that the players have to hear from you. They have to hear it from you because there is a lot of stuff our there— a lot of bad stuff. Our kids know that we will not tolerate those types of situations in our program.

We will also not tolerate drug use in our program. We drug test our kids. The day I got to Missouri, we started random drug testing with all our players. We did not have to do it, but we did it because it was the right thing to do. We kind of had a problem there in the beginning and we took care of that. I have never seen anybody do drugs and it help their life in any way. So, we randomly test 15 or 20 players every week.

We have players from all different races, religions, socioeconomic backgrounds, and just all different kinds of guys, so we have to have great respect for one another. If our kids do not have respect for the cultural differences within our program, we are never ever going to play together as a team.

The second thing you see when you enter our locker room is this.

YOU ALWAYS PROTECT YOUR FAMILY

- The team is first.
- Say the right thing.
- Do the right thing.
- Make good choices and decisions.

Because you represent your teammates.

I used to say, "Hey guys, do not get in trouble at night, make sure you do not do this and do not do that." Now, I tell our players to protect the family and protect the team and they know exactly what I mean. I will tell them we have to protect the team tonight and guys begin to nod their heads.

To our guys, protecting the team means the team is first. They know they should say the right things, do the right things, and make good choices and decisions because they represent their teammates and their families.

I use the terms a lot, and it is a very positive way of doing it. I may say to them that we have to protect the team tonight. I just think that it is a very positive way to specifically tell the players what that means. Both of those signs are on our locker room doors and our players see them every day.

I want to get into what I consider to be the foundation of our football program.

FOUNDATION: DON JAMES PROGRAM

- Organized
- Attention to detail: Have a detailed plan for every area of your program

- ✓ Academics
- ✓ Player development
- ✓ Recruiting
- ✓ Practice philosophy
- ✓ Mental preparation
- ✓ Developing team players
- ✓ The psychological approach to competing
- ✓ Game-week preparation
- ✓ 48-hour preparation
- ✓ Spring ball
- ✓ Summer ball
- ✓ Two-a-days
- ✓ Developing ownership
- ✓ Developing leadership
- Discipline
- Evaluation: Evaluate/critique every area at the conclusion (apply that the next time around). You are constantly evaluating and improving as coaches and as a program (just like you ask your players to do).

Don James is my mentor. He is the coach that I learned the most from. He did things the right way. He was a man of character and a man who had a formula for winning. So, I tell people I am a Don James disciple.

This was his program at Kent State where I played for him and at Washington where he won bowl games and championships. I took his program and implemented it at Toledo when I was there, and now, we have dropped it in at Missouri. That is where this has come from.

Don James was an organizational genius and that has not been lost on me. Solid organization is good because it makes the entire operation run better. It is good in the eyes of your players because you want them to play with excellence, and when you do things crisp and sharp and detailed, it is first class to them. That is all a part of the big picture in changing their attitudes on how to do things, so being organized is tremendously important.

My staff will hear me talking about attention to detail all the time. Every little thing is important. I do not agree with the guy who says, "Do not sweat the small stuff." I believe that the details involved in everything you do ultimately will determine the type of program that you have. We have a detailed plan for everything we do in our program.

We have a very detailed academic plan. It deals with going to class, going to study table, being responsible, being on time, and for everything regarding academics, we have a plan in place.

We have a detailed player-development plan. Our strength and conditioning coach has a staff of 15, and they are part of our team. He runs that program with discipline, attention to detail, and high intensity, and he does a great job developing strength, quickness, and speed, and then, measuring the results. When the kids can see those results, their confidence grows tremendously.

We also have detailed plans for recruiting. We have a practice philosophy and we have a detailed plan for mental preparation and how we are going to do that. We also have a plan for developing team players, which is to get the selfish kids whom we have been handed and you have been handed to become team players.

We are now doing a lot more with our players on the psychological approach to competing. We call it *The Pursuit of Excellence—The Mental Approach of a Champion*. We talk a lot to our players about making their strategies work for them, and about committing to excellence. This is the mental side of competing. It includes focusing in connection to meaningful goals, the idea of meeting those goals, mission excellence, quest for consistency, positive images, and on and on. We have three or four pages on every one of these things that we use to train our players how to think as athletes.

This is not the 70s when I played and you just had to get your mind right and go play. Now, there is so much out there to teach your guys about how to think. How do you handle adversity when you are playing in a game? How do you handle success? What about the laws of relaxation and intensity? What about distraction control? What about maintaining focus? How do you invest in and build team harmony? We spend a lot of time with our players now on competing, and the mental approach to becoming a champion.

We also have detailed plans for game-week preparation, for the 48 hours before a game, for all of spring football, for summer ball when our players are here for that, and, of course, for two-a-days. We also have plans for developing ownership and developing leadership within our team.

We have detailed plans for every one of those. It is my job to see that we run a very disciplined program and that all of that gets done. Then, we will sit down and evaluate everything we do in our program, and we are going to learn from it. From there, we bring all of the things we learned into the next year and apply them to make ourselves better.

It is my theory that that is how you improve as a staff and as a football program. We ask our players to get better, and we have to also get better as coaches. That is what I learned from Don James. This is the foundation of our football program and it is what we are about. It is the way we get better.

Now, when we arrived at Missouri eight years ago, things were not the way we wanted them to be. This chart sums up what the situation was then and what we did to begin to change it.

WHEN WE ARRIVED AT MISSOURI

- Mizzou had had two winning seasons in 17 years.
- Players had huge attitude issues.
- Most of the players had excuses for their failures.
- They did not know how to win.

WHAT WE DID

- Demanded a great work ethic
  - ✓ Made them invest more
  - ✓ Changed the work habits of our players
- Hung up three signs in the position rooms and coaches' offices
  - ✓ Attitude: Charles Swindoll

- ✓ No excuses: Can not have the excuse habit and the success habit
- ✓ Team bottom line

Missouri had had two winning seasons in 17 years. Players had huge attitude issues, most of them had excuses for their failures, and they obviously did not know how to win. I got on the phone with a respected old coach who really understood what we were facing there, and the main thing he told me was, "They don't know that they don't know." Boy, was that true! They did not know that they did not know. They thought they did, but they did not, and that was where we were at that point. So, here is what we did.

We demanded a great work ethic. We made them invest more, and we changed their work habits. In other words, we told them, "All of a sudden it is going to be a lot different. When we lift weights, it is going to be a lot different. Our six o'clock winning edge program is going to be a lot different. How we practice is going to be a lot different. The conditioning after practice is going to be a lot different. You are going to invest 50 percent more into this thing than you have ever done before."

Now, what does that do? That just separates the men from the boys. Those who are not interested in doing it at this level just kind of move out and go on. The ones who are committed and want to win and want to be good, they raise their level and continue on. That is hugely important. You have got to demand that they put the time and work ethic into it to be good.

The second thing we did was change our work habits in the weight room and how we practiced. I will talk more about that in a second. Then, we hung up three signs in the position rooms and the coaches' offices because there were three things we had to do before we were going to start winning. We had to change attitudes, we had to get rid of the excuse habit, and then, we had a thing called the team bottom line, which ultimately determined how to play every play.

ATTITUDE

The longer I live, the more I realize the impact of attitude on life. Attitude, to me, is more important than facts. It is more important than the past, than education, than money, than circumstances, than failures, than successes, than what other people think or say or do. It is more important than appearance, giftedness or skill. It will make or break a company, a church, a home. The remarkable thing is we have a choice every day regarding the attitude we will embrace for that day. We cannot change our past. We cannot change the fact that people will act in a certain way. We cannot change the inevitable. The only thing we can do is play on the one string we have, and that is our attitude. I am convinced that life is 10 percent what happens to me and 90 percent how I react to it. And so it is with you—we are in charge of our attitudes.

—Charles Swindoll

We have this sign in the locker room and every single coach has one in his position room and in his office. I have one in my office. It is a great thing, and teaching kids to be positive is a big issue today. You are in control of your attitude. The bottom line is that you control how you think. This is way beyond football, and it will help your kids forever. This is how they can deal with people for the rest of their lives. They turn and have a positive approach.

What is a bad attitude? We all have bad days, but when your bad day starts affecting the guy next to you, then you have a bad attitude. If you are in the locker room, and the guys around you are affected by what you are doing or saying, that is a bad attitude, and we have got to fix it. If we will correct bad attitudes when we see them, eventually we will change the culture.

The second thing we talk about is no excuses. Now, this is one of the best things ever written about that subject. I do not know who wrote it, but it is as good as it gets.

NO EXCUSES

Any excuse for nonperformance, however valid, softens the character. It is a sedative against one's own conscience. When a man uses an excuse, he attempts to convince both himself and others that unsatisfactory performance is somehow acceptable. He is, perhaps unconsciously, attempting to divert attention from performance—the only thing that counts is his own want for sympathy. The user is dishonest with himself as well as with others. No matter how good or how valid, the excuse never changes performance.

The world measures success in terms of performance alone. No man is remembered in history for what he would have accomplished. History never asks how hard it was to do the job, nor considers the obstacles that had to be overcome. It never measures the handicaps. It counts only one thing, performance. No man ever performed a worthwhile task without consciously ignoring many a plausible excuse. To use an excuse is a habit. We cannot have both the performance habit and the excuse habit. We all have a supply of excuses. The more we use them, the lower become our standards, the poorer our performance. The better we perform, the less plausible our excuses become.

Next time you want to defend your subpar performance, say instead (at least to yourself), "No excuses!"

Notice the startling effect this will have on your own self-respect. You will have recognized your failure. You will have been honest with yourself. You will be one step closer to the performance habit. You will be a better man for it. We will be a better team.

We live in an "excuse" world and kids have excuses for everything. So, we start off right from the beginning with the understanding that you cannot have a success habit and an excuse habit. It does not and will never work. In anything you do, whether in academics, your job, your marriage, whether it is with your team, or whether it is with your friends, you will not have success if you have excuses. We have to get rid of the excuse habit.

When kids get rid of the excuse habit, their self-esteem starts going up. They start feeling better about themselves, they become responsible for themselves, and as that happens, they become better people, better competitors, and better in everything they do.

I want to talk about the team *bottom line.*

TEAM BOTTOM LINE

- Be enthusiastic
- Be a six-second competitor
- Know your assignment
- Play tough and physical

One play at a time

Put all your energy, focus, and concentration into that one play. After it is over, you have 100 percent focus on the next play.

This is the third sign on the wall. We just hit them again and again with attitude, attitude, attitude, then no excuses, no excuses, no excuses, and finally, the team bottom line. This is how you play football at Missouri—one play at a time.

We are going to tell you how to play every play. First, you cannot do anything unless you have enthusiasm. Second, you have to be a six-second competitor. That is, when the play starts until the play is over, you are going as fast as you can, in control. Most kids are three- and four-second competitors, and we have to teach them to be six-second competitors. That is what we do on Tuesdays and Thursdays at six in the morning during the off-season.

The most important thing we do in the off-season is what we call the mats and the winning edge program. In the off-season, we train our guys to be six-second competitors. On the football field, we do the same thing, but we also do it in the off-season.

The next thing is to know your assignment. You have got to know what you are doing, and then, you have to play tough and physical. Those four requirements we evaluate on every play that you have. If you are lacking in one of those areas, then that play is not good enough. You are not giving that play what it needs. Our goal, then, is to get our whole football team playing like that.

What we want is to play one play at a time, with all our focus and concentration on that one play. After it is over, that play is gone and we will focus the same way on the next one. The bottom line is that is how we want you to play a play. The whole key is to get your whole football team playing like that, and that is not easy to do. But, when you get a locker room full of six-second competitors, you are going to play hard as a football team.

Those three things are the foundation that we are going to plug and push to get across. Everything we do within our program is going to be to get those points accomplished.

Next, I want to talk about our player development program.

PLAYER DEVELOPMENT

- Stronger, faster, quicker, tougher
- Set goals
- Personal record system (PR)
- Testing
- Winning edge program

In this program, we want to develop strength, and we want to get faster, quicker, and tougher. Every one of our players sets goals for what he wants to accomplish, and we will test for that this semester in about seven weeks.

We have a PR system, where PR stands for personal record. A bunch of you guys have been in our position coaches' offices and seen our PR boards where we display the individual position player's progress. I do not care what a player can do when he first gets here—I just care that every time he tests, he is moving up on that board. That is how I can determine if our football team is getting stronger, faster, and quicker.

You can sit there and say that you had a great off-season, that your guys worked hard, and that you are sure your guys are stronger, but you cannot measure how hard guys worked. What we want is to get a percentage of increase in bench press, power clean, and the other major lifts for the entire football team. Then, I can say before the spring football game that 90 percent of our guys are benching more than they have ever benched before, 95 percent of our guys have better power cleans, 99 percent of our guys are squatting better, and I will put them into clubs (the 300-pound-bench club, the 325-pound-bench club, the 350-pound-bench club, and so forth).

What that does is drive guys to get these numbers. Then, when they can all see it, they know they are getting stronger as a team.

We do the same thing with the 40-yard dash, and the same thing with the pro agility test. We want 95 percent of our guys to be quicker this year coming up than they were a year ago, so we test quickness.

That is what we do. Those guys will run up to the PR board after they bench-press and erase it, and they change it and put their new bench press up there. They will do that with all the other tests.

So, we have all of this in place in our player-development program. We do not just go out and lift some weights, set some goals, and say, "Good job, we are a little stronger and we are a little quicker." I can tell you how many guys run 4.3, run 4.4, or run 4.5 in our program. I can compare it to the last eight years we have been there. I can compare it to last year's team that was fourth in the nation to this year's team that was 16th in the nation.

What this does is to drive the players. They get into hitting their goals and keeping their personal records. It builds their confidence when they can see that we are a much stronger, much faster football team. We had more guys run 4.8 or better this year than we have ever had in our football program before. That not only makes you play better, but it also changes, from a mental standpoint, how players feel about themselves. I think you can see how that gets done.

Now, our winning edge program that we do on Tuesdays and Thursdays is probably the best thing we do. When I played at Kent State, Don James brought in this thing called the mats. We hated it. We had it at three o'clock in the afternoon then, and your day was dismal when you woke up if it was your day on the mats.

There are three stations in our winning edge program, and players rotate from station to station to station. They are organized in groups by position. One station teaches running fundamentals where players work on how to start and on all the techniques involved in running. The second station is an agility station where guys are working on change of direction. In that station, guys do ladder drills, start drills, the three-cone pro agility drill, and finish drills.

In all of this, everybody is going to start behind the line, do it as fast as they can, and do it the best they can, or they will do it over again. You do it right or you do it again. That is being a six-second competitor. You start, you finish, and, in between, you do it as fast as you can.

The third station is the thing we call the mats. We have curtains up around the mats. On the mats, let us say you have three lines, with about 10 guys in a line. We have a coach in front running the drill, a coach in back, and coaches on each side. It is about the size of a wrestling mat.

This is the single most important thing in training athletes that we do. The coach will get the first three guys up, break them down, and give them a command to start chopping their feet. If they do not do it with a full effort, they get back in the line. This is an intense drill. From chopping their feet, they go through a four-direction wave drill, then back to chopping their feet, roll up, and the coach sends them off the mat. When they go off the mat, the next three are up and ready to go. The drill lasts about six seconds for each group and if they do not do it perfect, they do it over again.

In all, there are about 13 different types of drills that we do on the mats. I can tell you about it, but until you see it, it does not do it justice—not even close. That is the best thing you can do to teach your kids to be mentally tougher, to teach them how to compete and fight through as they get tired, and to do things right from start to finish. That is the most important thing we do in terms of getting our players to play hard and be six-second competitors.

There are only certain ways you can become a better football player. One is player development, and I would like to think that Missouri has one of the top 10 player-development programs in the country. A second way is knowledge of your position, and the other way is fundamentals. Those are the only three ways I know, from the time the season is over until we kick off next year against Illinois, that we can get better. If that is all you can do, you need to make sure that you are doing all three of them at the highest level that you can get done.

I am not going to spend a lot of time on recruiting because it does not apply to a lot of you guys, but these are the things we look at. We have an extensive evaluation system. We do not look at stars. We could care less if a guy has three stars or five stars. It never comes up during our evaluations. We do what we do, and we feel good about how we do it. This could be good in that you can tell players what college football coaches are looking at.

RECRUITING

- Year-round organizational play
- Recruit good people
- Speed potential
- Evaluation system

Tough Questions

- Does he have the ability and the desire to be a great college player in the Big 12?
- Is he liked and respected by teammates and coaches? (1-10)
- Is he tough? How tough is he? (1-10)

- Is he a leader? Vocally or by example? (1-10)
- Is he a great competitor? (1-10)
- Does he do what he is supposed to do when he is supposed to do it? (1-10)
- How do you rate his character? (1-10)
- Good citizen? Ever been in trouble? (1-10)
- Work ethic and training habits? (1-10) Practice player? (1-10)
- Attitude? Is he coachable? How does he react to criticism?
- Concentration and ability to learn football? (1-10)
- Any medical problems? Surgery? Concussion? Back? Knee? Shoulder? Asthma?
- Does he have children?
- Has he ever been arrested?

This is not really about catching a ball or fundamentals or speed, it is more about the total person. We ask these questions to the whole staff and then we vote whether we want the player or not. I really think if you have good people who can run, the two most important ingredients are being great competitors and being tough. If you have those two ingredients, you have a chance to have a good football team.

The next thing I want to discuss is game-week preparation.

GAME-WEEK PREPARATION

- Sunday–Wednesday: Specific detailed plan for player game preparation
- Thursday–game time: 48-hour preparation

For Sunday through Wednesday, we tell our players what we expect from them on each day. We specifically tell them where they should be and what they need to get done on each day as far as football is concerned.

Then, in our 48-hour preparation, I have a team meeting on Thursday, and when we are done with our Thursday practice, we begin the process of getting mentally prepared so that when the kickoff comes on Saturday, we are ready to play. We always want to be prepared to play at our highest level.

We tell our players that with your A game we can beat anybody, but with your B game, anybody can beat you. How do you play your A game? You have to practice well and do all the other things well in preparation, but in the final 48 hours, somebody is going to have his mind right and be ready to play better than other people.

We tell our players what they should do on Friday afternoon after classes, and on Friday night before the game, and what they should do on Saturday morning. We will detail what they should do to be ready to play their best game. We tell them that if they cheat for 48 hours, they will never play their A game. That is not going to happen.

There is a way that you practice, and there are only certain things you can do to get better as a football team—player development, improve players' knowledge of their positions—and the other side of that is how you practice, because somebody is going to practice better than someone else. I want Missouri to be in the 10 percent that practices better than the rest.

PRACTICE PHILOSOPHY

- Play like you practice
- Teach fundamentals
- Teach and develop practice habits
  - ✓ Every rep on that field fundamentally is done right
  - ✓ Right technique/speed/assignment/intensity
- Demand a competitive spirit
  - ✓ Set up competition in every drill
  - ✓ Make kids compete individually
  - ✓ Make it fun

We teach fundamentals. We do not call it individual period any more, we call it fundamental period. That is when we work on fundamentals, and that is the big ingredient in becoming a better player at your position. Players have to be made to understand that they cannot just go through the repetitions. They have to focus on doing each rep exactly right if they are going to improve.

Every one of us is a creature of habit, so we want to develop good practice habits, and that means doing everything fundamentally right. When a player does not do a thing right, we make him do it again. I cannot stress enough how important it is to practice the right way. There are 10 percent of teams that do it better than everybody else and those are the teams that are going to play better.

In everything we do in practice now, we try to create competition, especially in spring football and in two-a-days. When we do a 1-on-1 pass rush drill, one guy is going to win and one guy is going to lose. We keep score, and at the end of the drill, either the offense won or the defense won the drill. We do the same thing with receivers and defensive backs. We make it very competitive.

We will do that with 11-on-11 controlled scrimmage periods, we do it with our inside run period, and we do it with 7-on-7. There is going to be an offense or defense that is going to win. We are going to have winners and losers, and at the end of practice, whoever wins gets to wear black jerseys the next day, and the coaches and players who lose have to do up-downs. I am on neither side, so I do not have to do anything—that is called the "Pinkel Plan."

Anyway, men, that really changes our practices. You will see our players talk about how much fun they had in practice. You are practicing to become a better team, and developing a competitive spirit is how you do it, and you have some fun in the process.

Now, I want to talk just a few minutes on developing ownership.

DEVELOPING OWNERSHIP

- 2000s kids are different.
- To get ownership, I had to change. Instead of me demanding ownership, I got the players involved with decision making.
- Let the players' voices be heard and still do all the right things for the program while maintaining discipline.

I want players that love Mizzou when they are on the team. It is our *football team*. When I first got there, the first four or five years, it was not *our team*, it was Coach Pinkel's team. There was no ownership. They wanted to win, but it was not their team.

Now, if you talk to our players, it is *our team*—this is how we do things, and this is what we are about. How did we get there? Well, I changed because these kids are different.

They now want to know what is going on. It is a different world now than it was back when I was growing up. The bottom line is that is how you get them as freshmen and how I get them as freshmen, and that is how they are. We just have to learn to deal with it.

The point is, we just were not getting ownership before. So, what we did was instead of demanding ownership, I got the kids involved in decision-making. Now, nothing ever got done in our program without me wanting to do it, I just ran it through the seniors, whom I work with now, so they were a part of what we got accomplished. Now,

virtually everything we do I talk about it with the seniors. It is little, but it is huge. Ownership is entirely different now.

Now, how do we get ownership? It is through communication, and it starts with building trust. I tell our coaches that we want our players to passionately care about our program, but if we do not passionately care about them as people, they will never, ever trust enough to love this program. So, we work real hard on relationships. As coaches, we have to be honest, be an encourager not a discourager, never talk about other players, and always be positive.

That is all I have right now, guys. I do not have all the answers but I do believe in what we do. There are certain ways to win games, and there are certain ways to lose games. The key is to be well coached, and to put your players in a position to win.

Remember, you are always welcome at the University of Missouri, and remember, you have tremendous influence on your kids. Thank you very much for being here and thank you for what you do for kids.

ALIGNMENTS AND ADJUSTMENTS IN THE 4-3 DEFENSE

University of Delaware

Thank you. I am going to jump right into my topic today. If you have any questions, please ask them. Do not just sit there. However, do not ask me how to defend the Delaware wing-T in the amount of time I have at this clinic.

At Delaware, we primarily are a 4-3 quarters team. We play that front and zone blitz from it. That is the bulk of what we do defensively. This season, we gave up 3.83 yards per carry against the run. In the passing game, we gave up 5.71 per pass. What we were excited about was the opponent only completed 40 percent of their passes. When you can stop someone's passing game 60 percent of the time, that is impressive.

It does not matter what defense you run; you have to develop some concepts to build on. When we align our defense, we give the Mike linebacker a tight-end rule. If there is one tight end in the game, the Mike linebacker makes the "tite" call to the direction of the tight end. If there are two tight ends or no tight ends in the game, the tite call goes to the passing strength of the formation.

You must make calls for even distributions. If there are two tight ends and two wideouts, the formation is identical on either side. The same thing is true of a double-wide slot formation. With an even distribution set and the ball in the middle of the field, the tite call goes to the left, and the passing strength call goes left. The football is on the hash marks 72 percent of the game. With the ball on the hash, the tite and strength call go to the wideside of the field. You must have communication in any defense to line up properly.

You have to handle motion because it changes the passing strength. "Zoom motion" is the flanker starting on one side of the formation and going across the field. A "zin motion" is the flanker going in motion but keeping the motion on his side of the ball. He comes in motion to the ball and brings the motion down to a minus split to his side. The zin motion will possibly change the coverage, and the zoom changes the passing strength.

If the tight end trades his position, that changes passing strength and play calling. The yum motion is the tight end in a tight slot position, going in motion. On yum motion, we do not change the front, and the coverage squats.

The point is: we give the defense a concept to deal with formations. If you can get the defense aligned to every formation, it gives you less to work on in practice every week.

We give them an unbalanced rule. On an unbalanced set, we only recognize the set if they have two backs in the backfield or five players to one side. That is an unbalanced set for us. A zebra set aligns the X-receiver on the line of scrimmage to the three-man surface. The Z-receiver is to the two-man surface and off the line of scrimmage. The Z-receiver is opposite in the formation. In this formation, we have five players to one side of the set, which means it is unbalanced. If the Z-receiver is opposite and there is one back in the backfield, we call that "Chester."

The next thing we do is adjust the defense to all different sets. We start with the pro set. We present the formation and talk about what happens with zoom, trade, and yum. We are looking for communication on the defense. The Mike linebacker gives the tite call for the front, and the strong safety gives the lucky or Ringo call for the passing strength.

We cover the twins set with zoom motion and tight-end trade. The jet set for us is three wide receivers and two backs in the backfield. The T-2 set is two backs, two tight ends, and one wide receiver. We use motion to create a 3x1 set and a 2x2 set and establish the communication that has to take place. The players have to make all these adjustments on their own.

In a game, the worst thing that can happen is your defense not being able to adjust to things that go on. That is when you get fired because you look like you are not coaching.

We align in an unbalanced set and trade the tight end to go back to the twins set. We align in a one-back set and motion into the empty set. We align them in an empty set and scatter the formation. That means that more than one person is shifting his position on the field.

That sounds simple, but you would be amazed at how many teams cannot get aligned on time. We do not huddle on defense. We have not had a defensive huddle in four years. By not huddling, it gives the defense more time to recognize the formation and the coach more time to get the proper personnel on the field.

I have talked about how the Mike calls the tite call. The tackle, rush, Mike, Sam, and strong safety align to the tite call. The nose, end, Will, and free safety align opposite the tite call. The corners stay on their side of the field.

If we get a tite left call, the rush end aligns in a 7 technique on the tight end (Diagram #1). The tackle aligns in a 3 technique on the guard, and the Mike linebacker aligns in a 10 alignment at four-and-a-half in the strongside A gap. The Sam linebacker aligns in a 60 alignment on the tight end. The nose plays a shade or a 1 technique to the openside of the formation. The end aligns in a 5 technique on the outside shoulder of the offensive tackle. The Will linebacker aligns in a 30 alignment at four-and-a-half yards in the B gap to the openside. The strong safety aligns to the tite side, and the free safety aligns to the openside.

When we play this defense, we play with a 7 technique for the rush end, and at times we cheat

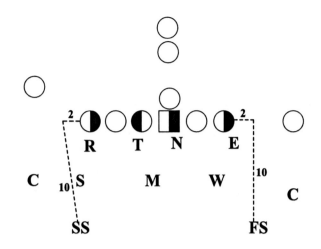

Diagram #1. Base 4-3

him to a 6 technique head-up on the end. We never play a 9 technique with the rush end. If you play with the 7 technique, the declaration of a block comes quickly for the strong safety. If you play with a 9 technique, it takes the strong safety more time to figure out what is going on.

In the twins set (Diagram #2), the Mike linebacker gives a tite left call. The secondary call is Ringo. The front alignment is the same, with the exception of the linebackers. The Will linebacker moves out to a position on the slot receiver. He is the apex of the triangle formed by the offensive tackle and the slot receiver. That means he splits the distance between the slot receiver and the tackle. The Mike linebacker slides to the openside in a 30 alignment, and the Sam linebacker aligns in a 30 alignment behind the tackle.

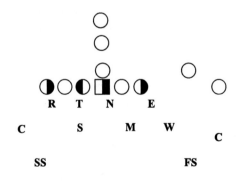

Diagram #2. Twins Set

The free safety goes to the split-end side, and the strong safety plays on the tight-end side. If we get a minus split to one side or the other, we check to cloud, and that side will become two-deep coverage. To the tight-end side, the corner rolls up to the flat, and the strong safety plays the half field coverage behind him. To the twins side, we play quarter coverage.

The strong safety communicates to the corner to play the cloud coverage, and the corner tells the Sam linebacker he is "hard." That means he is rolled up for contain and the flats. With two backs in the backfield, we tell the linebackers they can bow. That means they can stack over the guards.

The corner and free safety do not play the read scheme in our quarter coverage. We play lock-up man coverage on the slot and wide receiver. We play pure man with the corner on the wide receiver, which is the #1 receiver. The free safety plays man coverage on the slot receiver, which is the #2 receiver. We play a combo scheme on those receivers.

The free safety gives the Will linebacker a lock call. That tells the Will linebacker he has the #3 receiver pick-up and force on the run. The Will linebacker plays anyone coming out of the backfield in pass coverage.

If you do not get aligned properly, you have not communicated properly. You can run a 4-4, 4-3, or a 3-3 stack; they are all successful. The difference is whether you have a repertoire and make adjustments. It is not what you run; it is how you run it.

The safety alignment is 10 yards deep and two yards outside the #2 receiver. The strong safety is two yards outside the tight end, and the free safety is two yards outside the offensive tackle to the openside. On the snap of the ball, they step down and never read the quarterback. They read the tight end and the tackle.

The strong safety looks at the corner and calls read. That means the corner has the #1 receiver man-to-man on everything except a crossing route or a five-step hitch pattern. The read call tells the Sam linebacker he has to pick up coverage on the #3 receiver. The Sam linebacker does not care about the tight end. He reads through the linemen to the tailback. The Mike linebacker reads the triangle formed by the two guards and the center.

The Sam linebacker knows that on pass, the #3 receiver is coming from the backfield or from the other side of the field on a cross. He drops into a 10-yard zone area and reads the patterns. The Will linebacker does the same thing.

The Mike linebacker takes his read off of the #3 receiver. The Mike linebacker always opens to the #3 receiver and plays the hook area. If the #3 receiver goes vertical, the Mike linebacker runs with him. The Sam and Will linebackers never drop any deeper than 10 yards. They have a five-yard rule and break on anything from zero to five yards.

The two safeties never jump the #2 receiver from zero to 10 yards. They only pick the #2 receiver up when they pass 10 yards. That is the system we play. That is an overview of quarter coverage as we play it.

The jet formation is two backs and three wide receivers (Diagram #3). For the Mike linebacker, this set is a no-tight-end rule. He declares off the passing strength of the formation. To get that call, he listens to the strong safety. In the diagram, we would call lucky. The Mike linebacker calls tite left. The alignment is the same for the two-receiver side. The Sam linebacker splits the difference between the slot receiver and the offensive tackle. He gets a lock call from the strong safety and is responsible for the force on the run and the #3 receiver on the pass. The lock call puts the strong safety and corner in man coverage.

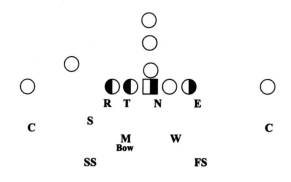

Diagram #3. Jet Adjustment

The lock call lets the strong safety play the crack on the Sam linebacker. He has man coverage on the #2 receiver. If he sees the crackback block on the

Sam linebacker, he is the support player to the outside. However, we tell him he never comes up until he sees contact. He yells to the Sam linebacker that it is coming, but he does not react to it until it occurs.

If the run flow goes away from the Sam linebacker, he has the cutback lane. The rule states that anytime one of the linebackers leaves the box, the other two linebackers can play bow or box. To the split-end side, the free safety calls read. That tells the corner he plays man on everything except a five-yard hitch pattern and the cross. The read tells the Will linebacker he has #3 pick-up and force.

In this formation, you have to determine who you want to play the isolation play. We have two ways we can play the isolation play. We play quarter-quarter-half in the secondary, which will change how we play the isolation on the backside.

If we have a read call to the split-end side, the free safety has man coverage on the #2 receiver (Diagram #4). The #2 receiver is in the backfield. He reads the tackle to his side. If the tackle fans to the outside and blocks the end, the free safety comes to the line in run support. The playside guard and center will combination on the nose. The Will linebacker attacks the fullback and spills the tailback to the free safety, supporting from the outside. If we know the opponent runs the isolation play, the free safety aligns at eight yards and cheats down to six yards.

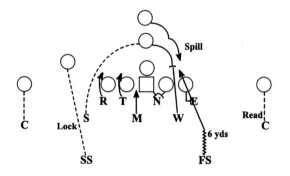

Diagram #4. Isolation Weak vs. Read

The Mike linebacker stays back in the A gap and becomes the cutback player. If we have a cloud call to the splitside, we have to play the isolation differently (Diagram #5). We lose the free safety in

run support on the isolation because he has to play half-field coverage over the top of the corner. The corner rolls to the flat on his side. The corner gives the Will linebacker a "hard" call. The Will knows there is half coverage to his side. He boxes the tailback to the inside. He takes on the block and forces the ball into the inside. The Mike linebacker comes over the top and fits inside the Will linebacker on the tailback.

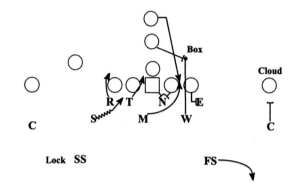

Diagram #5. Isolation Weak vs. Cloud

The Will and Mike linebacker communicate an alert word so the Mike knows to fill inside the box technique of the Will linebacker. The 3-technique tackle slants into the tight-end-side A gap. He fills the A gap to the backside, and the Sam linebacker has the cutback lane in the B gap to the backside. It is too far for the Sam linebacker to fill the A gap. If the nose is strong, you will have no trouble getting the Mike linebacker into the B gap to that side. If the nose is poor, the guard can chip the nose to the center and block the Mike linebacker. That is when you have some problems.

We tell the nose on a double-team to play one of the blockers and not both of them. He has to keep the integrity of the gap he has. We want him to defeat the center because eventually the guard has to get off on the Mike linebacker. When he leaves the double, the nose should make the play on the back. If he takes on the guard, the center should not be able to block the Mike linebacker.

If we get a cloud call, the corner has inside leverage and is reading the offensive tackle (Diagram #6). If we call slice, we get an inside slant by the 5-technique end. He slants into the B gap and spills the play to the outside. The Will linebacker fits outside and boxes the ball back to the inside. The Mike linebacker flies over the top and fits inside the Will linebacker, and the corner fits up into the run, also. He sees the block by the tackle and reacts to run.

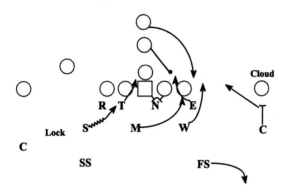

Diagram #6. Iso Weak vs. Cloud/Slice

We do not have a problem playing the run game to the weakside; the problem occurs on the pass. That is why we call the cloud adjustment into the splitside.

We get the two tight ends and two wide receivers look many times. That is an equal distribution set for us (Diagram #7). The calls are made by the position of the ball on the field of play. If the ball is in the middle of the field, the call is left and lucky. If the ball is on the hash mark, the call is a wideside call for the front and the secondary. The nose cannot play a shade with a tight end to his side. He moves to a 1 technique on the backside guard. The 5-technique end moves out to a 7 technique on the second tight end. The Sam and Will linebacker are in a 60-stack alignment on the tight ends.

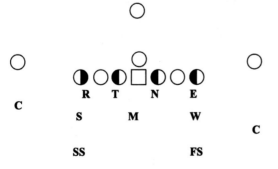

Diagram #7. Law of Distribution

The strong and free safeties give the read call both ways. The free safety likes this because he

can read the tight end instead of the tackle. The block key comes immediately from the tight end. If we get option, the 7 techniques have the quarterback unless the tight end blocks down on them. In that case the outside linebacker has the quarterback, and the safeties come for the pitch. If we get a crack from the outside on the linebacker, the corner comes outside on the pitch. If the tight end arc blocks, the end has the quarterback, and the linebacker or safety has the pitch, depending on what happens with the arc block.

The 7-technique player has some cardinal rules he must observe. He can never expand the C gap. He can never be knocked off the line back into the linebackers. That is all we ask him to do. The 7 technique aligns on the end but has to see the offensive tackle. If the tackle blocks down and he feels no pressure from the tight end, he has to think option. If he sees the dive play to his inside, he is 50 percent on the dive and 50 percent on the quarterback. We have someone on the dive, and the end must play quarterback. If he sees the ball in the dive back's hand, he can fall back inside and help with the tackle. If he does not see the ball, he sits and waits for the quarterback. If the tight end blocks the linebacker, we have no one to take the quarterback. The safety can get to the pitchback, but the end must make the play on the quarterback.

If we have a 2x2 formation, with two quick receivers to the right and the tight end and a wide receiver to the left, we make our calls (Diagram #8). We call that a dual set. The Mike linebacker calls tite left, and the strong safety calls Ringo. Everyone in front lines up normally, except the Will linebacker. He has a detached receiver and applies his rule. To the two-wide-receiver side, we play lock. If the distance between the slot and the tackle is too wide, the Will linebacker calls slice. On the slide, the end slants inside into the B gap, and the Will linebacker has the run support on run his way.

To the tight-end side, we play read coverage with the corner, strong safety, and Sam linebacker. We get a lot of 11-personnel groupings. That is one back, one tight end, and three wide receivers. This ends up in a 3x1 set most of the time. With the tight

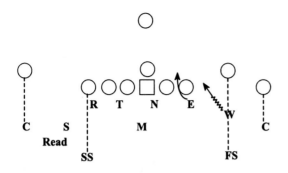

Diagram #8. Dual/Slice

end and two wide receivers to the left and the third wide receiver right, we call tite left and lucky. However, we do not play a pure quarter coverage on this set. We go to solo coverage (Diagram #9). There are many variations, but this is the standard one. The corner to the single-receiver side plays man coverage on the split end. The strong safety tells the corner and Sam linebacker to lock the coverage. The strong safety and corner have locked man coverage on the two wide receivers. The Sam linebacker in lock coverage has the #3 receiver. He plays him up to 10 yards. The free safety tightens his alignment toward the tight-end side. He keys the #3 receiver, who is the tight end. If the tight end goes vertical, the free safety takes him vertical. If he goes to the flat, he becomes the middle-third player.

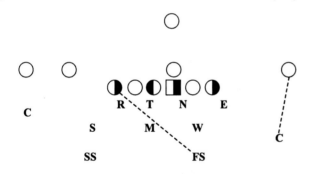

Diagram #9. Solo

The inside linebackers play the way they normally play. Since there is only one back in the backfield, there is no threat of an isolation play. The Mike and Will linebacker read the remaining back. If he goes to the weakside, the Will linebacker has him in man coverage. The Mike linebacker walls anything coming into the middle and does not allow it to come into the middle. If the back goes to the strongside, the Will walls anything coming into the middle, and

the Mike linebacker plays the hook area to that side up to 10 yards. The free safety has anything on a crossing or vertical over 10 yards in the middle. That is the general principle of the solo coverage.

The offense is smart, and we got hurt using that principle. We got hurt on the bootleg. We now tell the free safety he has the vertical in man coverage and any crosser coming across the field. What hurts this adjustment is the option backside. There are three variations for 3x1 coverage, and this is our base coverage.

With two tight ends and two backs in the game, we go to a T-2 adjustment (Diagram #10). The Mike linebacker makes the tite call to the passing strength of the formation. The strong safety announces the adjustment. He announces and does not holler. No one pays any attention to a holler. The passing strength call is lucky. We signal the package in the game from the sidelines. Our base alignment of the front is the same as the dual set with two tight ends. To the flanker side, the strong safety calls read. To the backside, the free safety calls cloud. The corner gives the Will linebacker a "hard" call.

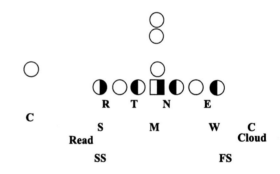

Diagram #10. T-2 Adjustment

The corner keys the tight end on this adjustment. If the tight end blocks down, he plays it like a crackback block and replaces the force. He has to come up and probably take on the fullback or a pulling guard. We do not sit in the defense and play base against the set. We move people and blitz.

You must have one base defense that you can hang your hat on. The players have confidence and can play it against anything. When things go wrong and they have made mistakes in other defenses, it has a calming effect on them. If I ever go into a game and the offense does something different, I get out of the zone blitzes and go to base. It seems to calm the players down.

When the offensive set is an unbalanced set, there are a number of things we need to know about the receivers in the set. The rule for unbalanced is two backs in the backfield and five players to one side. If the formation has a twins look on the outside and a three-man surface, we go to hurricane (Diagram #11). In a hurricane, you stay home and get into the basement. That is the message to the linebackers. They stay in the box and play normal. The front aligns as they usually do

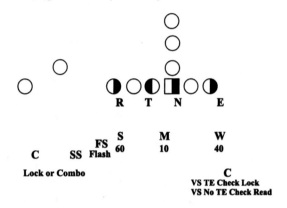

Diagram #11. Hurricane

The strong safety and corner to that side play lock on the twins set. The free safety comes to the twins side and becomes the apex player between the slot receiver and the tight end. The free safety calls flash. That tells the Sam linebacker he has the fourth receiver to that side.

On the backside, the corner has to know if he has an eligible receiver in front of him. If the corner has an eligible receiver, he locks him in man coverage. He calls read because the safety has the first back coming out of the backfield. If there is no eligible receiver to his side, he calls read and plays football.

Gentlemen, I appreciate your attention.

DEFENSIVE BACK FUNDAMENTALS AND DRILLS

Iowa State University

It is great to be here. I love to talk at clinics. I just got the job at Iowa State. I grew up about 20 minutes from Iowa State University in a suburb named Ankeny, Iowa. Getting involved in the Iowa State job was emotional for me. My dad was a high school coach for 35 years in the state of Iowa.

I was on the Auburn University staff last year, and when they brought in Gene Chizik as the head coach, he let the old staff go. So I was sitting in my house in Auburn without a job and the search service called me, wanting to know if I would be interested in the Iowa State head coaching job.

I knew I would have to take the emotion out of the whole process in dealing with the job. This would be especially true when dealing with the trip back home and throughout the interview process. I grew up on a farm in Iowa, and I learned that lesson as a kid growing up.

One morning I came down to breakfast, and there was no food on the table. I was real aggressive about the situation. I asked my mom, "Where is breakfast?" She replied, "There is no breakfast for you until you go out and do your chores." I banged things around and went out to do my chores. First, I went to collect the eggs. As I got to the chickens, I kicked at the first one I saw. I got that job done. Then I went to slop the hogs. The first pig I came to, I gave him a kick in the rear. I was cold and hungry. I was in a hurry to finish the chores. I still had to milk the cows. I went to the barn, kicked "Betsy" in the side, and went on to milk the cows.

I went in the house, and there was a bowl of dry cereal on the table. I asked my mother what was the deal. She replied, "I saw you kick at the chicken, so there are no eggs for you. Then I saw you take the whack at the pig. There will be no bacon for you for a while. I saw you kick ol' Betsy, so there will be no milk for you for a few days. That is all you are getting from me for breakfast."

By that time, my dad came walking down the stairs. As he walked across the kitchen, the cat came over in front of him. He kicked the cat as he came to the table. I looked at my mother and said, "Mom, are you going to tell Dad, or am I?" The moral of the story is that you must take emotion out of it in dealing with these situations.

Our winter practice started on January 12. That was my first opportunity to address the team. I got the job on December 20, 2008, and the players had already gone on the semester break. I did talk to several of them by telephone before that first meeting. At that first meeting, I wanted to establish what the expectations were for the team. This is what I told them: "Take a hard look at what you truly expect to get out of life because that is what you will get. You will get what you expect, seldom do we exceed our expectations, and when we do, we are surprised."

I went over that statement three times. I wanted to make sure they knew what the expectations of the program were going to be from day one. We were 2-10 in the 2008 season. We were 0-8 in the Big 12, and we lost the last 10 games of the season. So I went over the point that we wanted to set our goals very high and that we wanted to make sure everyone understood what would be expected from them.

Iowa State was coached by Dan McCarney for 12 years. Then Gene Chizik came into the program for the last two years. Now, it is my job to build the program to be successful. We are going to build the program with players that have been recruited by both of those former coaches, and with players we bring in this year.

Another thing I wanted to establish with the program was this: I wanted the players to know that we were going to build the program with the understanding that it is "our team!" It does not matter who recruited them, if they were rich or poor, or any other reason to exclude them from the team concept. This is our team! We know if we do not approach the job in a unifying manner, we are not going to have success. I have a quote from Vince Lombardi that stresses this point: "Build for your team a feeling of oneness, of dependence upon one another and of strength to be derived by unity."

It is very important to keep the players informed and aware of what is going on in the program. The more you know about what is taking place and the more you keep them informed, the better they will respond. On the other hand, you must prepare them for the unexpected as well.

I want a hungry football team. If you looked at our last games of the year, we were playing hard. Even with a 2-9 record, we still were playing hard in the fourth quarter. I was not concerned about that when I took the job. I saw the hunger they showed at the end of the season.

There is a difference in *wanting* and *needing*. It includes going to class on time, and doing what you are told to do. We wanted them to develop this attitude: "Begging for what you need, not buying what you want."

The process of building a program takes time. It is not a short-term deal. Another way to express this is an expression to help our players understand this point: "The reason most people fail instead of succeed is that they trade what they want most, for what they want at the *moment!*"

Where do we start in trying to turn the program around? This is where we start: mental toughness!

When I was at the University of Pittsburgh, this is what we did. We sat down as a staff and came up with this definition for mental toughness. This is how we defined mental toughness: Mental toughness is the ability to prepare, practice, and play at a high level of concentration and effort in order to perform like a *champion!*

We tried to include every aspect of the game and included them into that one meaning. It included the physical and the mental aspects of the game. This is what we think it takes to be mentally tough:

- Maturity: recognizing and acknowledging the fact that you are or are not operating at maximum capacity
- Physical conditioning: you must be in superior shape
- An intense, burning desire to be the very best

Every team in your league is doing an off-season program. Everyone in the other conferences is doing an indoor program. The thing is, you must be dong the program better than your opponent. The mental toughness accomplishes that point.

I constantly remind our players of what it takes to be mentally tough. One day, I am going to ask them to write it down for me to see if they are listening to me on what it takes to be mentally tough.

HOW TO BE MENTALLY TOUGH

- Go harder and longer in practice every day. Every day as you start to feel tired and feel like taking a break mentally or physically on the playing field, suck it up and go all out. "One play at a time!"
- Talk to yourself, and do not allow the assassin from within you to defeat you.
- Be enthusiastic in your approach to practice and the game.

We have six stations that we do in our off-season program. It is a part of the concentration aspect of mental toughness. One of the stations is what we call four cones. They start two yards behind the first cone. A coach will call out "Set," and the player jogs up to the first cone. Then, he sprints forward to the next cone. Then, he shuffles over the top to the third cone. Next, he backpedals down to the fourth cone. Then, he turns and runs from the last cone to the original starting point.

If the player steps up too early to start the drill or jumps before the "set," it is a matter of not concentrating. If they cut the cone short on one of the turns, or knock one of the cones over, that is a concentration issue.

We have another station that we call a 5-5-10 station. They start with the left foot on a line. They are going to shuffle to their right. They lead with the right foot, going first to the right, and then with the left foot as they shuffle back to the starting point. Then, they are going to turn and sprint. Then, they start going backwards. They do a five-yard pedal. Then, they step with the right foot, break, come forward, touch with the right foot, and then turn to their left and sprint 10 yards.

The players always have to think. Anytime they make a mistake on the concentration stations, it costs them five up-downs. There has to be consequence when they make a mistake. That is the mental aspect of the drill. If they can do it wrong, they are going to jump offside, or they are going to block the wrong man.

We run the six stations, and they have a minute-and-a-half between each station. If they make four mistakes during the six stations, they have 20 up-downs as a group. When they do this, they lose their rest time between the stations. I told you I thought they were a hungry football team, but I do not think they know what it takes to win. Just wanting to win a big game is not enough. They must need to win the big game. To do that, they must do things right.

Every drill has an end point. It may be a line, a cone, or a bag. If they coast to the finish on any drill, that means they have not given maximum effort. If they do not go full speed all the way through the drill, they are not giving maximum effort. If we see that happen, we add the up-downs.

We work our way through the stations, and it is hard on the players. However, we are teaching them the mental toughness necessary to be successful. That is what we think we must do to get over the hump.

WHAT MENTAL TOUGHNESS DOES FOR US

- It allows us to go home every night, knowing we did everything possible to be successful today.
- It keeps momentum on our side.
- It physically wears out our opponent.
- It helps us to be successful on third down, win the sudden change, conquer in the fourth quarter, and so forth.
- It makes us great human beings, and it makes us a great defensive team.

Here are a couple of my favorite words. The first is *strain*. There is a difference in going hard on a drill and straining on a drill. Straining is giving every ounce of energy you have on a drill. Your teammates can tell when you are straining. Your face turns red, and the veins show up in your neck. Sometimes, it may be a stumble as your run a drill or you elbow someone to keep from hitting the ground on a drill. I got this word from Florida State back in the 1990s when I visited a practice in the spring. When we run our drills, I want to see the players straining. I will go over the drills in a tape later.

The next word I like is *urgency*. I use this word over and over. I want the players to show urgency in everything they do. We use the word a lot, and the players know what we mean when we tell them they must play with urgency.

I am going to get into some of the defensive back information. But, I want you to know it is important to give the players something to make them think, especially in the game today with so many distractions involved. That mental part of the game can diminish the physical part of the game very quickly if we do not stay on top of things with our players. We use all of the points I have just talked about daily in our program.

For every clinic I participate in, I always talk about "Play one play at a time." In addition, I talk about the "five phases of a play." Here are a few things I think are worth getting out of this clinic.

This is how we install defenses: one play at a time. It is an even keel. The good Lord made us in such a way where it is hard for us to pat ourselves on the back when something goes great. In addition, it is hard for us to kick ourselves in the rear end when we do something bad. We must let the play go, and move on. You cannot hang your head when you get beat on a play. You must move on to the next play. On the next play, you may be able to pick off a pass and make it a big play. Let the play go, and move on, one play at a time.

There are five phases to every play in football:

- Call: know and understand the call.
- Recognize the formation.
- Align properly.
- Keys: Run and pass.
- Execute.

The better the football player understands his role, the better the team is going to be. This goes for everyone on the team. We want to eliminate guesswork. Over the years, we have found that more success on offense comes from misalignment by the defense.

We have talked about 60 percent of those five parts of a play, and the ball still has not been snapped at this point. So, we stress the mental and the intellectual aspects of the game in the five parts of a play. If we have been successful up to this point, our chance for success has improved.

Next comes keying the ball. You know what you are teaching them on defense. Make sure they are following the coaching points on keying the run or the pass. The best side of the ball to teach this is from the offensive side of the ball. This is where you can see the eyes of the defensive players.

A secondary coach may have to go behind the defense to see the total picture at times. He has to be able to coach from both sides of the ball. As a coach, if you have a problem with keying the football, you had better get on the offensive side of the ball so you can see the eyes. When you see the players are not keying properly, you must fix the problem at that time. "Get your eyes on your man." If the defense is not keying where they should, they are not going to play fast enough.

At first, all 11 of the defenders want to look at the ball. The tackle must learn to see the breastplate of that offensive tackle. The defensive back may need to see the footwork of the wide receiver. The point I am making is to make sure your players are keying what they are supposed to be keying.

The last point is to execute. Football is a fun game. However, we still must talk to the players about doing their job. Execute your job!

In working with the secondary, we refer to the "Big Four." The secondary is the last line of defense. We stress to them that we can win or lose games, depending on how they react to the Big Four. I think there are certain things each position must accomplish for the defensive team to have success. You may not have four points with the linebackers, or the down linemen. Here is what we stress to the backs in the Big Four.

THE BIG FOUR

- Sure tackling
- No deep balls
- No coverage busts
- Cup the ball

Be sure tacklers. We want to get the offensive man down. We cannot miss tackles. Secondary players must be the surest tacklers on the field, because there is no one behind us to back us up.

We cannot allow a deep pass over our head. This is how we determine if it is a deep ball. We say it is 20 yards for a pass, and 10 yards for a run. If it is a pass over 20 or a run over 10 yards, we call it a big play. It does not matter how far the pass traveled to get to a receiver; it is the total yardage on a play.

We cannot allow mental mistakes or coverage busts. We cannot be playing half coverage on one side, and thirds coverage on the other side. We cannot bust a coverage and leave someone open in a zone.

Saying we want to cup the ball is another way of saying contain the football. It's like a coffee cup; we want to keep the ball inside the cup and in front of our secondary.

During the season, we come in on Sunday, and we go through the big four. The lower those numbers are for each category, the better we have played as a defense. There is a direct correlation to this unit and these four points. Our defensive line could have played poorly, but we got the ballcarrier down every single time he came into the secondary. If we can be successful in those four areas, we have a chance to win the game. The better the secondary plays, the more success we are going to have.

Next, I want to cover some fundamental defensive secondary axioms.

SECONDARY AXIOMS

- Never take an inside fake.
- Play the ball, not the man.
- Deep defender never breaks on short-arm action of the quarterback.

We never take an inside fake. When the quarterback goes back to set up and fakes the ball to the back going up inside, it has no bearing on what my responsibility is. As a defensive back, that inside fake does not change things for me.

We play the ball and not the man. You cover the receiver. You cover the route. Then, you play the ball. A defender cannot play the man and play with his eyes on the quarterback the entire time of a play. The reason for that is the fact the receiver is going to separate from the defensive back, and he has no chance to play the ball. He has to execute the coverage, then he breaks to the man, and then he plays the ball.

Deep defenders cannot break on short-arm action of the quarterback. If we see the short-arm action, we cannot break up on that move. Deep defenders cannot break on the arm action of the quarterback and still play deep.

TO BE A GREAT DEFENSIVE BACK

To be a great defensive back, you must have all of these qualities. They are necessary for all secondary players:

- Stance
- Eyes
- Backpedal

It all starts with the stance. The stance starts in the ankle, rises to your knee, and on up to your hips. You must flex your ankles, bend your knees, and you must sink your hips. I love buzzwords and phrases. Flex the ankles, bend your knees, and sink the hips. It is not just a waist bend. That is not where the stance starts.

We all have players who have stiff joints. We can improve on the stiffness by starting with the ankles. Give them exercises where they have to stretch the ankles, and have them work on keeping the heels flat on the ground. Give them exercises where they have to work on bending the knees. Have them sink the hips as they bend the knees.

When we are in our stance, we want our numbers over the knees and our knees over our feet. When we start to move out of our stance, the numbers should stay over our knees, and the knees should stay over the feet. Each player is built differently. They have been told since youth league football to get down low. For players with long legs, bending down low is not good for them.

The first thing players do when they are bent down too low is to rise to their natural pad level. You have to find the natural pad level for each player. If a player has to change his pad level when he starts moving, the stance is not helping him. He has to find his natural pad level.

The eyes play a big part in playing defensive back. Where do you want them to key? I use a phrase to describe young players coming into our program: "You have high school eyes." All they want to look at is the quarterback. All they want to look at is the football. The vision has to be trained to where you want it to be to executed. On certain coverages, you want the vision on the quarterback the whole time. That is okay for that one defensive call. We say the eyes need to be where they need to be.

The backpedal is important in playing in the secondary. Some coaches teach shuffle. Some players struggle to backpedal. To be a great defensive back, to keep your shoulders parallel to the line of scrimmage, I think you must be able to backpedal.

Here is what we set out to accomplish in our individual fundamentals:

- Movement
- Tackling
- Ball drills

We have three phases of movement. We want to move, we want to pedal, and we want to shuffle, change directions, and get our hips open. Everything that we do as a safety or corner, we want to replicate in our individual movements. We want to have a movement phase.

We want to tackle. We want a physical phase of our individual fundamentals. I will cover the tackling drills we use in the film clip. We include in the physical phase getting off blocks. We work on taking on different blocks. In addition, we work on rerouting a receiver.

The next phase in our individual fundamentals is our ball drills. If we are going to cheat on the individual periods, it is going to be in the ball drills. I am never going to cheat on movement and tackling phase.

Let me get into some meat of the lecture. We talk about backpedal, and it is what we refer to as line progression. I said you must be able to backpedal to be a great defensive back. I think you can teach the backpedal. It starts with a good stance, and leaning with the butt. If you are going to backpedal properly, you do not lead with your shoulder blade. You lead with your butt. The hips and the butt should lead the way. When you are teaching this drill to the young kids in early practice, you teach it from the side so you can see it. Make sure the butt and hips are leading the way.

We want to snap from the knees down. We pedal back and forth until I feel the butt is leading the way. If we do not have the butt leading the way, we cannot advance to the next phase of the drill.

Once we have the butt leading the way, we want to snap from the knees down. A pedal is not a run. As you pedal, you do not use the entire leg as you do when you are running forward. You snap from the knee down as you pedal. As you snap, you are reaching back and you are gaining ground. It is a pedal, a snap, not a run.

Arm movement come next. I am not big on what type of movement, but there is momentum that goes with the movement. It should correspond to increasing your speed. Some players will snap from the elbow as they get into the backpedal. We like to snap from the knees down, moving the arms.

As we snap from the knees down, we want to take the top of the grass with our cleats. Take the tops of the blades of grass off the ground. You do not pick the foot up high as you pedal. As we take the top of the grass with our cleats, the length is going to decrease as we go back. We have to put our feet down quicker as we retreat. We want to gain ground as we pedal.

We set up the drills where we can watch the backpedal from the side. We want to start as many drills as we can on movement instead of sound. We react to movement, and not sound. On certain tackling drills, you have no choice but to go on sound.

I will show the drill at the end of the lecture. Most of the drills are simple drills, and you will see what we are doing once we cover the drills and then show the tape.

There are four phases of the backpedal:

- Control
- Speed
- Zone-turn
- Turn and run

If you are going from a hitch route to the post route, you are going to go through these four phases.

Control pedal is keying the route and deciphering. We are trying to decide if it is a run or if it is a pass. If it is a pass, is it a running pass, or a hot pass, which is a three-step drop and throw? Most passing teams show you within the first three steps what they are going to do. They come out from the center and look immediately to the flat where they are going to throw the ball. It is a hot route. If we can read that on the first step, we want to be able to respond on that one step. This is when we are doing the control phase. For most techniques, we key the quarterback. Once we read the quarterback, we leave him. We do stay on the quarterback all the way through the play. After we read him, we play the man and then play the ball.

The second phase of the progression is the speed aspect. We use the speed pedal when we have a dropback pass. The passes we are going to defend here are the intermediate or beyond. We want to hold the backpedal as long as we can. As the speed increases, the pad level stays the same. That is the control and the speed phase.

Next is the zone-turn phase. Just as the stance is different for each athlete, the cushion is different. When the receiver has broken my cushion, we have to get the hips open and turn. If he does not get the hips open, the receiver runs by the defensive back. Each secondary player has a different cushion. We are not going to be in a zone-turn very long. It is perpendicular to the line of scrimmage.

The fourth phase of the backpedal is the turn-and-run phase. The receiver had eaten up the cushion on the defensive back. Now, the defensive back has to turn and run with the receiver. He needs to stay with the upfield shoulder, protecting the goal line. Now, the eyes are on the man as opposed to looking back at the quarterback. He has to get back to cover the receiver so he does not look at the quarterback.

Next is our hot drill (Diagram #1). We have two defensive backs. We have the option to put out a wide receiver. We assume he is outside even if we do not have a player in that position. This is the area that the eyes of the defensive backs go. The quarterback comes out from the center to show the defensive backs what it is going to be like in a game.

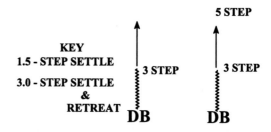

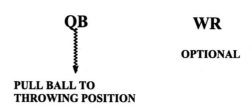

Diagram #1. Hot Drill

There are two types of hot passes. They are the immediately rise up and pass, or the quarterback takes a step-and-a-half and then throws. We find about 90 percent of them are very quick, and 10 percent are one-and-a-half step.

It is the job of the coach to know what the steps are going to be each week so the defensive backs can go over them. We key the eyes of the quarterback. As soon as he shows hot, they settle and identify the route. We settle, backpedal, ID the route, and then drive.

The next movement drill is the W Drill (Diagram #2). This is where we work all of our change of direction. At one time, we did this drill with a football. Then, we did it with a hand movement. Now, I do the drill with the body. I simulate a receiver running in place.

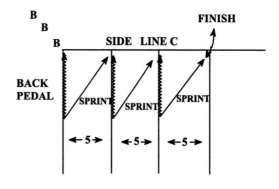

Diagram #2. W Drill

We have four cones placed five yards apart. On the movement of the coaches, the first defensive back starts his backpedal on the first line. When the coach does a stutter with his feet, the defensive back breaks from his backpedal to the next cone. He repeats the routine to each cone. We want him running all the way through to the last cone. We do not want them jogging past the cone on the last two yards. They must sprint past the cones. When the first player reaches the second cone, the next player starts his backpedal. When the first player reaches the last cone, we have three defensive backs in the drill. Another phrase we use is: "Finish drills to finish plays." Just as there is a start and stop to every play, or a snap and a whistle to end every play, we use the term finish the drills as you finish a play in a game. We are going to do the drill until they do it right and finish the drill.

We work against the in route, out route, and post route. We do not have to run the entire distance on the plays. We break the receivers at different levels.

Another thing we do in the W drill is the zone-turn break (Diagram #3). We had told the defenders it is against a dropback pass. When the receiver starts his movement, I want him into his speed pedal as opposed to control and then speed. We work against the in, out, post, and centerfield routes.

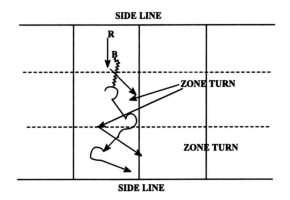

Diagram #3. Zone-Turn Break

When the defender does his zone-turn, he opens his hips and rotates them in the other direction. He can also do a speed turn. Instead of opening his hip and rotating to the other side, he turns his head and shoulders to the other side. There is a momentary lost of sight of the quarterback, but it is faster for the defensive back.

Next is our box drill. This is a movement for every position. We have a 10x10 box (Diagram #4). We set up four cones. I have two defensive backs in the box and a coach on the line. We call out "feet." The players pump their feet. Then, we call "back," and they pedal. Then, the coach points to one of the four cones. The two defensive backs turn and sprint in the direction of that cone. They are running toward that cone as urgently as they can.

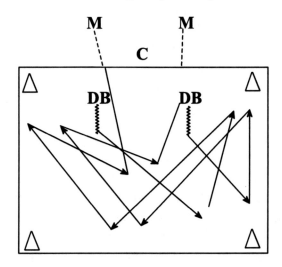

Diagram #4. Box Drill

Next, I am going to change the two defenders. Their eyes have always been on me. Their chest is always open toward the coach. Now, they are backing up to the first cone. They are dropping to the curl area. With two steps, we have changed them. It is quick two-steps, and we can change the direction of the defenders. When we finish the drill, they sprint forward, and a manager throws them a ball. We may go for five movements, and no more than seven changes of direction. We want to make sure they finish the drill strong, just as they would in a game.

Let me get to the tape with our drills.

THE SHOTGUN THREE- AND FIVE-STEP PASSING GAME

University of Georgia

Thank you, gentlemen. It is a pleasure to be here. This past off-season, I got a chance to spend some time in Southeast Asia. I spent time with the Marines, Army, Navy, Air Force, and Coast Guard. I stayed at several Air Force bases. I spent the night in the middle of the Persian Gulf on the *USS Nassau.*

I got a chance to meet a lot of 18- to 25-year-old men and women. They were there defending our country. I cannot tell you how impressed I was with what I saw. There are a lot of similarities between the military and football. The difference is what happens in a loss. If we lose a game, we shake it off and get ready for the next one. If the military loses a game, we are all in trouble. We play home games in football. However, we do not want any home games when it comes to war.

I have the greatest admiration for you gentlemen from the Marine Corps who are here today. I did not grow up in a military family and do not have much to connect me to that kind of life. However, I know military life is an outstanding career. I have seen the young people that are serving in our military. I see their morale, unity, cohesiveness, and organization. It is a massive operation, and I was totally impressed.

I am here to talk about some X's and O's in the quick-passing game. I want to talk about the difference between being under the center and in the shotgun. We made the transition to that some years ago when I was at Florida State University. The strategy and competition of the game of football is what got me into coaching. I was not good enough to keep playing, so I started coaching.

The more I coach, the more I realize the responsibility we have to the players we coach. How bad do these guys need us? How sad are our country's young people? They are sitting around watching TV and playing video games. They are trying to get out of any kind of work. Their parents do not make them do anything they do not want to do. They want to be their friend instead of their parent. That is what we live with every day. These guys need us desperately. This country needs football coaches desperately. They need you to show their kids the way. You have to show them how to work and fight through something tough.

I know that winning is awesome and that competition is what gets us excited. There are a lot of things wrong with football, but if we did not have football in this country, we would be in sadder shape. We are developing leaders for this country in all our communities. I want to applaud you coaches for what you do.

I think we need to take this job very seriously. If you are a young coach just starting out, you are like what I was years ago. All I wanted to hear was X's and O's. I want you to remember we have a tremendous obligation to the young men under our authority. Leading is serving the needs of the people we command. We serve our players by loving them, disciplining them, and helping them grow into the kind of men they should be.

I had the pleasure of working for Bobby Bowden. I call him "Coach," and he is like a boss to me. I look up to him. He not only gave me my first job, but he is my spiritual mentor. He is the most influential man in my life outside of my father. I want to thank him publicly for everything he has done for me.

After a few years coaching at Florida State, I got a chance to be the play caller. Coach Bowden had called the plays for years and done a good job of it. He came to a point in his career where he felt he could turn that responsibility over to the staff. The first season I called the plays was 1992. That was the year Charlie Ward was to be the starting quarterback.

We decided in the two-minute drill we would go to the shotgun. We did it from a five-receiver look. In our first game against Duke, Charlie threw four interceptions and four touchdowns. We were good enough to overcome those turnovers. In the second game, we played Clemson. He threw four more interceptions. The fourth interception was late in the fourth quarter, which was returned for a touchdown. I do not know the player's name, but we called him Barcelona because that was the site of the summer Olympics and he was a sprinter on that team.

Our defensive linebackers coach was sitting next to me in the press box. I called the play, and we had a lead at the time. I thought I was feeling stress from the bad call because I could not breathe. It was not the stress; it was the linebacker coach's hand around my neck, choking me. With two or three minutes left in the game, we were down four points. We got in the shotgun and used a no-huddle offense. We went right down the field, scored a touchdown, and won the game. We won the game because of the no-huddle, shotgun offense.

Later that season, we played Miami. We got behind and eventually lost the game on a wide-right field goal. However, we came back in the game with the no-huddle and shotgun attack. Miami began to bring linebacker pressure, and we did not protect very well. We decided to keep a back in the game with the quarterback in the shotgun.

We played Georgia Tech later in the season and were down by three scores going into the fourth quarter. We used the no-huddle, shotgun with one back in the backfield. We still had trouble protecting because Georgia Tech was bringing blitzes off both edges. We inserted the second back in the backfield. With two backs in the shotgun set, we protected better and had more offense with our screen game to the backs. We drove the ball 80 yards twice for two touchdowns. We onside-kicked the ball and recovered. We drove 60 yards for the winning score. It was a miracle.

When I got home after that game, my wife made a comment. She told me that Charlie did so well in the two-minute drill, we should start out the game with it. I told her that was a good idea. That was the birth of the no-huddle, shotgun offense at Florida State.

The next game was Virginia. It rained, and we did not want to take the chance with a wet ball. We did not use it until the next home game against Maryland. We used the no-huddle, shotgun offense from the start to the finish of the game. In the game, we had 10 drives that lead to 10 touchdowns. We had 858 yards of total offense. Charlie had over 400 yards passing and over 100 yards rushing. We were going fast in those days. At Georgia, we are not doing that, but I wanted to give you some background about how this offense came about.

At the start of the 1993 season, we decided to use the shotgun as our primary offense. We had the ability to go under the center, but the shotgun was the primary set. The problem we had to solve as a coaching staff was to make the three-step passing game from under the center match the shotgun. We were having timing problems in the shotgun. For the quarterbacks to catch the ball and throw was not a natural move for them. They lacked the rhythm and balance to throw the football that way.

The receiver's footwork was the same but the ball was not getting there on time. We were missing the windows that we usually got in the quick game. We decided to make the receiver's footwork fit the shotgun throws and change the footwork of the quarterback under the center to fit the timing of the receivers.

I am going to start out with a route we call "run it." It is a fade/stop pattern. It is an eight-yard route for us. We get off the jam of the defensive back, run as hard as we can for eight yards, and hit the brakes. The quarterback aligns five yards from the center. He catches the ball, gets into a three-step rhythm, and throws the ball. That is the footwork he uses in the shotgun. If he is under the center, he uses a quick five steps. Every step in that drop is quick.

The reason we run this route goes back to the way we used to run the hitch route or a speed-out.

The conversion route with these patterns with press coverage was a fade or takeoff. We ran the hitch route at six yards, and the quarterback took three steps. If we got press coverage, we threw the fade. Years ago, there were not many teams using press coverage on every down.

Defenses started playing press coverage on every down with the robber scheme built in. Mickey Andrews at Florida State fell in love with that scheme. Every down, we had a cornerback standing on top of our receiver, not allowing the quick hitch pattern.

The patterns we used to throw on first down were taken away by the pressed corner. Every time we called a hitch route, we ended up throwing a fade. They played man coverage with outside leverage and funneled everything inside to the low-hole player. They did not give the offense the easy throw on the hitch and slant. The receiver had trouble getting off the press, and the quarterback had trouble throwing the fade.

That was one of the reasons we changed the footwork from a three-step drop to a quick five. The quick five gives the receiver more time to escape the jam, get more separation, and let the quarterback see what type of ball he needs to throw on the fade. However, if you call a hitch and have to convert the route to a fade, you will not complete a high percentage of those passes. That is not what you want on a first-down play.

We are looking for a high percentage route. That is why we began to use the "run it" route (Diagram #1). It is good against press or bail coverage. The only coverage it is not good against is cover 2 and the rolled up corner. We have a way to run the pattern against cover 2, but you cannot blind call this route. If we get too much cover 2, we are wasting our time.

Our wide receiver's outside foot is back in our stance. It does not matter where his feet are aligned. All he is trying to do is get off the jam and run hard up to eight yards. When he gets to eight yards, he hits the brakes, and turns in to the quarterback. The receiver wants to give the defensive back a

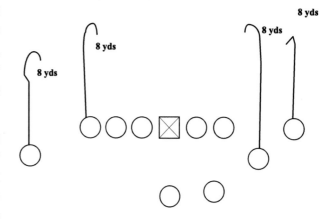

Diagram #1. Run It

move up the field that forces him to get out of the framework of his body and move his feet. He rips through the hands of the defensive back, gets to eight yards, and puts on the brakes. If the coverage is soft technique or bail coverage, the receiver makes the defensive back think he is going deep.

The quarterback takes his three steps and gets rid of the ball. If the quarterback waits until the receiver stops, he gives the defensive back a chance to make a play on the ball. For this pass to be successful, it must be thrown on time and rhythm. When the receiver plants and faces the quarterback, the quarterback throws the ball at the outside breastplate. If the receiver looks covered, he is not. As soon as the receiver hits the brakes, the ball is on him. By the time the corner hits the brakes, there is nothing he can do to stop the pass. This is the type of pattern you would run into the boundary.

To the wideside of the field, this pattern works better as a two-man pattern (Diagram #2). If we have a twin set into the wideside of the field, we use a "void" pattern. We generally get a corner in a press or bail look with a strong safety aligned on the slot receiver. We throw the pass off the curl/flat defender. The slot receiver runs an eight-yard pattern at the inside shoulder of the flat defender. If the curl/flat defender stays in the curl area, the slot receiver protects the throw to the wide receiver by stopping and occupying the defender.

If the strong safety buzzes the flat, the slot receiver chases his hip. That gives the slot receiver

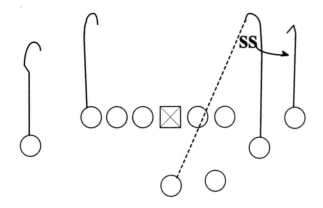

Diagram #2. Void

width. At eight yards, he turns back and catches the football. The reason he chases the hip is to get width from the inside linebacker.

We can run the same thing into the boundary. If we have a tight end and wide receiver into the boundary, the pattern is the same. The tight end works upfield on the outside linebacker. The read is the same as the strong-safety read to the wideside of the field. The tight end runs at the inside hip of the Will linebacker. He chases his hip if he widens to cover the flat. The whole object is to hold the curl/flat defender in that area to give the quarterback a clear throwing lane to the wide receiver.

The read we give to the quarterback is to take the short throw. In college, we still have a wideside and shortside of the field. Our goal is to throw to the shortside of the field. If there is any type of soft coverage, we throw to the outside receiver on the fade/stop unless the flat defender gets under the route.

If we see the free safety working into the boundary or down the boundary hash mark, we throw to the wideside of the field. If the free safety works to the boundary, the coverage is some type of rolled-up coverage. We throw the ball to the wide receiver into the field.

The obvious question is: how do you keep from throwing into a cover-2 secondary? If we try to run the ball, we have to figure out how many defenders are in the box. We have five linemen and a fullback to match up with a six-man box. If there are six defenders in the box, we run the ball. If the defense

puts another defender in the box, we throw the ball. That sounds simple.

It used to be when you came to the line of scrimmage, we knew from the pre-snap read the defense, but not anymore. Defenses disguise everything they do on defense. They show one thing and run something else. They try to disguise their coverage as long as they can. That is when the "freeze play" concept came along.

We use the "freeze play" to help us determine what to do. We use our cadence to entice the defense. We use voice inflexions to get the defense to jump or begin to commit players to the box. Once we see them jumping or moving in the secondary, we have an opportunity to change the play. If they are committing defenders to the box, we have the ability to check to a quick-passing game.

Everyone has their own system to run the "freeze play." The quarterback in the huddle calls the formation, freeze play, and the cadence. We come to the line of scrimmage with no play. After he goes through the cadence, he gets a clue as to what the defense will do. If the defense jumped into the neutral zone, the center snapped the ball and we got a free five yards. If they did not jump, we audible to the play we want to run.

You do not want to blind call plays unless you are getting the same coverage almost every time. If you play a team that will not run cover 2, you can blind call every play. If we read press coverage with one high safety, "run it" is a great play.

If you come to the line of scrimmage and read the blitz coming off the edge from the formation side, that does not mean you have the quick throw into the boundary (Diagram #3). The zone blitz has become extremely popular in college football. If the defense brings pressure from the field, they like to drop the opposite side end. We do not want to throw the ball to the defensive end under the wideout to the boundary. The safer throw is into the field.

We have the fade/stop to the outside receiver and the "void" route to the inside receiver. If the strong safety walls the slot receiver and tries to

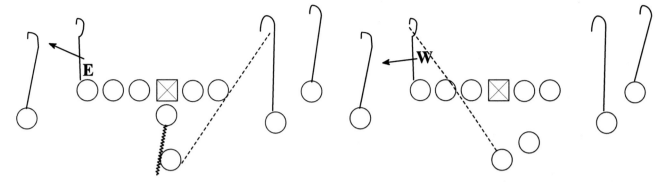

Diagram #3. Zone Blitz   **Diagram #4. Double Void**

keep him out of the middle, the quarterback throws the hitch to the outside receiver. It is critical that the "void" route and "run it" route be the same depth. If the slot runs his route at five yards and the outside receiver runs his pattern at eight yards, the strong safety will be in the throwing lane to the wide receiver.

We run the pattern at eight yards because we got the concept from Chan Gailey, who coached for the Pittsburgh Steelers. I thought that would be a good place to start. It works like a charm. If the receiver gets a free release, we run the pattern at eight yards. If the receiver gets jammed hard, it may end up six-and-a-half or seven yards.

If we run the stop route at five yards, we do not have time to sell the corner on the deep route. This is not a lollygagging route. The receiver has to run the pattern as hard as he can to sell the defensive back that he is going deep.

You see us in the three-wide-receivers, one-tight-end, and one-back set many times (Diagram #4). We like two wide receivers to the wideside of the field, and the tight end and split end into the boundary. The thing I like about this set is it gives us a "void" route into the boundary. If we get the flat defender buzzing the flat, the throw to the tight end is easy. This gives us protection for the stop route to the boundary.

We can run this route from the two-tight-end set. It is the same 2x2 set.

The next play is one of the best plays we have run over the years. We can make this a huddle call or make it a blind call. This play is a high-percentage

pass and easy to throw. I like this pass because the quarterback does not hold the ball long. Offensive line coaches like that part of the play.

I like it because you can throw it against almost any defense. It teaches the quarterback how to read defense even though it is a simple read. The quarterback can make quick decisions and get the ball out. You can call the play anything you want. I will call it "slant" (Diagram #5). The outside receiver's outside foot is back in their stance. They take five steps and break the pattern on a 45-degree angle. If the inside receiver is on the line of scrimmage, he runs an "arrow" route to a point. The point is three yards deep and three yards from the line of scrimmage.

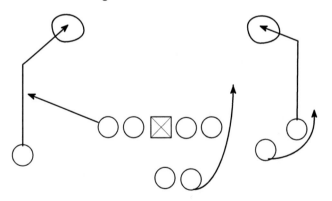

Diagram #5. Slant

The inside receiver can run the arrow route from off the line of scrimmage, but we like the "scat" route. On the scat route, the slot receiver aligns three yards off the line of scrimmage. He loses two yards from his alignment and stretches the field outside. When he reaches the numbers on the field, he works downfield. On his fifth or sixth step, he gets his head around to the quarterback. He is running full speed and stretching the field as much as he can.

The advantage of the scat route is the receiver's pads are square to the line of scrimmage when they catch the ball. Their pattern affords them space and allows them to make defenders miss tackles. If the receiver catches an arrow route, he is across the line of scrimmage. Generally, someone will hit the receiver immediately before he gets a chance to turn the ball downfield.

Because we throw the ball behind the line of scrimmage, most defensive coaches view that as a no-cover zone. They do not cover it and try to react back to the ball. That creates space between your skilled runner and the defenders. Open-field tackling is one of the most difficult things to do on defense.

The back in the backfield runs an "M route." The name of the route comes from the San Francisco 49ers. Bill Walsh ran both his running back on these routes, and it looked like an "M." The back starts out by losing a little ground. He tries to slip down the middle of the football field. That gives us two receivers in the curl areas, two in the flat areas, and one down the middle. The offense wants to stretch the defense, and we can do it with this play.

If we have a one-back set, the offensive line does not have to protect for a long period of time. The quarterback throws the ball quickly (Diagram #6). With one linebacker in the middle, we make a middle call. The two guards and the center are responsible for the two inside down defenders and the Mike linebacker. The tackle to the boundary has a double read on the defensive end and Will linebacker. He uses a pass set and blocks the defender who rushes inside. If both of them rush, he blocks the inside threat and releases the outside rusher. The tackle to the fieldside has a back to his side and blocks the defensive end. The back has a read on the Sam linebacker.

If there were two linebackers in the box, the back double reads the Sam linebacker and strong safety. The quarterback sees the rush and gets rid of the ball. We do not hold the ball long with this type of protection.

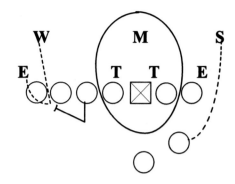

Diagram #6. Protection Scheme

We call the read for the quarterback a "robber" read (Diagram #7). The set you need to run this route is a 3x2 set. If we align in a twin set to the field with a split end into the boundary, we can have a tight end in the boundary slot or a back in the backfield.

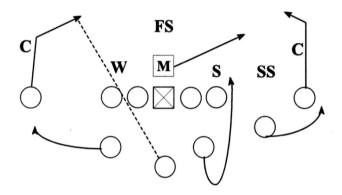

Diagram #7. Robber Read, One High

The defense we see is a five-under man coverage with a free safety. The front brings a four-man rush scheme. The corners press the two wide receivers. The strong safety mans up on the slot receiver to the field. The Sam and Will linebackers take the backs in the backfield man-to-man. The free safety in the middle of the field is free, and the Mike linebacker is the low-hole player in the middle of the field. He is a free defender in the middle underneath coverage.

The corners play with outside leverage on the wide receivers and force them to the inside. Everyone tries to force all the receivers into the middle of the field to the two free players. The safety is high, and the Mike linebacker is low in the middle of the field. The defense tries to force all the receivers to the free players so they can splatter them. By playing outside leverage, the corners cannot stop the slant route. However, the defense feels the Mike linebacker will explode the receiver coming inside on the slant.

We run the route as a mirrored concept. We have slants coming from both sides. The quarterback's read in a one-high safety look is the Mike linebacker. He cannot cover both sides. We read his movement and throw opposite. If the coverage is cover 3, we read the same player. If the coverage is cover 3, we have a curl/flat concept, and we win.

If the coverage is cover 3 and the Mike linebacker covers to the weakside, they can cover the curl/flat to that side. However, to the other side, they have a problem. With one safety high, the Mike linebacker tells the quarterback which side to throw. When the quarterback receives the ball, he looks at the Mike linebacker. If he goes to the strongside, the quarterback throws to the weakside. His immediate intention is to throw the weakside slant.

The quarterback does not throw the ball off the drop of the Mike linebacker. His drop tells him the side to throw. He knows if the Mike linebacker went strong, the Will linebacker is the only defender to the weakside. If there is anyone in his vision as he looks at the slant, he throws to the flat. His last choice is to throw the ball away. Zone blitzes have made it tough on the quarterbacks, but he can see the coverage.

We have the same routes working the strongside and weakside. The ball goes to the slant or flat routes with a one-high safety. The ball will not get to the M route. The M route is the receiver we use against a cover 2.

If we get a pre-snap cover-2 look in the secondary, the robber-read concept changes (Diagram #8). The read for the quarterback is the free safety. He watches to see what he does. If the free safety goes strong, the quarterback throws weak. If he goes weak, the quarterback throws strong. If the safety stays on the hash mark, the quarterback looks strong, however, the quarterback does not know what coverage he may see into the strongside. The look to the strongside makes the defenders think he is going to the

fieldside. However, he knows there is a good chance the ball will go to the M route.

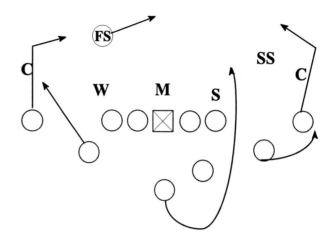

Diagram #8. Robber Read, Two High

In a cover-2 defense, the quarterback's read and the patterns take a little longer to run than cover 3 or the one-high safety look. If the defense runs a zone blitz, they bring five rushers. If they blitz the Mike and Sam linebackers and drop the defensive end, we can block all of them with our protection scheme. They have five rushing, three deep, and three underneath defenders and one of them is a defensive end.

We block all the rushers and throw quickly. The defense cannot cover the slant, arrow, or scat patterns. This play kills the zone-blitz scheme if they play cover 3 in the secondary. The quarterback cannot predetermine where he goes with the ball. He has to read the key and determine the side.

Are there any questions you would like to ask before I continue? The question asked was: *Why do we play a tight end with your split receivers instead of another wide receiver?*

I like the tight end with the three-wide-receiver set. There are two reasons we like that type of set. The last three or four tight ends who have played for us are now in the NFL. That is one reason we like the tight-end set. We have been blessed with tight ends who can block like offensive tackles and run patterns like backs. The tight end does not have far to run to stretch the defense into the boundary. We feel he can stretch the defense as well from a tight position as he can from the split. With the tight end aligned to the tight formation, it gives us the option of having a six- or seven-man protection scheme. If he is split, he can stretch the defense quicker, but he will run out of field before the ball gets there.

Question: Explain the numbering of your receivers.

Do not get confused by the way we identify our receivers. If we are aligned in a standard pro set, the flanker is the Z, the tight end is Y, and the split end is X. The backs in the backfield are the H-back, the halfback, and F-back is the fullback. When we go no-huddle, our formations are right or left. The Z-receiver and Y-end were always to the wide field. The X-end and H-back were to the boundary side.

If I wanted a fourth receiver in the game, we called him "Ted." We took out the F-back. If the tight end replaced the F-back, he was also called the "Ted." The tight end ended up being called the "Ted" rather than the Y-receiver. The tight end became "Ted" because of the no-huddle, hurry-up offense. The Y-receiver in the twins set is not the tight end. If we had both the H-back and F-back in the game, we put the H-back into the wideside of the field. He is the faster back and can stretch the field faster.

I need to cover one more thing. When we run the slant route against press coverage, we have two ways to do it. The key to the receiver's first move on the press corner is to perform it outside the frame of the defender's body. If the receiver does his moves in front of defensive back, you will not move him. If the receiver does his move outside the framework of the defender body and up the field, the defender has to move. If he does not move, we can beat him on the fade. The first move is a good hard jab step to the outside of the defender (Diagram #9). After the jab, we slip by on the inside. We push up the field for five yards and break the slant.

The other way we beat the press is to break outside. We take three steps to the outside as if we were running a fade. When we get the defender turned, we break underneath him and up the field to the break.

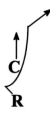

Diagram #9. Jab/Slip

If the coverage is a soft corner, we take five steps and make the break at a 45-degree angle. When we throw the slant, the quarterback's aiming point is from the belt buckle to the armpit on the body of the receiver. I do not want a receiver to reach for a ball on the slant route. Even if it is slightly ahead of him. That leaves him too exposed for a hit. I want the ball on the body on the slant route.

When the quarterback throws the ball on the scat route, the aiming point is one foot in front of the receiver's jersey number. On the arrow route, the quarterback throws the ball at the receiver's chest. If he throws the ball at the receiver's chest, the ball will catch up to him. Do not lead him on the arrow route. Throw the ball at him, and it will catch up to him. If the quarterback tries to lead the receiver, he ends up losing yards or falling down.

I like this pattern against any defense we see except quarters. In quarters, the defense can double the slot and fly a defender out to the flat. They also have a linebacker sitting to the inside on the in route.

This play is good in first or second down and third-and-medium. On third-and-long, it is not such a good play.

I am speaking at the FCA luncheon. I hope you can attend. Thank you for your attention.

Donnie Roberts

BEING MULTIPLE IN THE THREE-MAN FRONT

Lehigh University

Thank you. I am going to talk about our 3-4 multiple defense. I work with the three down defensive linemen. I feel comfortable talking about defensive line drills and techniques. I will tell you what we do in our three-man front. I will cover the way we teach the defense and cover some of the things we have been very successful with when running this defense.

I had not been a 3-4 defensive coach until three years ago. We had a new defensive coordinator come in, and he made the change. He liked the multiplicity of the 3-4 defense. We are very multiple in what we do with our 3-4 defense.

In our philosophy, there are certain things that we want to make sure we get accomplished. First, we want to be fundamentally sound. We start with the philosophy that everything we do is going to be fundamentally sound.

One special thing we do with our defense is to stress one area of fundamentals during the week. Each of the defensive coaches takes a specific area related to the game where we want to teach fundamentals. We do that every single day. There is never a time when we have to say we are going back to fundamentals. We do not go back to fundamentals; we want to keep on working daily on fundamentals.

We take a 10-minute period and do fundamental rotation drills once each week. We stress particular aspects that we feel we need to work on for that week. The idea is that we want to be fundamentally sound at all times.

We start with our three-point stance. We will cut down on the stagger more, being in a 3-4 defense. We want the back foot up, where the back-foot toes touch the back part of the toes on the front foot. That is against a balanced stance, where we can move left or right. For the most part, you will see us in a balanced stance.

We stress keeping the eyes on the target. What is the target? The target is where the down lineman wants to place his hands on the offensive blocker. If the eyes are on the target, the hands will hit the target. If the eyes are not on the target, he will not hit the target. The hands will follow the eyes.

We work on our takeoff and the blow delivery. We work on the block escape, and we work on pursuit to the ball. The idea is not to grab and shove the blocker. The idea is to gain control of the block. We work on a progression of things the defensive line must follow in taking on offensive blockers.

- Takeoff
  - ✓ Read, attack
  - ✓ Attack, read
- Blow delivery
  - ✓ Eyes: Eyes on target; see what you want to hit.
  - ✓ Hands: Stab and grab; hit the target with the hand and "squeeze grapes."
  - ✓ Feet: Feet follow; reach and gather. Explode out of the hips.
- Reestablish the line of scrimmage. Gain.
- Leverage on your man—horizontal and vertical.
- Effort, desire, compete! Finish plays.
- Defeat blocks:
  - ✓ Gain control of the block first.
  - ✓ Find the ballcarrier.
  - ✓ Shed and release from the block.
  - ✓ Accelerate to the ball. Tackle. Playmakers.
  - ✓ Do your job first.
- Be a difference-maker. Create havoc every play. Mental toughness!

"Trust your techniques. Do all the little things."

We have three ways to disguise our fronts:

- Stem front/Raider
- Random
- Slant

DISGUISING THE FRONTS

- Stem is to show one front and move to another front prior to snap.
- Raider is to show pressure: Show-and-go, or show-but-play.
- For down linemen, it is: Moving alignments prior to the snap.
- To attack and change fronts on the snap is a major part of our package.
- Random is changing the shades by the defensive linemen. This is to keep the blockers off balance and force them to use a different blocking scheme. If we get caught in a random as you are changing your alignment, the rule is to slant to where you were supposed to be before you moved.

Let me cover our base fronts. First is the field Hawk cover 3 (Diagram #1). We have Stud, Sam, Mike, and Will linebackers. We have a left tackle and a right tackle. We have a nose man. We have two corners, a strong safety in the slot, and a free safety to the field. We are going to use directional calls on the coverage. When we run field Hawk, we are telling the defense where the "me" linebacker is going to line up. "Me" is the Stud linebacker. If we call "you," it would be the Will linebacker. Here, we are declaring to the tight end.

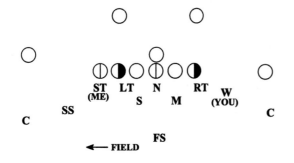

Diagram #1. Base Front—Field Hawk Cover 3

Our contain man is never a force player. The force player comes from a linebacker or a secondary player. The defensive lineman never has force on the call. We make a distinction between contain and force.

We never want our defensive front three to be in a true shade alignment. We do not want to line up where we give the offense a blocking angle on us. We are not a two-gap team. The more the individual players gain experience, the more we allow them to play head-up. Everyone is responsible for one gap.

On the backside C gap, we play it with inside leverage. The tackle can line up in a 4 technique, where he can go either inside or outside.

We play the left tackle in a heavy technique. We want him to knock the blocker off from getting to our linebacker inside. He is playing a heavy technique.

The noseguard plays a backdoor technique. He has the backside A gap. We have almost gone to a cheap, two-gap technique.

The Stud linebacker is in a two-point stance. He wants to friction the tight end on his down block. He is a contain player.

We can change the force with our calls on nitro force or with thunder force, when the safeties become the force on the call (Diagram #2). We call stack-4 nitro and change the force to the safeties.

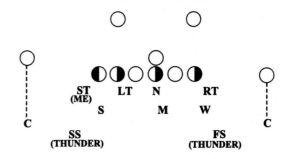

Diagram #2. Stack-4 Nitro

Our Eagle fronts are our weakside reduction fronts (Diagram #3). The same communication comes out. Eagle is a formational call. It gives us a tight-end call. We contain the quarterback with the

Will linebacker on the tight-end side, and the Stud linebacker contains on the shortside.

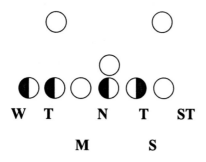

Diagram #3. Eagle 23

Our Ram front is similar to our Bear front (Diagram #4). We play a double Eagle with the tackles in 3 techniques, and the nose in a zero alignment. The Stud and Will linebackers' line up opposite the way they did on the Eagle.

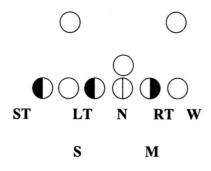

Diagram #4. Ram

On our Bear front, we do not do a lot out of it (Diagram #5). It is one of the fronts that we stem to and run stunts off the front. It was very good for us when we first installed it. We had a great deal of success when we ran it. This is what we call cover-1 roll. We are playing cover 1 on the front. We bring both the Sam and Will linebackers off the edge. The Stud plays man-to-man on the tight end, depending on the type of block he gets.

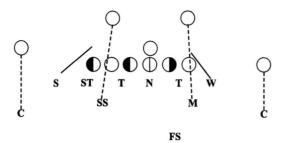

Diagram #5. Bear-1 Roll

Our odd front is different from the other fronts in that we now have other personnel in the game (Diagram #6). We can play different coverages from this defense.

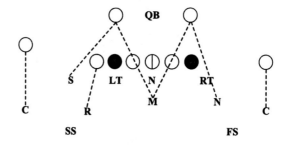

Diagram #6. Odd Two-Man

I want to move on to our line moves. The first line move is our slant (Diagram #7). The slant is a four-man run stunt, involving the "me" (or outside) linebacker and the three defensive linemen. The slant is run from the "me" side to the "you" side. We can run this stunt on any Hawk formation or directional front.

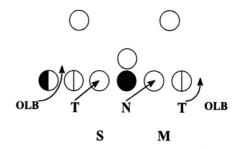

Diagram #7. Slant

The slant is a four-man move stunt. We always move from the "me" to the "you." We tell the tackle he must make the trip. His aiming point is the earhole or the facemask of the offensive guard. When we say "make the trip," it means we must have our tackle get his face across the face of the offensive guard.

We want the tackle to put the inside foot back in the direction he is going, with the weight on his outside foot. They must explode off the ball and get across the face of the guard.

The angle is a two-man run stunt, involving the "me" defensive tackle and the noseguard (Diagram #8). We are going from the "me" to the "you" side. The nose and tackle on the backside have to make the trip. This stunt can be run from any Hawk formation or directional front.

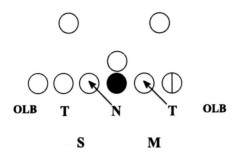

Diagram #8. Angle

We want to get our defensive men moving all over the place. In our crash move, we are running a two-man game (Diagram #9). It is a two-man stunt, involving the "me" linebacker and the "me" tackle. The slant is run from the "me" side to the "you" side. It can be used from the Hawk or directional fronts.

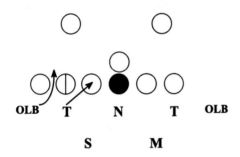

Diagram #9. Crash

Looking at the next stunt, we run the toss stunt (Diagram #10). This is a two-man stunt, involving the "me" linebacker and the "me" defensive tackle. The slant is from the "me" side. The tackle goes first, and the linebacker goes second. The outside linebacker must make the trip on the toss. Coaching point here is that the toss is called off against a tight end and a wing.

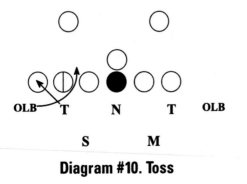

Diagram #10. Toss

Over on the other side, we run the sting (Diagram #11). It is a two-man stunt with the "me" linebacker and the "me" tackle. It is run on the "me" side. The linebacker goes first, and the tackle goes second. It can be used on Hawk and directional fronts. The sting stunt is off versus a tight end.

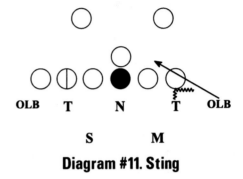

Diagram #11. Sting

On our tan stunt, it a two-man stunt, involving the "me" tackle and the nose man (Diagram #12). The defensive tackle goes first, and the nose man goes second. The tackle must hit the center on his move. The nose man cannot allow the ball to split the gap. It can be run from any Eagle formation or directional front.

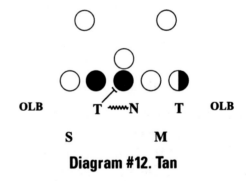

Diagram #12. Tan

Nuts is a two-man stunt run, involving the "me" tackle and the nose man (Diagram #13). The slant is run with the nose first and the tackle second. This stunt can be run from any Eagle formation or directional front.

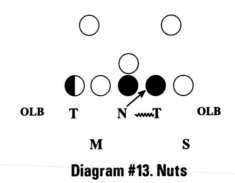

Diagram #13. Nuts

The last move I will cover is our pick move (Diagram #14). It is a two-man run stunt, involving the "me" tackle and the nose. The slant is run on the "me" side as a tan or nuts by definition. The stunt can be run from any Eagle formations or the directional fronts.

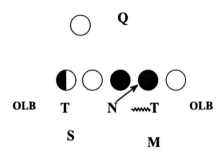

Diagram #14. Pick

Moving on to special techniques, we run two that I want to show you. First is punch (Diagram #15). We want to attack through the man and penetrate into the gap. The tackles and nose play one-half man backside against the reach-block.

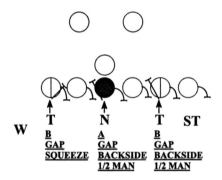

Diagram #15. Punch

The tackles' alignment is the 4 technique. They aggressively attack the offensive tackle and penetrate through them. If the offensive tackle reach-blocks, he is to play one-half man backside, with B-gap responsibility. If the offensive tackles use cutoff blocks, the tackles are to leverage the B gap, and squeeze to the offensive guard.

The nose aligns in the zero technique. He aggressively attacks the center, penetrating through him. He plays backside one-half man of the center's block.

The other special technique we like is the scan (Diagram #16). This is a three-man rush and an eight-man drop. The defensive line reads the slide.

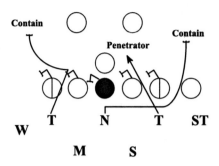

Diagram #16. Scan

Tackles are in a 4 alignment. The rules for the tackle are:

- Slide toward him: Attack the B gap and contain the quarterback. If the offensive tackle doubles back on him, he spins out and contains the quarterback.

- Slide away from him: Attack the B gap and chase the offensive guard. If the guard turns back toward the tackle, he should cross his face.

The nose man is in the zero alignment. He reads the center's slide. He loops away from the slide to contain. If the center gives no true read, he works strong.

We are not a big cover-zero team. We play a lot of cover 1 with a lot of zone pressure. We like the three-deep with three men under. We can play four-deep and two men under. For the defensive line, this is what we do on those pressure calls:

- Incorporate base techniques into pressure package.
- Create havoc.
- Be fundamentally sound; know your role.
- Know how pressure can tweak your technique.
- Get to your point.
- Stay on course.

BASE PRESSURE PACKAGE

We start with the field Hawk ham on the pressure calls (Diagram #17). The defensive tackle to the callside plays a 4 technique. He is in a reckless slant away from the call. The nose is playing his zero technique. He slants away from the call. The defensive tackle away from the call plays a heavy 5 alignment and contains in the cage.

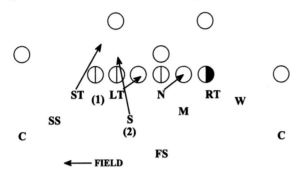

Diagram #17. Field Hawk Ham

We can run field Hawk storm. We bring the Stud linebacker inside the 6 technique. We bring the Sam linebacker outside and have him contain. It is a matter of changing the assignments for two players.

If we want to tweak the base pressure calls, we can use individual moves for different plays. Here is an example. We want to run a stunt for the nose. We call the stunt "naw." The nose lines up in his zero technique. He aggressively attacks the center, and then works into the A gap, away from the call. The base technique with spike can also be run with ham and storm.

If we call Ram backers, we are going to bring the Sam and Mike linebackers in the A gap. The tackles slant outside to the offensive tackles. The nose plays run first and lets the linebackers clear, and then he drops into the hole.

On Ram charger, we have the Stud and Will linebackers blitz from the outside. The tackles are in a 3 alignment. They stab the B gap and come under the offensive guard if they fan block.

On our Eagle smack move, we play the tackles in a 5 alignment (Diagram #18). They slant outside. The nose lines up in a 1 technique to the tight-end call. He slants to the "me" call. The defensive tackle away from the tight end lines up in a 3 alignment, slants outside. Where we have the numbers on the linebackers in the diagram, the 1 indicates the first man to stunt, and the 2 indicates the next man going over the stunt.

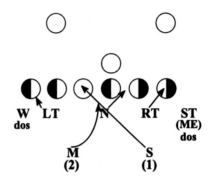

Diagram #18. Eagle Smack

We can take our read game and add them to the calls to come up with different stunts on the front line. We can run several moves with them and not involve the other defenders. We run enter, which is a stunt between the backside tackle and end. The end goes first, and the tackle goes second.

We can run Tex, which is a stunt between the end on the tight end and the tackle on the tight-end side. The tackle goes outside first, and the end comes across the line and comes down inside to the quarterback.

If we call mixer, we have a pass rush with all four linemen involved. The 1 and 6 techniques work together to run an enter move, and the 3 and 6 techniques work together on a "Tex" game.

I am sure you will be able to recognize the points we covered in the tapes. I want to thank you for staying here for this lecture. If we can do anything for you, let us know. Thank you

COACHING POINTS FOR TODAY'S ATHLETES

University of Alabama

Thank you. I am pleased to be here today to talk to a group that I truly respect. I think high school coaching is tremendously important in today's world. Words like honesty and integrity do not seem to mean as much in our society anymore. However, it means something to us. I appreciate what you are doing more than you know. I want you to understand that.

There is nothing I am going to say tonight that I invented. There is nothing here that I did not learn from someone else. The reason it excites me to come here and visit with you is to have the opportunity to share some ideas with you. What you do is special. Other than my parents, the person who had the greatest impact on my life was my high school coach. The principles that he taught our team had a great impact on where I am now and what I am doing.

Some of the most basic things I learned about coaching I learned from him. What you do is special, and do not lose sight of that. I know you have fewer students in the schools, but there is more pressure to win and higher expectations. It is more difficult to stay focused on the task you have to do. You have to stay focused on what you need to do to help your team be as successful as they can be.

It is not easy because what we do is different than what everybody else does. The human condition, from which we are all built, is to survive. What we have to do is take people who just want to be average and make them into elite athletes. We want to help them be as good as they can be and be special in what they do. Sometimes, we assume that everyone thinks that way.

The best way to approach that in this day and time is not to think that way. With the kids we are dealing with today, that is not the way it is. Usain Bolt, the Olympic champion in the 100- and 200-meter dashes, said it best. He said, "I do not know who I am racing against. I focus on running my best race. I do everything I can do in preparation to run my best race, and I couldn't care less who I am running against." We have to take the players who just want to be average and make them the best players they can be.

To win a championship, everyone has to play to their capacity. They have to run their best race. We are taking people who do not think that way and are affected by a world that is all about results. It is instant coffee, instant tea, and instant gratification. I watch my children play Nintendo. They get blown up, push the restart button, and start again. There are no consequences for losing.

When I was a kid, we played checkers. When you screwed up, you lost one of your checkers. You got immediately positive or negative self-gratification for what you did or did not do. These kids do not grow up that way. When it does not go right for them, they get frustrated and go do something else. It is up to us to make it about them. We have to get them to think about it from their standpoint because they are all self-absorbed in how they grow up and how they see things. That is the world we live in.

Barry Sanders and Walter Payton were great role models. They did everything you were supposed to do, but in this day and age, they would not get the positive self-gratification that Deion Sanders gets. He is another great player, but because of the circles he flies in, he is the one on ESPN and the one who is something special.

We are trying to do things that will reflect sportsmanship and things of that nature. However, those are the things that do not give self-gratification. What you do is special, and I could not appreciate it more. If it were not for what you do, I could not do what I do. What you do is important in your community. Do not lose sight of that. I know you have external pressure to win games, but stay focused on the important things.

Jesse Jackson came to speak to my team. After he spoke, he told me that Tiger Stadium on Saturday night was closer to being with God than being in his church. What he was saying was everybody on that team had a common goal. The rules are clearly defined, and there absolutely is no bias. The rich sit with the poor, and there is no racial prejudice. There are blacks with whites hugging and jumping up and down. He told me he could not get that within his church. The games are important to the community for their social development.

I know you work hard at what you do, but the emphasis should be on being the best that you can be. It should not be about winning and losing games. Because we live in a results-oriented world, it is extremely difficult not to focus on winning and losing. We have all been there at one time or another. When I went to LSU, we were 1-2 and had just lost to UAB. I was getting killed for being the highest paid coach in the country.

I was getting killed on talk radio. My little girl who was eight years old was sitting in the back seat on the way home after the game. She heard what they were saying and wanted to know if we were going to move again. The next day, I went to work and stopped at the self-serve to get some gas. When I went in to pay, the attendant notice the Big Ten championship ring I was wearing. He asked me what it was. I told him it was a Big Ten championship ring, and we were going to do the same thing at LSU. He said, "We are never going do it as long as Nick Saban is the coach." We have all been there.

When you are developing a program, the first thing you need to have is some kind of mission statement. I worked for Bill Belichick in Cleveland, and he spoke at our clinic last year. He put up a sign, and it was the only one in the entire building. It reads: "Do Your Job." That went for everyone in the organization. He defined what everyone's job was and a standard of excellence that everyone should do in completing the job. He defined the quality control of how to evaluate whether the job was done. That was his speech, and it was an hour long. To do your job, everyone has to know what they are trying to accomplish. That is why you need a mission statement.

University of Alabama Mission Statement

We are going to create an atmosphere and an environment where we can help our players be successful. First as people, second as students, and third to graduate from school and develop a career off the field. We want them to succeed as football players, have an outstanding college career, be the best they can be, and see if they can develop a football career at the next level. We want to use the resources that we have personally and as an institution to launch their career when they leave the program.

Everybody in the organization knows that statement. There is not one person working in our building that does not know what we are trying to accomplish. That goes for the medical staff, strength and conditioning staff, people in the academic center, secretaries, or the janitor. If there is anyone in our organization who is not working toward that goal, they should not be there because we are not working together as a team.

We have the greatest opportunity to teach some of these young people through athletics the principles and values they have not learned. We can teach such things as commitment. How many people do you know who have made commitments to some things and did not have the perseverance to see them through? How many people do you know who cannot even decide what they wanted to do? They have to know what is important to them. That leads to passion and desire for what they want to do. Most good players have a tremendous amount of passion and desire to be successful. Many people think they do not have that passion.

Jason Taylor is the best competitor you will find in the world. I was standing on the sideline, and he was standing beside me like a nine-year-old kid. He kept asking to go in the game. He has tremendous passion to be the best player he can be.

I have one special story I tell my players to illustrate commitment. Jaromir Jagr was a hockey player in the National Hockey League. He wore number 68 as his jersey number. He played on the Czechoslovakian Olympic hockey team in the 1984 Olympics Games His team ended up in the finals playing the Russians for the gold medal. In 1968, the Russians had invaded Czechoslovakia. His grandfather and many other Czechs were killed in that encounter. That is why he wore the number 68. It was a constant reminder of the fateful year. His coach came into the locker room to get the team ready before the gold-medal game and asked Jaromir if he was ready to play. Jaromir replied, "I've been ready to play this game all my life!" He said his commitment as a hockey player was to beat the Russians in the Olympics for all the people they killed, including his grandfather, in 1968. That was Jaromir's commitment.

Everyone has to have some passion. But to have it, you have to know what you want to accomplish. We have to help people find that out sometimes because they do not know. It is the only way they are going to work and invest their time like they need to. It is a simple process. Muhammad Ali always talks about winning and losing fights. He said when he was committed to training for the fight, he won. When he did not train and did not have that passion, he lost. You reap what you sow. That attitude is something we have to develop with our players. We have the opportunity in football to teach these kinds of things.

There are many people who do not get that opportunity if they are not involved in athletics. You need to think about that before you get rid of one of your players. I am slow to do that. I make them irrelevant in our program. I tell my players all the time, you will be irrelevant to this team if you do not do what you are supposed to do like everyone else on the team. They know what the rules are and what is expected of them. If they do not do it, they are irrelevant. You do not have to kick them off the team. Tell them in front of the rest of the team, which means you are not going to depend on them.

That does not mean you give up on them. They will appreciate it, and when they come back to you, they will be better than before. You will not have all the resentment you would have if you kicked him off the team. It takes a lot of perseverance, and the players today are different. When we recruit a player, he may be rated a four-star or five-star player by someone who has never coached a down. They have not seen a film on the kid. He is someone who just delivers the mail. The players are saddled with those expectations.

He cannot live with those expectations. If he cannot live up to the expectations of someone else, he becomes severally frustrated. Sometimes, the standard is impossible. We have to understand that. I ask a receiver what his goal is. If he says he wants to catch 50 balls, I tell him bull crap. What I want him to say is that he will do everything he can to be a complete player at his position.

I want him to come off the ball, run good routes, separate, get open, catch the ball consistently when it is thrown to him, and be a good blocker. I want him to do all the things it takes, and I want to make it about him.

It takes a lot of perseverance. You cannot be frustrated and get upset when things go bad. There is a book out there called *The Road Less Traveled*. A priest gave it to me when I was defensive coordinator at Michigan State. He told me it was a spiritual development and a positive attitude book. He told me to read it, and it would help me a lot. I got the book and the first statement in the book is a negative statement. It said, "Life is difficult." The book was about so much more. If you think things are going to be difficult and you are going to have to overcome adversity, it is a part of building character and being successful.

You have to keep a much more positive attitude when things do not go good for you. That is important for young people to understand because they do not get it. When we show our disappointment in players, what do they do? When a receiver drops the ball, do not tell him to catch the ball. Coach him, and tell him to look the ball in or get his hands in a different position. That is what we are supposed to do. We teach and inspire learning as coaches. But have the ability to sustain and learn from the mistakes you make.

I just read Tony Dungy's book. It is called *Uncommon: Finding Your Path to Significance.* Everyone in here should read the book. He is looking for the uncommon man, and he is talking about the same things I am. It is uncommon to have honesty, integrity, demanding work ethics, and discipline. That is not how people are anymore. More and more people do not hold to those principles and values. His message is to be the uncommon man and do these things that are important to being successful.

I tell recruits not to commit to us until they have considered all their options and are sure this is where they want to come to school. It is not good for the player to make a commitment, give his word, and then go back on it. I do not want to put the players in that position. None of us in the profession think a commitment is worth anything. After a player makes a commitment to a school, the recruiting does not stop. Teams come right in and try to get him to decommit. If the high school coach lets his player commit to a school, and he goes to some other school, the high school coach is guilty of that, too. That is the way it is, but it is not the way the profession should be.

You cannot be successful in our business if you cannot overcome adversity. If you have ever heard me speak before, you have heard this story. However, I am going to tell it again. In 1981, I was coaching the secondary at Ohio State. We had won seven and lost two, and we were getting ready to play a great Michigan team in the last game of the season. They were undefeated and had five All-Americans on their team. Anthony Carter was on that team. We played the game at Michigan in front of 106,000 fans. We were a 17-point underdog.

Our team practiced poorly all week. Our coaches did not have the right kind of enthusiasm for a big game. The bottom line was this: the coaches and players just did not think we could win the game at Michigan. We were all getting criticized by the media and the fans. We were more concerned with how the outcome of the game would affect us as individuals. Everyone felt we were going to Ann Arbor on Saturday to get our tails beat.

Woody Hayes had left Ohio State after the 1979 season. He did not come back to visit the team in 1980. But the day before we left for Michigan in 1981, he came back to talk with the team. It was the first time he had addressed the team since he left in 1979. Woody Hayes stood before the team, and this is what he told them: "There can be no great victory without adversity. When you have a big challenge such as this, it is a great opportunity for a great victory."

He turned everything around from the negative to the positive to motivate the team. He made the game an opportunity. He mentioned all the obstacles we were to face at Michigan. He related all of our obstacles for the Michigan game to the war in the Pacific in World War II. The victory in the Pacific was considered one of the greatest victories in the history of mankind. Why was that such a great victory for the United States? It was because of Pearl Harbor. We had lost our Pacific fleet. Rebuilding the Pacific feet and taking the fight to the Japanese made it one of the greatest victories of all time. It was the adversity experienced and overcome and the positive attitude of the American people that contributed to the victory.

That is when you have to focus on the right things. I remember this game more than any game we have ever played. We won 14-9 against the number-one scoring team in the country. They had the ball in the red zone five times and scored nine points. I was 27 years old and was pumped up, wishing we had some more games to play that season. Earl Bruce was the head coach, but Coach Hayes came in after the game and said he was glad that was the last game of the season. I was puzzled by the response. He said there was not a damn team in the country we could beat next week.

You cannot have great victories if you cannot overcome great adversity. The only way you can overcome adversity is if you take advantage of your failures. It is like the commercial Michael Jordon did for Nike. He said he took 26 game-winning shots and missed all of them. He played 384 NBA games in which he lost. He missed 2,032 shots. In the commercial, he opens the door to the locker room and said, "Because I failed is the reason why I succeed."

There are examples like that all over the place. If you take their role models and find others ways say the same things beside you saying it, it can pay dividends. We showed our players an interview with Allen Iverson. We had some players who were being irrelevant. They were missing class and being a bad actor. We showed Iverson. He said when he was at Georgetown playing for John Thompson, that his coach was always right. He should have always done what his coach said, but he never did. When he was with Philadelphia, he said Larry Brown was a great coach. "I should have always done what my coach said, but I did not."

During his career, he has been suspended from the team for missing practice, gun charges, and a long list of offenses. He admitted all the bad things. He was in Denver at the time of the interview, and there had not been anything bad written about him in two or three years. During the interview, he has two one-year-old girls sitting on his lap. He said, "Do you know why I changed my way of life? Because I did not want the two little girls growing up thinking I was a thug."

Sometimes, you have to make everything about the players. I had a player walking by the fraternity houses on campus. They were having a fraternity party and some of the members yelled some obscenities at him and called him some names. He went up to the house, took on one of the drunks, and whipped him good. He is going to be a first-round draft pick next year, coming out early as a junior. He is a sophomore right now.

There were no charges filed, although there could have been. I called him into my office. When he told me the story, I agreed with him that I may have done the same thing. But consider what you are putting at risk. You could make between 30 and 50 million dollars next year when you come out as a number-one draft pick. You can help your mother, sister, and family like you have never been able to. I

agree with you that you were right, but was it worth it to be right? The guy at the fraternity does not know you and does not care about you. It was nothing personal; he was just drunk.

He agreed that being right was not worth what it could have cost him. Once we made the problem about him and laid out the consequences for him, it made a difference to him. We have to be positive in our approach of how we get people to handle negatives. I ask players all the time what they are selling today. I watch our players walk out to practice every day. I can tell who broke up with their girlfriend or who flunked a math test just by watching their body language and how they are affecting everyone around them.

They have to ask: is what they are selling what they want to sell? Is it what they want other people to think? If you have a negative attitude that creates those thoughts in other people, it is a big negative. I am asked what I am selling today. It is important to be positive. The worst thing about being a competitor is showing the other guy you are frustrated. That is all about the perseverance we are talking about.

You should create an attitude where a player is trying to dominate his opponent every play in the game. His best play has a history and a life of its own. When that play is over, he is trying to do the same thing on the next play. That is the character attitude you work for. That attitude is called being relentless.

Why is Freddy Krueger scary? You cannot kill the guy. He is relentless. A relentless competitor is one that comes back repeatedly and handles adversity and frustration. He plays with intensity and is never affected by what happened on the last play in his approach to the next play. That is why I say each play has a history and life of its own.

The scoreboard is an external factor. If we are up 14 points in a game, do we play different than if we were down 14 points in a game? If we believe the way I do, the scoreboard has nothing to do with it. That is what you have to do to be a great competitor.

We should use that approach. We use the approach to gain results and that leads to the scoreboard. The scoreboard affects the player's performance. We played a national championship game at LSU. After we beat Georgia in the conference playoff game, all we heard was we had a chance to win a national championship. It would be the first time in 45 years. The first meeting we had leading up to the game, I laid out our plan. I did not talk about winning the national championship. I talked about dominating the opponent they were going to play against. I wanted them to play every play as the best play they could play. I want them to assume the opponent was the best player they had ever played against. That was all that I told them besides, "Let's go to work."

The score of the game was not relative to the way we dominated the game. We had 500 yards of offense to their 100. Our thoughts were never about winning the game; it was about dominating the player they played against.

Every one of us has had a player they feel has no pride and does not care. He cares and wants to do well. There has to be some reason he is not doing his best. We cannot treat our players all the same. There is one difference in coaching in college and the pros. You have what you have. High school is probably like the pro league. In pro ball, when the owner takes a player, he is going to play. You have no choice.

In college, I coached them all the same. The players who did what I coached got to play, and the players did not sat on the bench. In pro ball, if a player cannot backpedal the way you want, it does not matter. If the owner gave him 1.2 million dollars, he is going to play. You have to coach the things that will make him play. Those things are attitude, character, and athletic ability. Emerson Walls of the Dallas Cowboys had more interceptions than anyone in the history of the NFL. He could not backpedal a lick; however, he had great ball skills. You have to coach every player differently and find out what makes that player have the qualities you want in him.

I heard Martin Luther King give a sermon one time. He said there is only one guy in Montgomery, Alabama whom he would let shine his shoes. That guy has such pride in his performance that he will do the best job he can do every time he does it. It does not matter whose shoes he is shining; that is the way he does it. I have so much respect for that guy. He is the only guy in the world I want to shine my shoes. He went on to say if you are a street sweeper, sweep them the best that you can do. Sweep the streets like Michelangelo painted the Sistine Chapel and like Shakespeare wrote poetry. If you can do that, you have accomplished the best there is in life. That is as simple as it gets.

That was true 50 years ago, and it will be the same 50 years from now. Those kinds of values do not go away. It is respected by people. If your team plays well with toughness, good effort, and great intangibles, you can say you are going to win every game. We lost to Florida in the SEC championship game, the same way Oklahoma got beat. When Tebow put Florida on his back, we did not play good enough to beat them. We got beat in the fourth quarter just like Oklahoma did.

When we played Florida, our mistakes let them win. We did not play with the intangibles that it takes to win. Everyone respected us even though we lost the game. When we played Utah in the Sugar Bowl, we stunk. Rightly, we were criticized. It was my fault that I did not get the players ready to play. We did not respect the team we played. If you can get your players to take pride in their performance, you will get it every time.

I cannot talk to you enough about how important it is to develop a competitive spirit within your team. There is no "I" in team, but there is in win. If you look at the "I" in win, it stands for three things with me. It stands for intensity, which is the mental energy and how you go about what you do. The second "I" is immediately, which is a sense of urgency. You must do it now and not wait. The third thing is intelligence. You have to be well prepared and play smart.

I want to talk about the "Pyramid of Success." I cannot take credit for it because the players came up with that idea. I know they put a lot of thought into the project and researched the topic. This is what they decided. These are certain things we feel are important for us to have a championship team.

The first one was "team." Together, everybody accomplishes more. Trust and respect were the two words they wanted to associate with that thought. Togetherness on your team starts with everyone respecting each other. We do not talk about players competing against each other. I want our players to be the best they can be, and I focus on that.

Everyone has a job, and I expect him to do it. This is the greatest team game in the history of sport. Everybody has a job to do, and everyone has to execute his job. If you lose, it is never about the other team. You made mistakes. It is always that way. When we evaluate the performance of the defense, it is never one player. If there is a breakdown, it is the defense's fault—never one player. Soon, the players will begin to take blame for their shortcomings on the defense. Every down-and-distance in the game is a win or lose for us. It is effort, toughness, and knowing what to do—that wins for you. That takes no ability to do those three things.

When they see it in black and white, they start becoming a team, and the trust builds in your team. Leadership to me is reinforcing the principles and values of the program. You have to define those in the beginning so everyone knows what they are. They have to know what is expected, not only in how they play but how they act. I am old-fashioned. In my meetings, no one wears a hat. When they come into the office and there are secretaries in the room, they take their hats off. We do not wear earrings when we are traveling or representing the team. You do not have hair coming out of your helmet over your shoulder pads. This is how Alabama represents itself, and everybody expects to see Alabama this way.

If a player want to play with his hair down to his butt, he better play somewhere else. That has never hurt any of our players. I go to the players and ask them why they think we are doing these things? Why do they think we have rules about going to class? It is no different for anyone on the team. There is no disrespect intended. It gives them a better chance to be successful in life. We want them to continue developing while they are here. We want

them to get the degree and graduate from school. If they do not do that, they will not play for us.

In my entire career, I have only suspended seven players. Five of them played in the NFL. They were suspended four games for not going to school. We did not lose any of the games in which they were suspended. The only player you could suspend that would cost you a game is the quarterback. However, if you pick a player to play quarterback and he will not go to school, you have picked the wrong player. That is not on him; it is on you.

For the rest of them, it does not matter. Our nose tackle was probably the best nose in college football. He did not play against Tennessee and LSU, and it did not matter. We still won. He weighs 370 pounds, and no one weighs as much as him. He would rather do a back handstand and flip than a forward roll because he does not have to get his big butt off the ground. Moreover, he can do that.

The second item in the pyramid is: "be responsible for your own self-determination." The only person I have seen walk into a team meeting in the NFL and the entire room went totally silent was Jim Brown. I coached in the NFL for eight years. I have seen many people walk into rooms, and he is the only one who had such high esteem that everyone stopped talking. Being responsible for your own self-determination is another way of saying, "Do your job." When you make that kind of choice, you understand the consequences that go with it.

"Commitment to work to dominate the competition" is the third thing. In the off-season when players are working out and they think they are working hard, I tell them they have one of these machines at LSU, too. They are doing the same thing at Tennessee, and I know Auburn is working on them. What we do at 4:00, they do at 6:00 in the morning, and they are working hard, too. I want to know if you are working harder than they are. The fourth quarter is all about conditioning, pride, effort, and all the intangibles we have talked about.

To play with great effort, toughness, and know what to do, you must be in great condition. That goes to the great quote by Vince Lombardi. "Fatigue makes cowards of us all." You must have a well-conditioned team, and they all have to be committed to do the work.

I am old-fashioned. When I was in high school, we never had a pulled muscle. We did not have a trainer. We did not stretch. We ran up the hill, did some exercises, and scrimmaged. After the first play, you did not see the defense for the rest of practice because the dust was so thick. There was no grass on the field. We did not lift weights, but we had good coaches.

When I was in high school, I was the starting quarterback as a sophomore. We needed to win our last game to get into the state playoffs. It came down to the last play of the game. We had a fourth-and-12 for the touchdown. The coach called a time-out. We had time for one play. I went to the sideline, hoping the coach would call the play. Instead, he asked me what I thought would work. I told him I was not sure. He told me the left halfback was the fastest player in the state, and the split end has made All-State three years in a row. He told me, "I do not care which play you run as long as one of those two players get their hands on the ball." I ran a play-action pass. I faked the sweep to the running back and threw the ball to the split end for the touchdown. That left a great impression on me. I realized it was not the play that was important; it was the players. I never forgot that.

The last thing in the pyramid is "positive energy." You must have great team chemistry, and your team must play with positive energy. It rubs off and affects other people. It is so important in being successful.

Everyone should step back and ask: what is it I want to accomplish? What is it I have to do to do that? What am I willing to do to accomplish that? I must put all my positive energy into doing those things and stay focused on it all the time. Very few people can actually do that. If you are one of the people who can do that, you will pass many people in your effort to succeed. There is no one in this room who likes to be around a negative person. It is a fault that all of us must try to overcome. Our attitude and approach affects what the people around us do. The players on your team have to know that what they do affects other players, and that affects team chemistry.

You are a teacher. You must let your players know the only thing the last play is good for is a learning experience for the future. Experience is nothing but an accumulation of all your mistakes. Whatever you did on the last play is something learned for the next play. We should use that approach in teaching. We are not paid just to criticize and brow beat.

I coach the defensive backs. I tell them if they cannot take me getting on them, they will not be able to take getting beat for a touchdown in a game. The defensive back is one of the most exposed positions on the field. Everyone knows when you make a mistake. That is not important. What is important is how you will respond to the next play. I get on the defensive backs in practice but never in a game. I tell them, when it does not bother them, I will not have to get on them again. They will have developed mental toughness.

If the players will do these things, you will have a team full of champions on and off the field. When you have that, you win championships.

There is one other thing I would like to say to you. Our place is always open to you. When you talk about people sharing, that is how I learned. I have had some great mentors. Don James was my college coach. He was a fantastic coach and a great guy. He got me into coaching. George Perles at Michigan State gave me my first job with any responsibility as a coordinator. He was a great people person and a great defensive coach. Bill Belichick is the most organized and has the best plan of attack of anyone I know.

We want to do everything we can professionally to help you develop as a coach. When you visit, we learn something from you, too. I appreciate your time and I enjoyed visiting.

DEVELOPING THE GAME PLAN

University of Nebraska

I am going to talk about developing our game plan and about our scheme in that concept. Coach Bo Pelini does a great job of allowing coaches to coach. Each of us has a responsi-bility in drawing up the game plan. After the game is over on Saturday, we rarely meet as a staff on Sunday. We have a responsibility for the next game, and we let the old game go. There is nothing we can do about what happened yesterday.

The only things we can do are to prepare for the next game and correct the mistakes we made in the last one. We divide the staff as far as responsibilities. We do not meet as a staff, but each individual coach starts to work on his part of the game plan. I start to work on the pass pattern and passing game that we expect to see from the upcoming opponent. One coach will work on the running game, and another coach works on our opponent's protection scheme. On Monday, we have a staff meeting in the morning and compare notes.

The hardest thing I had to learn as a young coach was how to break down an opponent. What I wanted to know was "What was I looking for, and what was I coming up with?" Over the years, I have learned that offenses have a set of plays they will use. They do not have a hundred plays they run. They have a few plays designed to be run from certain formations. It is your job, as you break down an opponent, to find out what that team's favorite plays are. It will probably be four or five running plays and four or five passes.

They run those plays in a certain way. They may call an out/curl on one side and tag a pattern to the backside that makes that play look different from the base pattern. What you have to decipher is the actual play. You want to know what they are trying to do. The second thing you want to know is how the opponent plans to attack you as a defensive coach. You have to know if they are a power running team. If you play a 4-3 defense, how are they going to block the power? You have to learn that first.

We want to attack an offense and make them adjust to what we are doing. However, you cannot develop a plan and make the adjustments in a game if you do not know how they are blocking the power. In the staff meeting, we get on the chalkboard and start to draw things up. In the beginning, it looks good. However, when you get into situations that have to be covered, you may have multiple adjustments. You have so many adjustments there is no way to teach it all to your players. That goes back to the old adage: It is not about what we know; it is what we can teach. It takes an experienced coach to put the ego away and teach what you can teach.

We call our defenses against personnel groupings. With a 21 grouping, two backs and one tight end, there are five or six calls you can play against 21 personnel. Think about practicing the five or six calls you have to make against the five or six plays they run. If you run an over cover 2 against the power, think how many times you have to rep that play to get your players to play it right. Be very careful when you are trying to design a package.

I am going to talk about what we do and how we develop a concept. We are big on concepts. Someone asked me what type of coverage we play. We do it all, but we package it within a defensive concept. When we start in the spring practice, we teach concepts. We teach quarter coverage and cover-2 concepts. When we play it in a game, we call it one word. We might call "Gator." It may be the quarter coverage concept on one side and something else on the other side.

To start, you have to develop a pre-season plan. That is what you are doing right now. What you do right now in your pre-season prepa-ration is vital.

DEVELOPING A DEFENSIVE GAME PLAN: PRE-SEASON PREPARATION

- Developing a big board
- Defenses by personnel groups (e.g., fronts, coverages, stunts, blitzes)
- Color code by effectiveness (e.g., run, pass, both)

Developing the big board is what we are working on as a staff. On the big board, we have listed at the top the personnel groups we play against. In the 21 personnel grouping, there are two basic plays that go with that grouping. They are the power and split belly. We want to know from the big board what fronts and coverage will fit those kinds of plays. We color code the best adjustments in each listing.

BIG BOARD

12	20	21	22
Base	**Base**	**Base**	**Base**
Over-2	Over-2	Over-2	Under-4
Over-1 free	Over-1 free	Over-1 free	Under-1
Over-3	Even-3	Over-3	Over-3
Blitzes	**Blitzes**	**Blitzes**	**Blitzes**
Snake	Snake	Snake	Snake
Cat	Tomahawk	Cat	Smoke
Devil	Seminole	Devil	
Stunts	**Stunts**	**Stunts**	**Stunts**
Read	Tom	Read	Tom
Nut	Jet	Nut	Ram
Spike	Ram		

This will give you an idea of what we have on the big board. What you see is an example and not all that we have on the board. The top line in the chart is the personnel grouping. We color code the most effective coverage, blitz, and stunt against each grouping. If you walked into our staff meeting room right now, this big board is already developed. We have not played a game yet, but we are developing the big board for next season.

If we played a game next Saturday, we know the calls we could make in that game right now. We are going back and looking at last year's game and practice tapes to decide what we can do. We are trying to address the weaknesses that teams took advantage of in games.

Right now, we are talking through any basic adjustments that need to be added to the playbook. When we looked at our tapes of Oklahoma, Texas Tech, and Clemson, there was a common theme about the way those teams attack us with the slot formation. In the pre-season, we are looking at the changes in our basic adjustment in that formation. We want to make those adjustments now instead of waiting until we play a team that gives us that look.

You want to create a glossary of key words, buzzwords, and phrases. In the meeting room, you are going to come up with many words that mean something to you. Write them at that time. As time goes on, and after you take a vacation, you will forget what those words mean. In our playbook, we have a glossary of what our defensive terms mean. That keeps everyone on the same page. I think that is huge. A term like leverage is an important word for the defense. The players may not know what the coach is talking about when he says to keep outside leverage. That is defined in our glossary.

In our pre-season, we do the big board and the glossary. That is what we are working on right now.

We do not meet as a staff on Sunday. We work individually, fulfilling our responsibility. We come in on Sundays, and our whole goal is to develop an adequate scouting report. I believe a lot of coaches do things to make themselves feel good. If you make an elaborate scouting report with a book full of information, that is the wrong approach. Everything on the scouting report is irrelevant if the player does not know what he is looking at or have the time to read it.

When we start to break down film on the opponent, we concentrate on personnel alone. We want to know the opponent's number-one personnel group. If we play a team, and their number-one personnel group is 11 personnel, that is the first thing I look at.

If we have 121 plays of 11 personnel, I break down the passes by personnel. From there, I try to simplify that by breaking them down into formations. I am trying not to look at individual personnel. I am looking at the whole group. If they get into a 2x2 formation, I am looking for similarities and the plays they run from that formation. I am trying to narrow my focus on something I can tell our players when the offense comes out in that set. I try to narrow my focus before I get to the play.

After I narrow my focus, I look at the play. I organize the plays and look at them all. If we label some play "flat," for example, I will look at every single flat pass to see if there is some tendency I can see. As I do these things, I write myself notes as I am watching. I look at split relationship and anything that will tip me to a tendency. I even look at the offensive line to see if they are sitting higher on a pass.

We collect all this data, put it into a computer, and come up with this next sheet. This is an example of our data on a 21 personnel grouping for a particular game.

You can see from the chart they aligned in the 21 personnel group 23 times, which amounted to 63 percent of their offense sets. Of those times, they were in the pro set over half of the time. When they got in the pro formation, they ran the power-O 50 percent of the time. They also aligned in the slot and doubles formations. They were in the doubles formation only three times and the slot eight times. I watch these plays on film and take note of how they block. This is a run sheet.

We take these sheets and make our adjustments to each one of these formations and tendencies. We will have a call for every single item on this sheet. We have a base call for the pro, slot, and doubles formation. If they come out of the huddle with 21 personnel in the game and align in a

Personnel Grouping	For- mation	Run	Pass	Number of Plays	Percentage
21				23	63
	Pro			12	52
		18 power-O		6	50
		13 lead		3	25
		14 zone		1	8
		17 counter option		1	8
		18 toss		1	8
	Slot			8	38
		14 split zone		3	38
		18 power-O		3	38
		18 toss		2	25
	Doubles			3	13
		15 zone		2	67
		18 stretch		1	33

spread formation, we have an automatic alert call. We do not want to work the fits we have prepared against something that does not fit.

After we teach these things, we go back to the big board. We have talked about what works best against the 21 personnel group, and next we put it on the big board and color code the fronts and coverages we want to work. The colors tell us what we feel works best against that personnel group. However, we have an alert to everything we do.

You need to go through adjustments and fits. You need to draw the play and show the players where they fit. On Monday night, we draw up the fits and what we expect from everyone on the play. On the 18 power-O, we run an over-nail-2 (Diagram #1). The defense is an over front with the tackle in a 3 technique. The defensive end and 3-technique tackle run a nail stunt, which is an inside slant to the A and B gaps. The coverage is cover 2. The defensive end must get his hands on the offensive tackle to keep him off the backside linebacker.

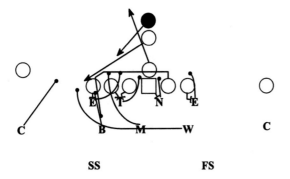

Diagram #1. Power-0 Fits

We go through the personnel, the plays they run, and how they block them. We have to figure out when they are going to run them. With 21 personnel, their number-one play is the power-0. The first thing I look at is down-and-distance. If they change the play, will it change on the down-and-distance?

We use the same sheet as we did with our personnel grouping and go through their play selection on first down. We do not go into the range of the personnel sheet. That will tell you the percentage of times they ran the power on first down. We consider formation, motion, shifts, run,

Personnel Grouping	Formation	Run	Pass	Number of Plays	Percentage
21				18	58
	Pro			13	72
		18 power-0		7	54
		13 lead		3	25
		14 split zone		1	8
		17 counter option		1	8
		18 toss		1	8
	Slot			5	38
		14 split zone		1	29
		18 power-0		4	80

or pass. We are trying to get a handle on what they will do on first down from this personnel group.

FIRST-AND-10

If you notice from the example, they still run the power-0 more from the pro set. However, in the slot set on first and ten they ran the power-0 four out of five times and they did not run it out of the double set on first and ten. On first-and-10 from the 21 personnel grouping, they ran the power-0 11 out of 18 times. On first-and-10, we have to stop the power play.

There are all kinds of ways to break down the down-and-distance situations. The standard is first-and-10 on the first possession or first-and-10 after a first down. The next situation is second-and-short, -medium, and -long. Some teams say second-and-long is seven yards plus. Second-and-medium is four to six yards, and second-and-short is one to three yards.

We have played teams that once they got to second and less than four yards for the first down, they were 90 percent pass. Our thinking was to go from second-and-short to second-and-long, and eliminate the medium situation. Another team played second-and-long as a running down. That meant they wanted half the needed yardage on second down with the intent to run again on third down or get into a good play-action situation.

You can print out a running game plan and see what the offense is doing. You can find out when they are going to run the ball more than they throw it.

You cannot do everything. On Monday, we have our graduate assistant chart our practices, using the call sheets and the plays run against those calls. He records that information all week. On Thursday, before we start practice, we look at the sheet. You may like a certain call against the power, but as you look at the call sheet, you find out you ran the adjustment twice the entire week. You have to ask yourself if you are comfortable with running a stunt twice the whole week that you plan on using in the game on Saturday. That is what you have to decide. Our rule is if we have not run it at least 10 times in practice, we will not run it in the game.

FIELD-AREA TENDENCIES (GOAL LINE, RED ZONE, COMING OUT, ETC.)

This area is the next consideration. We use the same sheets for the film breakdown. We divide the field and see what they do in those areas. We played a team from the MAC this year that had a great punter. When they were inside their territory in third-and-long, they were very conservative. They wanted to punt the ball every time and not take a chance. That will show up on the field-area tendencies.

We use the same sheet for red-zone plays. We record the plays they run and percentage on what down they like to run them. With the technology out there today, you can do that quickly. Doing film cutups and breakdowns is relatively simple with the right equipment. In our example, we found the team from the 21 personnel group ran no power-0 in the red zone. Since the offense is not going to run the power-0, we do not run the nail stunt in the red zone.

We are very multiple in our secondary coverage. We play many schemes, but we teach them as concepts in the spring every year. In the spring, we may call cover 4, but we will never run just that coverage. On one side, we may play a cover-4 concept, and on the other side we may play another concept. We have a universal call for our pass coverage. An example would be "Gator," which we played in the bowl game. The reason we came up with that name was we were playing the game in Florida. We played Clemson, and their number-one personnel group was 11 personnel. They played with one tight end, one back, and three wide receivers.

We played them in Gator coverage. We do not try to fit one pass coverage to this scheme. Clemson was a team that had different tendencies in formation A, as compared to formation B, or formation C. In 11 personnel grouping, there are three formations in which you can align. You can align in a 3x1 pro set, a 3x1 slot set, and a 2x2 set. What we tried to do was develop a concept based on those formations and those personnel.

The coverage was combination coverage. To simplify the call, we played Gator. We played one coverage. That was on us to do the work to find out what they were doing. An example of playing tendencies is in protection. If you find a team is putting their back on one side and turning the center away from him in their protection scheme, we feel we can take advantage of that. The problem is, if you call the blitz and they do not come out in that formation or do not put the back where you think he will be, what do you do? Are we stuck with running the blitz? We are not.

Our blitz and pressure calls will be alert calls. We are not going to run a blitz when we know they can protect it. Our huddle call is "blitz-A alert." If we do not get the set we want, we get out of the blitz. Our game plan against Clemson was based on their formations. If they came out in formation A, we played our 4-3 over with cover 2. If they came out in formation B, we played our 4-3 over with cover 1 or cover 3, and if they came out in formation C, we blitzed. That is how we came up and developed Gator.

We knew they could come out and give us a no-back set from that personnel group. We played the game a series at a time. We told the players to play Gator this series, but if they came out in an empty look, we went to cover 1. We try to get our team in the best coverage for our players. We do not want to put our players in a disadvantage situation. There is nothing worse than to run a blitz and give up a big play.

We will change up by series. On one series we may blitz, and on the next series we will play zone to that look. The next series we may man up to the situation. The problem is, doing so presents a huge communication point. However, we have signals from the sideline, where they know what is going on.

PRACTICE ACCORDINGLY

Begin with what they do the most:

- Personnel group
- Formation
- Play
- Down-and-distance

You want to make a team beat you left-handed. When we played Georgia Tech, they had a great wide receiver and had a tremendous power play. Everything we did that week in practice was geared to stopping the power and Calvin Johnson. We beat them 7-0. Our entire goal is to eliminate what the offense does best. Make a team get out of their comfort zone.

You have to talk through how the opponent is going to adjust to what you are doing. Coaches are smart. The last man with the chalk wins. Try to think through as you go into that game plan of what the offense could possibly do. There is one thing we do not do. We do not practice the "what-ifs" into our players. When we coach, we coach the rules and not the exceptions to the rule.

An opponent is not going to beat us with something that we have never seen. It happened at Colorado this year. They ran a play we had never seen before, and it hurt us. We stopped them and held them to a field goal. When we got the team on the sideline, we made the adjustment.

We give a scouting report to our players. We give them a formation sheet. On the formation, we show the plays they like to run in the areas they like to run them. We put their favorite passes on the sheet. There are visual charts. We list the down-and-distance they throw the pass and the frequency with which they throw it. The chart is what we make our scripts from during the week.

PUT IT ALL TOGETHER

- Know your plan.
- Trust your plan.

When you get it all together, you have to know your plan. When you are on the sideline and the game is going on, you have your sheet in front of you, but you must have a feel for what is going on in the game. You have to get yourself into the play. You must trust your plan. When a play busts, figure out why it broke down. The problem may not be with the stunt or the execution. It might be your athlete could not get the job done because of the other guys. They are on scholarship, too. You may not have the athletes against a particular team to do what you have coached them to do.

I played for Coach Osborne when we played Miami in the Orange Bowl. We were running the trap play and it was not gaining many yards. He told us to keep running that play because it was a good play, and we had practiced it all week. He told us, if we make the blocks, it will work. It finally broke for a touchdown.

That is what I mean about trusting your plan. We spent the entire week working on a plan that took seven or eight hours to develop. You cannot give up on it just because it failed on one play.

Here is an example of one entry I have on my call sheet. The situation is second and three to five yards for the first down:

- 2nd-and-3 to -5: R=49%, P=51%
- 21 personnel: R=48%, P=52%
  - ✓ Calls
  - ✓ Base
  - ✓ Blitz
- 11 personnel: R=33%, P=57%
  - ✓ Calls
  - ✓ Base
  - ✓ Blitz
  - ✓ Nickel

We have down-and-distance and personnel groupings for each situation. Tendencies do not lie. Just because it is short yardage does not mean it will be a short-yardage play. If they have a high percentage of passes in that situation, you have to trust your plan and defend the pass.

BE WILLING TO ADJUST YOUR PLAN (HALFTIME)

Do not be too stubborn to adjust the plan. Analyze whether their players are better than your players are. If they are better than you are, you have to alter and adjust at halftime. There is nothing more demoralizing than a team throwing a play-action pass for a touchdown in the first half. You go in at halftime and come out for the third quarter, and it happens again. If a team runs a reverse or a reverse pass for a touchdown in the first half, that play should never hurt in the second half. You should have that adjustment solved at halftime. That is critical.

Every coach has a different style, but Coach Pelini is very calm at halftime and allows the coaches to coach. We meet as a staff at halftime and talk about what adjustments must be made. After that, we meet with our position groups and make the adjustments and corrections. I think we were a better second-half team this year because we were able to make adjustments.

At times, we felt we had a good game plan and it was not working. That is the time you address your players with a strong hand. You have to get after them if they are not executing the game plan. Does anyone have any questions?

When we game plan, we game for a particular team and not for the whole season. I hope that some offensive coordinators prepare for cover 2 because we may not run it against them. Our secondary is multiple and can play a number of different ways and schemes. That is because we do not teach an entire scheme but a concept, which allows us to play combinations of different coverages.

I really appreciate your time. Thank you very much.

Tom Schmulbach

FROM THE WING-T TO THE SPREAD OFFENSE

Augustana College

The first clinic I ever attended was the Kellogg's® Coach of the Year Clinic. At that time, it was the Duffy Daugherty and Bud Wilkinson Coach of the Year Clinic sponsored by Kellogg's. I went to the clinic and saw my position coach from high school having dinner with John McKay. I thought to myself, that would be nice to know people like that. It is nice to meet and know people like that, but it takes a lot of work to get to those places in life.

My topic is "transition from the wing-T to the spread-zone read." This year, we had a crisis at our school. We decided to change our offensive scheme. That is something we debated and talked about for a long time. If you know anything about Augustana College, you know we are known for hard-nosed defense and running the ball on offense.

Three years ago, we set the national record for the fewest passes thrown in a season with 37 throws. Eleven of those passes came in the same game. That same year, our quarterback set the record for most rushing yards in a game by a quarterback. He rushed for 357 yards. We got a new head coach in 2000, and he was not used to those kinds of staggering statistics. We won a game two years ago and did not attempt a pass.

With all that said, there were many winning seasons. With all the wins we have had, why should we go to a spread offense geared to throwing the football? We looked at the personnel on our team and felt the offense fit the athletic ability of our quarterback. He was a special kind of athletic. He was not very big, but he was great in open spaces. He could make plays and win ball games for us. We had an excellent split end and running backs that caught the ball well. They could make people miss and turn those five-yard gains into 15-yard gains.

Personnelwise, we thought it was the right thing to do.

The second thing we explored was the trends in the world of football. High school players only see the spread offense these days. In high school, most teams run the spread offense. The pro game centers on the quarterback throwing the ball. The fact that the game has become wide open and fun to play has brought more athletes into the game. We felt we should play the game they were playing so the transition from high school to our program was not such a radical change.

When we looked at our schedule and the teams we had to beat to win championships, we decided that we needed to do more things offensively. We were winning seven games a year, but we could not seem to break into the championship series and win those other three games. We felt we needed more offense.

We felt that if we had a program that was attractive to athletes, we had a better chance to recruit more athletes that are skilled. The good wide receivers did not consider Augustana because we did not throw the ball. From a coaching point of view, we felt this system would allow the players to do what they do best. It would allow offensive linemen to block, running backs to run the ball, and receivers to catch the ball. We were not asking a running back to block or a wide receiver to do something that he is not trained to do.

We looked at all those things together and decided to change the offense and go to the spread game. The next thing we had to decide was how to install what we wanted to do. Were we going to make it fit or burn the boat? Were we going to try and make the spread fit into what we were doing or were we going to start from scratch and throw out the entire offense?

In 2007, we tried to fit the zone option into the Augustana wing-T offense.

2007

- Fit parts of what we did into a spread look (33 percent)
  - ✓ Option
  - ✓ Power
  - ✓ Belly
  - ✓ Toss (rocket)
  - ✓ Three- and five-step quick game and sprint out pass
- Run traditional Augustana wing-T offense (67 percent)

We ran the spread 33 percent of the time and fit it into what we were doing. We ran the option, which fit the spread offense. Our blocking was similar to the spread game. We ran the power from the spread, but we did not feel we could run the belly out of the spread. The offense was basically our offense with a new look.

2008

- Spread/zone read (85 percent)
  - ✓ Inside zone
  - ✓ Outside zone
  - ✓ Offensive additions: Wrap, counter, option
  - ✓ Quick and sprint out pass
- Augie offense (15 percent)
  - ✓ Power
  - ✓ Belly

In 2008, we ran the entire spread offense 85 percent of the time. It had nothing to do with the old rules and was a total commitment to a zone-read concept. We kept the Augustana offense as a short-yardage and goal-line package. We probably used it in more situations than that, but we had personnel that knew the system.

I had been the backfield coach for most of the 27 years I have been at Augustana. We have had two line coaches in that time. When we went to this offense, the head coach, Jim Barnes, asked me if I would like to coach the offensive line. I played that position in high school but had never coached a day in the offensive line. I want to show you some of the differences we did from the wing-T offense to the spread offense.

TECHNIQUE DIFFERENCES

Wing-T

- Four-point stance
- Crowd the line of scrimmage
- Weight forward, heels up
- Beat the cadence
- Have an assigned man to block
- Never retreat
- Two tight ends/tackles

Spread/Zone Read

- Two-point stance
- Back off line of scrimmage
- Flat-footed stance, staggered
- No cadence
- Have a zone concept to get to a man
- First step often back
- No tight ends

We went from a four-point stance to a two-point stance. Our guards are in a three-point stance, and the tackles can get in a three-point stance if they choose. We went from a mind-set that we were always going to beat the cadence and get off the line of scrimmage an instant before the ball was snapped to no cadence. After the quarterback goes through the sequence of signaling the play to all the receivers, he gives the "get-ready" signal to the center. The center snaps the ball when he is ready. After the center checks the defense, he says, "Go," and snaps the ball.

The line blocking was a big change. In the wing-T, we were assigned a man to block. In the spread, we know the direction we are going but we're not sure of the defender until he shows up. The first step off the line of scrimmage was totally different in the two concepts. In the old offense, we played with two tight ends for most of the game. Those tight ends were probably tackles. The spread offense did not have a two-tight end formation. We had to go back and name the formation we used.

We reduced the splits in our offensive line somewhat. In the wing-T, the splits were three-foot splits. When we went to the spread offense, we cut the splits to anywhere from 18 inches to two feet.

After we did our stretching, we had a perfect-play drill. In the drill, we emphasized what we were doing. We started practice with the concept in mind. We had to run five plays perfectly before we went on to the next drill. In the five plays, we had to run a screen, draw, three-step pass, inside zone, and outside zone.

When we researched the offense and looked at it, we needed to put together a philosophy. We spent most of the winter trying to come up with something. We felt like this was a good place to start.

OFFENSIVE LINE PRINCIPLES

The outside zone (stretch) is a frontside-gap scheme. All frontside linemen take a drop-step and work up their track. Our splits are no more than two feet, and we back off the ball as far as possible. This should prevent defenders from splitting our combinations as well as give our linemen more time to adjust to stunting defensive fronts. This is a horizontal play. It forces defenders to defend the sideline. Backside linemen, on the stretch, will cut block. This play will only work if we believe we can put two defenders on the ground every time.

The inside zone (belly) is a power cutback play that creates movement off the line with the potential of two quick double-team blocks. The base rule is if a defender covers you, block him. An uncovered player will drop-step, check level one, and work to the second level.

Both series' make the quarterback responsible for the backside edge player. He can put the backside second-level player in a double bind with the use of bubble and flash passes.

In our inside-zone scheme, we had the bubble pass and the flash pass built in to the play. We run the zone play, but the quarterback has the option to throw the bubble or flash pass out of that play.

The thing we probably adjusted to fit our scheme was the levels off the ball. We will be up and down the levels in our offensive line alignments. We are off the ball to the legal limit on some plays, while on other plays, we are closer to the line of scrimmage. It took us some time to learn about the backside cut-block scheme. One of the goals for our offensive linemen is to have a certain number of defenders on the ground during a game.

When we changed to the zone-read scheme, we had to change our stances. At the start of practice every day, we had a five-minute, "stance-check" period. During that period, we taught the stance.

STANCE CHECK

- Walk to the line of scrimmage.
- Feet: Keep a wide base with the feet parallel.
- Stagger: Outside foot in a toe-to-heel relationship.
- Sit: Back is flat with hips lower than the head, off hand rests outside the knee, holding the knee in.
- Hand: Drop hand down from the eyes inside of the knee.
- Pick the hand back up.

These were the points we emphasized in the drill. We worked on it every day. We wanted them to be able to pick up the hand in order to emphasize not putting too much weight on the hand. We want the off hand outside the knee, holding the knee in and straight down the field. We want the feet straight ahead, so he does not develop any duckwalk type of movement.

When we taught the progression of the block, we started out with the stance. Once we taught them the stance, we worked on the footwork that goes with blocking. We had to relearn how to punch and finish to each block. Punching and finishing is a matter of pad level and eye location. It is pad-under-pad and middle-to-middle.

Before we got into this in spring practice, we did a lot of research. We bought every video we could. We had videos from West Virginia, Utah, and C.W. Post. We read every book we could and went to Michigan for their spring practice. We felt good and thought we had a good start on what we needed to know.

APPROACH

- Belly (right and left covered)
  - ✓ Stance plus one
  - ✓ Stance plus two (two commands)
  - ✓ Stance plus two (one command)
  - ✓ Stance plus three, go-to-go
  - ✓ Full go/hammer
- Stretch (all linemen are considered uncovered on the stretch)
  - ✓ Stance plus 1
  - ✓ Stance plus 2

When we started teaching the techniques, we began with the approach to get into the block. We started with what we call stance plus one. We got in the stance and took the first step in the approach on a defender. We practiced those steps for the covered and uncovered linemen. If the defender was outside the blocker, he took his first step to cover the foot of the defender. If the defender was inside the blocker, he took an in-place step with his outside foot and got the inside hand up on the defender.

The second part of the drill is to take the second step, but we do it with a command for each step. The next progression is the *stance plus two*. It is the same drill with one command. The blocker takes his first two steps on the command. Next, the third step was added. We did all the step movements to both the left and to the right.

When we did the stretch play, we considered all the linemen to be uncovered and worked on the steps in that manner. We used whistles for the commands to move.

The next phase of our blocking was to work on the punch progression of the block. We started to teach this from the knees in the beginning.

PUNCH PROGRESSION

Two-Hand Punch

- From knees with hands on thighs, blocker will punch the defender in the chest. Defenders will be in a two-point stance with hands on knees.
- Stress hip roll and hand placement with thumbs up.
- Finish the drill moving forward.

Second-Step Drill (Teach Second Step and Punch Out of a Stance)

- Go: First step, second step, punch, then reset second step
- Two: Five reps of second step and punch
- Reset
- Go: Two steps and punch and reset to stance
- Go: Three or more reps

In the hand-placement portion of the drill, we place our hands at different places depending on the type of block we are using. We place the hands on the outside numbers, the armpit, or one hand on the shoulder pad and one on the sternum. The second-step drill is done from the feet. We step and punch.

These are the thoughts of a team that went from one scheme to the other. We thought we knew what we were doing. We prepared, read, and watched tape. When the season started, it was a whole new ball game. Here are our initial thoughts on the inside zone.

INSIDE ZONE THOUGHTS

- We would like to always start with two double-team blocks.
- We will stay on that block until a second-level player draws us off.
- You must decide whether a 3 technique on the backside guard is covered or uncovered.
- Your backside tackle is considered uncovered. How does he handle the outside linebacker?
- How much surface do you take/hand placement?
- Do you ever want to wrong-step a defender?
- Most big plays are backside plays.

We had to teach them that the play started with two double-team blocks, but they had to get off those blocks when the second threat came. One of the big points we had to decide was on the 3 technique. On the backside, is a 3 technique on the guard considered covered or uncovered? When we started, we decided to consider him uncovered. We thought the tackle was quick enough to cut him off. We had to learn about the backside tackle block on the backside linebacker. At the beginning, if he did not flow into the play, we left him alone and went to the frontside. Later, we started to find him and block him because the cutbacks were coming that way.

We had problems early with hand placement in the double-team block. We found the post blocker was covering up the surface of the defender, which made it awkward for the drive blocker. He had no surface to place his hands. We had to rethink our approach to the post blocker to take two-thirds of the defender and the drive blocker took the other one-third of him.

Wrong-stepping on the defender refers to an inside technique on the blocker. We had to decide if we wanted to step to the inside defender before we went into our zone step progression. We decided not to wrong-step on any zone play.

A drill we use to teach these techniques is a 2-on-1 drill. We align two offensive blockers on one defender. We work on the covered and uncovered look working for a takeover block or a block up to the next level. The linemen go through their zone steps and block the defender. We can stunt the defender once we learn the drill.

We use an identical drill to teach the double-team and slip technique. We align two offensive blockers and two defenders. We emphasize the double-team first and then, the slip to the linebacker.

We emphasize that the uncovered lineman, as he takes his steps, must be aware of the defender on the covered lineman. He has to see the inside movement because that will become his block. In our double-team blocks, you must have four eyes on the linebacker. If the linebacker comes underneath the double-team, the post blocker has to come off on the linebacker. If he goes over the top, the drive man slips to him. The linemen want to stay on the double-team until the linebacker forces one of them off.

This drill also teaches the proper track for the linemen to go to the second level. If the defender on the covered lineman does not move to the inside, the lineman climbs to the second level. This drill gives us the best teaching look at the double-team and individual tracks by the blockers. The two offensive blockers can be the guard and tackle or the center and guard.

The next play is the *outside zone play*. We had some thoughts on that play also.

Outside Zone (Stretch) Thoughts

- Frontside tackle and guard reach and climb or they climb and reach. They have a maximum of five steps to decide (sometimes improvise cross).
- Center can reach all the way to the 3 technique. If the 3 technique squats, anyone inside of him is old news.
- Backside guard and tackle cut— we want two on the ground.
- Convince every lineman that he is an elite athlete.
- When defensive people start worrying about who is going to block them, we've got 'em.
- Don't assume linemen know where the ball might or can go.
- Again, backside is the key. Grading plays versus grading wing-T.

On the outside zone play, we consider all offensive linemen uncovered. The frontside tackle and guard take their drop-steps and have to decide whether they are going to reach or climb block. We want them to decide on the block in three steps. However, we say by five steps, they have to know.

By the middle of the year, I expect our center to reach a 3-technique defender. That is especially true if that defender is slanting to the inside. Anytime a blocker reaches for a defender and he slants inside, leave him alone. He is yesterday's news and will not be part of the play.

It is tough to convince linemen that they are elite athletes. They are not elite athletes, but we had to convince them they were college athletes and were skillful. What I noticed about linemen is they did not like to hit the ground. They played on their feet and did not like to dive at someone. We had to convince them they could chase linebackers and defensive backs and get things done.

When the defensive lineman starts to play the cut block, you know he is worried about getting blocked. That becomes his first thought instead of his assignment.

Take your offensive linemen and show them where the ball can go on the zone play. Walk them through the play and show them where the ball can go. When we start teaching the inside zone, we start in the frontside A gap. However, it could break back into the backside A or B gap.

The backside is the absolute key to the success of the play. I realized that when I started grading our old wing-T plays. If the backside people can get their defenders on the ground, the running lanes behind the frontside blocks become huge.

We taught the backside cut blocks with bags. We had the dummies come straight across the line of scrimmage, take two steps down the line, or run flat to the line of scrimmage. The cut block is like tackling. The blocker gets as close as he possibly can and takes one more step before he throws. The cut block is no good if the lineman just dives at the feet. He has to run through the block and knock people down. We do those drills every day. The linemen began to understand that they could hit the ground and get up quickly.

When we run plays against air, our backside blockers dive on the ground and do a somersault. They are beginning to take pride in the fact they can get on the ground and get off it quickly.

We work our pairs on the outside zone play as we did the inside zone (Diagram #1). If we have a wide defender or outside movement, the lineman may have to drive the defender to the outside. The inside lineman has to climb to the second level to cut off the linebacker. If he cannot cut him off, he may have to go wider to get him.

Diagram #1. Wide

If the defender squats at the line of scrimmage, the inside lineman pushes the outside lineman off that block, and the outside lineman climbs up for the linebacker (Diagram #2).

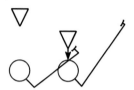

Diagram #2. Squat

If the covered lineman's man goes inside, he forgets him and climbs to the next level (Diagram #3). He hands the defender off to the uncovered blocker. At times, the blocker may cut the slanting defender. We use the momentum of the slanting defender to take him off his feet.

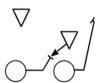

Diagram #3. Slanting

We went to Michigan for three days. We spent hours talking to their staff about this system. We watched all the cut-ups and film and did everything we could to learn all we could. We got a rulebook from West Virginia. We had just enough knowledge by the start of spring practice to get ourselves in a lot of trouble.

INSTALLATION THOUGHTS

• Michigan, spring ball, every video we could find, books, called friends, just enough knowledge to be in real trouble.

- Playing against triple-stack teams early plus our own defense helped us answer some difficult questions early.
- After three games, what was our best play?
- "Seven in the box equals touchdown" myth, not three yards at a time.
- I won't waste another second trying to figure out how to block seven in the box with five.
- Bringing in a tight end or an extra back is not the answer—that changes coverage dynamics.

After three games, we did not know what our best play was—that was scary. Our best offensive lineman was our left tackle, and the left guard was very aggressive. Our best play was anything we ran to the left side.

If you think seven in the box equals a touchdown, do not believe that. It is a myth. Everyone tells you with seven in the box, you can throw it deep and get a touchdown. Teams that play cover zero do not give up deep balls all the time.

The next thing is a personal pledge I hope I keep. I will not waste another second of my life trying to figure out how to block seven in the box with five offensive linemen—you cannot do it. Everyone's answer was to insert an extra back or tight end but you cannot do that. You cannot punch the pause button in the middle of a game to get someone into the game. If that is the answer, then you have changed the dynamics of the system. If you bring a tight end into the game, there are only three receivers on the outside and another man in the box.

Before the season started, I tried to list all the things we needed to do. I listed the things we needed to do every day. I listed the things we needed to do at least once a week. I listed things that we could do in pre-practice or warm-up. I also listed the stations. My inventory list will be much bigger next year.

2008 DRILL INVENTORY

Daily List

- Stance plus one, two ,three
- Boards blocking progression
- Punch progression
- 2-on-1 covered/uncovered
- 2-on-2 covered/uncovered
- 1-on-1 pass protection
- Group pass protection
- Protection with running backs
- Sled session
- Center skills

Weekly List

- Tuesday
  - ✓ Game week fronts
  - ✓ Offensive installation
  - ✓ Blocking in chutes
  - ✓ Inside drill vs. defense
  - ✓ Backside cutoff block
- Wednesday
  - ✓ Screen/draw package
  - ✓ Screen technique
  - ✓ Draw technique
  - ✓ Pass pro versue defense
- Thursday
  - ✓ Pulling counter/boot
  - ✓ Audible review
  - ✓ Fumble drill

Pre-Practice

- Stance check
- Warm-up movement
- Fit and finish
- Hand fights
- Drive the bus
- Fit and wave

Stations

- Board agility
- Cage drills
- Sandbag pass sets
- Around the square with bags

We have some concerns with our transition. This year, we were very good with our Augustana offense. The double dive and power play were good for us because our players knew it from previous years. However, I think we will get less effective in our Augustana offense as we practice less on that scheme. We hope to offset that by becoming more effective in the zone scheme. We had been good in the previous offense because we had an overabundance of fullbacks and tight ends. We do not have those personnel any more.

When we ran the Augustana system in practice, the offensive linemen would smile, and they were glad that we were going to that part of the game. That was a worry to us because we did not want to rely on that offense. The day our linemen realized they could be nasty people and play zone was the day we got better. When they realized at the point of attack they could be as nasty as ever, they started liking the zone offense. We hit the defender as hard as we used to, and it was a way we could get to the defender.

In the past, we never worried about toughness. If you could get through our practices, you were tough. We had to continually tell our linemen that this was not a finesse system. I asked our offensive linemen at the beginning of the year a question and it scared the hell out of me. I gave them four traits and asked them what they thought was the most important to offensive linemen.

- Do you want to be the most physical linemen?
- Do you want to be the hardest-working offensive linemen?
- Do you want to be the best-prepared linemen?
- Do you want to be the best technicians in the conference?

They answered they wanted to be the best technicians in the conference. That scared the hell out of me because I did not have a lot of background in the technical aspect of the offensive line. Luckily, my assistant line coach is a great technician. I let him do all the technical work, and when it came time for the contact, I stepped in.

I tried to convince them if they were the hardest-working group that all of the traits would come about. They thought I would think the most important thing would be most physical. They thought my answer to the problems they were having would be to knock the defender out. I think the hardest-working is the part of the game that controls the rest of those traits.

I let them make up all the calls they use in the offensive line. I do not know all the things they make up between one another. If they make up the calls, they remember them. If I make them up, I remember them, but I cannot play.

At the end of the year, we were the best offensive line in the conference. If we can continue to improve and be physical, we will be a good team. We give awards in practice for the best catch and best hit of the day. We give them old hit records which were hits in their day. We give the Supremes, Temptations, and records of that nature. It is quite an award and they make a big deal out of it.

That is it. I appreciate you staying with me. Thank you very much.

COACHING THE CORNERBACKS

University of Arizona

I appreciate the opportunity to be here to share some ideas about defense. I want to talk a little bit about philosophy and the team concept. That goes back to the way I was brought up, and the way I was taught to do things. That has held true everywhere I have been in coaching. Whether it was Kansas State University, the University of Oklahoma, or the University of Arizona, those ideas have remained the same. I hope I can give you something that will be useful and you can make it fit your program. I grew up in a football family in Ohio. However, my migration took me west instead of east.

I have been fortunate to be involved with turning three programs around. I was with Coach Snyder at Kansas State when we turned that program from a doormat into an unbelievably successful program. I was with my brother Bob at Oklahoma when we restored that program into a position of respect. I am now the head coach at Arizona, and we are on the road to recovering the successes that program had at an earlier time. What we did in those programs is very special.

At the University of Arizona, it was hard to turn that program. We play in an extremely tough conference, and we needed players to compete at that level. We have gotten the program established, and hopefully we can compete for the conference championship for years to come.

I do not want to spend a great deal of time on philosophy, but there are some reasons you need to hear these things. These are things that I believed were important at every place I have been, and they have proven to be successful.

We want to keep what we are doing as simple as possible. We want the players to play and react and not think too much. We must have things built into our program that add deception and address the fine points of offense and defense, but we want to be simple in our approach. We have time restrictions in college, so we must keep what we are doing simple.

We base our basic philosophy on defense around a seven- and eight-man front with zone blitzes. How we adapt our personnel to that philosophy is our staple on defense. We will blitz a number of different ways and create deception out of our base fronts. In the secondary, we make preparation during the week of how to best handle great quarterbacks and receivers. When we play great quarterbacks and receivers, we do not want to match up our corners with them all day long. How we handle those quarterbacks and receivers and adapt our personnel to those situations is big part of our philosophy.

I want to start with some basic concepts that are important to the success of a program.

PHILOSOPHY

- Great defense
- Turnover margin
- Red-zone offense
- Special teams

HOW DO YOU ACCOMPLISH THESE THINGS?

- Cultivate leadership—particularly with the seniors.
- Play hard on every snap—average play should be four to seven seconds.
- Preparation—do your job.
- Team first—don't be selfish, and maintain positive energy.

The attitude of your football team is built around discipline. If you want to have a good football team, you must have a good defense. I believe the success of a program begins with defense. You depend on your defense when the game is on the line. It develops the toughness that goes with a successful program.

The second thing that is important is turnover margin. We were 5-7 in 2007, and 8-5 last year. Last year, we lost four games by seven or less points. We were competitive in every game. We went from sixth on defense in 2007 to second in 2008. Only the Southern Cal defense was better. The turnover margin this year was the reason for that big turnaround.

The third area we talk about is red-zone offense. We want to know how successful we are in certain areas of the field. We were second in the league with red-zone offense. We scored 33 out of 37 times in the red zone. That helped us win games and gave us some consistency in the red zone throughout the year. We are successful in red-zone scoring opportunities.

The last category is special teams. We want to excel in this area. In our special teams, we were either first, second, or third in all areas of the kicking game except kickoff return. In our field goal, punt team, punt-return team, and kickoff team, we were first, second, or third in the conference.

To accomplish those goals, you must have leadership. Leadership comes from your seniors. This senior class played a tremendous part in the transition from the previous staff to our staff.

To accomplish any goal on the field, you must play hard. A play in football lasts only four to seven seconds. You cannot win games if your team does not play hard in the games and in practice. We want our players going as hard as they can on every play. We try to develop depth so that we can rest our players. We do not want to take any plays off. If they need rest, we rest on the sidelines, not in the games.

Players have to prepare to do their job. Preparation is something that is personal to each player and coach. I prepare to do my job and know what is going on, and I expect our players to do the same thing.

The last thing is to put the team first and forget about your ego. Players cannot be selfish and must be a positive influence for your team to be successful. Players must sacrifice their individual interest for the betterment of the team.

Those are some base ideas about our philosophy. The next thing I want to do is give you an idea of what we do defensively. We play a number of defensive fronts based on what we see in the opponent from week to week.

This year, we played an "over or under" defense with a three-deep secondary about 70 percent of the time (Diagram #1). We define our safeties and determine who the eighth man in the box will be at all times. In everything we do, we have the capability of playing two-deep if we choose. We can also play zero coverage from this defense. There are a lot of different things we can do from this front.

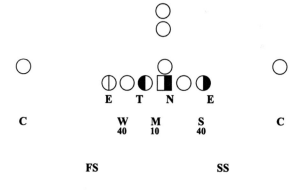

Diagram #1. Over, Cover 3

In this defense, we play a 3 technique to the tight-end side with a nose shade on the center to the splitside. The defensive end aligns in a 6 technique head-up the tight end. The 6 technique is the hardest technique to play. The end to the openside plays a 5 technique. We play the Will linebacker in a 40 technique over the offensive tackle to the tight-end side. The Mike linebacker aligns in a 10 technique over the center. The Sam linebacker is head-up the tackle to the openside in a 40 technique.

We make the "G" adjustment with the nose. The G adjustment moves the nose into an inside eye alignment on the openside guard. The linebackers read backs and angles of those backs. They also read flow of the backs. We read the near and far sets of the fullback. We are a one-gap team. We also drop the safeties down into gap responsibilities. We have the ability to move the nose around and get into some stack alignments.

We align our linebackers based on what the offense does. If we get flow into the openside, the linebackers are gap responsible. If they try to isolate the Sam linebacker, he stuffs the play with his inside shoulder and forces the ball to the Mike linebacker (Diagram #2). The Mike linebacker fills to the B gap on flow to the openside of the formation. The Will linebacker has the A gap to the tight-end side. The 6 technique fills the C gap to that side, and the strong safety has responsibility for the D gap.

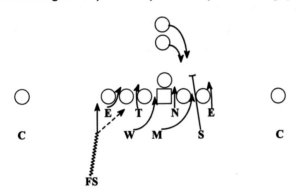

Diagram #2. Weakside Flow

The strong safety plays slow as he comes to his gap. If the 6 technique gets cut off from the C gap, the strong safety fills that gap. We want to play the cutback and not let the ball get backside.

If the fullback goes in short motion to that side, we bump the linebackers with his motion. If he goes to the strongside, we adjust a step that way. When teams start to move their fullback, they are trying to gain leverage on the linebackers. If they are a split-flow team, we respect the first move with our linebackers and react back. If we cannot stop them late, we are not a very good football team. If they release the fullback out to the weakside, the Sam linebacker picks him up. If we play man-free in the

secondary, the run reactions are the same for the defense.

The next play I want to talk about is the power play to the tight-end side. The offense will double-team your 3 technique, block back with the center, and pull the guard through the off-tackle area. The fullback is a kick-out blocker on that play (Diagram #3). People who run the power use the play-action pass to take advantage of a cover-3 team. They use maximum protection, clear out the coverage with the split end, and bring the flanker on a deep cross into the vacated area. This play also looks like the stretch lead play. That is why it is a difficult play to defend.

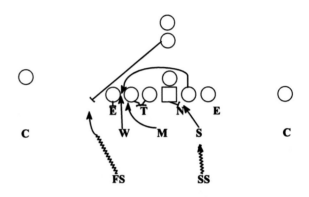

Diagram #3. Power Play

The Will linebacker flows into the C gap, keeping his outside arm free. The offense tries to base block the tight end on the defensive end. We want the Will linebacker to fill the C gap, with the ability to get outside if the defensive end gets blocked down. The Mike linebacker fills from the inside out. This is a hard read for the Mike linebacker. They see the angle of the fullback, but they may not see the pull of the offensive guard. A lot of people shoot the Mike linebacker when they see this scheme. We do not. We want the Mike linebacker playing the inside eye of the pulling guard as he turns up into the hole. The Will linebacker plays outside the guard. We want the Mike linebacker playing tight to the pulling guard because offenses want to run the ball back inside the linebacker.

It is easy for the Mike linebacker to overpursue the power play. He gets in too big a hurry to get outside, and the ball comes back behind him. The thing we want to do is attack downhill at this play. If a team runs a counter play, the principles for playing the counter are the same as playing the power.

If the offense aligns in a twins set, we have two ideas about how to play this set (Diagram #4). The offense puts the twins set into the wide field most of the time. We can walk the strong safety up on the slot receiver. The rest of the defense remains the same, with the exception of the free safety and backside corner. The corner aligns in a 4x4 alignment outside the tight end. The free safety moves toward the twin-receiver side and aligns in the fieldside B gap.

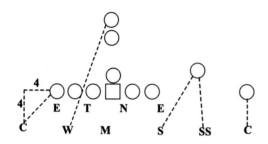

Diagram #4. Twins Set, Cover 1

The first adjustment is 1 coverage, which is a man-free concept, against this set. To the twins side, the Sam linebacker and strong safety play a man-to-man "in-and-out" technique on the slot receiver. The field corner plays the split end in man coverage. The boundary corner has the tight end if he releases on a pass. The Will linebacker has the first back coming out of the backfield to the tight-end side.

If the tight end blocks, the corner is the run support player to the outside. The free safety is a B-gap player to the twins side, but he has to help the boundary corner on the post route into the middle. The boundary corner plays the tight end for a flag or fade route and has help to his inside from the free safety.

The defensive fits of the linebacker do not change with the twins set. If they run an isolation play to the twins side, the Sam linebacker plays the

lead block the same way as he did in the pro set. The Mike linebacker has the same fit on the isolation and the power. On the power play, the Will linebacker is fitting outside the pulling guard, and the Mike linebacker fits inside the pulling guard. The Sam linebacker is still the cutback player on the power play to the tight-end side.

The second adjustment to the twins set brings the strong safety back in a two-deep alignment (Diagram #5). The free safety moves to the tight-end side in a two-deep look. The Sam linebacker moves outside in a stack position behind the defensive end. We play a 3 coverage. The boundary corner has the flat, and the free safety has the zone behind him. The strong safety is the half-field player. The only play to the twins side that presents a problem is the bubble screen that way.

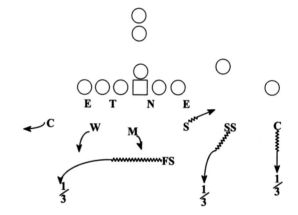

Diagram #5. Twins Set, Cover 3

The strong safety keys the slotback. If he bubbles to the outside, he can get into the support area quickly. The corner can see the block coming from the outside receiver to the inside and can react back into the play. The corner rolls up and plays the flat area, and the strong safety has the half coverage over the top. The Sam linebacker is in a position to help on all inside routes by the slot or split receiver.

We can also run blitzes from both of these looks (Diagram #6). With the strong safety in the rolled-up position, we like to bring him off the edge. We slant the line to the tight end and bring the strong safety off the edge.

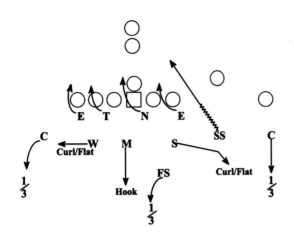

Diagram #6. Strong Safety Blitz Man

We can also run the same stunt and play zone coverage. We can still bring the strong safety off the edge and drop the defensive end into the boundary (Diagram #7). The boundary corner drops to the half field, and the defensive end drops into the boundary flat. The free safety moves to the twins side half, and the strong safety blitzes off the edge.

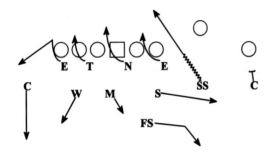

Diagram #7. Strong Safety Blitz Zone

In our defensive scheme, we play a boundary and field corner. We do not play left and right. Our base alignment for our safeties is a two-deep look. We disguise our coverage and have constant movement in the defensive secondary. They are walking and moving all the time.

As I said before, the 6 technique is the hardest technique to play. He aligns head-up the tight end and has to play his block. However, he has to be aware of what the tackle is doing. Teams want to use the tight end and tackle in combination blocks on the 6 technique. He has to feel the tackle and know what he is trying to do. We do not want the 6 technique to get penetration up the field on runs toward him. We want him to control the tight end and see the tackle.

If the tackle's shoulder moves to the inside, he has to be able to recognize what type of block it is. When he becomes good at his position, he knows from the angle whether it is a scoop block on the 3 technique or a down block. If the tackle steps down on the 3 technique at an angle, it is a combination block on the 3 technique. If he steps flat to the line of scrimmage, it is a scoop cutoff block on the 3 technique.

The Mike linebacker and nose work together. If the center comes off on the Mike linebacker, the nose should make the play. They have to work as a team. The nose cannot allow the center to get to the Mike linebacker. He has to make the center concentrate on him and not get a free release. The 3 technique has to make the guard block him. He cannot allow the guard to come off the line of scrimmage into the A gap. He cannot allow the tackle to single-block him. If the ball is run in the B gap, he has to be a factor on the tackle.

If the fullback moves into a weakside wing position outside the offensive tackle, the Sam linebacker moves up to the line of scrimmage (Diagram #8). We describe the fullback off set in the I formation as a "far" and "near" positions. If the fullback off sets to the split-end side, we call that a "far" position. If he sets to the tight-end side, that is a "near" position. If he shifts or moves in motion, the Sam linebacker moves back to his original position and plays his technique. If the fullback moves to the near side of the formation, all the linebackers adjust to that side. If they run the power-G, the Will linebacker is outside the guard pull, and the Mike linebacker is inside the guard pull.

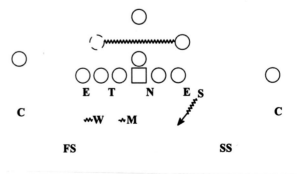

Diagram #8. Near Motion

If the fullback sets in the far set, the Sam linebacker widens somewhat. Teams like to run the outside stretch lead play from this set (Diagram #9). The Sam linebacker reads the angle of the fullback and gets to the outside across his face. The Mike linebacker fits inside the Sam linebacker. The problem is the backside 6 technique. He cannot let the C gap on the backside widen. We do not want the free safety filling inside on that type of run.

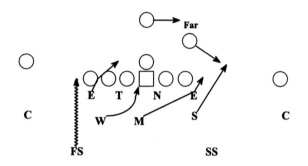

Diagram #9. Far Set

The "over switch" call is the strong safety adjustment to the twins set. The strong safety drops down on the slot receiver in the twins set. The backside corner moves tight to the line of scrimmage in a 4x4 alignment. The corner has the tight end, and the Will linebacker has the first back out of the backfield (Diagram #10). In the diagram, the offense aligns in a twins set to the field and a wing set to the boundary with one back in the backfield. If they motion the wing back into the twins side, they create a 3x1 set to the field. Everyone to the backside must play their cutback lanes. If the ball starts to the tight end and cuts back, the strong safety has to cover the D gap.

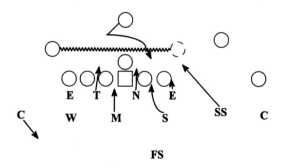

Diagram #10. Over Switch

With this kind of adjustment, we use combination coverages. We man the twins side and zone the backside. We can play quarter coverage to the twins side and man coverage to the tight side. We have ways to change the coverage to fit the opponent's tendencies.

In the college game, the hash marks are important to defensive football. We play our defense into the field quite a bit. We play a lot of "field weak-3" (Diagram #11). This is another way to get into an eight-man front. On this defense, we put the nose and Sam linebacker into the wideside of the field. The Sam linebacker plays a 9 technique on the tight end. The 3 technique moves out to a 5 technique, and the nose moves to the field shade on the center. The Mike and Will linebackers move over, and the free safety drops down into the Will linebacker's position.

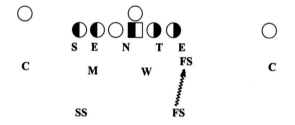

Diagram #11. Field Weak-3

We use this defense when the offense trades the tight end or gives us a lot of movement from one side of the set to the other. If they trade the tight end into the boundary, we are in "over-3" and have not moved anyone. The linebackers and free safety adjust back to their original position. In the "field weak" call, we are playing an "under" defense in this alignment. All the fits for the Mike, Will, and free safety are the same as Sam, Mike, and Will linebackers in the "over" defense. The Mike linebacker has outside leverage on the pulling guard. The Will linebacker has inside leverage on the pulling guard, and the free safety has the cutback scheme.

If we play "field weak-3" with the twins set, the Sam linebacker and nose go into the wideside of the field (Diagram #12). To the boundary, we align in a

3 technique and a 6 technique. The boundary corner comes down to his 4x4 alignment. The strong safety comes down on the slot receiver, and everything else is the same.

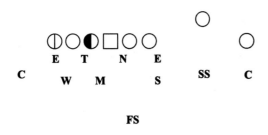

Diagram #12. Field Over Switch

If we want to change our coverage and bring pressure, we bring the free safety off the tight-end side on an edge blitz (Diagram #13). The shade nose and 3-technique tackle run a short stick slant away from the tight end into their adjacent A and B gaps. The 6 technique runs a long stick across the C gap into the B gap. The free safety disguises his blitz and comes off the edge outside the tight end. The corners and strong safety play three-deep coverage. The Will and Sam linebackers play a curl-to-flat zone, and the Mike linebacker plays the middle hook area. We play three-under and three-deep with a five-man pressure scheme.

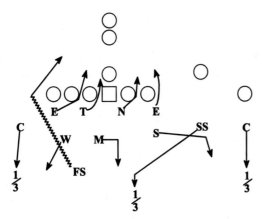

Diagram #13. Free Safety Hot

Because of the slanting of the defensive line, the fit rules for the linebackers on a running play will obviously change. Against a twins set, one of the blitzes we use is "over hot fox" (Diagram #14). The slants by the defensive line are the same as the free-safety edge blitz. The corner is the blitzer on

this stunt. He disguises his blitz and comes off the edge. The Sam linebacker cheats out to the slot receiver and plays curl-to-flat on that side. The free safety cheats down into a linebacker's depth alignment but will cover the deep third to his side. The Will linebacker has curl-to-flat coverage into the boundary.

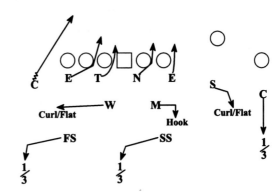

Diagram #14. Over Hot Fox

The Will linebacker's alignment on this blitz is in the A gap to the tight-end side. He has to get into the curl/flat area but should not have any trouble as long as the back in the backfield stays there. If the back moves to a position that outflanks the linebacker, he has to move that way. The Mike linebacker has a hook-to-curl drop on a pass. The strong safety is the middle-third player, and the field corner has the outside third into the wide-side of the field.

We run another blitz called "over slant hot" (Diagram #15). We align in our over defense. The 5-technique defensive end to the openside slants into the B gap. The shade nose slants across the center's face into the tight-end side A gap. The 3-technique tackle blows his B gap, and the 6-technique defensive end widens his alignment and comes off the edge.

The Sam linebacker disguises his blitz and comes off the openside edge outside the offensive tackle. The strong safety drops down into the vacated area and plays the Sam linebacker's curl-to-flat coverage. If the play is a run instead of a pass, the strong safety has the run responsibility of the Sam linebacker. On flow away from him, he fills the backside A gap. The Will linebacker has the flat-

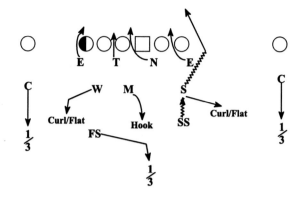

Diagram #15. Over Slant Hot

to-curl area to his side, and the Mike linebacker plays the middle hook area. The corners play deep outside-third coverage, and the free safety has the middle third.

These blitzes give us a way to bring pressure from the field and the boundary and to remain solid and sound to all running plays. When we blitz players off the edge, they want to come as tight as they can, but they must be aware of what is happening. They must read as they blitz. If the flow goes away, the blitzer has to look at the shoulders of the running back. If the shoulders are going away, the blitzer continues on his blitz path. However, if the shoulders are square, he has to slow down because eventually the ball will cut back and he is the cutback player. He must be aware of the back shoulder. If the back shoulder goes away, the blitzer continues on the path and goes to the ball. If the back shoulder comes back, he has to squeeze inside and play the cutback.

When we play our field defense, it looks like an under defense. From this front, we can play quarter coverage into the field with the field corner and strong safety. In the over defense, the free safety cheats to the line of scrimmage and is a D-gap player because the tight end aligns to his side. On the "field weak" defense, he becomes an A-gap player because the tight end is on the opposite side.

Our free safety is a big physical football player. That is why we have him rolling down into the run support most of the time. However, the strong safety can also play in that role. This defense is only one concept of our scheme.

The linebackers must know where the free safety support is at all times. They have to know who is coming down into run support and where he will fill. When they take on isolation blocks, they want to funnel the ball into a linebacker or the free safety.

We play a 6 technique on the tight end rather than a 9 technique. We feel it does not create as big a bubble over the linebackers. These are some of our ideas about defensive football. Football involves a lot of common sense when it comes to making adjustments to what the offense does. All we do is figure out ways to make it simple for our players.

I appreciate you coaches being here. I hope you have a better idea about how to implement our style of defense. We try to get the eighth man in the box a number of different ways. Football is very complicated with all the formations and sets offenses can show the defense. We try to keep it as simple as we can, but you have to be smart to play the game today. I know Arizona is a long way from here, but you are welcome to come see us. Thank you very much.

SCREEN PASSES AND FIVE-MAN PASS PROTECTION

Rutgers University

It is a pleasure to be representing Rutgers University. Today, I want to talk about the multiple screens game, and later I will talk about our five-man protection we use with our empty set. Let me begin with a short philosophy of what we are trying to do in the screen game.

MULTIPLE SCREEN PACKAGE

- Teaching philosophy.
- Everything in great detail.
- All components of the game are important.
- Teach positively.
- Fundamentals of the game.
- Excel at the little things.
- Success at the big things will follow.

Remember: It is not what we know as coaches; it is what our players can execute during a game.

When you start to teach the screen, you must have a clear understanding of what you are trying to accomplish. That goes back to the team philosophy of being secure with the ball, but at the same time being aggressive. We want to pay attention to the details of the play. All components of the game are important because if one component breaks down, the play will not be successful. The quarterback has to throw the ball, and the receiver has to catch it, but that is only the beginning to any successful play. You need the protection and downfield blocking with exact timing to make plays. The vital components of the screen are the offensive linemen. The guard, tackle, and center have important roles to play in this type of offense.

As with any part of coaching, nothing is gained by extreme criticism. You must coach with a positive attitude and have an upbeat tempo to everything you do on the field. Players respond to positive instructions better than negative browbeating and criticism. Teach and encourage your players.

The screen game is like any other phase of the offense. Its success depends on the execution of the fundamentals of football. When things go wrong with what you are doing, go back to the fundamentals of the game. Football is a simple game with respect to the fundamentals. There are certain things to be done at the beginning to lay the foundations for other skills to be built upon.

Leave no stone unturned, and excel at the little things. If you take care of details in the beginning, success at the big things will follow. This next point is extremely important. You must remember it is not what you know as a coach that is important. Unless you are going to play the game, what you know does not count. The success of any play depends on what the players know and can execute during the game.

We believe there are five ways to get the ball into your best players' hands. The screen concept is one way to get the ball into the hands of one of your best athletes in space. If those athletes get space, they can make something happen. This year, our screen game was a primary outside-in game.

We run directional screens, which are traditional halfback screens one way or the other. However, the directional screens seemed to go better the year before. I guess that was because Ray Rice was on the receiving end of most of the directional screens we threw. We run the pop screen, which is the outside-in screen. We also run a variety of different hitch screens. That was probably our best screen this year.

The screen has an impact on the rest of your offense. It neutralizes the effect of teams trying to rush the passer. For teams with an aggressive front four, it keeps the threat of a screen in the back of their minds, which slows down their pass rush.

Here are some aspects of the screen game you have to consider:

- Throw from the dropback, play-action, and moving pocket.
- Practice the component parts.
- Bring the parts together.
- Drill like any other play.
- Choose the one you feel best about.
- Too many screen concepts lead to average-at-best plays.
- Make it your play.

Make the screen game a complement to what you do in the passing game. You must throw the screen from the dropback, play-action, and from the moving pocket. Those drops are part of your passing game, and it has to be part of the screen game. There has to be carryover value in the screen game. It has to be an extension of the passing game. You cannot throw the screen from some part of a passing game that you do not use. It must come off your passing drops and patterns.

We treat the screen play like any other play in our offense. We are better at the screen play because we practice it more. You have to practice all the components of the plays that go into the game. You cannot practice the play and not get into the details in group practice. In addition, the blocking has to time up with the throws.

Too many screens will water down the effectiveness of your screen game. The screen is not effective if you run it too much in a game. The screen has to be deceptive and a surprise for it to achieve maximum success. If the defense expects the screen play, they can break it down quickly.

You have to do a great job of selling the game to the coaching staff. The coaches have to buy into the importance of the game in the offense. The timing of the screen pass is tremendously important to the success of the play. The quarterback has to get to the release point and deliver the ball so it is caught in the proper area.

The components of the screen are your big people running and blocking in space. With a traditional directional screen, you have three big players running in space. That involves the onside guard, the center, and the backside guard getting out and running ahead of the ballcarrier. The outside screen requires the onside tackle to get outside and make a block on a defensive back.

In the screen game, we try to gain a numbers advantage on the defense. We want the defensive line not to be a factor in the screen game. We want to get multiple blockers on a few defensive players.

When we run our screen game, we like to create a diversion to get the defense's attention. We use shifting and motion to get the defense moving. By using motion, it gives us an idea of what the defense is trying to do, and it better defines the blocking scheme.

In the directional screen, the screenside tackle blocks his pass-protection scheme that fits what the quarterback action is (Diagram #1). He wants to set and allow the defensive end up the field. He brings the defender deep and drives him by the quarterback to the outside to allow the release of the back. He has to be aware of any line games run by the defensive linemen or a zone-blitz scheme. If the linebacker comes outside, he blocks him as he would the defensive end. He must be aggressive and stay engaged with the defensive end.

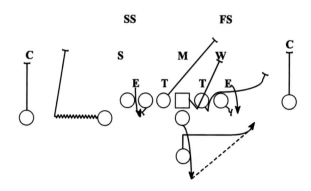

Diagram #1. Directional Screen

The screenside guard executes his pass block, punches the defender for two counts, and releases on the screen. He has dual responsibility; he blocks the first man to the outside and secures the catch. If there is no one there, he continues flat and kicks out on the outside. If there is no one there, he leads down the field. We want to do our work on their side of the line of scrimmage.

The center and playside guard can exchange responsibilities, depending on which linemen gets out first. If the center is uncovered, he gets to the outside first, secures the catch, and kicks out on the outside. The guard will lead upfield. The backside guard blocks, punches, and counts before he releases downfield. We release him over the line of scrimmage and not behind the line.

The screenside guard, center, and awayside guard, must kick out or man read to the screenside, wall off the near linebacker, and peel back on the man keying the screen. We call him the "rat killer." If there is anyone chasing the screen, he picks him off. The offside tackle has to control the defensive end to his side and block the same rules as the screenside tackle. He has to control the backside of the play.

If the backside guard feels the defender has read the play, he stays with him and rides him wherever he can. He can tell the defensive lineman has read the screen because he will redirect his charge. When he stops rushing and redirects in the direction of the screen, the backside guard cannot release him. He does not release him to run free to the outside.

It is important for the screen blockers to stay on the move. We do not want them to stop and wait on things to happen. If they stop, they are dead in their attempt to block moving targets. Once they break their momentum, they have trouble restarting their engine.

The tight end on the screenside or the awayside is taught to hunt the safety. He wants to block the middle safety or the near safety. If the middle of the field is open, he blocks the near safety to his side. If the middle of the field is closed, he blocks the middle safety. If it is man coverage, he runs off the coverage.

The wide receiver to the screenside must outside release and block the deepest defender on his side. If the corner rolls to his side, he has to outside release on the corner. If he inside releases, he opens the defender's eyes to what is happening. We want the defender's eyes away from the play. If there is man coverage, run it as far as they will go. Once they react to the screen, block them. If we have a crack screen called, the screenside wide receiver blocks the inside shoulder of the first defender to his inside.

The effective screen game begins with protection:

- Protect first.
- How does protection impact being able to release?
- What responsibility (if any) does the back have?
- Prefer to slide the protection to the side of the screen.
- Does the play hold up versus pressure?
- The timing of the screen is critical to its effectiveness.

We must protect first and have no free rusher coming to the quarterback. Defensive linemen are taught if they feel something is up, then something *is* up. The offense line cannot give the screen away through their actions. They have to block the defensive linemen like any other pass play. If the offensive linemen tell the defense we are running the screen, no one rushes.

How will the protection ultimately determine the way the offensive linemen releases, and what blocking responsibility does the back have? When we run our screen game, the offensive linemen must know how they are going to release for the blocker. If we keep the rushes moving to the outside, that is the easiest way to release to the outside. The offensive linemen must develop the punch and throw movement to release from a block.

We try to minimize any blocking responsibility for the running back on a screen play. We tell the running back, if his blocking responsibility is an immediate threat, he has to block him before he can release.

We prefer to have the screenside as the side we are sliding our protection. If we slide the protection to the right, we have the screen go to the right. It is difficult for the offensive line to slide the protection one way and release the other way.

When we run the screen game, we want the defense to use some kind of pressure scheme. If you have the screen call and the defense comes with a pressure blitz, we have an opportunity for a big play.

In our dropback passing game, our screen timing count is "1001, 1000, go." We have to be able to speed up the time in the five-step drop. However, in the play-action drops, we must slow the timing down. In a play-action situation, we have to give the linebackers time to recognize the play-action and retreat. They will initially jump to the run fake and then retreat.

In every screen package, there are some problems areas. The first problem has to do with the timing of the play. That is one of the screen components leaving too soon. When we run this play on air, we count aloud so everyone can hear. If anyone leaves too soon, it gives the screen away to the defense.

Leaving too soon gives the play away to the defense, and leaving too late means no blocking when the ball gets there. One of the big problems for this play is the near linebacker reading the screen quickly. He gets into the screen before the blockers get there. If a defensive lineman sees the play, he redirects his charge and runs the play down. That is what we call a "rat." The backside guard is the rat killer. He is the one who has to peel back on the rat. If the defensive end to the side of the screen stops rushing and drops, he is right in the middle of the screen.

POP SCREEN

- Use outside-in screen selectively.
- Use it when you feel the defense has zone tendencies.

- Work to get the ball to the best player in space.
- Put your linemen in a numbers- and leverage-advantage situation.

On this screen, we cut down the number of big players trying to get out into the screen. The screen is made up of the tackle, guard, and center. However, the center and guard are not involved with running outside.

Blocking Responsibilities

- Screenside tackle: Set, punch, and throw defensive end. Run flat to block the corner.
- Screenside guard: Set, punch, and throw. Seal the box. Ambush the defensive end.
- Center: Set, punch, and throw. Wall any linebacker threat. Adjust to safety level.
- Backside guard: Set, punch, and throw. Block any threat to outside. Adjust to safety level.
- Backside tackle: Control defensive end, and run him up the field. Adjust late to the safety on your side.

The tackle to the screenside pass sets and punches the defensive end (Diagram #2). When the end starts up the field, the tackle throws him up the field and releases to block the corner. The screenside guard sets, punches, and throws his defender up the field. He takes over the block on the defensive end that the tackle threw up the field. The center sets, punches, and throws his defender, and releases on any linebacker threat to the outside. If there is no linebacker, he adjusts to the safety level.

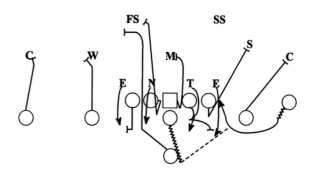

Diagram #2. Pop Screen

The backside guard sets, punches, and throws his blocker, and blocks any threat to the outside. If there is no threat, he adjusts to the safety level. The backside tackle blocks the defensive end up the field. He comes off the block late after the ball is thrown and tries to get to the safety on his side.

When we talk about the linemen throwing their defender, they are using the momentum of the defender to keep him going up the field. They push their defender in an upfield direction and come under them for their blocks.

The wide receiver catches the ball, moving back to the inside. If there is a second receiver to the screenside, he blocks out on the defender, covering the wide receiver. The tackle coming from the inside blocks the second defender in that area, which is generally the Sam linebacker. If the screen is thrown to the single receiver, the tackle blocks the corner.

HITCH SCREEN

The third concept is our hitch screen. This is a run-action screen. It is an inside-out screen off a hard run-action. The people involved in the screen are the screenside guard and tackle.

Blocking Responsibilities

- Screenside tackle: Three steps inside, plant, and run flat to block the corner
- Screenside guard: Three steps inside, plant, and seal the box. Ambush to linebacker level
- Center: Execute run-action.
- Backside guard: Execute run-action.
- Backside tackle: Execute run-action.

The screenside tackle takes three hard steps into the B gap (Diagram #3). He plants on his third step and reverses his direction. He runs flat to kick out the corner to his side. If there is anyone in the B gap, he pushes off them to get back to the outside. The screenside guard takes three steps into the A gap, plants, and reverses his direction. He seals the box. He has to block anyone in that area. It does not matter if it is the end or linebacker. He has to seal the box area.

If we throw the screen into a two-receiver side, the inside receiver blocks the defender over the hitch receiver.

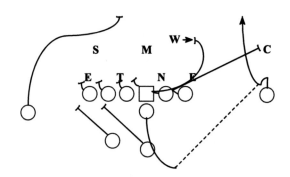

Diagram #3. Hitch Screen

We throw a crack screen to the running back. It is a one-man screen (Diagram #4). The wide receiver to the screenside cracks on the first defender to his inside. The screenside tackle gets a punch release on the defensive end and runs to block the corner to that side. The tailback swings to that side and the quarterback gets him the ball. It is a quick hitting play. There is no delay by the back.

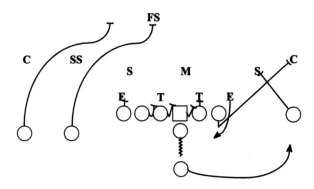

Diagram #4. Crack Screen

The linemen block their pass assignments on this play. The only offensive lineman involved in the crack screen is the playside tackle. We can run this play from any number of sets with motion.

Before I stop, I want to cover our five-man protection scheme. We use this to protect in our empty-set passing game. We can use a five-step drop or align in the shotgun. The launch point for the quarterback is five to seven yards behind the center. This is mostly an empty concept for us. The tight end can be attached to the formation, or he can be detached. We can use this concept out of any formation or personnel group.

FIVE-MAN PROTECTION PRINCIPLES

- Offensive line has four "bigs" and who we designate as the Will linebacker to next defender outside.
- Launch point is five to seven yards directly behind the center.
- Traditional slide protection look specific.
- Carry over with other protections.
- Designate attackside and backside.

If the defense is a 4-3 defense, the two guards, two tackles, and the center are responsible for the four down linemen and the linebacker designated as the Will linebacker (Diagram #5). To the backside, we slide the protection. The linebacker who is designated as the Will linebacker may not be in the Will linebacker's position. It could actually be the Mike linebacker, but his alignment makes him the designated linebacker.

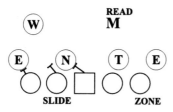

Diagram #5. Five-Man Protection

We slide the protection to that linebacker and read the other linebacker. That leaves the attackside tackle and guard in a zone scheme. The tackle does not think man protection. He is going to take the most dangerous rusher. If they blitz the linebacker from that side, there will be an unblocked man coming.

The tackle vertical sets and takes the most dangerous threat to the quarterback. If the linebacker does not come, he blocks the defensive end. If the defensive end slants inside and the linebacker comes outside, he blocks the defensive end. If the linebacker blitzes the B gap, the tackle blocks the linebacker. Whatever they do, the tackle takes the defender with the shortest distance to the quarterback.

If the guard has a 3 technique aligned on him, and the tackle has a defensive end on his outside shoulder, the guard and tackle are working in

combination on those three defenders. If the linebacker blows the A gap, the guard takes him. If the linebacker blows the B gap, the tackle takes him. If he comes wide around the outside, no one takes him unless the defensive end drops into coverage. If all three defenders come in the scheme, the defender farthest from the quarterback is unblocked.

It is logical to think, in a five-man protection, that if the defense brings six defenders, someone is not blocked. We want that someone coming from the farthest distance away.

The quarterback is reading the attackside and can see the unblocked defender. He has to throw the ball. We do not want to take the sack. He throws the ball or throws it away.

When we designate an attackside and a backside, we do that by using right or left numbers, or right or left words. We protect the backside. The quarterback must read the attackside. The tackle and guard to that side are blocking a zone scheme.

If the defense is a three-man front, the center has the nose by himself (Diagram #6). To the attackside, the guard and tackle take the Mike and Sam linebackers and the defensive end in a zone scheme. If the Mike linebacker blitzes inside, the guard takes him, and the tackle blocks the defensive end. If the Sam linebacker and defensive end come, the guard blocks the defensive end, and the tackle takes the Sam linebacker. If they all come, the rusher farthest from the quarterback is the unblocked rusher. The other side is blocking the same scheme.

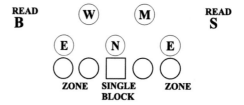

Diagram #6. Five-Man Protection vs. Odd

If only one of the defenders rushes, the guard helps the tackle or the center. The center and guards pass line stunts between them. The tackles and guards are in a pure zone scheme and pass off the ED and defensive-end stunts.

THE QUARTERBACK IN THE WEST COAST OFFENSE

University of Nebraska

We are a West Coast football team. What does that mean? What is a West Coast team? It is Paul Brown's, Bill Walsh's, and many other coaches' offense. I learned the offense from Mike White when we were at the University of Illinois. That is where I started. I have been in offense my entire coaching career.

The West Coast offense is awesome. It has held up over the test of time. I love it because it is a quarterback offense. It is an offense geared toward teaching the quarterback. Conceptually, there are some good points on the offense. The big picture of the offense is how it pertains to the quarterback, and that is what I am going to lecture on here. A ton of quarterbacks have been successful in this offense. It all goes back to how the quarterbacks have been managed and how they have been taught.

I am going to talk about the things others taught me. It is not about me, it is what I have learned from other people. I hope this will help you.

We are a 50/50 run/pass-ratio team. This really helps the quarterback. We are multiple in our personnel groupings. We are multiple in our formation structures. We use motion, we use the shift game, and we use the shift/motion game. At times, we can really be funky with this part of the game. A lot of this is because we are trying to hide our intentions. What the defense sees is not what the defense is going to get. We selfscout our offense. We spend a lot of time trying to change up and to look different. We do this for a purpose. It is to help our quarterback. He is conceptually taught our system. Everything is driven by concepts in the way the offense is put together. A lot of people say that the West Coast is all plays—it is not just plays.

I want to tell a personal story to illustrate the concept that the offense is about. After I left the University of Illinois, I coached at Miami University (OH). When I started coaching quarterbacks at Miami, I was the nextdoor neighbor of Weeb Ewbank. Not many of you know who Weeb Ewbank was. Weeb Ewbank is in the Hall of Fame. He was the head coach for the Baltimore Colts and the New York Jets when they won the Super Bowl. He coached Johnny Unitas and Joe Namath. He was a Miami grad. He retired and came back to Miami to live. I got him out of retirement. He helped me coach quarterbacks for three years. He was around me for five years. He was with me from day to day for three years.

I got a personal insight into what the West Coast offense is all about with Coach Ewbank. He was the first quarterback to play at Miami. After him, came Paul Brown. Paul Brown was a great coach with the Cleveland Browns and the Cincinnati Bengals. He owned the Cincinnati Bengals. He is in the Hall of Fame as well.

For three seasons, I took Coach Ewbank to Wilmington, Ohio to watch the Bengals during preseason practice. I was 31 years old when we made our first trip to Wilmington with Coach Ewbank. When we got to the practice field, I would have to take Coach Ewbank to see Coach Brown. We would go for the weekend to watch practice. The Bengals had some good teams in that span when we visited preseason camp.

Coach Ewbank and Coach Brown would talk football for hours in those sessions. I was in the background, and it was neat to hear them talk about the offense the Browns were running. Coach Brown was really the inventor of the West Coast offense. He was the coach that took the time to teach me the offense. The one point that I got from Coach Brown was very important about the offense. The key to the offense is the method in which the offense is taught to the players and the quarterback. It is how the quarterback is managed and how he is drilled. That is the emphasis of this lecture today.

I gave you the brief history because the offense has held up over time. It is a great offense to coach.

PRINCIPLES OF THE WEST COAST OFFENSE

- High percentage passes that attack the field both horizontally and vertically
- Changeup protections
- Sequential football
- Friendly to offensive line and quarterback

We have three protections. If you broke the offense down, you would find that in man protection, we could be in our sixman protection or seven-man protection. It all looks different. It is hard for the defense to figure us out because of our protection schemes. We can play slide protection, and we can play man protection on the frontside and zone protection on the backside. We can run gap protection. We have three schemes of protection, but there are not a lot of things to learn on the protection.

We are going to change up our protections. With that school of thought, we are able to look multiple to the defense.

We are going to change up the quarterback's launch point. That is huge in this offense. We do not want to let the quarterback sit in one spot on his launch point. We want to change up his passing clock. We can run the three-step, the quick five-step, a big five-step, and a quick seven-step drop. Do not freak out on the quick seven-step drop because it is just one more beep than the five-step drop.

We change up the rhythm, the protections, and the launch points. When we do that, we make the defense work more and we make our quarterback more efficient—we have made him better.

You may say that is a lot of volume. If all of this is conceptually taught, which is the premise of the West Coast offense, it is not that much offense to learn. It is easy to learn the offense. It is a streamlined offense. It is sequential football, which means that one thing leads into another concept.

The West Coast offense is friendly to the offensive line. More important, it is friendly to the quarterback. It is a great offense to be a quarterback in.

This is the key to the West Coast offense. This is what I learned from Coach Brown. I was a young coach at the time, and I thought everything about football was just plays. I learned that the game was more than just plays from Coach Brown. I want to mention some of the accomplishments of Coach Brown.

He was an education major. He first made his name when he coached high school football at Massillon, Ohio. He was the first coach to use the classroom as a coaching tool. He was the first coach to design and use a playbook. He was the first coach to use film. What he did was to find unique ways to teach football.

The West Coast offense revolves around how you teach your quarterback. The key to the West Coast offense is understanding this concept. It is not the plays—it is the method in which the offense is taught. Here are the keys.

It is a group installation and concept overview. One voice puts in the play to the offense. That voice is the offensive coordinator. I put in the plays so the position coaches can sit with their players and get in the important points that I want to make on each play. We cover what is important to make the play work.

After we do a group install, we take the players to position rooms and the assistants detail the play we just covered. Next, we do a walkthrough with the players. Finally, we take it to individual drills. In the individual drills, we work on fundamental teaching and technique teaching for the play.

From there, we break the team into small groups where we do smallgroup drills and isolation drills. We go 1-on-1, 3-on-3, and 3-on-2. We will work on the routes we installed that day in our 1-on-1 drills. We also do a 3-on-3 drill, which is an inside-pass drill. It is the tight end and two backs, or it could be the tight end and the inside receiver in the single-back set. It is a read drill for the quarterback. It is a great drill.

The 3-over-2 is a perimeter aspect of the drill. It is the outside receiver as #1, the inside receiver as #2, and our back. It is half-line oriented. We do a lot of full-speed reads, and we do a lot of half-line reads. It is a great drill to teach what we are trying to accomplish. This drill is good for the quarterback as it is working on timing and ball placement. The drill is good for the quarterback in that it helps him with his decision-making skills.

What you are seeing is the "whole-part-whole" teaching concept. One of the first things I learned as I was majoring in education was the whole-part-whole teaching concept. That is what teaching the West Coast offense is. That is how Coach Brown broke the offense down for me.

One day, Coach Brown made a comment to me to the effect that because I was an education major I should be able to comprehend what he was teaching. He asked me if I knew about the *KISS* teaching theory. I told him I did know what the KISS theory was and it stood for *Keep It Simple, Stupid.* He said, "No, it is not that, Stupid." I asked what it was and he said, "It is *Keep It Simple and Sound."* That is what the West Coast offense is built around. It is real simple, and it is logical thinking.

When we go to the walk-through, I stress to our staff that we do not want to do a walk-through but that we want to do a "run-through." I learned this from Coach Ewbank. He asked me why we would teach the play in the classroom, and then, when we go outside, run the play in a 7-on-7 drill. He suggested we run the play "on air" first. I have done the teaching process that way ever since that conversation with Coach Ewbank. When we do that, it reinforces what you have just taught. It also helps the quarterback in the way the plays are presented to him.

In our 7-on-7 drill, we put it all together. We work on a half-ball read, or a middle-triangle read. When we do the 7-on-7 drill, we do not allow the defense to blitz. That is important for the development of the quarterback. There is a place for blitzing, and I will come back to it later. We work against straight coverage in the 7-on-7 drill.

The next teaching aspect is the team sessions. We work on the following aspects in this session.

TEAM SESSIONS

- Base coverages
- Base blitz pick-up
- Nickel coverages
- Nickel blitz pick-up

When we get into our nickel coverages, it is against a different defender. Does our offense change? Not really. We may match a different personnel group or introduce a different concept or get into four receivers instead of three receivers.

The nickel blitz pickup is different. We get a lot more man coverage out of our defense. We get more pressures against our own defense. We are working the whole-part-whole method of teaching.

Our next phase is team situational football. We work on coming out when we are backed up to our goal line. This is our "orange zone." This is the fringe area next to the red zone. Next, we do red-zone offense. In our coming-out session, we work on normal and nickel downs.

What happens in a given day of practice is this. We are going to practice individually, then, we go 1-on-1, 3-over-2, and then, 7-on-7.

TEAM SITUATION FOOTBALL

- Coming out: Normal and nickel downs
- Orange zone: Normal and nickel downs
- Red zone: Normal and nickel downs

When we get through all of the nickel aspects at the end, they are separated by down-and-distance.

When we get done with an install phase, the players have had it installed, they have had a walk-through, they have had it detailed, and, by the end of the day, they are going to see everything they are going to see in football. We set up our practice that way—that is how we divide practice.

I want to talk about the way we build our offense. We have a "quarterback school" where I get one hour a week with the quarterbacks. That is all we can do, and that has to be through film study. We have an orientation book. The first week we spend on defensive football. The second week we get into teaching football. I teach bracketing in that session. I teach them about horizontal bracketing, vertical bracketing, and the checkdown.

Here is the way we teach bracketing. What is horizontal bracketing? We take a single defender and line him up. Then, we place a receiver outside of him and one inside of him, in his area of responsibility. We teach the quarterback the bracketing aspect of the concept. With one receiver inside the defender and one receiver outside of the defender, we have outnumbered him. There is one defender and two receivers.

This gives us the ability to play a game we call "monkey in the middle" (Diagram #1). If the defender goes outside, we should throw the ball inside. If the defender stays inside, we should throw the ball outside. It is a very simple way of presenting the passing game to the players. That is horizontal bracketing.

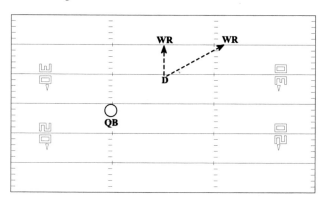

Diagram #1. Horizontal Bracketing

Vertical bracketing is a single defender with, once again, a receiver spotted outside of him and a receiver spotted over the top and inside of him (Diagram #2). I learned from Mike White that the two levels in coverages are always there. It does not matter what the coverage is, the *inner zone* and the *over zone* are always there. This is what vertical bracketing attacks.

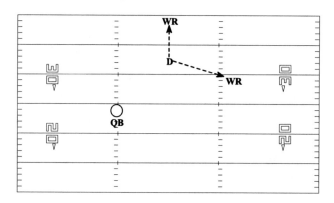

Diagram #2. Vertical Bracketing

The inner zone is the rush between the linebackers. The over zone is between the third level, between the linebackers and the deep secondary. Those two things are always involved. We do a lot of high/low reads and low/high reads. If the defender plays high, we throw low. If he plays low, we throw high. It is real simple.

It shocks me to find out how many coaches tell me they have not heard that concept. Once they understand this, they get into the passing game.

The third phase is the checkdown (Diagram #3). I go back to a story that Coach Ewbank told me. He said, "You know that football is just math, right?" I asked him what he meant. He said, "It is real simple. The defense has one man and you have two men. If they have two men, you have three men." This is where the checkdown comes into play.

The only way the defense can stop the offense in the bracketing aspect is to add an additional defender. The offense must make sure we have that third man in the bracket. That is where the checkdown comes into play.

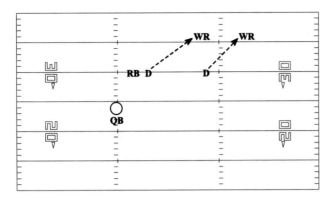

Diagram #3. The Checkdown

This is how we teach the quarterback this concept. We play monkey in the middle. We have a primary read in the bracket with a second progression read. We have receiver #1, and receiver #2 based off the single defender. They go to the brackets and work on making the correct throw.

This system gives you a chance to throw high percentage completions in the passing game. You have simple reads, and it does not screw anything up. The receivers are in positions where it is easy to find them.

The next phase we start teaching the quarterbacks is the *alerts*. We refer to this as "alerts/opportunity ball."

TYPES OF ALERTS

- Explosion ball: Down-the-field throw based on the defense's coverage or technique
- Free throw: Individual 1-on-1 throw created by both formation structure and concept (box rule)

ALERT DEFINITIONS

- Technique alert: Big ball opportunity created by defensive leverage and technique. That is an explosion ball.
- Coverage alert: Big ball opportunity created by defensive coverage. This is another big ball play.
- Individual alert: Free access throw created by structure and coverage. This is how we get our best athletes matched up on certain defenders.

The great thing about the West Coast offense is that we have those alerts, but we also have a foundation for the quarterback to operate. If the quarterback is in doubt or he is not sure, he depends on his foundation. I will show you want I mean by that because that is a lot of talk about theory, so I will show you this in our films.

We start teaching the quarterbacks and receivers the key elements of the West Coast passing attack. We want them to know this is what we want to be. We want to solve the equations related to the following situations.

KEY ELEMENTS TO THE WEST COAST PASSING ATTACK

- Timing = Quarterback's feet
- Spacing = Vertical and horizontal bracketing
- Attack the lesser defenders with match play

Who is responsible for timing? It is the quarterback. Specifically, it is his feet. Everything goes back to his feet. Who is responsible for spacing? The receivers are responsible for spacing. This includes all of the eligible receivers in the game.

We are always going to attack the lesser defender. We are going to make match play on them. This is in the dropback game as well as the play-action game. Play-action catches the defense in run/pass conflicts. In the dropback game, you are attacking the lesser defenders and making match play. We always attack adjustment defenders such as nickel backs, Will backers, Buck backers, and Mike backers. We attack the boundary defender.

We like to spread teams out and isolate those defenders and play high/low or play inside/out or monkey in the box.

We have key equations that we work on. We get our players to buy this and to believe in the equations.

KEY EQUATIONS

- Timing = Protection
- Timing and spacing = Completions
- Timing and ball placement = Yards after catch (YAC)

Timing = Protection

Our quarterback is responsible for protection. He is no different than the center, guards, tackles, tight ends, or running backs when it comes to protection. How is the quarterback going to do it? He is going to win with his feet. Protection should not matter if he gets the ball out of his hand when he is supposed to get it out. He does not want to hold the ball too long.

We tell the quarterback he must have a clock built into his passing rhythm. The clock must sound an alarm to him on these times on the different pass drops. The number of seconds he holds the ball is vital on our protection.

Timing and Spacing = Completions

- Understand the importance of the drop.
- Your footwork is your timing as a quarterback.
- Be religious with your drop mechanics.
- Perfect the fundamentals of your drop. Trust it—make it second nature.
- Always get to balance—on drop, on pocket movement, and on a scramble.

Next in the equation is timing and spacing equals completions. If the quarterback's feet are faced up with the feet of the receiver, we get a completion.

This is the way we approach the game. We put a lot into this. We try to be cognizant of this, and we look for it in our films. I will talk about it in a 7-on-7 drill and when we are watching the films as a unit. I talk about where the quarterback should let the ball go on the different timing steps. I stop the film and look to see where the receivers are at that time. I look to see if the receivers get the spacing that we need to be successful. If there is a mistake, we can go back and work on this in the next practice. We try to tie all of this into the training we are giving to our receivers.

Timing and Ball Placement = Yards After Catch

- Throwing off the clock catches the defenders in a reaction mode.
- Ball placement: Placing the ball to keep the receiver between the defender and the ball (leverage).

If the ball is out of the quarterback's hands on time and the ball placement is correct, we are going to increase our yardage. Our offensive goals include this point. We want to have 50 percent production in our passing game to come after the YAC (yards after catch).

The way we evaluate this is simple. On ball-control passes that we throw for five yards or more, we are expecting to pick up 10 yards or more on the play. We work on different unit circuits. We can get a lot of reps in that session. We get good fundamental training in the unity session. We work on this in that session.

We spend a lot of time talking about the points I have covered up to this point. For us, this is the passing game. This is it. It is not the how part or the route part. They are important, but the reason the offense works is the way we work the offense and how we practice the offense. This is what we try to build with our kids.

We want the quarterback to know the passing clock as well as the coaches know it. We use this in all of our drills with the quarterback.

PASSING CLOCK

- One-step drop = 1.0–1.2 seconds
- Three-step drop = 1.5–1.8 seconds
- Five-step drop = 2.0–2.4 seconds
- Seven-step drop = 2.8–3.0 seconds
- Quick eight = 1.5–1.8 seconds
- Gator eight/nine = 3.0–3.4 seconds

We have timed these plays over the years. I have a G.A. that just finished clocking all of our plays from last year. We call the G.A. the "professor of clockolgy." He has it down to a science.

The quick eight is on a sprint-out pass where we do not block the contain man. The Gator phase is when we get the quarterback outside of the containment on a scramble play.

We have a clock that we take on the field to time these drops. The clock is set and is in a basket. A bell rings when the time has elapsed on the time frame we are working on. If we are running a three-step drop, we set the clock at 1.8 seconds. The ball needs to be out of the hand of the quarterback before the bell rings.

If you are interested in this clock, you may want to check with Neil Gilman. He came out to our practice, saw what we were doing, and made one that works fine with this drill. I think there is another company that has a snapper that is set on a clock that does the same thing on the snap. I want to use it in our 7-on-7 drills. The point is that we want to train the quarterbacks to be timing passers. It is big for us. It will help with the protection, and the line coach will always love you.

We always work on rhythm throws. I will work on this even when we are on drills with the receivers. I stand off from the quarterbacks and I watch the feet of each quarterback. As soon as his third step hits, I clap my hands and call out, "Ball." This is to get the quarterback trained to throw on time.

Here is how I break decisionmaking down for our quarterbacks. If they can understand this information, it will help them make good decisions.

Know your offense: Know the how and the why. The most important thing is to know the why. That is the bracketing. The how part refers to the plays. The why is attacking the single defender and making him wrong.

Coverage ID: Presnap read of the defense. This is how we break it down. It is real simple. I am not into cover 2 or cover 3. We say the middle is open, or the middle is closed. That is only two coverages for us. That is it. There are a lot of different variations.

Verify the coverage: We say to find *Waldo*—he is the free safety. We want to read the free safety. Look through the safety on the first step. When our quarterbacks come in on Monday, I ask them what the number is of the opponent's free safety. I want to know his number, and I want to know his backup. They have seen the films, and they should know all of this from those films. I ask the quarterbacks to tell me the spokes for the quarterback. I have them draw these on the chalkboard. "Spokes" relates to

how the quarterback drops or rotates when the ball is snapped.

We let Waldo take us to everything by his pre-snap and by his post-snap. Here are the ID keys:

- ID movement key
  ✓ Find the monkey in the middle with your peripheral vision. He cannot be right.
- Finish with your eyes
  ✓ Take the defender to where he wants to go with your eyes.
  ✓ Then, throw away from defender.
  ✓ If #2 is covered by adjacent defender, hit the checkdown.

Here are the things we ask our quarterbacks to know. This is how we teach him the offense. We have five coaching points:

- Package
- Clock
- Movement key
- Progression
- Protection rule

You may not want to include all five of these points. I have most of our players for five years, and I want them to know where everything fits in our offense. The formula is simple. Where does it fit?

It is either a vertical high/low or a vertical low/high. It is a horizontal outside/in, or an inside/out. It could be a middle-of-the-field read high/low or low/high. There is not a lot left that we have not covered. We keep it streamlined, and that is the point I want to get across to them. I want them to know the kind of read it is so they will play with their eyes.

The clock is when the ball should come out of the hands of the quarterback. That is the second coaching point. The third point is: Who is the movement key on the play? In other words, who is the monkey in the middle? We identify the defender as the playside, hook/curl defender. We are only reading one man, not the whole defense. We progression read the man. The defense changes so often that we do not make it complicated. We key the free safety.

The progression is what the quarterback is looking for. That is simple. The final coaching point is the protection rule. Every quarterback must know his protection rule.

We do not have to throw hot routes in this offense. We have not thrown a hot route in two years. We want to find the movement key and make that man wrong.

You must understand, the coaching staff digs out all the answers to make things work for the quarterback. We want him to be able to go out and play and not have to worry about figuring out what to do. We figure all of that out for him and teach him what to do in practice. We want it to be like a pickup basketball game for the quarterback. When you play pickup basketball, you just play. It all comes natural—you play. We want his talent to come out. We want him to be able to show his competitiveness. I want him to play without a lot of thought.

I want to give you one play and go over how we would coach it. The play is our bingo play.

TRIPS RIGHT: 72 Y BINGO X OUT

We are a tag team. We are not a numbers team, as far as our patterns are concerned. We learn by concepts. Bingo is a concept for us. This call should give the quarterback a trigger in his head where it fits in our offense. This is how he reads the call:

- Package: Full-field read, vertical high/low read
- Clock: Quick seven and close/From the gun: Quick five and close
- Movement key: Playside hook/curl defender
- Progression:
  - ✓ Alert: Post
  - ✓ Box alert: Out
  - ✓ Foundation: Basic/drive, burst
- Protection rule:
  - ✓ Two high: MID
  - ✓ One high: MID
  - ✓ Zero high: Audible

What does full-field mean to the quarterback?

He must make some determinations on the pre-snap of where he is going to go with the football. He is going to cut the field into a half. This makes him always right. He is going to read the vertical high/low reads.

The clock is going to be quick seven from underneath the center. If he is in the shotgun set, it is quick five and close.

The movement key is the playside hook/curl defender. I will show this when we look at the films.

His progression is this. He has two alerts on this play. He goes to coverage alerts to check down. The box alert is a checkdown call. His foundation is basic/drive, burst. If he comes up to the line and does not know what the defense is doing, he plays his foundation progression. We want our quarterback to always be right. We want him to take the chalk away from the defensive coordinator. We give him the whole field to read, and we are going to teach him how to do it in a fast, streamlined manner.

We talked about the protection rule. Two high means we are going to ID the Mike linebacker and, on one high, we ID the Mike linebacker. If we have zero high, we run an audible.

The rest of this is a clinic in itself. I will not get into the other aspects of the play.

Our quarterbacks always want to look for the deep pass. A lot of the West Coast pass offense relates to the deep pass. The offense gets a reputation of being a "dink-and-dunk" offense, but it isn't. It is not that if you set up the plays to take advantage of the defense. If you set up the offense, you can get the deep plays.

We are going to throw the post route if we get quarter coverage. The quarterback identifies the quarter coverage. He is going, number one to the post, and number two to the burst route on the checkdown. If he does not like the post route, that is fine. He must have a place to throw the ball if the defense takes away our individual receiver. I am not going to get into the patterns in this session because we are talking about working with the quarterback.

Let me finish with the key to the quarterback's success:

- Philosophy: Make fundamentals the nature of the quarterback. React and respond.
- There are two primary fundamental areas that the quarterback must master:
    - ✓ One piece passer
    - ✓ Find balance with the feet
- Core fundamental drills
    - ✓ Throw drills
    - ✓ Line drills
    - ✓ Bag drills
    - ✓ Balance drills
    - ✓ Pocket drills

I am big on fundamentals. I just read a book by Coach John Wooden, the former UCLA basketball coach. I like the way he thinks. He talked about the great teams he had at UCLA, and all of them thrived on these three principles:

- Relentless effort
- Fundamental execution
- Attention to detail

That is how we think. We are huge on fundamentals. That is why we say we want to make every fundamental become second nature to the quarterback. When something happens, he just reacts and responds. You have to drill this if you want to make that happen. That is how I set up all of my drill work.

I wanted to go over these drills to show you how we stress the fundamentals. This is a great offense, but it must be presented to the quarterback in a manner that will allow him to develop his talents. If you can do that, you have a good chance of having success.

THE OFFENSIVE LINE MIND-SET

Oklahoma State University

Good afternoon. I want to talk about line blocking on the inside zone play. We have led the Big 12 in rushing for the past three years. We do many things that are different.

We are a multiple-tempo offense. We are a balanced running team. Three years ago, we were number two in the nation behind Oregon State in balance. Two years ago, we were number one in the nation in balance. We were balanced in types of runs, protections, and run:pass ratio. Being balanced gives us a chance to be successful.

We do not need the best linemen in the nation to be successful. We try to win with execution and keeping all our players on the same page. Within that balance, we run the zone and power play. There are only a few concepts we concern ourselves with. We run the zone play both inside and outside. We run the counter and power. We run a lead play along with some options. The zone play is the play we have put together over the years.

I want to talk about how we install the zone play from a standpoint of schematics and mechanics. When we talk about schemes, it deals with assignments. The mechanics of a play is the technique used to get someone blocked. I want to get into some combination blocks and ultimately into what I call disruption.

If the defense aligns in an odd, even, or eight-man front, that is no problem. It is all the bastard things the defense does along with those alignments that give us problems. It is the twist, stunt, linebacker blitzes, linebackers walked up into the gaps, and things of that nature that give us problems. Obviously, we spent many hours on those types of things.

INSIDE ZONE TEACHING PROGRESSION

- Man (zero, 1, 2, 3) rules
- Track assignments
- Zone-drive steps, fit, and technique
- Covered/uncovered fundamentals
- Zone combination scheme
- Disruption (recognition and adjustment)

We give our linemen assignments. If they can count to three and play hard, they can play for me. The assignments are not difficult. I do not give tests on them, and we do not have a playbook. If I have to give a test or a playbook, the scheme is too hard.

The center IDs the zero point much like he does on pass protection. Wherever the center establishes the count, the guard will take the #1 defender from there. The tackle has #2, and the tight end blocks #3.

This allows us to run the ball without two zone-play calls. If we run the inside zone and the outside zone, we learn the assignment for each play the same way. This has been a tool to help our players get clear in their minds who to block. They do not have to learn fronts when you have this system.

It allows you the flexibility of moving personnel around in the offensive line. If your right guard has to play left tackle, he does not have to take a rep at left tackle to know his rules. He has the #2 defender to his side.

We have two types of zone tracks. We have a "zone-drive" track, which is more downhill. It is like a drive block. In this block, the offensive lineman wants to cover the body of the defender with the eyes on the outside half.

If we run the ball outside, we use a "zone-reach" track. The lineman splits the defender's crotch on the first step working for the outside armpit. He worries about playside leverage and not coverage of the body.

The tracks will dictate how the offensive blocker fits into the defender. His track is married to the running back.

As a coach, I am paid for five things. I tell my players they will play if they can do these five things. The first item is fundamentals. You have to be a fundamentalist and technician. The next three things come in order. They are assignment, leverage, and coverage. The last item is finish. You have to teach a player or a group of players to finish.

A player has to know who to block. That is his assignment. His footwork gets him into the correct leverage on the defender. To effectively block a defender, we must cover up his body. Those fundamentals come from the zone track.

Last year, we ran the zone play 268 times in different forms or fashions. When I say the zone play, we may have run the zone option, inside zone, outside zone, or zone pass. We run the same tracks over and over when we run these plays. That is why we had so much success. When you get that many reps on a play, you become good at it.

When I talk about the scheme, I am not going to spend much time talking about the tight end. The tight end has the #3 defender. He uses a power zone track and utilizes his mechanics on a first- or second-level player. He has a certain technique and fit on the power zone block.

Before I go any further, there are many coaches who have won multiple state championships. If you are having success with what you are doing, continue to do it. What I am talking about may have one technique or flavor that you can use to become even better at what you do.

This is the center's zero identification to the nub or openside of the formation (Diagram #1). If you run the ball to the nub side, the center counts three defenders from the ghost tight end going inside. He

counts from the outside to the inside. After he makes his count, he calls "nose right." That tells the linemen, the zero man is the nose guard in his right-side gap. The guard has the first defender beyond the nose, and the tackle has the second defender beyond the nose. The center counts from the outside to the inside to get the zero identification. The linemen count from the zero identification inside to the outside to get their blocking assignments.

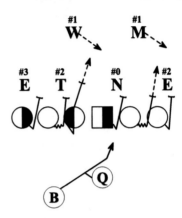

Diagram #1. Center Zero Identification

To the backside, the Will linebacker is #1, the 3-technique tackle is #2, and the 7-technique end is #3 in the linemen count.

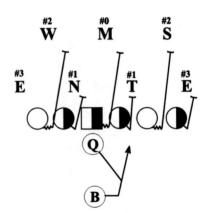

Diagram #2. Center's Zero Identification

If the tight end aligns right, the center has to deal with a 3-technique defender. The center makes his count and designates the Mike linebacker as his zero identification. The right guard has the 3 technique, the tackle has the Sam linebacker, and the tight end has the 7-technique defender. To the right side, the guard has the nose, and the tackle has the Will linebacker.

This is a simple way to do things, but it gets complicated when the defense starts to move and stunt. I want to spend time working on disruptions that occur in the defense (Diagram #2). I cannot tell my players they have a certain defender every time. If the defense starts moving defenders around as we get ready to snap the ball, we never want to get hit in the face. We cover up all the front side defenders and let the backside defenders run.

POWER ZONE STEP

I want to cover the power zone track. The power zone track represents the course or angle that each of our blockers use for executing our inside zone blocking scheme. The first step sets the track for the linemen and backs. The track we use to press our zone fits is a downhill, full coverage, and attacking (north-south) course. The backs and offensive line will be joined at the hip on the exact same track so that it will tie directly into the flow of the play.

COACHING POINTS

It is imperative for the success of inside zone scheme that blockers and ballcarriers:

- Buy into and understand the power zone-track philosophy
- Trust each other to not deviate from the power zone track
- Execute with proper "discipline and patience" to allow schemes to develop and take advantage of angles, movement, and out of position defenders

The back and blockers have to be on the same page. You cannot expect the linemen to grind and root-hog in the scheme and the back to run somewhere else. The backs and linemen have to trust each other to be where they are supposed to be on their track. This scheme is methodical and is done over and over.

The players cannot deviate from the power zone track. When the ballcarrier runs this scheme, he must have patience. He has to take advantage of angles, movements, and defenders who get out of

position. If he gets in too big a hurry, the play will not develop.

The drop-step is the first step in the track. It is like a pass set in my mind. If someone asked me what kind of pass set we teach. The type of set depends on how wide the defender is in his alignment. If we block the inside zone and the defender aligns in a 2 technique on the guard, his drop-step is tiny. If the defender is right on the blocker, he gets his hips, eyes, and numbers on the chest of the defender immediately. From that point on, the blocker adjusts to what the defender does. If he bucket-steps, the blocker is off his track from the beginning of the block.

If the defender aligns on the outside eye of the guard, he has to open his hips to get on his track. However, we do not give ground when we come off the ball. We have to cover up the defender as quickly as we can. If he is wide and in the gap, we use a longer drop-step to get the defender covered. We teach this so it times up the zone combinations with the adjacent lineman.

ZONE DROP-STEP

To ensure we secure the proper "track" and "zone drive" physical fit on assigned defensive linemen and linebackers, we use a zone drop-step upon the departure phase. The offensive lineman wants to go from stance to fit through the outside jersey number of the defender with key elements in mind:

- Time up the zone combination with adjacent uncovered offensive lineman.
- Time up the running back getting exchange and getting the ball to the line of scrimmage.
- Drop hips behind the line of scrimmage, keeping lineman in position where he stays in front of the defender.
- Allow lineman to gain leverage and to open up hips, and more importantly base on approach.
- Put lineman on proper track on zone play upon departure phase or approach.

The drop-step drops the hips behind the line of scrimmage. If you do not lose ground, we are even with the defender and inside-out on the block, which we do not want. That is what the defense wants in their scheme. We want to slide and cover up the body of the defender.

The zone drive block and zone reach are different for me. When we zone drive block we are worried about full coverage in getting to the outside shoulder.

ZONE DRIVE BLOCK

We use two types of zone blocking fits when attacking and covering a first-level defender:

- Zone drive block = inside (gut) zone
- Zone reach block = outside (wide) zone

The zone drive block is the technique where we secure a slow and full coverage fit on a first-level defender while maintaining leverage and "track integrity." The zone drive block is nothing more than our base drive-block progression with the exception of (three) key factors:

- Approach and fit is about 12 inches playside of the midline of the first-level defender.
- Technique to and through the defender is done while maintaining power zone track concept.
- 2-on-2 or 3-on-3 combinations are built-in zone concepts used throughout the power zone scheme.

If we run the toss sweep or wide zone to the right, the angle and aiming point is different. The step with the near foot is deeper, and the inside foot is faster. If we run the inside zone play, the first step has less depth, and the second step is slower.

Working in zone combinations allows the offensive linemen to take care of the disruptions that occur in the defense. The covered and uncovered linemen must communicate with one another to ensure defenders are passed off and slip blocking occurs. The steps by uncovered linemen into their zone must keep the blocker square and ready to take on an outside defender slanting into his gap. The uncovered linemen cannot allow penetration from an outside stunt. We never want penetration from the playside. Therefore, we cover up all frontside defenders and let the backside defender run.

ZONE-BLOCKING COMBINATIONS: POWER SLIP

- Covered lineman (outside blocker)
  - ✓ Aiming point: Playside armpit.
  - ✓ First step: Drop-step with near foot.
  - ✓ Second step: Punch-step to backside instep of down lineman.
  - ✓ Contact: Eyes, hat, hands on tight outside fit.
  - ✓ Finish: Drive through playside number with tight fit on the power zone track.
  - ✓ Technique: Zone drive block on the power zone track.
  - ✓ *Coaching point:* Near knee, near shoulder on the power zone track.

- Uncovered lineman (inside blocker)
  - ✓ Aiming point: Playside armpit.
  - ✓ First step: Open/jump step with near foot.
  - ✓ Second step: Shuffle-step to midline of down lineman.
  - ✓ Contact: Eyes, hat, hands through cylinder of down lineman to tight outside fit on linebacker.
  - ✓ Finish: Drive through cylinder of down lineman to and through playside number of second-level linebacker.
  - ✓ Technique: Power slip track block through playside gap to second-level linebacker, execute climb-drive technique.
  - ✓ *Coaching point:* Near knee, near shoulder on power zone track.

We use combination blocks to block two defenders. If we use a "gut" block, the guard and tackle are in combination on a defender. The uncovered lineman has to communicate to the covered lineman to make sure they are on the same page. That lets the linemen re-identify their blocking assignments. If the defense moves many times, it eliminates confusion as to the blocking assignments.

If I were the left guard, I would be in a left-handed stance. If he has a block on the linebacker, he steps with width as he opens his hips. He drags the inside foot to get his hips in front of any activity that may occur in the B gap. If a color or activity shows, he blows it up. He does not spend time going after the linebacker and lets the 5-technique tackle get three yards deep in the backfield. The defensive tackle will be stopped and not allowed to penetrate. A one-yard gain is better than a four-yard loss. If there is no activity in the B gap, the guard pounds his track and climbs to the second level.

I tell the guard to hit the ground running. When he finds no activity in his gap, he gets to the second level as fast as he can. I want to talk about techniques and fundamentals for a second. One of the biggest struggles I have had over the years is where to find enough time to get all this taught. Sometimes, when we practice in the stadium, I cannot find a place to work. I have the biggest group on the field, and I end up in the tunnel or in the 15th row. I feel like we are in the way.

I have had elaborate practice schedules. Sometimes coaches come to clinics and talk about all these things and do not have enough time to get it all taught. I have chiseled it down to the fewest individual things I need to do. Here is the way we try to organize our practices. We have several categories of schemes that we use for our running game.

- Power zone
- Wide zone
- Power zrap
- Lead/center

Those are the schemes we work on in run practice. I have five drills that I do every day. Every day, I work some kind of drill in the chutes. I work some kind of technique drill using angle boards and bags. I work some type of sled work because I am an old-school football coach. I work some type of 1-on-1 blocking. I block linebackers, down-blocks, reach block, or a cutoff block. The last thing I do is combination work in a 2-on-2 *half-line drill*.

If you are not organized, you screw around and leave something out. It is not important to spend a certain amount of time on these things daily, but it is important for you to touch on them every day.

We start our practice at 2:15 with a five-minute team meeting. We go to special-teams meetings for 15 minutes and position meetings for 10 minutes. The coaches meet with the quarterbacks for 10 minutes

before practice. During that time, the offensive linemen have a pre-practice session working on mirror drill, T-drills, hand sparring, hand replacement drills, and 3-on-3 twists and linebacker folds.

The practice begins at 3:30. We start with a stretch period followed by a PAT/field-goal period. The line goes through a flex period. We follow that with blocking as a line on scheme fits versus air bags (slow teach) for five minutes and crack/read double-screen reverse for five minutes. All my individual drills deal with run blocking. I do not spend that much time on pass blocking.

When we get into the second hour of practice, we get into the meat of team practice. We have eight minutes of inside drill against the defense. During the 7-on-7 period, the line works four minutes on 1-on-1 pass protection and four minutes on twist pass protection. From there, we spend eight minutes working a offensive line group drill on run blocking against the scout defense. The next drill is almost a repeat drill. We spend eight minutes on a running team drill against the defense. The last drill is a full-team drill against the scouts.

We end practice at 5:30. After practice, we have an offensive line post-practice routine. I like this period because most everyone has taken it to the house. We take off our helmets and work for an additional 10 minutes. If you are organized, it is amazing what you can get done. I take one or two of our running concepts and work on them. An example of something we may work on is cut or chop blocking.

The footwork for the cutoff block is the same as the zone-track scheme except we want to chop the defender at the line of scrimmage. If the right guard has a defender in his inside gap, he takes the same steps. He has to protect the integrity of his gap and make sure the defender is charging inside. His landmark is six inches beyond the defenders inside hip. As soon as the guard's foot hits the ground, he shows the defender his numbers and cuts him down.

If we plan on cut-blocking in a game, you have to work on it. When we work half-line drills, we spend too much time on playside blocking. There are two sides to every play. We can get the frontside blocked up just right, but the backside allows the tackle. You have to work on reps of the cutoff block to the backside. This is the time we concentrate on those types of blocking assignments.

This is the time to work on combination blocks that are new or need adjustment. You can work on your tracks on the first and second levels.

Before I run out of time, I want to show you some techniques we use to team pass protection. The first technique is a man-protection technique when the lineman is covered by a pass rusher aligned in an outside alignment (3, 5, or 9 technique). The lineman's assignment is to secure inside leverage on the rusher. It requires him to take a kick-step with his outside foot on departure. The kick-step allows the lineman to gain depth and width off the snap count before any type of collision. The lineman's aiming point is the inside half of the defender's jersey number and hip. The blocker already has inside-out leverage on the rusher. He kick-steps and "settles." He must be in a good proper protection stance and posture. The depth of the set depends on the type of protection and the style of the pass rusher, but the leverage is always stays the same.

OUTSIDE SET/FIT

- Violently explode off the snap.
- Execute quick, explosive kick-step for depth/width.
- Big-eye inside jersey number/hip through outside technique.
- Kick-step with outside foot, firm punch with inside hand.
- Maintain separation "wide base" on second step, slide step by covering as minimal ground on second step (G-slide).
- Maintain proper pad level by keeping good knee bend, butt down ("eyes below the defender's mouth" concept).
- Center of gravity: maintain weight distribution between your widely spread in-steps.

The next technique is a man-protection technique when covered by a pass rusher aligned head-up or in the middle of the protector (2, 4, or 6 technique). The lineman must secure inside leverage on the rusher. That requires him to use a post/drag step on the snap with his inside foot on departure from the line of scrimmage. The lineman's aiming point is the inside half of the defender. He aims for the inside jersey number and inside hip of rusher. He must constantly defend against any push by rusher through his inside hip. The middle set is all about speed, base, leverage, and hands.

MIDDLE SET/FIT

- Violently explode off the snap.
- Execute strong, forceful post/drag combination step.
- Big-eye inside jersey number/hip through outside technique.
- Step with near foot, firm punch with near hand.
- Maintain separation ("wide base") on drag step by covering as little ground as possible on each step.
- Maintain proper pad level by keeping good knee bend, butt down, using "eyes below the defender's mouth" concept.

If the rusher has an inside alignment, the blocker must explode off the snap. He has to post-step with his inside foot and maintain good leverage on the defender.

INSIDE SET/FIT

- Violently explode off the snap.
- Execute strong, forceful post/drag combination step.
- Big-eye inside jersey number/hip through outside tech.
- Step with near foot, firm punch with near hand.
- Maintain proper pad level by keeping good knee bend, butt down, using "eyes below the defender's mouth" concept.
- Maintain separation ("wide base") on drag-step by covering minimal ground on second step (G)

We use man pass-protection drills, where we emphasize sound protection "posture" while working movements (lateral) and the redirection of movements both to the inside (post) and to the outside (kick) (Diagram #3). We align defenders directly over the top (zero, 2, or 4 technique) of the offensive linemen and tell them to sprint left to right to left and so on. We ask the offensive linemen to "shadow" or stay directly in front of the defenders, using proper change-of-direction skills. We do two sets of the drill. (Equipment Needed: Six tall cones)

Coaching Points:

- First set with hands behind the back
- Second set with use of hands to stress extend, punch, and grab mechanics.

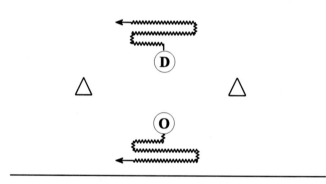

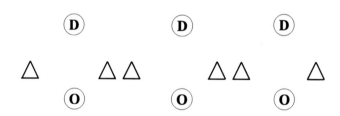

Diagram #3. Mirror Dodge Drill

The next drill emphasizes the shuffling movement to bring defenders to proper fit (Diagram #4). We bleed in the combination phase of the "extension and punchy" to stun or stop the defender's charge. The lineman adjusts to the charge of three various defenders. He shuffles and slides in correct protection posture to bring the proper fit and explode his hands through the hand shield. We do two sets of this drill. (Equipment Needed: Two tall cones and three hand shields per group)

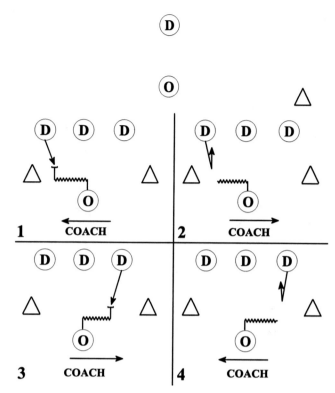

Diagram #4. T-Drill (Two Groups of 1-on-3)

This drill emphasizes the deflection and combative phase of the punch/extend technique and also the immediate replacement of hands to the defender's numbers (Diagram #5). I have one coaching point to pass on. The drill starts on the whistle and goes four to six seconds per set. The offensive lineman is in perfect pass-protection position and starts the drill with a slow walk. We want hand action in this drill with the defender working for inside hand position. (Equipment Needed: Six tall cones)

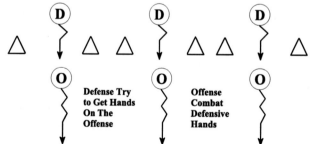

Diagram #5. Hand Replacement/ Spar Drill (Three Lines)

We use a drill that teaches offensive linemen to combat all "spin movement" and counter moves (Diagram #6). We align three offensive linemen up against three defenders. The offensive linemen get into perfect posture/position, moving inside-out and back-and-forth. (Equipment Needed: Six cones)

Coaching Points:

- First set: Center line spin
- Second set: Center line spin with bull rush counter
- Third set: Center line spin with hop counter

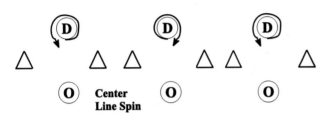

Center Line Spin

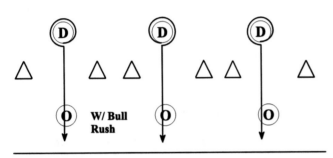

W/ Bull Rush

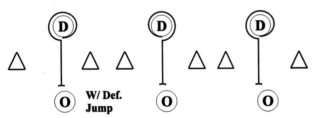

W/ Def. Jump

Diagram #6. Center Line Spin Drill

This man pass-protection drill emphasizes the base mechanics of blocking (Diagram #7). We shuffle and slide, while maintaining inside leverage with full surface fits.

In the drill, we periodically use extension punches and grab technique. The thing to emphasize is to shuffle-slide down the line to the inside post foot as well as to the outside kick foot.

In the old days, if you were a guard, you wanted to force your men into a 3 technique. For the tackles, we wanted to bring them to a slow 5 technique. For the center, we want to bring the rusher to the zero technique. That was the old way. It does not work today. The pass rushers keep on running against those blocks.

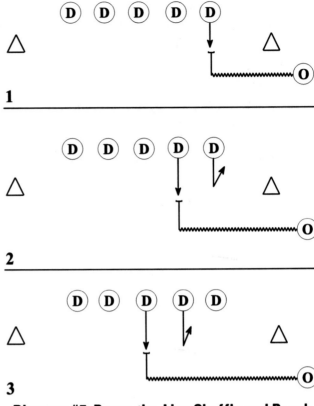

1

2

3

Diagram #7. Down-the-Line Shuffle and Punch

We started setting in the pass-rush lanes. If you are not on the edge, you take up too much space. We told the blockers we want them to be in an illusion set versus a defender on air. On air was not always the look. We want to give the defender the illusion that we are running outside.

We wanted the blockers to take their hands, shoulders, heads, feet, and everything they could to give the defense the illusion that we were going outside (Diagram #8). We want them to keep their head cocked, drag the inside foot, keep the kneecap inside the foot, and the rest of it is a game. We are going to get into the pass-rush lane every snap on the pass.

I want to talk about disruption quickly. I want to talk about things that disrupt us.

Disruption: Recognition and Adjustments

- Spikes (3 technique)
- Twists/stunts
- Sticks (5 technique)
- Linebacker dogs

NEW!

2009
COACH OF THE
YEAR CLINICS
Football Manual

Featuring lectures from several of America's most renowned coaches. Edited by Earl Browning.

$29.95 • 288 pages • 978-1-60679-062-5

Also available:

2003

1-58518-856-5
288 pp. • $24.95

2004

1-58518-896-4
280 pp. • $24.95

2005

1-58518-932-4
288 pp. • $24.95

2006

1-58518-969-3
304 pp. • $24.95

2007
1-58518-073-8
288 pp. • $24.95

2008

978-1-58518-719-5
272 pp. • $24.95

Title	Item #	Price	Qty	Total
	Tax on materials for California residents only.			
	Shipping & Handling: $7.50 for first item $1.50 for each additional item	PLUS CA Tax 8.25%	PLUS Shipping	
		TOTAL		

Name _____
Organization/School _____
Address _____
City _____ State _____ ZIP _____ Phone ( ) _____

Method of Payment: ☐ VISA ☐ MasterCard ☐ AMERICAN EXPRESS ☐ DISCOVER ☐ Check # ☐ P.O. #

Account # ☐☐☐☐ ☐☐☐☐ ☐☐☐☐ ☐☐☐☐ Expiration: ___/___ CVC #: _____

Email Address: _____
Signature: _____

COACHES CHOICE
www.coacheschoice.com

Send check or money order to: Coaches Choice
P.O. Box 1828 Monterey, CA 93942
or call toll-free: (888) 229-5745 or fax: (831) 372-6075

Diagram #8. Jump-Bait the Lane

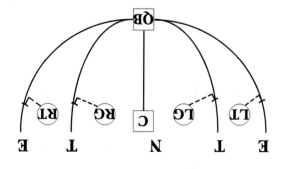

- Pirate stunt
- Bastard alignments
- Fire zone blitz
- UFO/add-in defender

We see the 3-technique spike and a 5-technique stick. Those are inside-slant stunts moving from one gap to the next gap inside. We also see the pirate stunt. It is an exchange of gaps that gives another add-in defender. It is a different look, but it is smoke and mirrors. We see fire zone blitzes along with twists and stunts. If your offense is a first-and-10 running team, you can look for a run twist and stunt in that situation.

When I talk about bastard alignments, I refer to two wide 3 techniques or two shade techniques on the center. It could be a double Eagle nose alignment. The 3-3 stack defense can be classified as one of those types of defense. A gap-eight alignment. The defense is another bastard alignment. The UFO/add-in defender is huge to understanding. When the defense starts rolling the secondary or walking down safeties into the box to gain the advantage on the blockers, you must have a plan.

When teams run a fire zone defense, it becomes a difficult thing to block. When you get the fire zone to the boundary, it screws all your numbers up. You have a hard time running the football if you are not ready to block it. You have to find a way to crease the scheme. Your linemen have to understand what they are responsible to block. They have to feel the stunt based on down-and-distance or alignment. If the shade nose is aligned in a 1 technique on the guard instead of on the center, that could be a tip.

Whatever it is, the linemen have to start to recognize it and communicate it to their combination blocker. If the safety cheats down to the outside, we should expect the defensive line to slant away from him. He comes off the edge and the defensive line moves one gap inside. We have to communicate that. We have to build a wall and drill against the defensive long sticker.

The scheme on defense demands the defender running the spikes and sticks get across the face of the offensive blocker. We have to coach our linemen to understand that and rein the sticker back inside. In our scheme we have stretchers and stakers. The backside blockers have to be stakers and wall off the defensive stunts. The playside blockers are the stretchers, chasing their assignments and stretching the defense. If we can stretch the playside and stake the backside, we create a crease in the defense. All it takes is one defender to lose on the backside for us to hit the seam.

If the play is to the openside of the formation, we want to stretch the openside (Diagram #9). The center, playside guard, and tackle are the stretcher and chasers. The center opens on the noseguard and runs him to the outside as he can. He is not trying to stop him from getting outside. The guard and tackle do the same thing. To the backside, the linemen want to get ahead of their blocking assignments and literally slow down their blocks to stall the movement of the backside defenders. They stop the flow of the defense, and the gaps open up. They can also chop the defender to stop his movement.

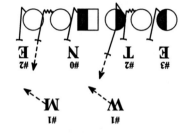

Diagram #9. Stretch and Stake

I appreciate your attention, and anytime we can do something for you, do not fail to call on us.